T5-ASM-923

BULL COOK AND AUTHENTIC HISTORICAL RECIPES AND PRACTICES

by GEORGE LEONARD HERTER and
BERTHE E. HERTER
Herter's, Waseca, Minnesota

BULL COOK AND AUTHENTIC HISTORICAL RECIPES AND PRACTICES

First Edition — 1960
Second Edition — 1960
Third Edition — 1961
Fourth Edition — 1961
Fifth Edition — 1962
Sixth Edition — 1963
Seventh Edition — 1963
Eighth Edition — 1963
Ninth Edition — 1964

*Published in the United States of America
by Herter's, Inc.
Waseca, Minnesota*

Dedicated To
Christian Herter

Bull Cook and Authentic Historical Recipes and Practices

In the lumber camp days and pioneer days the cooks learned from each other and the old world cooks. Each taught the other his country's cooking secrets. Out of the mixing came fine food, prepared as nowhere else in the world.

I am putting down some of these recipes that you will not find in cook books plus many other historical recipes. Each recipe here is a real cooking secret. I am also publishing for the first time authentic historical recipes of great importance.

For your convenience I will start with meats, fish, eggs, soups and sauces, sandwiches, vegetables, the art of French frying, desserts, how to dress game, how to properly sharpen a knife, how to make wines and beer, how to make French soap, what to do in case of hydrogen or cobalt bomb attack. Keeping as much in alphabetical order as possible.

Meats

HOW TO MAKE REAL CORNED VENISON, ANTELOPE, MOOSE, BEAR AND BEEF

Corned meat originated in the town of London, England in 1725. It was invented by a man named John Wilson, a chemist. The real secret of producing true corned meat is known only by a very few people and they guard their secret very carefully. Although some cook books and food editors of magazines from time to time publish recipes for corning meat these recipes are not even close to the real one. This is the first time the real authentic recipe for corning meat has ever been published.

You can corn venison, antelope, moose, bear or beef with this same authentic corning method. It makes all of these meats simply wonderful eating. People who will not eat wild meats just love them corned. Corning wild meats takes out all the musky wild flavor that most people do not like and even the toughest of wild meats becomes as tender as can be.

The canned corned meat called corned beef that you can buy in all of our grocery stores is not corned beef at all but simply a very poor preserved beef made in South America and sold under the label of corned beef.

In World War One, this South American so-called corned beef, was shipped to our fighting forces in Europe. They did not like it at all and gave it the nickname of "Corned Willie", meaning goat meat preserved by soaking it in corn whisky. The name stuck. In corning beef no corn or corn whiskey of any kind is ever used.

In stores the fresh corned beef you can buy is never really good. Packing houses invariably take the brisket of beef which is the cheapest, poorest possible meat and corn it so they can get a high price for it.

Here are the ingredients to make up 6 gallons of corning liquids. If this is too much cut the recipe in half or if too little double it.

10 ounces of sugar.
2 ounces of sodium nitrate. (Get from your druggist)
½ ounce of sodium nitrite. (Get from your druggist)
3 pounds of salt.
3 level teaspoons of black pepper.
1 level teaspoon of ground cloves.
6 bay leaves.
12 level teaspoons of mixed pickling spice.
If you care for onions, mince one onion 3 inches in diameter.
If you care for garlic, mince 4 garlic cloves.

Put the ingredients into a pickle crock or glass jar and add enough water to make a total of six gallons including the ingredients.

The ideal temperature for corning meat is about 38 degrees. During the fall or spring months this is not too difficult to get. In the winter you can use an unheated part of your basement for corning meat. During hot summer months it is hard to find a place around 38 degrees. Higher temperatures will not affect the end result of your corning at all but for every 15 degrees of a higher temperature than about 38 degrees add one third more salt. At about 83 degrees for example add 3 more pounds of salt making a total of 6 pounds of salt used.

Now place your meat into the liquid. If it tends to bob up put a heavy plate on it smaller than the inside of the crock to keep it down. Cover well. A good piece of the round is wonderful corned but you can take poor pieces of meat like the brisket and corn it to make it easier to eat.

Leave the meat remain in the corning liquid for 15 days. On the fifth and tenth days stir the liquid well and remove the meat and put it back in a reverse position. After the fifteenth day remove the meat. Use what you want for immediate use and store the balance in a cool place.

The meat at this stage has a dull unappetizing color but pay no attention to this. When cooked corned meat turns a beautiful fresh red meat color that is very, very, appetizing.

COOK CORNED MEAT AS FOLLOWS:

Place the corned meat in a pan with a cover. Add enough cold water to cover the meat. Bring to a boil and remove the scum from the water. Reduce the heat and simmer for about 5 hours or until nice and tender. Season to taste and serve as the main meat dish.

AUTHENTIC IRISH CORNED BEEF AND CABBAGE

In writing about corned beef it would be a great oversight not to list this world famous recipe. It is a great recipe and if you have not tried it you have missed one of the world's finest meals. This recipe was brought to Minnesota by early Irish immigrants. It is very popular throughout Minnesota and especially in St. Paul where the population of this second largest Minnesota city is over one-third Irish.

Cook the corned beef exactly as previously described but do the following: Use about a three pound piece of corned beef. For the last hour of cooking the corned beef add six whole onions about two inches in diameter and six carrots about 8 inches long. Three small cabbages about 5 inches in diameter or smaller. The smaller cabbages have an entirely different flavor than larger ones. A small cabbage has a true Brussels sprout flavor which it loses entirely as it gets larger. Large cabbage all have a strong cabbage flavor, not a Brussels sprouts flavor at all. Note all of the vegetables are cooked whole.

Serve the meat and the vegetables together on a large platter.

This is wonderful eating.

ENGLISH ROAST BEEF

A piece of roast beef is certainly grand eating. The early English immigrants from around Lincoln, England brought with them as fine a recipe for roast beef as I have ever eaten. They added sage to it after they arrived in America. Here is how it is made:

Buy a good roast about 3 inches thick. Salt and pepper it well. Place a good sized piece of butter in your frying pan and melt it. Now place the roast in the pan and over a medium heat brown it well on both sides. Now place the roast in a pan with a cover and pour the melted butter over it. Put a half a cup of water in the pan. Put one fourth teaspoon of sage and one fourth teaspoon of dry mint leaves on the roast. The sage they learned to use in this country as it is found only in North America. Put the cover on the pan. Place in your oven at 325 to 350 degrees and roast for about 3½ hours, if you like your beef well done. About 2 hours if you like it rare. Every hour look at the roast and add enough water to keep up the half cup level. When done to suit you remove the roast and put it on your serving plate. Now take a heaping teaspoon of butter and place it in a clean frying pan over medium heat. Melt the butter. Now take a heaping tablespoon of flour and add it to the butter. Stir until well mixed with the butter. Now remove from the stove and add one half cup of cold water. The water must be cold, not hot, or the flour and the butter will become lumpy. Mix in the cold water until the butter and flour and the cold water are a smooth paste. Now place the pan back onto the stove over a medium heat. Add one eighth teaspoon of sage and one eighth teaspoon of dry mint leaves. Now add all the liquid from the pan the roast was roasted in and mix it in well. Stir all the time and leave slowly boil until it thickens. Remove and serve this gravy with the roast beef.

This recipe now is used by The Cafe Exceptionale in Minneapolis and is called Yankee Pot Roast. Yankee Pot Roast helped the Cafe Exceptionale win first or second place every year in the North American restaurant ratings.

THE REAL SECRETS OF BUYING OR ORDERING BEEF STEAK

There are few things more falsely mixed up than the buying or ordering of beef steaks. I will start right at the beginning. The animal that all of our beef cattle originated from was the European bison or buffalo. It is an animal that looks almost identical to a Texas longhorn. There were a number in Germany a few years back and probably still are. There are a great many in Africa among the cattle being raised by the natives there at present. There are a few longhorns left in Kansas, Texas, and in Mexico at this writing. I just saw one in Dodge City recently.

European bison or buffalo tastes very little different from our American bison or buffalo. If anything American bison or buffalo runs more tender on the average and with a milder beef taste and odor. The only reason that American buffalo is not widely used instead of beef is that people in North America as a whole do not like wild animal meat. They still remember the buffalo as a wild animal but forget that our cattle were also all wild buffalo just a short time ago.

Here are the names and descriptions of beef steaks. The illustration on page 67 shows areas where beef steaks are found on beef, buffalo, deer, and antelope.

1. Round steak. This is from the heavy part of the rear legs and is one of the less tender steaks.

2. Rumpsteak. Has a strong beef flavor but is one of the less tender steaks. Thought well of in England.

3. Sirloin steak. This steak is between the rump steaks and the loin steaks. It is a great favorite among men, rarely eaten by women. Requires aging if you want it real tender.

4. Bifteck. French name for pin bone sirloin steak.

5. T. Bone Steak. A loin steak with the tenderloin on it.

6. Porterhouse Steak. A T-Bone steak with the largest section of tenderloin on it.

7. New York Cut Steak. A T-Bone with the tenderloin cut out. Restaurants serve this steak a great deal as it allows them to save the tenderloin and sell it separately.

8. Tenderloin Steak. This is the inner muscle at the top of the rib cage that is part of all T. Bone steaks.

9. Chateaubriand. The third steak cut from the heavy end of a tenderloin steak.

10. Rib Steak. Found on the loin after the tenderloin muscle ends. The most popular steak in France. It has a nice beef flavor entirely different from other steaks.

11. Entrecotes. French name for rib steaks.

12. Ranch Steak. Another name for rib steaks often used in the west.

13. Belgian Entrecote Steak. The meat section of a one foot long section of rib steak loin is cut out and sliced lengthwise not crosswise as rib steaks are always sliced in North America. Makes a long delicious steak considered by far the best of all steaks in Belgium.

14. Tournedos. These steaks are uniform slices cut from the heavy part of a tenderloin. They should run about a half inch thick.

15. Stripped Tenderloin. These are the eyes of beef taken from front shoulder roasts and other roast cuts. They are served with a strip of bacon around them held on by toothpicks as they sometimes are made up of several small eyes and have to be held together. They must be well aged or they will not be too tender.

16. Scotch Tenderloin Steak. Same as blade steak. It is the heart of the front shoulder. It must be well aged or it will not be tender.

17. Blade Steak. The rear of the front shoulder. It must be well aged or it will not be tender.

18. Club Steak. This is the poorest T. Bone steak.

19. Flank Steak. This is from the belly and is coarse and dry. It should be well aged and served with lots of melted butter or a mixture of half beef suet and half butter.

20. Cube Steak. These steaks are made from any part of beef that is inexpensive. The meat is run through a machine that cuts the meat, tenderizing it.

21. Hamburger steak. This can be ground from any lean beef. ¼ teaspoon of nutmeg should be added to each pound to give it a good clean beef taste. If prepared this way with nutmeg it is as good a steak as any.

22. Minute steak is the same as cube steak. It can be made of any piece of beef run through a tenderizing cutter type of machine.

23. Swiss Steak. The poorest round steak.

24. Kansas City Steak. This is a T-bone steak with the bone and tenderloin removed. Same as New York Cut Steak, Top Loin Steak, Loin Strip Steak. Gives the restaurant a chance to sell the tenderloin separately and make more money. Strictly a restaurant and butcher racket steak.

25. Top Loin Steak. Same as Kansas City Steak, New York Cut Steak, Loin Strip Steak.
26. Loin Strip Steak. Same as Kansas City Steak, New York Cut Steak, Top Loin Steak.
27. Delmonico Steak. The eye of a rib steak. Same as Ranch Steak, Rib Eye Steak, Spencer Steak, English Beef Eater Cut Steak.
28. Spencer Steak. The eye of a rib steak. Same as Ranch Steak, Rib Eye Steak, Delmonico Steak, English Beef Eater Cut Steak.
29. English Beef Eater Cut Steak. Same as Rib Eye Steak, Ranch Steak, Delmonico Steak, Spencer Steak.
30. Chuck Steak. Cut from the triangle chuck pot roast. Good but must be aged to make it tender.
31. Shoulder Fillet Steak. Taken from the top of the shoulder. Good but must be aged to make it tender. Same as London Steak.
32. London Steak. Same as Shoulder Fillet Steak.
33. Backstrip Steak. The strips of meat taken from each side of the backbone.
34. Africa Steak. This is the thin layer of meat and fat sliced off from the upper half of the rib cage. It is very delicious and the favorite of back country Africans in Africa.
35. Nubian Steak. A slice off from the side of a round of a hind leg about one inch thick and with about a half inch of fat left on the meat. Note that this steak is cut from the side of the round not cut across the round like round steak is cut in North America. This is a wonderful steak and the favorite steak in Africa.
36. Pinwheel Steak Tenderloin. This is a flank steak or "London Broil" steak run through a meat tenderizer cutter just once then rolled to form a piece of meat that looks like a tenderloin. A wooden pin is put through the roll to hold it together. Any unsightly ends of meat are trimmed off. Flank steak

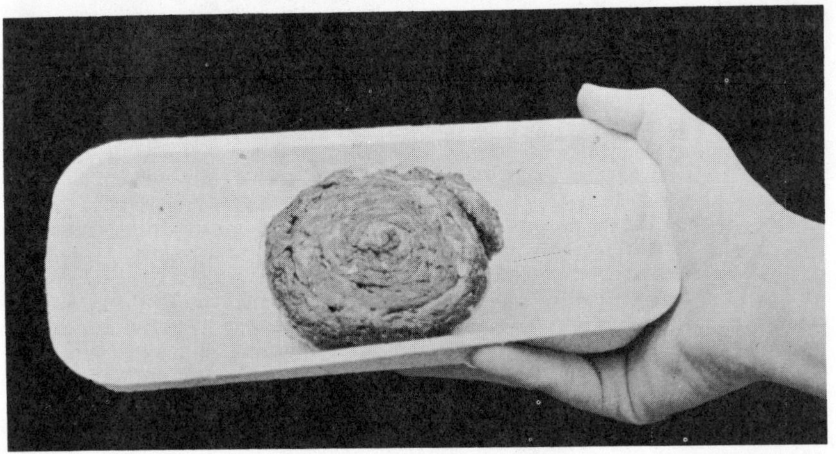

The pinwheel tenderloin steak should be priced as low as good hamburger. It is tender and has wonderful flavor.

is low in price and pinwheel steaks should cost no more than good hamburger. A pinwheel steak is tender and has a very good taste and flavor. Restaurants, however, now sell a lot of such steaks and meat packing houses now cut most flank steaks and sell it to them. If you are a good friend of your butcher he can get you some.
37. Skirt Steak Tenderloin. There is a thin piece of meat on the inside of

the front shoulder called a "skirt." The skirts used to all go into baloney and hamburger. Today the skirt is cut out and the tough sinew removed from each side of it. The skirt is then run through a meat tenderizer cutter just once. The meat is then rolled up to form a piece of meat that looks like a small tenderloin. A wooden pin is stuck through it to keep the meat from unrolling. Any unsightly edge pieces of meat are trimmed off. Skirt steak tenderloins are tender and tasty. Restaurants have found them to be very good sellers so meat packing houses now mostly cut them out and sell them just to restaurants. If your butcher wants to, he can demand them for you. They

The skirt tenderloin steak is wonderful eating and low in price.

should cost no more than good hamburger. Chicago restaurants, in particular, sell tremendous quantities of "skirt tenderloins." If you ask the waiter or even the cook in a restaurant serving skirt tenderloins, they rarely will know what part of the beef a skirt comes from. Most of the ones whom I have talked to thought that the skirts were made by slicing thin pieces from sirloin or New York cut steaks. This, of course, is not at all true.

In the United States there are the following grades of beef based on how fat the animal is. In all other parts of the world there are no grades on beef based on how fat the animal is and only in America the amount of fat on an animal makes the price higher.

1. Commercial or economy grade beef. This is beef that is not particularly fat.
2. Good grade beef. This is medium fat beef.
3. Choice grade beef. This is very fat beef.
4. Prime grade beef. This is extremely fat beef.

These American grades of beef were first established when really fat cattle were scarce as they were all grass prairie fed not corn fed. When cattle began to be corn fed the grades still lingered on and are still with us today. Over-fattening of cattle by feeding them corn gives them tremendous layers of fat on the outside of the meat and also puts veins of fat into the meat itself. The meat becomes over tender to the point of being grainless and soft like meat that has been tenderized with papaya juice dried or liquid which is the basis for all meat tenderizers. The meat loses much of its good beef aroma and tastes. European people consider over fat beef of the poorest quality and they are absolutely right. Commercial and good grades of American beef are far superior in all respects to choice and prime grades and strangely enough much cheaper in the United States but higher in Europe. You cannot fool a European by trying to sell him a lot of fat instead of meat like is being done in America today.

Buy commercial grade or good grade steaks, leave them set for 12 hours at about 75 degrees room temperature or a shorter time at a hotter temperature or a longer time at a cooler temperature. Aging beef is as simple as can be. Actually the time you leave it out is not important just leave it out until it begins to turn a darker red and it is really tender and aged. The toughest old bull steak left to age like this will be as tender as any that you have ever eaten.

As to what cut of steak to buy this is strictly a matter of personal preference.

In the United States the beef tenderloin and the T-Bone steak are by far the most popular; with rib steaks third; and sirloin fourth.

In Europe the rib steak is first by far and the tenderloin second.

In England the rump steak is first, the T-Bone second, and tenderloin third.

In Belgium the Belgian Entrecote steak is by far the first and T-Bone and tenderloin next in that order.

In Latin American countries the T-Bone is first, the tenderloin second, and the stripped tenderloin third.

ORIGIN OF THE WORD SIRLOIN STEAK

Comes from an old French word surlonge meaning top of the loin.

BEEF STEAK LEOPOLD I

You be sure to try this recipe as it does something to beef that nothing else even comes close to. Here is the original recipe:

Leopold I was born a Prince in 1790 in Saxe Cobourg, Bavaria, Germany. He was a great eater and made a great study of recipes. He became king of Belgium and was well liked by the Belgians. His first wife died in childbirth. He not only had a taste for good food but an eye for beautiful women. His second wife was Louise Marie of Orleans, a real beauty and daughter of King Louis Philippe of France.

Leopold and his wife, both were experts on cooking; but Leopold himself was the one who created the recipe Leopold I. As all really great recipes it is a simple one, yet it contains a cooking fact very few people know.

Pepper is a red berry found on a climbing East Indian shrub called piper nigrum. The flesh part of the berry when dry turns black and is used to make black pepper. The seed of the berry is white and this is used to make white pepper. After the flesh of the pepper berry and the seed are ground up to make white or black peppers for the grocery trade they have practically no taste or smell. They simply are irritants that give the impression of hotness. Grocery store ground pepper whether white or black has the bad quality of oxidizing rapidly, which causes it to lose all of its taste and flavor. The more moisture in the air the quicker either one oxidizes.

If you dry the whole pepper berry, the dried skin on the berry prevents all oxidization. To prove this to yourself buy a small pepper mill and some pepper berries which are usually called pepper corns. Grind up a few of the pepper berries onto a dish and smell them. They have a very different strong herb-like smell, never found at all in store-bought ground pepper either black or white. Your own ground pepper has this good herb smell but it is not nearly as hot as oxidized black or white pepper.

Now take your beef steak, whatever kind that you desire and lay it onto a plate. Salt it on both sides to taste. Now take your pepper mill and grind a thin coating of pepper berries over one side of the steak. Take your finger tips and press the pieces of the pepper berries into the meat as much as possible. Turn the steak over and do the same for the other side. Now broil the steak as described under broiling steak elsewhere in this book. Remove the steak when done as you desire it and quickly take a heaping spoonful of butter and spread it over the entire steak. The butter blends with the herb flavors of the pepper berries and gives the steak the best flavor you have ever tasted in a steak. It does something for beef that you just would not believe possible until you tasted it.

This is expensive eating but a recipe wonderful to use on some special occasion.

Beef Steak Leopold is available at many fine restaurants including the Brussels Restaurant at 115 East Fifty-fourth street in New York and goes under the name of Steak Poivre. At Maxim's in Paris, France, it is called Steak Albert. At Maxim's they use white pepper instead of whole ground pepper. They pour 1 ounce of hot brandy over the steak before serving it. It is very good too but I prefer holding to the original recipe to the letter.

BROILED STEAK

Steak is always a rare and choice eating item. Actually a perfectly broiled steak is very simple to make.

Melt enough butter to cover the bottom of a pan. While warm but not hot, soak up both sides of the steak in the butter for 10 or 15 minutes before putting in the broiler. Salt and pepper the steak now before putting it into the broiler, not after it is done so the salt and pepper goes into the meat.

If you use an oven have your broiler or oven at 500 degrees and leave the door half way open. If cooking outdoors cook over red hot coals, never flames. The butter is a protection against hard searing which ruins any steak, because the butter sizzling is a warning to the cook and the butter also gives a steak that nice, brown mahogany color. Do not use oil of any kind on steaks.

If your steak is a thick one and you want it well done you cannot broil it until the center is done because if you do the outside of the steak will be much too hard. On such steaks first prepare them of course exactly as described above and broil them until nicely brown on both sides. Turn off your broiler and leave your oven cool down to 325 degrees F. Place the steaks in a pan on a broiling rack and spread them generously with butter to keep them from drying out. Bake them slowly until they are well done. Baste with the juice that forms in the bottom of the pan. This runs from 30 to 45 minutes or more depending on the thickness of the steaks.

Always lift and turn a steak with a meat lifter, never a fork. A fork penetrates the steak and allows the blood and juice to come out. The blood and juice must stay in the steak to give it true steak flavor.

NEVER USE CHARCOAL FOR BROILING

Charcoal absorbs great quantities of poisonous gases. It is used for this purpose in gas masks. It will absorb 90 times its own volume of ammonia gas. Most charcoal briquets contain quantities of wood alcohol and acetic acid. These fumes are given off as the briquets burn and are extremely toxic.

Charcoal is a dark or black porous form of carbon prepared from vegetable or animal substances as by charring wood in a kiln from which air is excluded. In countries where coal and other fuels are hard to find or are too expensive charcoal is used for cooking fires.

Americans observed charcoal cooking in other countries and decided it must be a better method of broiling. Charcoal gives off various types of fumes depending on what it is made from but mostly just a dirty carbon odor. This carbon odor gives a taste to broiled food that is just the same as you would get by sprinkling carbon on the food. This taste is far more often undesirable than desirable.

For broiling meat, fish, or fowl over a fire always use hard coal. It gives off no carbon fumes like charcoal and it gives the meat, fish or fowl a much cleaner taste. Hard coal never obscures the flavor of meat, fish or fowl as charcoal definitely does.

The use of hard coal instead of charcoal in Minnesota for broiling has always been the accepted practice. Many other parts of America have also discovered this to be true. The famous restaurant, Gage and Tollner's in Brooklyn which unquestionably broils the finest fish and meat in the East uses nothing but hard coal for broiling, never charcoal.

BUTTER KNIFE STEAK

Butter knife steak is found in parts of England, Belgium, Germany, Denmark, Norway and Sweden. It is popular in Minnesota. In North America a number of restaurants feature it.

The recipe is as follows:

Buy a piece of sirloin steak 2¼ inches thick. Cut pieces out of it about four inches round. This makes them look like pieces of tenderloin or filet mignon. Spread out a layer of salt on a plate. Dip both sides of the piece of meat into the salt. Pepper the steak lightly on both sides. Have your oven at 500 degrees and leave the door half way open. Have the meat three or four inches below the heat. Brown on both sides, turn every 10 minutes and baste in its own juice or butter. Broil for 35 to 40 minutes, (18 to 20 minutes) for each side. This will give you a rare steak. For medium rare, move to four inches below heat. Broil from 45 to 50 minutes (23 to 25 minutes on each side.) For well done take the broiled rare steak and roast from one hour to two hours in your oven at 325 degrees.

Murray's, an Irish restaurant in Minneapolis, features butter knife steaks.

Steaks made in this manner in medium rare or well done are always very tender and a butter knife will easily cut them.

General broiling guide for steaks with your oven at 500 degrees and the steak three inches from the heat source is:

1 inch thick.

Rare: 10 minutes (5 each side).

Medium: 12 to 15 minutes (6 or 7 each side).

1½ inch thick:

Rare: 14 to 16 minutes (7 or 8 each side.)

Medium: 18 to 20 minutes (9 or 10 each side.)

HOW TO FRY A STEAK

A fried steak is delicious if prepared properly. At home you often do not want to dirty up your oven to broil steaks. It is, of course, far quicker to fry a steak. This is the only way a really good cook will fry a steak.

Take a large frying pan, cast iron or stainless steel with a copper bottom. Place rendered beef suet in it so that it covers the bottom about one-eighth of an inch deep. Get the suet good and hot. Salt and pepper your steak to taste. Put it in the frying pan with a meat ladle, not a fork. Sear it on both sides to hold in as much of the juices and blood as possible. Then fry until done as you desire it. Remove from the pan with a meat lifter, not a fork, and place on a paper towel for a second, then lift with your meat holder and place the other side on the towel for a second. Quickly place the steak on a warm plate and with a knife or brush or your finger, rub butter over both sides of the hot steak. Serve at once.

Beef steak, buffalo, and venison should not if possible be fried in butter as in order to cook them properly the fat must be good and hot. If butter is made hot enough for this it will burn. Beef suet gives just the right taste to the steak, does not burn and does not make the steak greasy. The steak however must be "finished" with butter as the butter adds the right touch to the steak. Many famous cooks prefer a fried steak to all others.

Many famous restaurants fry steak when you order a grilled steak as in most cases it tastes much better. In order to keep the customer happy they put in grilled lines on the steak with a piece of red hot fine steel rod.

MARIA LUISA ROQUEFORT STUFFED CHOPPED BEEF

Maria Luisa was an Austrian woman, the daughter of Francis I of Austria. She married Napoleon I of France becoming Empress of France. The French spelling of her name is Marie Louise, the same as it is spelled in English.

Austrian cooking has always been excellent and Marie Louise had been trained to know fine cooking by the very best Austrian cooks since the time she was a small girl. When she came to France she brought with her a complete collection of the finest Austrian recipes and blended them into French and Italian cooking recipes. Signor Qualiotti was Napoleon's cook and the creator of such things as Chow Chow mustard pickles, a great favorite of Napoleon's. Signor Qualiotti was quick to recognize the great ability of the Empress and learned much from her.

Marie Louise was a woman who instinctively knew good food combinations. Her Roquefort stuffed chopped beef, if you like cheese is one of the really fine dishes and like all really good recipes is simple to make if you know the trick. Here is the original recipe:

Take a medium sized handful of well ground beef. It can be ground stew meat, round steak, or any good lean piece of beef. Do not buy sirloin tip, or sirloin steak. Regardless of what a high priced restaurant owner may tell you, after lean beef has been run through a good grinder twice no one can tell whether it is lean stew meat or lean sirloin.

Make a thin flat pattie of the ground beef about six inches in diameter. The only way I know of that this can be done really well is as follows: Place the meat in the center of a piece of waxed paper. Fold the paper over on the pad of ground beef and then squash it out flat between the palms of your hand. Make two of these thin patties. Melt a heaping tablespoon of butter in a large frying pan. Put the patties into the pan and salt and pepper to taste at once. Cook them over medium heat on one side. When done on one side only turn the patties over. Immediately put a layer of thinly sliced Roquefort cheese all over the top of one of the meat patties. No need to buy French Roquefort as today's American-made Roquefort cheese is just as good or better. American-made Roquefort cheese goes under the name of Blue Cheese. Now cook the underside of the meat patties. As soon as they are done take the meat pattie with no roquefort cheese on it and place it on top of the one with the Roquefort cheese on it. Press it down slightly and remove and serve. This is served as the main dish with potatoes of any kind you might desire and a tossed salad.

In many restaurants this dish is served usually under such names as Roquefort Stuffed Chopped Sirloin Steak, or French Roquefort Stuffed Chopped Sirloin Steak, or Chopped Steak Napoleon. Invariably it is never prepared right and is difficult to eat. They take a large pad of ground beef not chopped sirloin steak and flatten it out. They then place a wad of Roquefort cheese in the center of the thick pad of meat and fold it over the cheese. They then press the meat around the cheese. Using such a method the inside of the meat never becomes cooked as the cheese acts as insulation and prevents this. Now rare steak many people like but rare ground beef no one likes in this country. Never order Roquefort Stuffed ground beef at a restaurant unless you tell the cook how to make it.

Roquefort Stuffed Chopped Beef and Chow Chow mustard pickles and French Fried Potatoes were one of Napoleon's favorite meals. When he was a prisoner on St. Helena Island he requested that he would be served this menu at least once a week. His request was never granted. I have always thought this was carrying punishment way too far.

MEAT PADDIES SHOSHONIAN

The resort town of Palm Springs, California was once the proud home of the Shoshonian Linguestic Indians. The town is located at the end of a

Palm Springs is in a desert valley between mountains.

long valley and is surrounded by mountains on three sides. Some of the mountains are so high that they have snow on them during the winter months.

There are a number of natural springs that come out of the mountain canyons. Around the springs are natural native palm trees of the "neowashingtonia

Snow-capped mountains around Palm Springs. The tree is a Joshua tree found only in desert areas.

filifera" group. There still are about 3,000 left that run about 2,500 years old. They have a small bluish fruit that is edible. When the Indians lived in

The natural springs of Palm Springs have now been made into a health "Spa" or health baths so to speak.

the area there were a few big horned sheep, mule deer, and jack rabbits. For the most part these animals tended to live around the spring areas. The Indians

Natural native palms on the Indian reservation at Palm Springs, California.

gathered mesquite beans, wild oats and grass seeds for food. They snared rabbits, deer, and sheep. The Shoshonian's were not very adept with bows and and arrows or spears.

A delicacy that they made whenever possible was meat paddies. They were made as follows.

Put a piece of meat on a flat clean rock and pound it to a pulp with a smooth rounded rock. Take cooked mesquite beans and pound them to a pulp using the same method. Now mix one third bean pulp with two thirds meat pulp. Form into a paddie and cook on a hot rock. Make a quick present day authentic version as follows.

Buy a can of pork and beans. Open and put in a large mixing bowl. Take a fork or good potato masher and mash the beans into a pulp. Take one third bean pulp and two thirds hamburger and mix well together. Season to taste with salt and pepper. Form into hamburger paddies and fry in butter. Serve on hamburger buns with onions, pickles or whatever relish you desire. It is really good eating.

Today there are a number of "atmosphere" restaurants in Palm Springs but none of them anything special.

Hollywood, thank goodness, is dead. Television has at least done incalculable good in destroying this evil group. Hollywood created an era where

One of the many restaurants in Palm Springs.

prostitutes were made national heroines simply because they bedded well with some studio owners. Marriage was treated as a farce and divorce became a ticket for a whore to move from one house to another. Millions of dollars a year were paid to incompetent people posed as actors. These incompetents were publicized as national heroes by the studio moguls.

In Palm Springs, today, a few aging so-called Hollywood stars are making a last feeble effort to ruin a town. They bilked the public out of billions of dollars yet will not let Palm Spring citizens even tell you where their homes are. They are gods, you know, in their own small minds. They took all the money they could get from the public but now are so self-styled important that the public cannot even gaze at them unless they pay. The President of the United States always lets people know where he lives but these show world punks are too self important to let the public, that gave them every penny that they have, have even a look at where they live. Among them are the U. S. O. heroes who fought World War II in officers club's and used the U. S. O. merely for free publicity for themselves or "exposure" as they call it. They had movies made of their so-called "free" U. S. O. shows and ran them on television. Here too, come the shylocks that for more "free exposure," will try to sponsor a campaign against any disease. We have really fine people only too willing to do this sort of work. If Palm Springs could get rid of the old movie and television self-styled tin gods it would be a fine resort area.

Palm Springs is a far superior winter resort area than such dreary places as Scottsdale, Arizona. Palm Springs has dozens of real mountains on its perimeter not just a hill like Camelback hill in Scottsdale. If left alone Palm Springs could be a fine solid town that any country would be proud of.

BELGIAN BURGERS

This is one of the rare recipes that produces food entirely different than anything you have ever eaten, yet is simple to make and requires no fancy ingredients.

This recipe was invented by Berthe Gramme in Belgium.

Take a hamburger bun and lightly butter both sides of it. On one side put mustard and catsup or tomato sauce on the bun. On the other side put a thin raw hamburger. On top of the hamburger put sliced raw onions and sliced dill pickle. Carefully put the two pieces of the bun together. Place in a small covered baking dish or wrap in aluminum foil. Put in your oven at 400 degrees and bake about 40 minutes. Remove and leave cool a bit. Take a knife and fork and cut the burger into about four parts and eat.

The butter, hamburger juice, onion juice and pickle juice, baked catsup and mustard blend into a taste you would not recognize. A very wonderful recipe, be sure to try it.

FINNISH HAMBURGER

When the Finlanders came to Minnesota they settled in the northern areas as it was very similar to their native Finland. The Finns are wonderful fish cooks and also meat cooks. The early Finnish method of preparing hamburger makes it a dish worth walking miles to get.

Take a large tablespoon of butter and put it in a large frying pan. Cut up a medium sized onion into small pieces and fry the pieces in the butter until they are just half done, not completely cooked. Salt and pepper a pound of hamburger well and add it to the onions. Stir the hamburger with a fork while you cook it so that it breaks up as it cooks into small pieces. When cooked spread it hot on buttered bread so that it melts the butter. Eat it while it is hot.

LUMBERJACK HAMBURGER

I have heard more famous cooks say that you could tell a good cook from a bad one by the way they cooked hamburger easier than any other way. There is a lot of truth in this as a good hamburger is hard to get.

This recipe is the old lumberjack method brought in by the French. It is as simple as could be but is today a forgotten art.

Put a large tablespoon of butter in your frying pan and have the heat on medium hot only. Melt the butter until it is brown. Remember brown, not just melted. Do not use lard, bacon grease, margarine or any modern shortening or oil, just use butter. Butter and beef form a taste that nothing else comes even close to duplicating. Now salt and pepper your hamburger before you make it into paddies. The salt and pepper thus penetrates the meat and gives it an entirely different taste than if you salt and pepper the paddies in the pan. Make your paddies by putting the desired amount of hamburger in the center of a large square of wax paper. Fold over the wax paper on the hamburger. Then press on the wax paper and flatten out the hamburger nice and thin. You cannot flatten out hamburgers thin enough with your hands. Thick hamburgers are dry and tasteless. As ground meat when it is cooked thick dries out badly. Now fry the hamburgers slowly turning frequently. When done remove. Now take the bread or bun you are to serve it on and put the faces that the hamburger will rest on down into the butter and meat sauce and fry the bread or bun for a minute. Now place your hamburger on the bread or bun. Add whatever trimmings you prefer such as pickles, onions, mustard, catsup, etc., or none at all.

I have eaten in nearly every country in the world and dishes with the fanciest of names but a hamburger prepared in this way is as fine a tasting food as you will ever find.

HAMBURGER CHATEAUBRIAND

Francois Rene Vicomte de Chateaubriand was born in France in 1768. He grew up to be just a fair author but an excellent eater. He gave the name Chateaubriand to the thickest best cut from the heavy end of a beef tenderloin. This name is still used for this cut in restaurants the world over.

His great contribution to eating however was not naming the Chateaubriand steak but in the use of cooked and dried oatmeal with meat. Oatmeal is a strange food. It contains more easily digested food and vitamins than any other grain. That is why of all grains babies do by far the best on it. Oatmeal also contains enzymes that do very strange things especially to meats.

Hamburger Chateaubriand is a very special recipe. Here is the original recipe.

Take one pound of ground beef. It need not be the best grade at all. Take one pound of ground pork liver. Beef liver will do just as well if pork liver is not available. You may have trouble getting your butcher to grind the pork liver for you, as they do not like to run pork liver through their grinders. They have to wash out the grinder afterwards so other meat that they grind will not have a tinge of liver taste. If he refuses to do it for you, just tell him that you will take your business to someone who will, and you will have no difficulty with him.

Take a large bowl and mix the ground beef and ground liver together with two cups of one minute rolled oats. This one minute rolled oats saves you from cooking and drying the oats. Season with salt and pepper to taste. The oats blends with the meat and actually becomes a part of it.

Make hamburger patties of the mixture and fry them. Serve as hamburger steaks or on buns with pickles, onion, mustard, catsup etc., whatever you prefer. The oatmeal firms the meat making it delicious and tender in texture and with a slight pink tinge.

Everyone likes these hamburgers even when they cannot stand liver. Those who like liverwurst, liver cheese, liver sausage just can't get enough of these hamburgers.

This hamburger Chateaubriand is the healthiest meat that exists. The liver in it builds up your blood better than any tonic ever devised.

MEAT LOAF CHATEAUBRIAND

Francois Rene Vicomte de Chateaubriand was born in France in 1768. He will be forever remembered for giving the name of Chateaubriand to the thickest beef cut from the heavy end of a beef tenderloin. His greatest contribution to eating, however, was inventing the use of cooked in dried oatmeal with meat. His Hamburger Chateaubriand is a classic and his meat loaf Chateaubriand is so good you never tire of it.

I am very fond of meat loaf. I like early American meat loaf made with ground beef and bread soaked in milk, and Belgian meat loaf made with ground beef, a little ground pork, eggs, cooked vegetables and cooked macaroni. In fact I thoroughly enjoy all the many good meat loaves made the world over.

Meat Loaf Chateaubriand, however, is excellent and one to be sure to try. Here is the recipe.

Put two eggs into a large mixing crock and mix well with a fork. Add one pound of ground beef. The ground beef need not be the best grade at all. Add one cup of dry one minute oatmeal. This saves cooking and preparing it. Add one level teaspoon of salt and one fourth teaspoon of black pepper, ¼ teaspoon of nutmeg. Mix all ingredients together well.

The following additions are optional and were not with the original recipe but I like them added very well and maybe you will. Add one chopped onion about two inches in diameter, and one small can of pimentoes juice and all.

Grease a meat loaf pan with butter and form your meat loaf in it. Bake for about one hour at 350 degrees. The oatmeal will keep the meat a slight pinkish color.

Eating a meat loaf like this is known among good eaters as eating high off from the hog. I certainly agree that it is.

BEEF STROGANOFF

Beef Stroganoff was invented by Serge Stroganoff, a court cook in the reign of Catherine the Great of Russia. Catherine was the daughter of the Duke of Anholt-zervst of Prussia, born in 1729. She was a cruel despot and full of personal vices but did a great deal to help Russian scientists, writers, and philosophers and to westernize Russia as much as possible. She also encouraged Russian cooks such as Stroganoff to adapt French cooking methods and also to create new Russian dishes. She was a great woman for romancing and during her more youthful days would have a different lover every night or so. She had them killed for some trumped up charge as she tired of them. She died of heart failure in 1796 in the arms of her last young lover, Prince Platow Louboff at the age of 67. She certainly was quite a woman.

The Beef Stroganoff as served in restaurants today is a far cry from the original recipe. Regular cook book recipes are also poor imitations at best and far from the original. You can get the same sorry, greasy result by just mixing a little sour cream into beef gravy and serving it on beef roast. Here is the original recipe and it is an excellent way of serving beef. Note that the original recipe contains no sour cream, tomato paste, puree, no mushrooms, or no beef tenderloin. Here are the ingredients:

3 level tablespoons of butter.
3 level tablespoons of chopped onion.
1 tablespoon of flour.
1½ cups of clear beef soup or consomme.
1 cup of sour buttermilk.
2 pounds of beef stew meat or two pounds of a good shoulder roast.
¼ teaspoon of black pepper.
¼ teaspoon of salt.

Take the beef stew meat or the roast and slice it up into pieces as thin as you can or about one fourth of an inch thick, at the thickest. The thinner the better. The pieces should not be more than about two inches square. Salt and pepper the meat to taste. Put 3 level tablespoons of butter into a frying pan and 3 level tablespoons of chopped onion. Add the meat. Over a medium heat cook until the meat is done.

Make a sauce or gravy as follows. Put two level tablespoons of butter into a large frying pan and melt the butter until it just barely starts to turn brown. Take off from the stove. Now add 1¾ level tablespoons of flour into the hot butter until the mixture forms a medium syrupy consistency not a thick paste. Remember not a thick paste. Add more butter if necessary. Now add 1½ cups of cold clear beef soup or consomme and stir in well. (You can make clear beef soup by simply boiling a piece of beef about four inches in diameter or so in two cups of water. You can buy consomme in cans.) Now place back onto the stove and over a medium heat bring to a slow boil. Stir continually. Now add one cup of sour buttermilk and stir in well. Be sure to use sour buttermilk not sour cream. Sour cream is terrifically greasy, in fact almost as greasy as using the same amount of butter and not at all suited for this purpose. Now pour the meat, onion and butter sauce into the gravy and gently simmer just enough so that it is well heated. Serve with mashed potatoes or boiled white rice and dark bread.

Note: To sour buttermilk simply cover a bowl of buttermilk and leave stand until it thickens. This recipe was often used with venison and bear meat as well as beef. The meat must be sliced as thin as possible. That is one of the secrets of real Beef Stroganoff.

MENUDO OF TRIPE

Tripe is the first stomach of a cow. It is used to hold the grass and grain before it goes into the cow's regular stomach. Many people have never eaten tripe and are really missing one of the world's really fine meats.

Tripe is featured at Antoine's Restaurant in New Orleans which is rated as North America's finest restaurant. They serve Tripes a la mode de Caen, which is one of the good foods that have made them so famous. Galatoire's Restaurant in New Orleans features Eggs a la tripe and they are delicious. Tripe can be bought in most of the meat markets of the southwest and south. If they do not have it any grocer will quickly get it for you.

Here is this famous recipe.

Fill a covered pot with three quarts of water, add one level tablespoon of salt and bring to a boil. Take three pounds of tripe and wash it and scrape it well in three changes of cold water. Then cut it up into one inch squares and add to the boiling water. Boil for one hour and twenty-five minutes keeping the water level the same. Then add three medium sized carrots cut up into one inch pieces and two medium sized potatoes cut up into one inch squares. Boil for 30 minutes. Add one large one pound can of cooked garbanzos or Ram's Head peas. Have the following prepared and add and boil for ten minutes more.

Take five level tablespoons of beef suet and melt in a frying pan. Cut up one, two inch onion into small pieces and brown them in the beef suet over medium heat. Add one half teaspoon of cumin powder, one level teaspoon of chili powder, one half teaspoon of paprika to the beef suet and onion. Stir them in well.

Put into large individual bowls and salt and pepper to taste and serve with crackers. It is really delicious.

In some parts of the Southwest tripe is served with hominy. Hominy is certainly good food but should never be used in menudo. Eating hominy in menudo is like shaking hands with an empty glove.

Antoine's recipe for Tripe a la Mode de Caen is as follows:

Wash and scrape three pounds of fresh tripe in 3 changes of cold water. Cut into strips about 2½ inches long by ½ inch wide. Take a Dutch oven of metal or ceramic and put ¼ pound of thinly sliced salt pork in the bottom. Then add the following. Two medium sized carrots about eight inches long diced, 2 onions about 2 inches in diameter sliced thinly, 2 large leeks sliced thinly, 2 large celery stalks grated. One large green pepper grated, one level tablespoon of finely cut up parsley. Sprinkle the following over the mixture. One eighth level teaspoon of thyme and ⅛ level teaspoon of marjoram, ⅛ level teaspoon of mace, ¼ level teaspoon of freshly ground peppercorns, 2 large bay or laurel leaves, 3 whole cloves and a level teaspoon of salt. Your Dutch oven should now be nearly full. Fill the pot with equal parts of consomme and apple cider. Put the lid onto the Dutch oven. If the lid is not absolutely tight seal up any cracks with a dough made from flour and water. Bake in a very slow oven for about 12 hours.

Remove and add the following: 6 small green onions or shallots diced and just barely browned in butter, 1 cup of tomato paste. Stir in carefully. Add one fourth cup of Calvados or apple brandy if you have it. This is not necessary. Serve in a deep warm platter or casserole and garnish with pieces of fresh parsley and squares of puff paste pastry or German toast. I much prefer the German toast with this famous dish.

KIDNEYS HENRY THE VIII

Henry the VIII was King of England from 1509 to 1547. He had six wives. The first, Catherine d'Aragon, the second, Anne Boleyn, the third, Jane Seymour, the fourth, Anne de Cleves, the fifth, Catherine Howard, and the sixth, Katryn Parr. He had the heads chopped off from Anne Boleyn and Catherine Howard. Katryn Parr his last wife was the only one who was more than a match for him. At the same time she was married to Henry she was spending more than an occasional night with Tom Seymour the brother of Jane Seymour, Henry's third wife.

Henry the VIII actually never amounted to anything and would not have made a good ditch digger. The only thing that he ever did do to his credit was to highly endorse the kidneys made by Elizabeth Grant, one of his many cooks.

Here is the original recipe and it is the only way to properly prepare kidneys. Today the cooking of kidneys is a lost art and most people buy them for their cats and dogs because they do not know how to cook them. Kidneys properly prepared are one of the finest meats and contain far more digestible food value and vitamins than such things as beef roast, or pork chops. In judging meats for food value and in many other ways animals have far more intelligence than man. A mountain lion will kill a deer and eat the liver, kidneys, stomach and heart first. These organs contain the highest food values and most vitamins in the entire animal. Unless the lion is very hungry it will leave such things as the roasts and steaks to other less fortunate predators who have to take what is left and like it.

Here is the original recipe of Elizabeth Grant:

Take three large beef kidneys and remove all fat from them. Put them into a pot of boiling water with three level tablespoons of vinegar in the water and boil for twenty minutes. Remove from the stove, throw away the water, add new water and boil for another twenty minutes. Remove and again throw away the water, add fresh water and boil for another 20 minutes. Remove the kidneys from the water and leave them cool. When cool cut out any tubes in the kidneys. Now slice the kidneys in one fourth inch thick slices. Take a medium sized frying pan and put two level teaspoons of butter and two level tablespoons of beef suet and melt. Add one chopped up leek or onion about two inches in diameter. Put in the slices of kidney and brown them lightly on both sides. Serve with a few fresh leeks or onions and season to taste.

Kidneys fried in this manner are one of the finest meats you have ever eaten. The secret in cooking kidneys is to boil them in three waters for one hour before they are fried. A good modern touch is to sprinkle the fried kidneys with paprika just before serving.

If you try to fry kidneys without first boiling them like the magazine food department cooks tell you they will smell like you are trying to fry a piece of an old toilet seat and they will taste just about as bad.

WHERE TO GET GOOD BUFFALO AND ELK MEAT

The Black Hills wild buffalo and elk herds need thinning out every year. You can buy really good buffalo or elk meat by writing to Custer State Park, Hermosa, South Dakota.

Two year old buffalo bulls just right for eating run in price as follows fully dressed out. These two year old buffalo are tender and have a good mild flavor even milder than most beef. A two year old bull will weigh about 600 pounds dressed. Half or whole buffalo 35c a pound.

Buffalo liver 25c a pound. Buffalo liver is much better tasting than beef or pork liver. Buffalo tongue 25c a pound. Buffalo tongue is a

A two year old buffalo has a milder flavor and is more tender than beef.

great delicacy. It is wonderful eating. Much better than beef tongue.

Two year old bull elk fully dressed out priced as follows:

Elk are a lot better eating than deer.

Half or whole elk 30c a pound.

Elk liver 25c a pound. Elk liver is delicious. Far better than beef or pork liver.

Elk tongue 25c a pound. Elk tongue is very good.

Get your orders in as soon as you can as they do not usually have too many to sell. Either buffalo or elk make a wonderful treat for a sportsmen's club supper or church supper. They ship the meat frozen express collect.

THE WORLD'S FINEST EUROPEAN TYPE BEEF

As I have before mentioned all of our beef cattle come from the European

African Longhorned Cattle

buffalo or bison. The Texas Longhorn was the closest to the European wild buffalo that we have ever had in this country. Their horns grow to a six or eight foot spread. A five year old steer will grow about a six foot

African Longhorned Cattle

spread of horns. Incidentally the longhorns that you see for sale today are all from Africa. In Africa today there are a great many longhorned cattle and the horns are all shipped over here to be sold for decorative purposes as genuine Texas Longhorns. These African Longhorns have horns much longer and with wider spreads than the genuine Texas Longhorns ever had.

The longhorn cattle were hard to handle because of their long horns. They also had bad tempers. Wolves and mountain lions are not able to attack genuine longhorn cattle as the cattle will actually attack them and kill them.

The beef from longhorn cattle is the finest European type of beef available in any of the various breeds. It is far superior in taste and tenderness to short horns, white face or even black angus cattle.

Every farmer and rancher should raise a few genuine longhorns just for his own beef if nothing else. If you have a freezer you can buy one and put it up in your freezer.

Genuine Texas Longhorns can be bought from the Wichita Refuge, Cache, Oklahoma. This is a United States Government refuge. They have a herd of about 330 genuine longhorns and sell off the surplus each year.

GETHSEMENE BEEF

On the night of the Last Supper we all know that Jesus and the Apostles had bread and wine for supper. The table was U shaped not a straight table as shown in most pictures of The Last Supper. Meat, of course, was also served as was the tradition of that time and it was prepared in the usual manner of the time. Whether the meat was mutton or beef no one knows. Chances are it was mutton as beef was not as widely eaten at that time. Here is the meat recipe used in Jerusalem at this time and it is a great recipe.

Take a 3 pound piece of beef roast. It should be economy grade and as free from fat as possible. It can be any cut. A good blade roast or rump roast is excellent. Place the roast in a good sized pot and cover it with water. Add two whole peeled onions about two inches in diameter, ½ level teaspoon of ground cardamon, ½ level teaspoon of ground cinnamon, ½ level teaspoon of ground allspice, ½ level teaspoon of ground nutmeg, 3 laurel or bay leaves, 1 clove of fresh garlic or ½ teaspoon of powdered garlic, 1 level teaspoon of salt and ¼ level teaspoon of ground black pepper. You can vary the salt and pepper to taste.

Boil for three hours over medium heat replacing the water that boils off. Then remove the meat and leave drain. Slice it as thinly as possible and serve. The meat will have a delicate pink color on the inside and be brown on the outside. It has a rich, herb flavor that makes the finest eating. There is no other recipe that produces meat with a flavor like this. Venison, antelope, moose, caribou, bear and mutton are all wonderful using this recipe. The recipe is the one that present day kosher corned beef comes from except that inexpensive sodium nitrate and sodium nitrite are used to make the meat pink to save on expensive spices to make it pink, yet kosher corned beef runs about $2.00 a pound. Irish corned beef came also from this old basic recipe and was brought to Ireland by the early Christian missionaries.

SAUERBRATEN

Sauerbraten was invented by Charlemagne who died in A. D. 814. The recipe was used as a means of using up left over roasted meat. Albert of Cologne in the thirteenth century a man like Charlemagne much interested in foods and gardening used the recipe with fresh meat. Albert of Cologne incidentally through a mutation of a loose leaf cabbage discovered the first really good hard headed cabbage in northern Europe.

The original sauerbraten recipes are far superior to the ones passed off today in Europe as well as in North America for sauerbraten. Prepared with the basic original recipes, sauerbraten is an excellent main course dish that most all people enjoy very much.

Here is the basic sauerbraten recipe:

Take a four pound beef or venison roast. Make a pickling solution as follows: 2 quarts of vinegar, 1 leak or onion about two inches in diameter sliced thinly. 1 level tablespoon of salt. There was no pepper, cloves or bay leaves in those days but adding them does help greatly. Add one half level teaspoon of pepper, 3 bay leaves and four whole cloves. Place the pickling mixture in a pot and put the roast into it. Put it in your refrigerator or a cool place. Leave the roast soak for four days turning the roast every day, then remove the roast from the pickling solution. Now put three level tablespoons of beef suet into a frying pan and melt. Put the meat into the pan over a medium heat and lightly brown it on both sides. Then remove the meat. Put the meat into a roaster pan. Take one half of the pickling liquid, one half cup of water, ½ tablespoon of honey (sugar will also do) mix together well and pour into the roasting pan. Put a cover on the pan. Roast the meat for 2½ to 3 hours at 350 degrees. Add water if necessary to keep the liquid level the same. When done remove the meat from the roasting pan and put on a meat serving platter.

Take two level tablespoons of flour and dissolve in a cup of cold water. Add water to liquid in the bottom of the roasting pan and stir in well. Put the roasting pan on the stove and boil gently to form a gravy. Add four level tablespoons of cottage cheese. Stir into the gravy until it just is barely mixed in then remove from the stove and serve.

Sauerbraten never did and should not ever contain such things as tomatoes, gingersnaps, sour cream, bacon or pork.

Sauerbraten as I stated before originated as a means of using up left over roasted meat, and actually is still preferred by many food experts to sauerbraten made from fresh meat. Here is how it is done. Take your left over beef or venison roast and put it in the pickling solution for 24 hours.

Take your left over gravy add three or four tablespoons of the pickling liquid to it or whatever amount suits your tastes and add also three or four tablespoons of cottage cheese to it or whatever amount suits your taste. Remove the meat from the pickling solution, break it up into medium sized pieces, and warm it up in the gravy. You will have a delicious meal.

Antelope, elk, deer, buffalo, soup ducks, bear, all make wonderful sauerbraten either using the fresh meat or leftovers. People who normally will not eat any of these meats invariably like them very much when made into sauerbraten.

CHURCH BUILDER CHICKEN

This recipe has done more good I believe than any other recipe in the world. It originated in Virginia but has spread over a large part of this country. It came to Minnesota with a pretty blonde girl, Ellen, daughter of Mrs. Thomas Powell of Emporia, Virginia. Mrs. Powell's daughter married Dale Schmidt, a Minnesota soldier, and came to live in Minnesota.

In Virginia, as well as everywhere else it has unfortunately always been hard work to raise money to build churches. Selling cakes, pies, candy, etc., has always worked fairly well to raise church money but not anything too spectacular. In Virginia, a recipe originally called chicken muddle was offered at church sales and it outsold everything and soon took the name of Church Builder Chicken. Church Builder Chicken has built not hundreds but thousands of churches. Today it sells for $1.25 a quart and is the biggest bargain you ever got. It is very fine eating, be sure to not only try it at your home but have your church try it. Have them label the jars Church Builder Chicken from the original Virginia Recipe:

Here are the ingredients:

1 good sized chicken.
½ lb. of uncut bacon.
2 large onions. (3 inches in diameter.)
4 lbs. potatoes.
5 cans lima beans or butter beans as they are called in the South. (drained) (No. 2 cans.)
2 cans of whole kernel corn. (drained) (No. 2 cans.)
5 cans of tomatoes. (No. 2 cans.)
½ level teaspoon of red pepper.
½ level teaspoon of black pepper.
1½ teaspoons of salt.

Proceed as follows: Take your chicken and cook in a pressure cooker until done enough so that the meat comes off the bones easily. Remove the meat from the bones, break up into bite size pieces and place the chicken meat back in the pressure cooker just for storage. Do not pressure cook it any further. Peel the 4 pounds of potatoes and boil them until well done. Usually takes about 20 minutes. Drain the water from the potatoes and mash them. Now dice your 2 large onions and put them with the chicken in the pressure cooker. Add the 5 cans of drained lima beans, 2 cans of drained whole kernel corn and 5 cans of tomatoes. Leave the top off from the pressure cooker and bring to a slow boil over medium heat. Then remove from the stove. Take the half pound of uncut bacon and cut it up into half inch squares. Place on a tray in the oven and leave until pretty well done. Now put the bacon cubes with the chicken mixture in the pressure cooker. Add 1½ level teaspoons of salt, ½ level teaspoon of red pepper, ½ level teaspoon of black pepper. Now put in the mashed potatoes and leave slowly boil over a medium heat for 45 minutes or until thick. Stir frequently to keep from burning.

Serve with good bread and butter. This recipe is one of those that pleases everyone.

JEFFERSON DAVIS SOUTHERN CHICKEN

After the War between the States many Confederate soldiers upon returning home found their homes and farms burned and completely destroyed and everything they owned gone. They were refugees simply not knowing where their next meal was coming from. Many of these soldiers were so discouraged with their plight that they decided to leave the South entirely and try their luck in the homestead areas. A great many of them went West, and some went to Minnesota where there was plenty of land for homesteading. Among those who came to Minnesota were the McLin brothers from the personal body guard of Jefferson Davis, the President of the Confederacy. They settled on a lake called Silver Lake a few miles from Waseca, Minnesota, and built log cabins for their families. They were wooden bridge builders by trade and farmed and built bridges to earn a living for their families. Other refugee Confederate soldiers settled on homesteads through the area. They were all the finest possible people, hard working and honest and won the respect of everyone. The Southern families soon intermarried with the early Minnesota immigrants and became a true part of the area.

The Southern families brought with them true Southern or as you should say "Dixieland" cooking. This cooking is far different than the cooking that

The home in New Orleans where Jefferson Davis died.

is done in the South today which as a whole is not anywhere near what it used to be. Dixieland as all Southern people know comes from the French word Dix meaning ten. A Dixie was a $10 bill widely circulated in Louisiana and the South before the War Between The States. A Dixie had a large "Dix" in the center of the reverse side.

True Southern cooking is English, Scotch, and Irish cooking blended with French cooking. Makes a wonderful practically unbeatable combination. Today's Southern cooking for the most part has gone down and in most cases is about as Southern as General Grant and simply is not anywhere near like, or as good as it used to be. I have a great many Southern friends and they heartily agree on this.

Contrary to opinion chicken is not naturally a tender meat. All of our chickens came directly only a short time ago from the Chinese and India, Red Jungle Fowl. Red Jungle Fowl look almost exactly like an overgrown Bantam chicken. Their flesh is stringy and dry with a tendency for toughness.

Southern cooked chicken used to be the finest you could get anywhere. Everyone knew this to be a well established fact. Today if you order Southern cooked chicken you usually get chicken pan-fried or deep fried in a heavy batter. There are worse ways of cooking chicken but you would have to look hard to find them. The batter on such chicken is greasy and heavy and if you eat it with the meat the batter and grease taste and odor is so pronounced that you cannot tell whether the meat is fresh or from some half spoiled chicken. When you get down near the bone you are just as apt to run into some pink uncooked flesh. No one usually has to tell you where the kitchen is when such chicken is being cooked. You can locate it by the smell of the strong grease from well outside of the house.

Jefferson Davis was a man who liked food well prepared and saw to it himself that his cooks knew how to cook. He prided himself on the meals in his house and they were excellent yet, not actually any better than in most of the Southern homes during this period. Southern cooking was then a thing to really dream about.

This is Jefferson Davis' own recipe, always used in his home for cooking chicken. It should certainly be revived:

Take a well cleaned chicken and carefully disjoint and cut off the the legs. Then split the chicken down the middle with a heavy knife. Cut the back from the breast pieces. In other words, the chicken should be cut up into serving portions. Place the pieces in a pressure cooker and cook for about 20 minutes. If an old chicken you may have to add 10 minutes to this time. This will really tenderize the meat taking away all of its natural tendency for stringiness. No other method will do this. In the old days no pressure cooker was used. Two large bars of cast iron were set along each side of the handle on the cover of the cooking pot. It took some longer to tenderize and precook the chicken pieces but the end result was identical. It was not known as pressure cooking the chicken but as steaming it.

If you boil a chicken in water before frying it you boil the flavor out of the meat and tend to make the meat dry and rubbery. If you just pan fry or French fry raw chicken pieces even though it is a tender springer it will tend to be stringy and rubbery.

Now remove the chicken pieces from the pressure cooker and dust them lightly with fine cracker crumbs. Remember lightly, not heavily. Most people do not eat the batter on chicken as it sticks to the skin of the chicken and they do not eat the skin either. Actually the batter simply serves to prevent the chicken from being cooked too hard on the inside.

Put four heaping teaspoons of butter into a large frying pan and melt over a medium heat. Save money any way you can, but do not try to save it by using margarine or cooking oils or fats to pan fry chicken. Chicken can only be fried in butter. Pan fry the pieces of chicken until light brown. Keep turning them frequently. This will only take you about five minutes. Remove and serve at once while good and hot. This recipe makes really fine chicken, one of the very best foods known to this world.

CHICKEN A' LA KING

Chef George Greenwald was working at the Brighton Beach Hotel, Brighton Beach in 1898. He was an excellent cook and worked hard to please his boss, E. Clarke King II. One summer afternoon he prepared a special chicken dish for Mr. Clark and served it to him for supper. Mr. King thought it wonderful and told Greenwald to put it on the menu. Greenwald did and called it Chicken a' la King. In those days society came to Brighton Beach a great deal. The new dish was a great success and soon became popular all over North America.

Here is George Greenwald's original recipe, for eight servings:

2 level tablespoons of butter.
½ green pepper medium sized shredded on a metal kitchen shredder.
1 cup of thinly sliced mushroom stems and pieces.
2 level tablespoons of white flour.
½ level teaspoon of salt.
¼ level teaspoon of black pepper.
2 cups of cream, just regular cream, not whipping cream.
3 cups of cut up boiled chicken.
¼ cup of butter, heated until soft and worked until creamy.
3 egg yolks.
1 teaspoon of onion juice.
1 tablespoon of lemon juice.
½ level teaspoon of paprika.
¼ cup of sherry wine.
2 ounces of canned pimento cut in small strips.

Put the two tablespoons of butter in a pan and melt. Add the shredded green pepper and sliced mushrooms and simmer over a medium heat for 5 minutes. Add the two tablespoons of flour and ½ teaspoon of salt and ¼ teaspoon of pepper. Stir and cook until frothy. Be sure that the flour is worked in well and the mixture smooth. Mix in 2 cups of cream, stir carefully until the sauce is thickened. Now pour into the top of a double boiler. Add the 3 cups of cut up boiled chicken being sure that all the skin is removed from the pieces. Heat well over the hot water in the double boiler. Beat the creamed ¼ cup of butter into the 3 egg yolks. Add 1 teaspoon of onion juice, 1 tablespoon of lemon juice and ½ teaspoon of paprika to the butter and egg yolks. Add them slowly to the hot chicken mixture stirring carefully until thickened and smooth. Add the shredded pimento. Remove from the boiler and add ¼ cup of sherry wine stirring it in carefully. Serve at once on pieces of hot buttered toast. You can also serve it in patty shells or in a nest of noodles. You can leave out the sherry wine if you do not care for a touch of wine flavoring.

This is an expensive dish to make but an excellent one for a very special occasion.

CHICKEN OR PHEASANT SUPREME OR KIEV

This famous method of preparing chicken or pheasant is not of Russian origin as the name Kiev would imply. It was invented by Appert, a Frenchman who invented the canning of food and is called Chicken Supreme. The name Kiev was given this method of preparing chicken or pheasant by early New York restaurants to try to please the many Russian immigrants. The name went back to Europe and is and was used in many places to describe Chicken Supreme. The correct name however is Chicken or Pheasant Supreme and should always be used.

Chicken or Pheasant Supreme is a great delicacy and its preparation is a secret known by only a few cooks. Here is the original recipe.

We are going to eat good tonight.

Take a pheasant or chicken and remove the breast and the skin on the breasts. Take the legs, neck, wings, back meat and use it for a soup or stew or fry and roast it. None of this meat is used in this recipe. Take the breasts and slice them about three sixteenths of an inch thick with the grain of the meat not across the grain. Slice into flat pieces as large as possible. Put these flat pieces onto a wooden board or counter top. Take a saucer and with the edge of the saucer pound the pieces of breast all over in one direction and then in the other direction. Be careful not to cut the breast into pieces with the pounding but give them a good thorough pounding. The breast should look like a piece of thin hamburger when you are finished pounding it. Now take a piece of soft butter about one inch square. Shape it roughly into the shape of a cone. Place the butter in the center of the pounded breast. Fold the breast over the butter with about a one inch lap. Press the edges of the breast tightly together with your fingers. Then with the edge of the saucer pound the lap lightly to seal it very well. Pounding the breasts makes the meat stick and seal together tightly. Take one large egg and break it into a bowl. Take the juice of half a lemon and mix it into the egg. The lemon juice will turn the egg into a very thin liquid. Add just a pinch of dried onion powder. Dip the pieces of chicken or pheasant breast carefully into the mixture. Take your fingers and smear the mixture on any places that are not well covered. Now roll the pieces in a mixture of one half white flour and one half bread crumbs. Heat beef suet in your French fryer to about 380 to 390 degrees, this is good and hot but not smoking hot. Put the floured breasts into the beef suet and fry for about five to seven minutes or until just done. Do not overfry them. It does not take long to cook them. Remove and serve at once as the main meat dish. When the person cuts into the pheasant or chicken the melted butter blended with the flavor of the meat squirts out forming a delicious sauce for the meat.

You can take about the last four inches of the leg bone of the chicken or pheasant and wrap the breast meat with the butter placed in it around it on one end. Then dip it in the batter and French fry it. This is purely presentation and has nothing to do with the recipe. Chicken or pheasant Supreme is delicious eating and what you might call a spectacular dish. A good one to use on someone who you desire to impress with your cooking ability.

Chicken Kiev is served very well at the Cafe Exceptionale in Minneapolis, Minnesota. This is the only restaurant in North America that does serve it well.

Charlie's Cafe Exceptionale, Minneapolis, Minnesota one of the world's finest restaurants. Has its own built-in bakery and butcher shop.

CHICKEN OR PHEASANT INDIAN STYLE OR CHICKEN CACCIATORE

Some recipe books and restaurants believe that words are the most important part of a recipe or menu. They give very fancy names to poor basic recipes that they dream up and try to fool you into thinking they are really something. "Chicken Tetrazzini" is a typical example. Tetrazzini means in "little pieces" in Italian nothing more. It usually is a very poor hot dish made of pieces of chicken, spaghetti and a flour chicken gravy. Sometimes heavy cream and sherry wine are added and the top sprinkled with Parmesan cheese. No matter what you add you end up with a gluey mess that certainly cannot be called good cooking in any sense of the word. You can use it for a paste for sticking paper together and that is all it is good for.

The American Indians, of course, were the first to use tomatoes, as tomatoes originated in Central America. They were also the first to use sweet and hot green and red peppers as they originated in Central America. The Indians cooked quail and turkeys in tomato and green pepper sauce centuries before any white man ever set foot on North, Central or South America. The early hunters and missionaries in Mexico were quick to pick up the use of the tomato and peppers with fowl and Hunter's Chicken was born. Mostly quail, turkey, prairie chicken and sometimes rabbit were used to make it. Immigrants who went back to Europe took the recipe back with them. In Italy they naturally called it chicken cacciatore which in Italian simply means hunter style chicken. The Italians also take very well to Indian corn bread and today it is an important food in many parts of Italy. I was talking to one of New York's most famous chefs a short time ago. He confidentially told me that corn bread originated in Italy and Italian corn bread was still the best made anywhere. When I reminded him that corn originated here in the Americas and was not even used in any part of Europe until fairly recently, he was quite taken back to say the least. I was not surprised at all as most of the supposed renowned chefs of today are not even fair cooks. The only thing that they are any good at is in making food look fancy.

The original hunter style chicken was made as follows.

Take a chicken of whatever size that you can get. Try to get a fairly good-sized one. Cut it up so that the legs, breast, wings and backs are separate. Put the chicken pieces into a good-sized pot and add two large cans of tomatoes and a cup of cut up sweet green peppers, one onion about 2½ inches in diameter cut up, ¼ teaspoon of ground sage, 1/16 teaspoon of ground red pepper or pepper to taste, 1 level teaspoon of salt and 1 level teaspoon of butter. If you like garlic put in a clove of garlic or ½ level teaspoon of powdered garlic. Cover the chicken pieces and other ingredients with just enough water so that the chicken meat will boil well. Boil over a medium heat for about an hour or until the chicken is very tender.

Place a generous amount of butter in a frying pan with two tablespoons of water and melt the butter. Remove and drain the chicken pieces. Fry them in the butter without flouring them until they are slightly browned. Pour any remaining butter into the pot with the vegetables. Serve the chicken separately on a plate with a bowl of the vegetables beside it. Use the vegetable mixture to dip the chicken in as you eat it and as a vegetable.

There is no olive oil or wine used in making chicken cacciatore nor are the vegetables ever served on the chicken.

PHEASANT CATHERINE DE MEDICIS

Catherine de Medicis was an Italian woman, cousin to Caesar Borgia, son of Pope Alexander the XI. The Borgia family were mainly bankers and were powerful not only in Italy but all over Europe. Catherine married Prince Henry, second son of the King of France, Francois The First. She had three sons, two of whom were not all there mentally. One son she married to Mary Stuart of Scotland. Prince Francis, brother of Prince Henry, was conveniently poisoned so Prince Henry became King of France.

Catherine was a high-tempered, very intelligent woman. She ruled France and her husband with an iron hand. Her face was not very good looking but she had beautiful legs. She invented women's panties so that she could ride a horse with her skirts up high showing off her beautiful legs. Up until this time women wore no panties of any kind. She brought with her to France the first melon seeds and started the French growing melons. Catherine brought the first forks with her from Italy and taught the French how to use a fork. Before this time they used a knife to bring food up to their mouths. Many good recipes were also brought into France by Catherine de Medicis and in turn she learned a great many good recipes from the French. Some authors state that Catherine de Medicis for the first time brought fine cooking to France. This is entirely untrue. The French were doing really fine cooking long before Caherine de Medicis was even born. Her husband soon became tired of being bossed around all the time by Catherine and got a fine good looking mistress by the name of Diane De Poitiers. Catherine tried to poison her numerous times but never succeeded.

Catherine De Medicis wanted political power above everything else. She got together a group of two hundred beautiful young girls and carefully trained them how to entertain men. This group was called the Escadron Volant. She would send them out singly or in groups to gain the favor and to entertain political rivals and men who she wanted to influence. The girls were all taught to eat green apples and to drink a cup of vinegar a day to keep them from getting pregnant. In those days green apples and vinegar were thought to keep a woman from ever becoming pregnant. If one of the girls became pregnant it was taken for granted that she had neglected to eat her green apples and drink her vinegar and the girl was promptly discharged.

Catherine was not what you might call a squeamish woman. At one time at the Saint Barthelemy massacre she had 10,000 men killed including Admiral Coligny, a famous French military expert.

Catherine's best recipe was Pheasant Catherine De Medicis. This recipe shows real cooking talent. Pheasants have very dry flesh when roasted or just fried much more so than a chicken. Pheasants came into Europe from Asia by way of the ancient country of Phase where Rion River goes through Grousia or Georgia goes into the Black Sea. This country was annexed to Russia in 1802. Here is the recipe.

Take a rooster or hen pheasant and pluck off all feathers, do not skin it. Cut off the legs and head and remove the entrails. Save the heart, liver and stomach. Place the pheasant and the heart, liver and stomach in a pot with enough water to cover it well. Add one onion about 2½ inches in diameter, cut up in small pieces, three bay leaves or laurel leaves, one level teaspoon of ground cinnamon, ¼ teaspoon of ground cloves, 1 cup of cut-up celery, salt and pepper to taste. Over medium heat boil for two hours or until the pheasant is very tender keeping the pot covered as much as possible and water to keep up the level of the liquid. Remove the pheasant and leave drain. Add three cups of flat egg noodles to the liquid in the pot and boil the noodles until tender. While the noodles are boiling remove the breasts from the pheasant, the legs and all meat from the wings and back and fry them in butter in a frying pan until just lightly brown. Do not put any flour, bread crumbs or starch on them. Now remove the noodles. Serve the liquid the pheasant was boiled in as a soup. It is extremely delicious. Serve the lightly buttered fried pheasant and noodles as the main dish on the same plate. The pheasant will not be at all dry as some of the soup fluid is absorbed by the flesh.

DOVES WYATT EARP

Wyatt Earp came from Lamar, Missouri. His first law enforcing job began there in 1870 when he was elected constable. After he became constable which was considered a solid, steady, job, he married his sweetheart, Willa Sutherland.

A typhus epidemic hit Lamar several months after Wyatt was married.

Willa was one of the first to contract this dread disease and within a few days she died a horrible, painful death.

Willa's death changed Wyatt overnight. From a quiet, conservative, friendly, small town law officer who carried no gun Wyatt changed to a gaunt, cold, blue-eyed, brown mustached gunfighter; one of the most cool and deadly that the West ever knew.

While at Lamar, Wyatt did some shooting with a shotgun and .22 caliber rifle. He barely knew how to shoot a revolver and was no shot at all with a revolver. In the words of the time he couldn't hit a bull over the butt with an ironing board as far as revolver shooting was concerned.

Wyatt left Lamar shortly after Willa's death as everything in Lamar reminded him of her. He bought a Colt .45 revolver, a new 12 gauge shotgun, and a Winchester rifle and traveled to the Indian Territory which is now Oklahoma. He got a job with a Government Surveying Crew to supply meat for the crew and guard the crew's gear. Wyatt had made up his mind to become handy with both revolvers and rifles. His job gave him plenty of spare time and he used every minute of it to dry fire with his guns. Wyatt believed that accuracy of fire was far more important than just fast drawing. He spent hours holding his arm stretched out full length with his revolver in his hand to get his arm muscles used to this position so that his arm would not shake even slightly in shooting. Wild Bill Hickok gave Wyatt and also Bat Masterson pointers on gun fighting.

Wyatt gained his reputation as a gunfighter in Ellsworth, Kansas. Texan Ben Thompson, of the West's finest gunfighters was in town. Ben had killed thirty-eight men in gunfights. He was an Ex-Confederate War Hero. He wore a high silk hat, white collar, flowing cape, gold watch chain, fancy vests and a stick pin in the design of a Confederate Flag. It was almost certain death to wear a high silk hat in the frontier towns but no one ever kidded Ben about it or his stick pin. In Dodge City, Wild Bill Hickok was in the Long Branch Saloon. A Mexican came in and asked Wild Bill for enough money to buy a meal. Hickok evidently thought that the man was trying to get money for a drink. He said to the Mexican, "Get out of here you drunken pepper gut or I'll throw you out." Ben Thompson was standing nearby and overheard the remark. Ben had lots of bad faults but never would tolerate anyone picking on anyone. Ben had been partly brought up by a fine Mexican woman and had great respect for Mexicans. He gave the man some money, then walked over to Wild Bill Hickok, tapped him on the shoulder and told him, "Be out of town in an hour or I'll kill you." Wild Bill Hickok didn't hesitate a moment; he left Dodge City at once.

In Ellsworth, County Sheriff C. B. Whitney carrying a double barrelled shotgun told Ben to leave town as he was an undesirable character. Ben walked over to a store, bought a double barrelled shotgun, loaded it with buckshot, walked over to Sheriff Whitney and put two loads into his chest. He then stated that he would like to see someone try to take him into custody. Wyatt Earp and the mayor of Ellsworth had watched the killing. Wyatt had nothing against Ben but told the Mayor that if he would lend him his gun belt and two .45 Colt revolvers that he would quiet Ben down before he hurt someone else. The Mayor gladly supplied the guns and belt. Wyatt walked out toward Ben and called to Ben to put his shotgun on the ground or he'd kill him. Ben did it immediately. Afterwards Ben said that he had a strong feeling Wyatt could kill him before he could get him with the shotgun although he knew nothing of Wyatt. Ben always praised Wyatt highly. This making famous Ben Thompson back down made Wyatt famous overnight throughout the West.

In 1873 Ellsworth, Kansas asked Wyatt to become its Marshall. Wyatt declined the offer as he felt he needed another year's revolver practice.

The next year Witchita offered him a Deputy Marshall's job. This he took as he felt he was ready.

In 1876 Dodge City offered Wyatt $250 a month plus $2.50 for each arrest he made. Wyatt took the job and served as law officer in Dodge City at the following times.

May 17 to Sept. 9, 1876 as assistant Marshall.

July 6 to November 29, 1877 as Marshall.

August 6, 1878 as assistant Marshall.

Wyatt was never a U. S. marshall or deputy marshall.

Wyatt spent a good bit of time in Arizona. He went to Arizona with Doc Holliday a dentist friend who had a bad case of tuberculosis. Holliday was also a gunfighter and had killed four men. Wyatt's brothers, Morgan and Virgil joined him later in Arizona. Wyatt's other brothers, Warren and James and half bother, Newton, did not come.

Wyatt at first hired out to guard bullion stages. For this work he used a 12 gauge double barrelled shotgun loaded with buckshot. He bought the Oriental Saloon in Tombstone and had Luke Short, Fort Worth gambler and Bat Masterson from Dodge City, deal-monte for him in the saloon. Luke was known as "the undertaker's friend". He killed such expert gunfighters as Charlie Storms in Leadville, Colorado and Jim Courtright in Fort Worth, Texas. He was soon offered the Deputy Sheriff's job at Tombstone, Arizona. This he accepted. Wyatt was now thirty-one years old.

Morgan Earp was killed by Charlie Stillwell. Wyatt located Stillwell. When Stillwell saw Wyatt he became paralyzed with fear and couldn't even draw his gun. Wyatt walked up to him with a double barrelled shotgun, put it on his heart and pulled the trigger twice. While in Arizona Wyatt killed, among others, the well known Curly Bill Brocious, cattle rustler, with a shotgun, and Indian Charlie, a noted gunman, with his Buntline Colt .45. A writer from New York State, E. Z. C. Judson, had the pen name of Ned Buntline. He was a dime novel writer of the Old West and had given Wyatt a Colt .45 with a 12 inch barrel. He also gave one to Bat Masterson and a number of other noted gunfighters. Only Wyatt spent day after day practicing with this long barrelled revolver until he could handle it fast and perfectly. The long barrel made the revolver many times more accurate than the short 4¾ inch barrelled Colt revolvers used by other gunfighters. Wyatt believed that an accurately placed bullet in the heart or head was the only thing that would stop a man. Bat Masterson cut his Buntline barrel down to 8 inches from 12 inches. The others who received these special guns foolishly cut the barrels down to 4¾ inches.

Looking for still other frontiers and to get away from his awful lonesomeness Wyatt went to Colorado, then to California and Alaska and back to California. Wyatt married Josephine Sarah Marcus, a San Francisco girl. He discovered the Happy Day Gold and Copper Mines and Kern County oil lands. He died a very wealthy man. If it had not been for his first wife Willa's death, Wyatt would have stayed in Lamar, Missouri and never fired a pistol.

I have taken the time to give you the brief facts about Wyatt Earp as he is an important part of American history and one of our great men. The Hollywood, television, and movie crowd in their movies of Wyatt have as usual not bothered to tell the truth about him. They present movies of Wyatt that are untrue from beginning to end. We need men today like Wyatt to put law and order in today's Hollywood and New York's television area more than we ever needed them in Dodge City or Tombstone.

After his first wife's death the only thing that Wyatt really ever enjoyed was good food. He was an outstanding cook himself of wild game. He went at learning to cook wild game just like he went at learning to shoot with a revolver, continual hard practice. In many parts of the West his cooking methods will be remembered long after his deeds with a gun are forgotten.

At Dodge, his boiled sliced buffalo tongue pickled in vinegar and his thinly sliced buffalo liver fried with bacon and onions were famous. His Wyatt Earp breakfast consisting of a half inch thick slice of beef or buffalo, eye of a rib steak with thinly sliced onions on top put between two slices of buttered bread with the butter well sprinkled with salt and served with two fried eggs fried on both sides was very popular and justly so.

When Wyatt ran the Oriental Saloon at Tombstone, Arizona both its liquor and food were excellent. Wyatt saw to that. Arizona then and now

White-winged doves at Tombstone, Arizona. They are about a third larger than a mourning dove.

has always had very good hunting. Mourning doves, white-winged doves, Gambels quail, turkey, deer, bear, and javelina were and are plentiful. Wyatt loved to shoot doves on the wing with a shotgun. He rightly considered them the most difficult wing shot of all. Wild doves are very good roasted whole or just the legs and breast fried if you like meat with a strong wild flavor. Wild dove tastes much like wild duck having a slight liver like wild taste. Most people do not however like this taste. Here was Wyatt's method of cooking doves. Using this method they have absolutely no "wild duck" or liver taste at all and are simply delicious.

Pick ten doves and cut off their wings, feet and head. Remove the entrails and singe off the hair feathers with a candle. Take a knife and cut the leg and back section away from the breast section. Put two level tablespoons of butter and two level tablespoons of beef suet in a large frying pan and melt them. Place the back and leg pieces and breast pieces in the frying pan and brown them well. Take a large pot. Cut up a medium sized cabbage in eighths and place in the pot. Add six large carrots, one level teaspoon of sage leaves, one cup of cooked lima beans and one large onion diced. Place the browned dove pieces in the pot. Add enough water to cover over the vegetables and birds about two inches deep. Add the butter and beef suet from the frying pan. Boil slowly (about simmering) for about an hour and a half. Remove the dove pieces and let them drain. Serve them with potatoes or brown rice with butter. Remove the carrots and cabbage from the water and serve as a vegetable. Add one cup of cooked macaroni to the soup or cooking stock and serve with buttered bread. This makes a delicious rare meal that everyone likes. I always put three level tablespoons of soy sauce in the pot before starting it to boil. Soy sauce has the magic quality of quickly removing all undesirable tastes from both meats and vegetables, and leaving in their place very desirable tastes.

The white-winged dove of the southwest is larger than the mourning dove and very good eating.

Charles Shibell of Tombstone once asked Wyatt what was the best shot that he had ever made. Wyatt did not hesitate a minute but replied, "The time I killed nine mourning doves out of a flock coming into a water hole with one shot."

BOHEMIAN WILD DUCK

The Bohemians came early to Minnesota and built up their fine towns such as New Prague. They are excellent cooks. The Bohemian recipe I like best is their method of cooking wild duck. It is a simple easy method and typically Bohemian. The Bohemians are hard-working conservative people and they know how to put everything to good use.

Save up the orange peel of six oranges. Cut up 12 strips of the peel about a fourth of an inch wide and an inch long. Poke small holes in the duck breast with the point of your knife every 1½ inches square and force the orange peel down into the holes. Take the balance of the orange peels and lay them on top of the duck until the duck is completely covered with the orange peel. The more the better. Tuck the orange peel down the sides as much as possible to hold it close to the duck. Put a natural dark brown duck marsh long grained rice dressing in the duck and roast with your usual method. The orange peel flavor and aroma blends with the duck and gives it a clean, fresh, different taste that is delicious. This method makes even a bluebill that has been feeding on minnows taste good.

DUCK GENGHIS KHAN

The great Genghis Khan, greatest ruler of all time, 700 years ago nearly dominated the world. He came closer to doing it than any man ever has. The Khan came from Mongolia, an ancient, ancient land. It and Tibet were the first lands out of the sea when the earth was formed. In Tibet the world's largest pyramids still exist made by the most ancient race to ever inhabit the globe.

The great Genghis Khan liked Chinese cooking above all other. In America we know little of Chinese cooking as we think that chow mein and chop suey are Chinese or Japanese foods. They both were invented in San Francisco by a Greek named John Metaxa who behind the scenes owned a restaurant in the Chinese district but had Chinese people pretend to own it and run it. The only thing about chow mein or chop suey that is Chinese or Japanese is soy sauce if you use it on them. Soy sauce is popular in Japan.

The story that chop suey was invented in the 19th century by Lo Feng-Luh aide to a Chinese statesman Li Hung Chang is entirely untrue. Lo Feng-Luh was also appointed as personal envoy to England's Court of St. James by China's Dowager Empress. Chop suey was very popular in America long before he ever saw America.

Here is the Great Khan's favorite duck recipe and it is typical oriental cooking. This recipe as you will note contains rhubarb. Our word rhubarb comes from the French word rhubarbe. Rhubarb originated in the eastern Mediterranean, Asia Minor, the Middle East and China. The earliest records of the use of rhubarb were in 2700 B. C. in China. Only the stalks of rhubarb are edible. The leaves and the roots contain substances that cause violent illness or death if eaten in any amount. Through the ages thousands of people have been purposely poisoned by feeding them cooked rhubarb with roots mixed in with the cooked stalks. Countless children have died from eating rhubarb leaves.

Early mongols believed that rhubarb restored a man's strength after spending a night with a woman.

Rhubarb first came to Europe by way of Italy. It was cultivated at Padua, Italy in 1608. In 1778 rhubarb was first used in England to make tarts and pies. Rhubarb was brought to Maine from England in 1790. It was used somewhat for tarts and pies but never has become very popular in North America.

Back to our recipe. Take a duck wild or tame, and remove all skin and fat from it. Make a mixture of about six cups of chopped up rhubarb, three level tablespoons of cinnamon, and one and a half cups of sugar or honey. Stuff the duck tightly with this mixture. Place the duck in a deep covered pot. Add one cup of water. Now fill the pot with the rhubarb, cinnamon and sugar mixture. Be sure to cover over the entire duck at least one inch deep preferably two inches deep. Place in your oven and roast until well done. Look at the duck occasionally to make sure that it is not burning. Add a little water if there is any danger of this. Remove from the oven when done.

Make the following sauce for the duck. Put two heaping tablespoons of butter into a frying pan and melt with medium heat until it just starts to brown. Remove the frying pan from the stove. Add two level tablespoons of flour. Mix the flour in well with the melted butter. It will make a thin paste. Now add a cup of cold orange juice and one level tablespoon of sugar or honey, mix well into the flour and butter. Mix until they are smoothly blended. Put the pan back onto the stove over medium heat. Stir until it begins to thicken. Add one-fourth level teaspoon of salt. Salt the duck lightly and serve in small pieces, generously covered with the sauce.

Duck whether tame or wild is very greasy and has quite an odor. By skinning the duck and removing all the fat on the surface of the duck's body you remove nearly all of the strong duck odor. The rhubarb, cinnamon and sugar cure the duck's meat as you roast it giving it an entirely delicious different taste. The orange sauce served with the meat lends just the right flavor. A duck prepared in this manner is rare delicious eating.

Oranges originally came from South China and Indo China and are much used in oriental cooking. Sweet and Mandarin oranges have been eaten and used in China from the beginning of the world. Chinese writings tell of oranges as far back as 2,200 years before Christ.

Oranges did not get to Europe until after the beginning of the 15th Century. Columbus brought orange seeds to America. Orange used as a sauce base or gravy base is wonderful on ducks, and geese. Be sure to try this recipe.

WILD OR TAME DUCK MAXIM'S

Not too many pepole care for wild or tame duck the way that it is usually prepared as it is either too musky or livery or too greasy. The old Maxim's restaurant in Paris, France, used this famous recipe and everyone liked it. In those days Paris was a fabulous town. People greeted you on the street by not saying "How are you today" but by saying "What are you going to eat today." The old Paris was very much like New Orleans. Even today in New Orleans some people carry an empty whisky bottle of coffee in their pocket made up to their own particular formula and stop and take a drink of it every so often. The coffee may contain a little brandy, a little orange peel or even a drop or two of anise. I was talking to a friend in New Orleans one time, and had another friend walk up to the first one and ask for a drink of his coffee. The man with the coffee obligingly pulled out a flask of coffee and gave him a drink as a matter of course. Enough of this city talk; here is the original recipe for duck Maxim's.

Take a wild or tame duck and remove the skin from the breasts and then remove the breasts. Slice the breasts with the grain, not across the grain, in as large slices as possible and as thin slices as possible. Try to keep them not more than three sixteenths of an inch thick. Skin the legs and remove the meat. Slice the leg meat also into thin slices. Put the sliced duck pieces into a pot of boiling salted water and boil them for fifteen minutes. Remove the slices and drain them on paper and throw away the water. Put the sliced duck pieces into a pot. Cover with frozen or fresh orange juice, either works as well as the other. Leave stand in the orange juice for an hour. Put several pieces of bacon into a frying pan and fry them until crisp. Remove the bacon and put in the duck slices and lightly fry them in the bacon grease. If you do not like the taste of bacon grease use butter.

Duck prepared in this manner is eating you will always remember with great pleasure.

BIRDS SAINT THOMAS AQUINAS

Saint Thomas Aquinas was born in 1225 and died in 1274. He was a very brilliant kindly man, an Italian by birth. He enjoyed eating food immensely. He became so heavy set that his stomach kept him so far away from tables that he could not reach his plate. He was practical as well as brilliant and kindly and quickly solved his problem. He simply sawed out a half circle in his eating table so that his stomach could fit comfortably into the sawed out section.

He, like all Europeans who like good food, understood and appreciated the wonderful food that can be made from many species of birds. Here in North America we have foolishly neglected to preserve the recipes of our forefathers for preparing birds. Today throughout Europe birds are eaten and enjoyed more than ever. In the early days of our country birds were eaten extensively. In Pennsylvania the Germans made the finest main meat dish from fat Bob-o-link breasts in a thick, rich, gravy.

The French in the New England states made Pate de Allouette. Allouette means meadow lark in French. They ground the steamed meadow lark breasts and mixed them with cottage cheese and powdered tarragon spice. The Irish, English and Scots made delicious meat pies from black bird breasts. The Scandinavians made simply wonderful meat paddies from ground bird's breasts, mixed with dried bread and grated yellow cheese.

I have eaten birds of many kinds prepared in various manners and enjoyed them all a great deal. They are a real delicacy. My favorite birds though for eating are meadow larks and robins. Both are excellent, being far superior to such good eating birds as quail, woodcock, pheasant or partridge. Robins are, I believe, even better than meadow larks.

The recipe for cooking birds that I write here is the one used and recommended by Saint Thomas Aquinas. It is a basic one for bird cooking and has never been improved upon. Be sure to try it at your first opportunity.

Get three young robins for every person. If possible get them in the early part of the summer as at this time they are at their very best. Anyone that has a berry patch, cherry, plum or apple orchard is glad to have you take them as they are bad destroyers of fruit. Make a cut with a sharp knife along the breast bone and peel off the skin with the feathers on it from the breasts of the birds. Cut out the breasts. Wash them well in cold water. Place a good sized chunk of butter in your frying pan. Dip the breasts into flour and put them into the melted butter. Just brown the breasts nicely on all sides, do not attempt to completely cook them. Salt and pepper to taste. Now remove the breasts and cook them in a pressure cooker for 8 to 12 minutes. At the time of Saint Aquinas the birds were placed on a grate over a pot of boiling water. The cover was then put on the pot and the birds steamed until done. The pressure cooker does the same thing, only quicker. Remove the breasts when done and serve as the main meat dish. You can serve them with a gravy made from the butter left in the frying pan, with fried onions or just as they are. They make rare delicious eating.

NORWEGIAN FRIED HAM

It is simple to fry ham as we all know but to get it just right is a 100 year old trick that few cooks know.

Take your frying pan and put a half a teaspoon of butter in it. Then take beef hamburger and make a good sized paddy and fry it in the butter. If you do not have hamburger, any small piece of beef frying meat will do but be sure it has some fat on it. Remove the beef when well fried.

Now fry your ham in the mixture of butter and beef residue. The beef flavor blends into the ham and produces the best ham you have ever tasted. You just have to try it to note the vast difference.

ALWAYS SLICE HAM AS THINLY AS POSSIBLE

Ham sliced thin has a much different better taste than if sliced thick. The reason for this is that ham in thick slices contains a porky undesirable taste and odor. Slicing it thin releases most of this taste and odor making it taste entirely different. Even in making a ham sandwich slice ham as thinly as possible and make the sandwich up of many thin slices of ham rather than one thick slice.

In the Middle South and Deep South in the hill country everyone has long known that ham must be sliced as thinly as possible in order to have the best of taste. The good ham in these areas is all home cured on farms and is of excellent quality and very firm. It can be sliced so thinly that you can nearly see through it. It is the finest ham available in North America by far and entirely different than the soft ham made by the large meat packing companies. The large meat packing companies use an embalming process of putting quick curing liquids through the veins of the ham under pressure. It is a very fast process and actually adds weight to the meat, by making the meat soak up excessive liquids. A home cured ham, of course, loses weight as it is cured and hence the large meat packers would not think of using such a method. The loading of hams with embalming liquids has become so over done in many states that state laws have had to be passed to limit the weight a large packer can add to ham with embalming liquids.

HOW TO PREPARE JAVELINA FOR EATING

Javelina are in general a wild boar-type of animal found in the Southwestern States, Mexico and Central America. They are, however, a much higher form of animal life than pigs or wild boars. They have a stomach system much more highly developed and are far more intelligent. Their body is built entirely different than a pig or wild boar. The hind legs or

A pair of prime javelinas.

hams are very small, not large like those on a pig or wild boar. The front legs have the most muscles or meat on them, in a pig or wild boar the front legs have the least muscles. The head of a javelina makes an excellent trophy. They are an animal that will attack on occasion when wounded or attack when found in large groups and disturbed.

Due to a lack of knowledge on how to care for javelina meat they are often considered by amateur hunters to be unedible. Nothing could be further from the truth. Javelina makes rare excellent eating even superior to European wild boar.

Here is how to prepare javelina for eating. If possible avoid shooting javelina so that the bullet goes through the stomach or intestine. This is a precaution that should be taken in shooting any game that is to be eaten. Stomach and intestine juices give any meat a bad odor and taste. Intestine juice is nothing but manure and soaking any meat in manure ruins it. About in the middle of the back toward the rear of the javelina whether it be male or female is a musk gland. If this has been damaged in anyway by a bullet the carcass is worthless for eating. With a sharp knife immediately open up the abdominal cavity from the anus to within about three inches of the tip end of the lower jaw. Clean out all of the body organs and intestines. Put the liver and the heart in a plastic bag and tie a string around the top and put it in your pocket. The heart and liver are excellent eating. Now skin the javelina at once. Be very careful to cut out the musk gland on the back as you come to it. Do not use the knife that was used to cut out gland for butchering—unless it is washed. If you desire the head for a trophy, skin out the head leaving the ears on the skin. Skin around the eyes and lips carefully and leave the nose on the skin. Leave the 3 inch piece of the lower jaw skin in one, do not split it to the tip of the jaw. Save both jaws with their teeth in them. The skull is no longer used in modern taxidermy, so you do not have to save it. Sprinkle the inside of the skin heavily with borax. If you have no borax use salt. If you leave the skin on a javelina until you get it home the meat will pick up a musky odor from the skin. Put the carcass in a clean muslin or cheese cloth sack. When you get home send the skin in to be tanned for leather. Javelina leather makes the finest gloves available in the world today. At home cut off the two rear legs or hams and the two front leg hams. Saw off the ribs with a hack saw and saw the loin in two down the center. Saw and cut out the pork chops. Cure the meat as follows:

Here are the ingredients to make up 6 gallons of curing liquid. If this is too much cut the recipe in half or if too little double it.

10 ounces of sugar.
2 ounces of sodium nitrate. (Get from your druggist)
½ ounce of sodium nitrite. (Get from your druggist)
3 pounds of salt.
3 level teaspoons of black pepper.
1 level teaspoon of ground cloves.
6 bay leaves.
12 level teaspoons of mixed pickling spice.
If you care for onions, mince one onion 3 inches in diameter.
If you care for garlic, mince 4 garlic cloves.

Put the ingredients into a pickle crock or glass jar, and add enough water to make a total of six gallons including the ingredients.

The ideal temperature for curing meat is about 38 degrees. During the fall or spring months this is not too difficult to get. In the winter you can use an unheated part of your basement for curing meat. During hot summer months it is hard to find a place around 38 degrees. Higher temperatures will not affect the end result of your curing at all but for every 15 degrees of a higher temperature than about 38 degrees add one third more salt. At about 83 degrees for example add 6 more pounds of salt making a total of 12 pounds of salt used.

Now place your meat into the liquid. If it tends to bob up put a heavy plate on it smaller than the inside crock to keep it down. Cover well.

Leave the meat remain in the liquid for 15 days. On the fifth and tenth days stir the liquid well and remove the meat and put it back in a reverse position. After the fifteenth day remove the meat.

The meat at this time has a dull unappetizing color; pay no attention to this. When cooked the meat turns a beautiful fresh red meat color that is very, very appetizing.

After the meat is cured use what you want fresh and freeze the rest.

If you have a full grown or old boar or sow, cook the meat as follows. Put about a half inch of water in the bottom of a pressure cooker. Sprinkle the meat heavily with cinnamon and rub it well into the meat. Stick six whole cloves into the meat. Put the meat into the pressure cooker. Add on top of the meat one medium cabbage, six large carrots, one medium sized onion sliced, one cup of cut up celery and three bay leaves, and three level tablespoons of soy sauce. Cook until tender. Even the toughest old sow or boar will cook tender in a pressure cooker and the meat will be delicately flavored and have no wild or musky odor at all.

If you have a young small or medium sized boar or sow cook it as follows: Place the meat in a large pot. Add one fourth level teaspoon of ground cinnamon, one fourth level teaspoon of ground cloves, three bay leaves, four level tablespoons of soy sauce, one medium sized onion sliced up. Cover with water. Pepper to taste but add no salt. Cover the pot and boil slowly until tender. Usually takes several hours. This will give you tender, delicious meat with no strong or musk flavor or smell at all. People who would never eat javelina will ask for seconds when prepared in this manner. The soy sauce and cinnamon are century old Chinese tricks to destroy the odor and musk taste in pork and they work magically well on javelina.

HOW TO MAKE LIVERWURST OF DUCK, GOOSE, DEER, RABBIT, SQUIRREL, PHEASANT, MOOSE, OR CALF'S OR PORK LIVER BY JOHANNES KEPLER

Johannes Kepler was a well known German astrologer. He was born in 1571 and died in 1630. His work on astronomy has long since been forgotten but his creating liverwurst will never be forgotten.

Liver such as that taken from ducks, geese, deer, rabbits, squirrels, pheasants, moose, antelope, or calf, cow, bull or pork liver all make excellent liverwurst. In cleaning game such as ducks, rabbits, squirrels and pheasants most people throw away the livers. It is a sin to waste this precious meat. Be sure to save it and use it. Here is the correct way to make liverwurst:

Always freeze liver if you are not going to make it up right away as liver is like fish flesh and spoils very rapidly.

For the weight of liver that you have take the same weight of fresh pork meat. Be sure that the pork meat has some fat on it. Now grind up the two together in your meat grinder. Mix them together well.

In one gallon of water add one-sixth ounce of sodium nitrate and three thirty-seconds of an ounce of sodium nitrite, and 2 level tablespoons of salt. Place the ground meat into this liquid. Break it up into as small pieces as possible and leave in the liquid for one day. Now remove the meat from the liquid. Add black pepper and salt to taste. Add one level teaspoon of liquid smoke to every two pounds of the meat. If you care for onion or garlic flavor add at this time, to taste. Now place in a baking pan. Bake at 325 degrees for about four hours. Remove and leave cool. The liverwurst is actually ready to eat now and you will rarely get a chance to do anything else with it. However if your family does not eat it right away, remove the loaf and put it through your meat grinder. Mix in just enough lard to make it hold together well. You probably will not have any casing to stuff the liverwurst into, so just form it into rolls and put wax paper around it. Hold the paper in place with string. Real liverwurst like this doesn't last long enough around the house to pay to put it up too fancily. Liverwurst cannot be made of just liver alone as liver has much too strong a liver flavor.

SWEDISH MUSKRAT

The person who named the muskrat should forever be ashamed of himself. If he had given it a nice name such as water opossum, water rabbit, or something of this nature their carcasses would be worth more than their pelts are today. The name muskrat simply is not appealing to most people from an eating standpoint.

Early Swedish pioneers brought with them their mighty fine cooks and they developed some dishes that have never been equaled. Stewed muskrat was one time a popular Minnesota dish as well as stewed beaver.

Swedish muskrat however is one of the best dishes you will ever eat. Muskrat flesh is mild, and very tasty. It is one of the best eating meats in the world. Muskrats eat only marsh roots and clams and their flesh reflects this mild, clean diet.

Take the hind legs or hams of six nice muskrats and clean all fat from them. Boil them for 45 minutes in water with salt and pepper added to taste. Remove them from the water.

Put a generous amount of butter in a large frying pan and melt. Slice a medium sized onion in the butter and cook until half done. Sprinkle nutmeg over the muskrat hams and rub it in. Place the hams in the butter. Brown the muskrat hams well. Put one cup of cooked celery and celery leaves in the pan and mix with the onions. Salt and pepper to taste. Serve altogether on a large plate. This is a serving for only one hungry man.

JAPANESE METHOD OF MAKING A PORK ROAST

The first Japanese originally came from China and they brought with them traditional old Chinese cooking methods. The Japanese are great lovers of pork and through the centuries have developed a great many tricks in cooking pork. They were using sugar sauce on hams over 2,000 years before sugar was even known to Europe. Europe has had sugar only a relatively short time. Sugar came to Arabia in the 13th century, to Sicily in the 14th century, to Portugal in the 15th century. It was really late in the 16th century before Central Europe had sugar. In 1747 the German chemist Marggraf was the first to discover sugar in sugar beets and this made sugar plentiful in Europe.

The Japanese trick that I like in making a pork roast is as follows: Before putting your roast into the oven sprinkle it all over with cinnamon. Rub the cinnamon in well. Poke some holes into the roast with a sharp nail, or skewer and work a little cinnamon down into the holes into the heavy parts of the roast. Cinnamon has almost a miraculous effect on pork. If the pork is strong, and much pork is, it takes away any strong porky odor entirely. On good pork it gives it a delightful, fresh taste. This method was standard procedure at lumber camps after a number of Japanese cooks served pork roast this way just once.

BARBECUED PORK RIBS STONEWALL

Thousands of years ago there were pig-like animals and also horses in North America. Something killed off all of the horses down to the last one and all of the pig-like animals except the javelina. The Spaniards brought in horses from Europe when they came into Mexico. The Indians killed some of the Spaniards; and the horses of the dead Spaniards ran wild and again populated North America with horses. The European people domesticated pigs from European wild pigs. The Spanish brought the first pigs to North America. When the French came to Canada and to the Mississippi they brought pigs with them; and the English Colonists on the east coast brought in large numbers of pigs with them also.

All of the early colonists were quick to find that pigs liked corn very well and that it quickly fattened them and gave the meat an excellent flavor much less musky than pigs raised in Europe that practically had to forage their own food. Acorns too were plentiful in some areas and feeding the pigs on acorns produced an excellent pork as the colonists quickly discovered.

For some reason the colonists who settled in the South, such as the areas now known as Kentucky, Tennessee, Arkansas, Louisiana, North and South Carolina, Georgia, Virginia, and Alabama took to eating pork the most and were the first to use on pork, sauces that contained tomatoes.

In the Old South barbecued rib cooking developed into a real fine art. Today, sad to say, barbecued ribs prepared by the original first recipes are next to impossible to find not only in the South but in any part of North America.

Here is the recipe of a gentleman named Thomas Jonathan Jackson born 1824 and killed 1863. He was a very brilliant military leader. If he had not been killed he probably would have emerged from the War Between the States as one of the great generals of all times. He was a fierce soldier who once he had planned his strategy allowed no room for retreat. This earned him the well deserved nickname of "Stonewall." He was an orphan boy and a deeply religious man and spent all of his time possible in prayer. General Jackson was well liked by Union as well as Confederate forces. Typical of this man is the story of the little old lady, Barbara Frietchie, waving a Union flag as he rode by with his troops and his quick order that he would shoot any man that took the flag from her, said a word to her or spat in any direction.

General Jackson was an excellent cook and spent a great deal of time seeing to it himself that what food his soldiers had was prepared properly. This is the recipe he used for barbecued pork ribs. It has never been bettered and seldom equaled. Takes quite a lot longer to do than today's methods but it is well worth every minute you take to make the ribs right.

Go to your butcher and buy your pork ribs. Spare ribs which are cut up on the back have more meat on them but plain pork ribs are also excellent. Take a good sized glass or ceramic bowl or stainless steel bowl and add 8 cups of water. To this, mix in two and a half level teaspoons of salt, one level teaspoon of saltpeter, one fourth level teaspoon of ground cloves, and one eighth teaspoon of black pepper. Do not worry about the saltpeter dulling any sexual desires as this small amount has absolutely no effect on your sexual desires at all. A great deal of store-bought ham canned meats and sauages that you buy today has far more saltpeter in it than this. Now put your pork ribs into this solution and leave them stand in it at room temperature or about 70 degrees for twelve hours or overnight. If it is hotter than this, put the bowl in the basement or some other cool place and leave stand for three days. Eight cups of this mixture will only cover about two pounds of pork ribs. Make up enough of the mixture using the same proportions to cover the amount of pork ribs you buy. This soaking in this solution will not only give the meat a clean musk free taste but will keep the meat pink and tasty after being roasted, not brown and gray and porky tasting as you nowadays invariably have barbecued ribs served to you.

Now place the ribs on a raised wire rack and place them in a large pan. The wire rack must be high enough from the bottom of the pan so that the drippings from off the ribs collecting in the bottom of the pan will not touch the ribs. Add one cup of water to the pan. Put a cover on the pan if you have one, if not cover the pan with aluminum foil and press it around the edges of the pan well so that you have a good seal. Place the pan in your oven at a temperature of 300 degrees and roast for three hours. Open the oven, and pour off all grease that has collected in the pan. Now take a spoon and cover one side of the ribs just lightly with the barbecue sauce which recipe is in the latter part of this one. Put back the ribs into the oven for another half hour. Remove and turn the ribs over and cover the other side slightly with the barbecue sauce. Put the ribs back into the oven and roast for another half hour. Then remove and cover generously with the barbecue sauce and serve. The reason you put a little sauce on each side of the ribs and roast the ribs for one-half hour is simply to impregnate the meat slightly while roasting with the flavor of the sauce.

This slow four hour roasting of pork ribs is done to get the grease out of the ribs without hardening the meat. No other method will accomplish this, but this one. Most recipes today tell you to put the ribs into an oven at from 450 to 500 degrees for 15 or 20 minutes and then lower the temperature and roast them. This is exactly what you do not want to do. The meat on pork ribs is tender, delicate, and not very thick. You must not give it a hard crust as doing this hardens and spoils some of the already not too plentiful meat on the ribs. Do not attempt to cook pork ribs over an open fire as this also tends to harden and destroy the delicate meat and to badly dry it out ruining its good taste.

Jackson was one of the first I believe to discover that smoke flavor was entirely made up of the tar deposit that smoke left on anything it touched. This wood tar is readily dissolved in water and can be added to the sauce and gives it the much desired smoke taste without destroying the delicate meat over an open fire.

The barbecue sauce is prepared as follows:

Take one onion about two inches in diameter and dice it. Dice two cups of celery. Put three level tablespoons of butter into a large frying pan and melt it. Add the diced onion and celery and brown them lightly. Add two cups of tomato sauce. This can be made by removing the seeds from tomatoes and grinding them up. You can buy Hunt's tomato sauce today in grocery stores which is the same thing. The 8 oz. cans will equal two cups. Add two level teaspoons of prepared mustard, 2 level tablespoons of brown sugar, two level tablespoons of lemon or lime juice, two tablespoons of liquid smoke, two tablespoons of vinegar, 1 level teaspoon of salt, ¼ level teaspoon of black pepper, 1/16 level teaspoon of cayenne pepper or 6 drops of Tobasco sauce, ½ cup of water, 2 level tablespoons of chili powder, grind up three cloves. Bring to a boil and then simmer for one-half hour. Note: This barbecue sauce contains no Worcestershire sauce, no catsup, like today's recipes do. It definitely must contain celery as described.

Pour the sauce generously over the pork ribs and serve. Note that this sauce is not cooked with the ribs at all as it must not pick up any of the grease or lard from the ribs. Grease or lard not only destroys the flavor of the sauce but makes the sauce hard to digest giving you a heavy greasy filled stomach that can make you feel very uncomfortable for as much as a day.

EISBEIN MIT SAUERKRAUT

In 1899 two German bartenders, Conrad Kolb and Henry Schroeder decided to start a beer tavern at 125 St. Charles Avenue in New Orleans. After they started the tavern Kolb wanted to combine a restaurant with the beer tavern but Schroeder did not want to, so Kolb bought him out. The partnership did not even last a year. After buying out Schroeder, Conrad Kolb immediately enlarged the tavern and put in a restaurant. His wife was the cook. They served both German and French foods and the restaurant was a success right from the start. French and German foods make an ideal combination just like French and German marriages. In the city of New Orleans there is a large German population. Many of them have intermarried with the French. As the years went by they enlarged the restaurant by taking over two nearby buildings. The inside of their restaurant looks like an old world German restaurant and I know because I have been in many of them. Beer steins are used as decoration, the woodwork is heavy timbers. An elaborate system of pulleys and leather belts operate old fashioned fans. A manikin of a Tyrolean man turns a great crank that seemingly operates the intricate fan system. Today the fans are, of course, no longer needed as the restaurant is fully air conditioned. Lowenbrau beer is on tap but this I do not care too much for as it is a little too heavy. The Jax beer made in New Orleans is a light beer made with more hops than most American beers and I found it to be very good and superior to Lowenbrau. Today Kolb's is owned by several lawyers and they smartly have maintained Conrad Kolb's atmosphere and recipes.

Kolb's German restaurant and the Pearl Oyster Bar in the background, New Orleans.

A good many people from the Midwest are of German descent and visit New Orleans in the winter. After a few days on highly seasoned seafoods they want some good roast beef and they usually end up at Kolb's for it.

When I go into Kolb's I often order Eisbein Mit Sauerkraut or pig's knuckles with sauerkraut and boiled white potatoes. They prepare them well.

Kolb's recipe in general is as follows.

Take young pig's knuckles and wash them carefully in water with about a cup of vinegar per quart. Boil them in beef consomme lightly seasoned with ground cloves, pepper and salt. Use about a half teaspoon of ground cloves to two quarts of water. They serve the boiled pig's knuckles with sauerkraut lightly fried in butter and boiled potatoes and this is very good. However, I have the cook take my sauerkraut and mix in catsup until the sauerkraut is all lightly coated and crumble up three strips of well fried bacon into the sauerkraut and mix in well. Then warm the mixture in a pan. I take a little of the beef consomme that the pig's knuckles were boiled in and mix it with the boiled potatoes and two or three pats of butter.

CHILE-CON-CARNE MARY OF AGREDA

Chile-Con-Carne is very popular in the Southwestern part of the United States. It is a Spanish recipe not at all Mexican and it is not popular in Mexico. The recipe was created by the first missionary to Texas, New Mexico, Arizona and Southern California, a very wise and mysterious woman called Mary of Agreda, Spain. She taught this recipe to the Indians in these areas and the recipe remains practically exactly the same in the Southwest today. The essential ingredients in Chile-Con-Carne are the spices cumin or cummin or cumino. All are just different names for the same spice and oregano. Cumin is the seed from a dwarf carrot native to Egypt and Syria. Oregano belongs to the European mint plants. Its dried leaves are used. The reason that most Chile-Con-Carne made in the Middlewest and East is so very poor is that it does not contain either of these spices.

The Spanish people are wonderful cooks. Spain has also been occupied by the Phoenicians, Greeks, Romans, Moors, and Arabs. The Spaniards added the best of their cooking ideas to their own making Spanish cooking fabulous and very different.

Shortly after the printing press was invented the Spaniards printed a cook book. This book was called "Lubre de Coch" and was printed in Catalan dialect in Barcelona by a man named Maeste Rubert in 1467. This book was so popular all over Europe that it was reprinted many times during the 16th century. In 1525 Emperor Charles V of Spain ordered this book translated into Castillian Spanish, the national Spanish language. He had it printed in Toledo. Charles the V conquered Germany, Austria, part of Belgium, most of France and Rome. He became Emperor of Germany in 1519. He captured Rome in 1527. In 1555 he became a monk at the Monastery at Yuste, Spain and died in 1558 at the age of 58. In every country he conquered Spanish cooking became part of their cooking and still is today. Thus beautiful dark haired German, Austrian and Belgian girls are mostly of Spanish descent. Many monuments were built for him throughout Spain but his greatest monument is the fine brandy Carlos V which was named after him.

Spain politically and geographically is made up of eight distinct regions. These regions were separate kingdoms until they were loosely joined together by the rulers Ferdinand and Isabella. Even today each region has its own dialect and its own special food recipes. In the Southern regions, fruit and fish are plentiful and a great deal of olive oil is produced and used. Along the Mediterranean large quantities of rice are raised and used in recipes; in the North livestock, vegetables and fish are plentiful and widely used.

The Basques, both the Spanish and French, are the finest cooks in Spain. Many of America's finest restaurant cooks are Spanish or French

Basques from the French and Spanish provinces along the Pyrenees and Bay of Biscay.

Here is the original recipe for Chile-Con-Carne. Chile-Con-Carne means "Meat with Chile" in Spanish.

2 pounds of beef, mutton, venison or antelope. Original recipe called for venison or antelope only.
1 pound of fresh pork. Original recipe called for javelina instead of pork.
4 cloves of garlic chopped up fine.
2 tablespoons of lard or beef suet or antelope fat.
3 bay or laurel leaves.
1 quart ripe tomatoes or 1 large can of tomatoes, juice and all.
1 onion about 2 inches in diameter chopped up fine or one large leek chopped up fine.
1 cup of chile pepper pulp or six level tablespoons of chile powder mixed with one level tablespoon of flour.
1 level tablespoon of oregano.
1 level tablespoon of salt.
1 level teaspoon of cumin, cummin or cumino powder.

Cut the meat up into cubes about one half inch square. Take a good sized covered cooking pot. Melt the beef suet in the pot. Dice the onion or leek and garlic and brown them in the beef suet. Put in the meat and 3 level tablespoons of water and cover and steam well for 5 minutes. Rub the tomatoes through a colander and add. Stir in the chile pepper pulp and cook for twenty minutes. If you use chile powder mix the powder and the flour into enough cold water to form a thin paste then mix into the beef suet, onion and garlic after they are browned. Stir until smooth, then add the meat. Now add the oregano, cumino and salt and cook slowly for about 2 hours. Add a little water to keep from burning but add as little as possible.

When done serve on a plate or in a bowl poured over bans or frijoles in Spanish, prepared as follows.

2 cups of red beans sometimes called Mexican beans.
1/3 pound of salt pork or three level tablespoons of beef suet.
¼ level teaspoon of oregano.

Pick the beans over carefully throwing away any bad ones. Then soak the beans overnight in room temperature water. In the morning drain off the water, put the beans in a large cooking pot and then cover them with fresh cold water. Add salt pork or beef suet and the oregano. Boil over medium heat from 4 to 6 hours or until the beans are nice and tender. Add water as water boils away. Remove from the water and drain and serve by pouring the Chile-Con-Carne over them.

If you are in a hurry use two pounds of canned red beans. In this case drain and put in a pot and fill with cold water. Add beef suet or salt pork and the oregano and boil for five minutes, then drain and serve with the Chile-Con-Carne poured over them.

Never under any circumstances cook beans with the Chile-Con-Carne as you will end up with a sticky mass of nothing that does not even resemble Chile-Con-Carne. The Chile-Con-Carne usually will be just right for hotness with the chile pulp or powder but if not add ground red pepper to taste.

SERVE AN EXTRA NAPKIN THAT IS WET WHEN SERVING BARBECUED PORK RIBS OR CHICKEN LEGS AND WINGS

To eat barbecued pork ribs or chicken legs or wings it is necessary to pick them up with your fingers to really enjoy eating them. When serving these foods serve an extra napkin that has been soaked in water and partially rung out. Wiping your fingers on the wet napkin quickly removes all grease.

This is an old western trick and a very good one. For example, the better restaurants in the Rapid City, South Dakota area like Westwood do this.

HOW TO FRY PORK SAUSAGE GERMAN STYLE

It is indeed rare these days when you find a cook who knows how to fry pork sausage. The old immigrant German cooks who knew how to fry pork sausage have died off and their cooking secrets, sad to say, died with them. The new generations try to learn their cooking from food editors who themselves do not know how to cook.

The cooking editors of our home and women's magazines are good photographers and take beautiful pictures of colorful food dishes but they do not know how to cook. You cannot eat colorful photographs. If these food editors would go back and learn the fundamentals of good cooking they could, I believe, learn how to cook.

Not long ago, although I did not desire to, I got into an argument with a very nice woman. I told her cooking editors know little about cooking. The argument became heated, something I did not desire. Finally I said I would write a letter to every cooking editor of all the home and women's magazines plus the cooks of every brand of nationally known flour. In the letter I would ask for two recipes. I told her that none of these cooking editors would be able to send me these two recipes that would really work. I am not mentioning the names of these so-called cooks but you all know most of them well.

The recipes I asked for were these basic ones for really good cooks.

1. The recipe for making hard crusted French bread or Vienna bread.
2. The recipe for making real flaky pastry such as is used in making good Napoleons, cream horns, and real strudel.

I wrote the letters to the cooking editors and got answers from all of them. Most of the cooking editors simply wrote me that they did not know these recipes. The others tried to act authentic and technical and sent me copies of recipes for these items that they copied from cook books. Not one of the recipes they copied from cook books that they sent me would work. The recipes sounded fine, fancy and technical but simply would not produce what they were supposed to. The truth was that the writers of the cook books they copied from were just writers also and not cooks. Incidentally they copied from the best cook books in this country, too.

Now to get back to frying pork sausage. This recipe applies whether pork sausage is smoked or not smoked.

Place the sausages in a frying pan and just barely cover them with water. Put a cover on the pan and boil them for 5 to 10 minutes, depending upon how thick the sausages are. Now empty out the water from the pan and take out the sausages and put them on a plate. Take a small piece of butter and put it in the frying pan and melt it. Now place the pork sausages back into the pan and over a medium heat. Turn them frequently until the skins of the sausages are just slightly brown and remove and serve. Pork sausage made in this manner is a great treat. Pork sausage cooked in this manner does not have a hard brown shell on them that you get on them when you try to just fry them. Pork sausage cooked in this manner does not shrink badly in size but keeps its shape well and is tender and juicy on the inside. If you just fry pork sausage they shrink and become tough and lose most of their fine flavor.

Pork should never be eaten raw as our doctors all rightly tell us. In order to just fry pork sausage enough so it is good and safe to eat you have to actually burn its outside so much that it forms a hard shell. By first cooking the sausage in water you not only cook it and keep it tender and save all of its wonderful flavor and juice but you make the meat safe for eating by the same method a doctor uses to sterilize his instruments.

PRAIRIE DOG BAT MASTERSON

Bat Masterson

Bat Masterson was one of the early law officers at Dodge City, Kansas and a great friend of Wyatt Earp's. Bat was an excellent gunfighter. He was a short, stubby man with a friendly homespun appearance that made him look like anything but a gunfighter. In later years he became a New York sports writer. He was not a heavy drinker. He preferred lemon pop to alcoholic drinks and drank large quantities of it. His favorite foods were cold tongue sandwiches and wiener sandwiches. Bat created a wiener sandwich which became well known throughout the Old West and was justly thought of as a real delicacy. Everyone called it a Prairie Dog. It is one of the greatest wiener recipes ever made and will be remembered long after Bat's gun deeds are forgotten. Here is the original recipe.

Take a wiener and slit it open lengthwise. Take ground sage and rub plenty of it into the slit and onto the sides of the slit. Place the wiener in an oven and broil until done. Take a bun and on one side of it put mustard and thinly sliced dill pickles. On the other side sprinkle it well with Worcestershire sauce. The sage, mustard, and Worcestershire sauce blend together to give you a sandwich with a wonderful taste. Be sure to try this famous sandwich at your first opportunity. It makes the usual catsup and mustard wiener sandwich taste very poor in comparison.

BELGIAN JACK RABBIT OR SNOWSHOE RABBIT

Jack rabbits and snowshoe rabbits have wonderful meat and there are dozens of really wonderful ways to serve them. This 200 year old recipe is awfully good and different. Every so often I just have to go out and get a jack rabbit and fix it this way.

Cut up a jack rabbit or snowshoe rabbit in serving pieces and salt and pepper it to taste. Melt a generous amount of butter in a large frying pan and brown all sides of the rabbit pieces well. Remove the rabbit meat from the pan and put them in a baking pan with a cover. In the melted butter add half a teaspoon of nutmeg, one-half a teaspoon of cinnamon and one teaspoon of powdered or two teaspoons of fresh horse-radish. Stir well and then pour on top of the rabbit pieces. Add ½ cup of water.

Now put in your oven at 350 degrees and bake for one hour.

Take one tablespoon of flour and mix with 3 tablespoons of cold water and mix until there are no lumps in it. Remove the rabbit pieces from the baking pan. Add the flour mixture to the liquid left in the pan and stir in well. Boil gently for a few minutes until the mixture thickens, to make the gravy. Serve the rabbit pieces with gravy and potatoes.

BELGIAN SQUIRREL

There are very few people whom I have talked to who know something about eating who do not rate squirrel at the top of the list when it comes to eating wild animals. Squirrel meat is light-colored, fine-textured, with a mild delicate flavor. Squirrel meat is far superior to venison or moose and you do not tire of it as easily as you do such meats when you have it for a more or less steady diet.

I have eaten fried squirrel, roasted squirrel and stewed squirrel in the Central, Southern and Eastern states and I just love them in any of these styles.

If I get to eating too much squirrel, I make sure to have it Belgian style as I never tire of it that way. Be sure to try it this way. I know you will enjoy it a great deal. This method is really the standard Ardennes method of cooking rabbit and was used in this country by the Belgians on squirrels as well as cottontail rabbits.

Clean three squirrels, wash and dry them thoroughly. Cut them up into serving pieces. Put a generous amount of butter in a frying pan and melt. Put in the squirrel pieces and brown them on all sides. Do not cook them, just brown them. Remove the squirrel pieces and place them in a deep cooking pot. Slice two medium sized onions in the left over melted butter in the frying pan and brown the onions. When the onions are done put the onions and the melted butter on the squirrel pieces in the pot. Then add enough water to nearly cover the meat. Then add 3 tablespoons of vinegar, ⅛ level teaspoon of thyme and salt and pepper to taste. Cover the pot and place in your oven at 350 degrees for 1 hour. Now remove the pot and put 1½ dozen prunes in the water. Be sure to put them in the water so they sink. Then reduce the oven heat to 325 degrees and bake for 45 minutes. Now remove the pot. Mix 1½ tablespoons of flour in a cup of cold water and mix until it contains no lumps. Then add this to the sauce in the pot. Place the pot on top of your stove at medium heat. Stir until it thickens. This usually takes from 10 to 15 minutes. Timing in making a sauce or gravy is the important thing. Watch when the gravy begins to form bubbles. It is just right when a nape or a coating forms on your spoon or ladle when you dip it in to test the consistency of the gravy.

Serve the squirrel hot with lots of gravy. Serve with the gravy on potatoes or toast. It is just wonderful. A person who simply cannot stand wild game will learn to like it quickly after a taste of this dish.

DIAMONDBACKED TERRAPIN BOOKBINDERS

The old original Bookbinders restaurant in Philadelphia.

Interior of the old original Bookbinders in Philadelphia.

In 1865 Samuel Bookbinder started a restaurant down in the dock area of Philadelphia on 125 Walnut Street. He served good food at reasonable prices and the restaurant became a success. Sam had a flare for showmanship and although he could get all kinds of seafood close by, he wanted something that could not be gotten locally for a specialty of his restaurant. He finally settled on a snapper soup made from snapping turtles that he had shipped in from Waterville, Minnesota. To ship in turtles from the Midwest when there were all kinds of terrapin and turtles available right in Philadephia was quite a stunt to pull in those days. His sons, Sam and Dick, sold the restaurant. After the restaurant was gone they realized that the name Bookbinder was a very good restaurant name so they started a new

Bookbinders Philadelphia.

restaurant at 215 South 15th Street in Philadelphia. As you walk into their new restaurant you want to watch your step or you will fall flat on your face. The floor is rough planked and warped badly. There are three floors to the new restaurant. All are decorated with mounted salt water fish and fish nets. The back room on the main floor is decorated with duck hunting decoys and a rifle and a shotgun painted red and is one of the worst looking restaurant rooms I have ever seen. They should definitely redecorate this room or old Sam is bound to come back and haunt them.

Upper room of Bookbinders. Note the large beer glasses full of oyster crackers on the table.

In the front of the first floor is a sea food bar. Here you can buy sea food to take home.

On every table they have a large beer glass full of oyster crackers. Their diamondbacked terrapin turtle is very good. If you are going to Philadelphia wire ahead and be sure that they have it on their menu for you. The diamond-backed terrapin they use is raised on farms in the nearby areas. They look much like a Galapagos Island turtle or Arizona desert turtle. The common leopard turtles that are found by the millions in the East, South, Midwest and Southwest taste just like diamondbacked terrapin but, of course, haven't the name. They can be used in place of diamondbacked terrapin in any recipe. Here is old Sam Bookbinder's original recipe.

Get two diamondbacked terrapins about 12 inches long or two common leopard turtles about this size or the equivalent in smaller ones. Cut off their heads with a small hatchet right behind the skull. Put them into a pot of boiling water for five minutes. This relaxes the muscles and makes them very easy to clean. Now carefully cut off the belly shell. Skin out the legs, tail and neck meat. If you have hit a female you are very lucky. Save all of the partly developed eggs inside of her. They will look like small round yellow balls about the size of peas or small marbles. Throw the rest away.

Put the meat and the eggs, if you have them into one quart of boiling water. Add one level teaspoon of finely chopped parsley, salt and pepper to taste using celery salt. Boil for twenty minutes. Remove a cup of the

The "take home" sea food bar at Bookbinders. It is on the main floor. Here you buy what cooked seafood that you want and take it home and eat it.

stock and place it in the cup in the freezing part of your refrigerator. Take a frying pan, melt two level tablespoons of butter and add 1½ level tablespoons of flour. Stir into the butter until smooth and creamy. Add one fourth cup of the chilled turtle stock from the refrigerator. Never use hot turtle stock or it will make the mixture lumpy. Put on the stove over a medium heat and stir and leave cook until the mixture thickens. Add enough turtle stock until the mixture is about as thin as half and half cream and milk, no thicker. It is better to have the sauce too thin than too thick. Cut up the terrapin meat into small pieces no bigger than a pea, and add with the eggs. Season with celery salt and pepper again if necessary. Have a small shaker bottle full of sherry wine on the table. Serve in a soup bowl and shake a few drops of sherry wine over the meat and sauce after it is on the table.

Wine shaker bottles are very difficult to get these days. If you cannot find one save an empty soy sauce bottle or Lea and Perrine meat sauce empty bottle. Wash it out good, remove the label and use it for your sherry shaker bottle. I prefer Sauce Lance Herter for a table shaker bottle but the sherry is excellent.

The snapper soup served at Bookbinders and at the Old Original Bookbinders is not really snapper soup at all or even a close facsimile. I am sure that the snapper soup at both of these places has made old Sam Bookbinder not only turn over in his grave many many times but made him spin in his grave.

Dick Bookbinder shows a lobster to a customer for size. Here again note the beer glass full of oyster crackers on the table.

I was born within twelve miles of where snapper soup originated in Minnesota, where old Sam got both his snapping turtles and his soup recipe. They can't even fool me on snapper soup if they got up in the middle of the night.

The snapper soup served at the Old Original Bookbinders looks and tastes like a bowl of poor veal gravy. It contains such things as veal, chicken fat, etc. I have the recipe but would not waste space to print it. A number of our leading cook books know so little about cooking that they print it with great fanfare.

The snapper soup served at the new Bookbinders tastes and looks like a bowlful of flour paste with a little tomato sauce in it. I have this recipe too and would certainly not waste space on it. At both places there is no taste at all of snapping turtle in the soup. They could use most anything in place of what little snapping turtle they use and you would never know the difference. Reminds me of the cook who made chicken soup by holding a chicken over the pot for a few minutes.

Here is the original snapper soup recipe and it makes an entirely different soup that is extremely delicious and tastes like snapping turtle meat, not something else.

Get a medium sized snapping turtle about 12 inches long. If you live in the Midwest any old trapper friend will sell you one. They are not at all cheap, in fact, are very expensive. One will cost you about $3.75. If you are out of this area write the Waterville Chamber of Commerce, Waterville,

The oyster bar in the Old Original Bookbinders Philadelphia. Here oysters are opened by laying them on a wooden bar. This is not the way to do it, you need a heavy strip of curved lead about four inches to hold an oyster while you open it. They should send someone down to New Orleans to learn how it is really done.

Minnesota, ask them for the addresses of snapping turtle dealers and they will send them to you.

A good specimen of snapping turtle. They live only in fresh water. The best ones come from Waterville, Minnesota.

Cut off the turtle's head with a small hatchet, being very careful not to get bitten. A snapper can take your hand off in one bite. Put the turtle in boiling water for about seven minutes. Remove and carefully cut off the bottom shell. Skin out the legs, tail, and neck and remove the flesh. If you are lucky you may get a female. Remove the undeveloped eggs, they look like yellow marbles. Place the meat and eggs in a large pot over medium heat. Add two quarts of water, two level tablespoons of finely chopped or pureed parsley, ⅛ level teaspoon of nutmeg and salt and pepper to taste using celery salt. Boil for thirty minutes. Add one cup of mashed boiled potatos and a half cup of whole

A soy sauce bottle like this makes a fine bottle to keep sherry wine on your table.

milk. Four level tablespoons of finely chopped cooked pimentoes or pureed pimentos. The canned one are very good for this purpose. 4 level tablespoons of butter. Warm and serve at once. Have a shaker bottle of sherry wine on the table. After the soup is on the table shake a few drops of the wine into the soup. You can buy a whole fifth of sherry wine for $1.00 or less so it is cheaper to use than any other table condiment even mustard. You cannot afford to be without sherry on the table.

This orginal snapper soup, has a flavor all of its own. I have eaten it all of my life and never got tired of it.

In Philadelphia you often see the word scrod fish on a menu. This is a strict phony as scrod is nothing but a small codfish and makes better lutefisk than anything else.

FRIED SNAPPING TURTLE OR SMALLER TURTLE MEAT, SCANDINAVIAN STYLE

Put a generous amount of butter in your frying pan. Salt and pepper the turtle meat to taste and fry it exactly as you would a piece of beef.

If you have the meat from a very large snapping turtle soak the meat over night in a mixture of ¼ vinegar and ¾ water with about a tablespoon of salt for every cup of water used. In the morning, wash the meat well in cold, clean water and dry it. It is then ready to fry. This latter method makes the turtle meat very tender.

SNAPPING TURTLE STEW

See pages 267-268 for Turtle Dressing Instructions

Either snapping turtle meat or smaller turtle meat can be used. The flesh of smaller turtles is just as good as snapping turtle meat but it takes more turtles to produce the amount of meat you need.

Turtle flesh in general is much like beef but more stringy. It is delicious eating. Turtles are plentiful in many areas, in fact so plentiful in many states that in case of a hydrogen bombing they would furnish enough meat for a considerable length of time.

Take two pounds of turtle meat and cut it up in one inch pieces or larger, depending on the size of the turtles the meat was taken from.

Melt a generous amount of butter in a frying pan and brown the turtle meat well on all sides. Then remove from the flame.

Put sufficient water in your stew pot for the following vegetables but not an excessive amount, and bring to a boil.

Add one medium sized sliced onion.

2 cups of cut up celery and be sure to include the celery leaves as they contain the best flavoring.

1 cup of lima beans that have been soaked overnight to soften them or 1 cup of canned lima beans. Simmer for one half hour.

Now dump in the browned turtle meat and the melted butter. Add 3 diced medium sized potatoes.

3 medium sized carrots cut up.

One small can of tomatoes.

One half cup of chopped parsley and salt and pepper to taste.

Cook slowly for 45 minutes more.

Serve in good sized soup bowls.

JACK PINE SAVAGE VENISON ROAST

The old term for the men who lived in the bush was jack pine savage; it later changed to the more formal name of bushman. The jack pine savages produced some fabulous cooks. If you did not learn to cook very well you became so tired of the foods available that you actually got so you could not keep them in your stomach.

Venison is wonderful meat and a welcome change when you have a deer to eat once a year. When you eat venison every month of the year it gets to the point where it is difficult to eat. I have never known an Indian who would not trade ten times the weight in deer meat for either beef or pork or for that matter, although this may seem strange to you, dog meat, which is also good meat.

A lot of nice roasts and steaks on the hoof if you know how to prepare them properly.

This is the way the old jack pine savages ate their deer roasts and there never has been a method developed half as good.

First select a good piece of either the rump, round, or standing rib for best results. Trim off all of the skin, fibers, and fat and when I say all of the fat I mean every speck. Work it out of the meat with your fingers if necessary. Deer fat is not good to eat and its taste spoils the taste of the meat.

Make a formula enough to cover the roast of ½ vinegar and ½ water, a tablespoon of salt for every quart of water and eight bay leaves and 8 whole cloves if you have them. Leave the roast stand in this liquid for 24 hours. Take the point of your Bowie or Bull Cook Knife and run it into the meat every square inch to leave the liquid penetrate. Remove and drain off the liquid. Rinse lightly in cold water and dry off with a cloth. Put the roast where it is cold or in the freezer for an hour or two until the meat is cold and firm. Salt and pepper the roast well.

Get a piece of beef suet from your butcher and some bacon. Cut both in pieces about 3 inches long and one-fourth to a half inch thick. Take your Bowie or Bull Cook Knife and push the point of it down into the top of the roast, then push forward on the knife blade making an opening in back of it. Push the pieces of suet and bacon down into the meat as far as you can. Do this once to every square inch of the roast. It takes a little practice to get the knack of this. Now lay strips of both beef suet and bacon on top of the roast completely covering the top. Then place in a roasting pan.

Put about one fourth of an inch or so of water in the bottom of the pan. Roast in a slow oven 325 degrees F. until done. Do not overcook as overcooked venison is tough and dry. Baste frequently with juice from the bottom of the pan and keep the level of juice up to a fourth of an inch or more. If necessary add more water. It will take about 25 minutes or more per pound to cook your roast.

Venison has a bad tendency to be too dry. It must be cooked with plenty of suet and bacon to correct this. Salt pork works well too but the suet and bacon much better. Dry venison is very tough and has a goat like taste. You can roast onions, carrots, celery, potatoes and rutabagas with your roast if you desire. Roasting vegetables with the venison helps to keep it from drying out.

Always serve venison on a hot plate as it gets tallowy when it is cool.

QUEBEC VENISON PATTIES

Venison is a meat that you get very tired of quickly. Many people will not eat it at all. This old French Canadian standard venison recipe produces venison that anyone will eat and enjoy whether they like venison or not.

A young buck like this one or a real old buck past the sexual urge stage or a dry doe make the best eating venison.

Take five pounds of lean venison with absolutely no fat on it at all. Venison fat is strong and musky and not good eating. Mix in two pounds of ground pork, the fatter the pork the better. Mix in the following spices into the meat.

2 level tablespoons of ground black pepper.
3 level tablespoons of ground nutmeg.
3 level tablespoons of salt.
2 level tablespoons of dried powdered onion.
¼ level teaspoon of powdered garlic

Make up into patties and fry in beef suet or butter. Wrap the patties which you do not eat, at once, in aluminum foil and freeze them in your deep freeze. Do not keep them frozen for more than three months.

VENISON ARDENNES

This is an ancient Belgium recipe for venison and hard to beat. It originated in the famous Ardennes forests of Belgium where deer are more plentiful than any forest in Europe.

This famous recipe makes venison taste good to people who do not ordinarily like venison at all and to people who are tired of eating venison. It does not take long to get tired of venison.

Take two pounds of lean venison and cut it up into bite-sized chunks. Be sure that no fat is on the pieces. Venison fat is strong and bad tasting. Boil the pieces until absolutely tender in water that you have seasoned to taste with salt and pepper. Remove from the water and drain well. While you are cooking the meat prepare the following sauce or gravy so that it is ready to pour over the meat as soon as it is well drained.

Take four level tablespoons of white flour and mix it well in just enough cold water to form a thin paste. Be sure to use cold water. Put the mixture into a frying pan or sauce pan. Add one cup of brown vinegar, one cup of cold water, one onion two inches in diameter chopped up finely, ¼ level teaspoon of ground cloves, ½ level teaspoon of ground ginger, ½ level teaspoon of salt, ⅛ level teaspoon of black pepper. Heat over a medium heat stirring all the time until you form a smooth gravy or sauce.

Pour this over the bite-size cooked pieces of venison and serve at once. This is a real taste treat and will be appreciated by anyone who really likes good unusual food.

VENISON HAMBURGER COCHISE

Cochise was in pioneer times, head of the Apache nation and indeed a great man and chief. He fought hard about the same as you and I would defending our wives and children against invaders who stole your land and starved your family. He was a great fighter but also a great loser, something most of us are not often prone to be.

As I write this his descendant, Cochise is 79 years old. He is undoubtedly one of the greatest Americans who ever lived. He was with William Frederick Cody as a sharpshooter in his Wild West Show. They were showing in Paris and Cochise enlisted in the Lafayette Squadron in World War I and distinguished himself highly.

In World War II he lied about his age in order to fight for us again and served 67 missions in a B-17 bomber in World War II.

At one time trying to help his people he rode a horse from Washington, D. C. all the way to Arizona.

This American deserves a lot more than just tipping our hats to him. After taking the beating that his people took he was a good loser to come back and fight for his conquerors in two wars. Takes a big man to do a thing like this.

The original Cochise, like all Indians, was very tired of eating venison and other game. When the first settlers came with cattle the Indians became very fond of beef. It was a real welcome change. When new spices gradually worked their way West with the settlers the Indians became very fond of them also.

Chief Cochise developed a way to make venison hamburger really delicious that has never been equaled by the finest cooks in the world. This method gives the hamburger a clean, fresh taste, free from the musk odor of venison that makes many people dislike it and makes every one tire of it when eaten continuously.

Take three parts of venison free from all fat and sinews. One part of beef suet. Grind them together well. Now mix in one-half level teaspoon of ground nutmeg and ⅛ level teaspoon of ground cloves per pound into the meat. Makes delicious hamburger that everyone likes.

VENISON, ANTELOPE OR GAZELLE, ESCALOPES RHAZES

Rhazes was born in Persia in 865 A. D. Rhazes was an extremely brilliant, kind man, a great doctor and writer. He was the first to describ measles and smallpox, to observe the reaction of the eye's pupil to light. was the first to write a book on children's diseases and this book rem the standard guide for doctors for centuries. His medical discoveries reached Europe by way of North Africa and Spain and were immediately accepted.

The cooking at the time of Rhazes in Persia was excellent. The Persians were then already using most of the spices that we use today and some very wonderful ones which we do not know of today such as Guimauve which is a violet flavor. Bay leaves, mustard, parsley, rose seeds, garlic, onions, fennel, cummin and saffron were all commonly used at that early date.

Rhazes discovered that to make the best tasting chicken you must pen them up in a small pen and feed them nothing but buckwheat for two weeks before eating them. Escoffier, the great French cook, read this discovery of Rhazes and wrote up the idea as his own. Escoffier made a specialty of chicken fed on buckwheat. Rhazes also discovered that peeled eggplant pickled in vinegar was delicious. It still remains today as the finest way to serve eggplant. It is a much better method than frying it.

Rhazes' method of preparing venison, antelope, or gazelle is an all time classic. It is one of the finest ways ever devised to prepare the meat of these animals. People who will not eat these meats will ask for seconds and thirds prepared with Rhazes' method. Here is his exact method.

Take a good piece of round steak or front shoulder meat and slice it across the grain into as thin slices as possible. Preferably about one eighth of an inch thick. Boil the slices in lightly salted water for one half hour. Remove the meat from the water and throw away the water. Boil again for one half hour in fresh lightly salted water. Remove the meat and leave the meat drain well. Throw away the water. Put about 2 quarts of fresh water back into the cooking pot. Add four level tablespoons of vinegar, one finely cut up clove of garlic, or ¼ level teaspoon of garlic powder. 1 level teaspoon of fennel spice and one level teaspoon of cummin spice, one half level teaspoon of salt, ¼ level teaspoon of black pepper. Stir the spices in well. Add the meat to the mixture. Bring the water to a slow boil then remove from the stove and leave the meat in the solution for one hour or more. Warm the solution and remove the meat and serve it warm or remove the meat and put it in your refrigerator and serve it cold. The meat can be served with a regular meal, as a before the meal appetizer, or in sandwiches. I just love meat prepared in this manner served in a sandwich made of buttered rye bread.

WIENER SCHNITZEL HILDEGARD

In the Middle Ages Abbess Hildegard of Rupertsberg about 1079 in her writings Physica Sacia was the first person to explain that in making beer you must have hops in it. This famous woman invented many famous foods such as Wiener Schnitzel as well as some of the finest beers of all time.

Wiener Schnitzel is very much misunderstood. In many parts of Germany it is thought to be an American dish. While eating in 1957 at one of Berlin's better restaurants I said that I liked the Wiener Schnitzel very much. They said they were very happy I liked their preparation of an American recipe.

The best Wiener Schnitzel in Europe today is served at the Am Franziskanerplatz in Vienna, Austria. This restaurant is located in a house over 500 years old. The building used to be a convent for girls who had children out of wedlock. They could leave the convent only if a man requested them for marriage. The convent finally sold the building to the Franciscan Brothers. While they were there Empress Maria Theresia used to come there to pray and relax. Today the upper 10 of Vienna's society eat there.

Here is the original Wiener Schnitzel recipe. Wiener Schnitzel today is mostly made with veal but it was originally made from pork, veal or venison, and usually venison.

If you use venison, slice off pieces of round steak seven inches long and about four inches wide and only one-eighth of an inch thick, not any thicker. If you use veal, slice off pieces of round steak about 7 inches long and about 4 inches wide and one-fourth of an inch thick. You also can use veal chops with the bone and fat removed and the meat cut not more than one-fourth of an inch thick. If you use pork, slice off pieces of fresh or cooked ham round steak about 7 inches long and four inches wide and one-eighth of an inch thick, no thicker. You can also use pork chops with the bone and fat removed and the meat sliced not more than one-fourth of an inch thick.

Whatever meat you use, place the meat on a wooden board and give it a good beating all over with the edge of a saucer. Now take a block of hard wood about two inches square and at least an inch thick and place it on the meat. Take an ordinary hammer and pound on the block spreading out the meat. In the case of the one-fourth inch thick meat, spread it to one-sixteenth of an inch thick. Season the meat on both sides with salt.

Now take two eggs per five pieces of meat and break them into a bowl and beat them just until they are smoothly mixed.

Take a large plate and cover it with bread crumbs about one-fourth of of an inch deep. Remember, just bread crumbs not flour or salt.

Take a French fryer, with beef suet or just a frying pan and enough rendered beef suet to fill the pan about one inch deep. Heat the fat to the same temperature as for frying French fried potatoes.

Now with your hands dip the meat into the beaten eggs being sure that the eggs cover all of the meat. Now take a fork and with the fork, not your hands, roll the meat in the bread crumbs. When the meat is well covered with bread crumbs, with your fork place in the pan and fry in the hot beef suet. Fry only until the batter is a nice golden brown. This will only take a few minutes. Remove and place on paper to drain. Put on the plate to serve. Sprinkle the top sides with powdered mustard, not wet mustard. Take finely grated onion and sprinkle the top sides also. Serve at once while hot.

The secret of making Wiener Schnitzel is to get the meat pounded and spread out so that it is thin. If it is thick you have to keep it in the hot suet too long in order to cook the meat and the over cooking ruins the batter.

This is a very good recipe for veal and pork and one of the finest ways to serve venison.

WYOMING POLISH SAUSAGE, SALAMI, AND SMOKED VENISON

I have always enjoyed hunting mule deer and antelope in Wyoming. The hunting is in beautiful open country. You can get good clear shots at both deer and antelope. Even more than the shooting however I enjoy eating Wyoming prepared venison and antelope. Here is how it is done:

The butcher shops in Sheridan smoke the deer hams exactly like smoking a pork ham with the exception that all the fat is carefully trimmed away before smoking. The venison when smoked tastes very much like fine wild acorn fed pork. It is just wonderful and you can eat it for days without tiring of it.

Here is the exact recipe for Wyoming Polish sausage:

Take 17 pounds of lean, fat-free venison and 17 pounds of lean, fresh pork. Your mixture has to be this half and half mixture to be really good.

Grind up the meats and mix them together thoroughly. Mix in 4 ounces of water.

Now mix in 1½ ounces of black pepper, one ounce of ginger, 1½ ounces of nutmeg, ½ ounce of allspice, ½ ounce of paprika, 2 level teaspoons of garlic powder. (If you do not like garlic, substitute 4 level teaspoons of onion powder), 12 ounces of salt, ½ pound of dried milk.

If you do not want to go to the trouble of making the meat into sausages simply wrap it in pound packages in aluminum foil and freeze it for safe keeping. To use it simply make up into paddies and fry like hamburger or hamburger steak. It is delicious.

To make up into sausages you can do it in two different ways depending on whether you have smoking equipment or not. Either method is equally good.

1. If you do not have smoking equipment proceed as follows:

Mix in three level teaspoons of liquid smoke. (Check the instructions on the liquid smoke bottle as the amount necessary to use varies from brand to brand. Herter's French Canadian Liquid Smoke is best.)

Stuff the meat in casings if you have them. Keep the links about 6 to 8 inches long. If you have no casings simply make the meat into paddies. This works just as well.

Smoking is just a baking process. Put what you will use for two weeks in your refrigerator. Wrap the balance in aluminum foil and freeze.

2. If you have smoking equipment proceed as follows:

Stuff the meat in casings if you have them. Keep the links about 6 or 8 inches long. Keep the links connected until they are dry. If you do not have casings make up the meat into paddies and place them on metal trays or wire screen that will go in your smoke house or smoker. Smoke over a low maple, apple, mesquite, or hickory wood fire from four to six hours. Keep the fire low at about 120 degrees. This is not hot enough to cause much dripping or shrinking.

Remove and put a two week's supply in your refrigerator. Wrap the balance in aluminum foil and freeze at once.

To cook put the paddies or sausages in a frying pan and add enough water to cover up one-third of the way on them. Put a cover on the frying pan and boil for 15 minutes. Remove, pour out the water from the frying pan and then put the paddies or sausages back into the frying pan and brown them slightly on all sides. Makes wonderful eating.

SERVING VENISON

There are many excellent ways to prepare venison, the one iron clad rule however, that you must follow is to serve all venison on warm heated plates. Venison cools very rapidly and becomes tallowy and unpalatable, if not served on warm plates. This applies to all venison, steaks, roasts, chops, hamburger, etc.

Round or oval aluminum plate platters are the best plates ever made to serve venison on and should always be used if at all possible. Your venison will taste very much better served on such plates.

THE ONLY CORRECT WAY TO CUT UP VENISON

If you cut up your venison yourself follow the illustration on page 67 as much as you possibly can.

If you have a butcher cut up your deer show him this illustration and tell him it must be cut up in this manner. Butchers know how to cut up a deer properly but rarely do so. If they realize you know how it should be done, they will be sure to give you a good honest job. Never

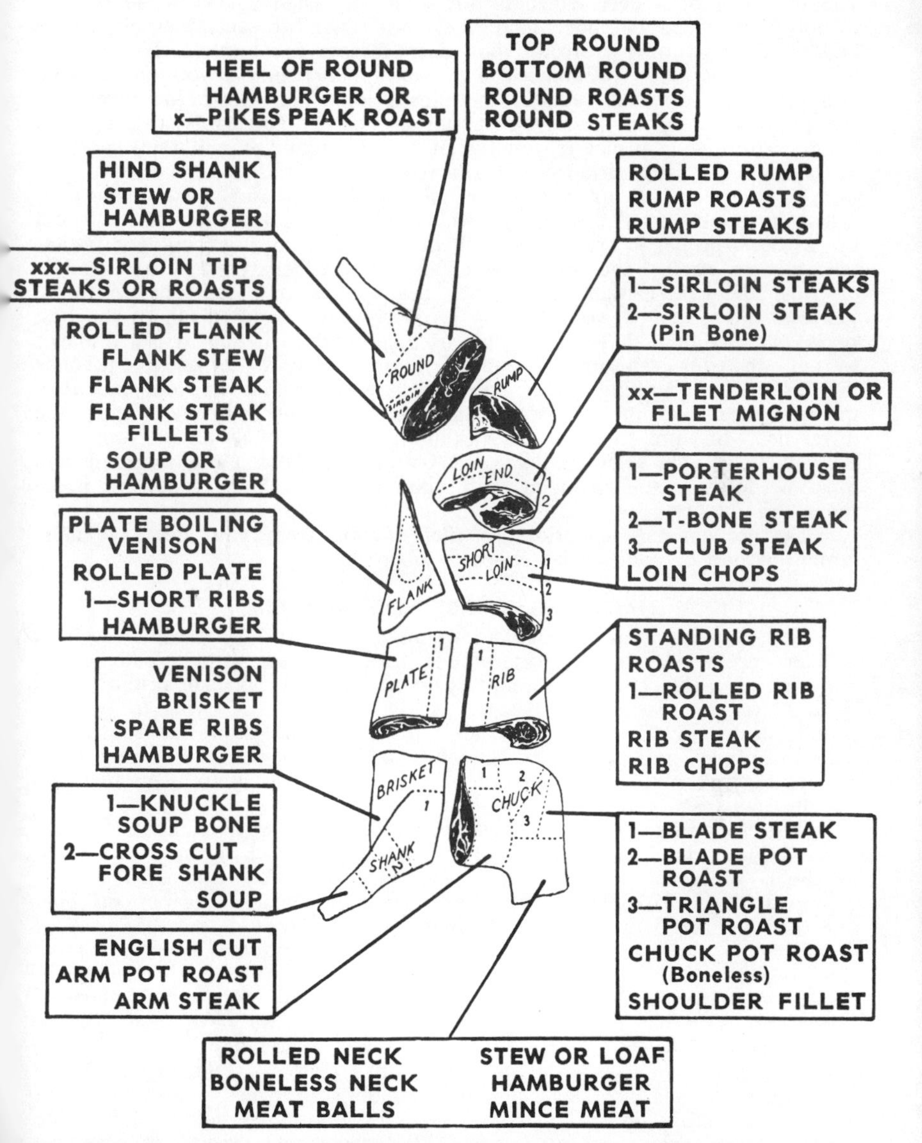

-Not cut from Antelope or Small Deer, left as part of adjoining cut.

—Do not remove, leave as part of Steaks, unless the deer is very large.

‹—Not cut from Antelope or Small Deer, do not remove, leave as part of Round.

TE—On Small Deer or Antelope backbone not split, yields Chops or Roasts, no Steaks.

take a deer to a butcher you do not know. It is sad, but very true that most butchers, when they see a deer carcass with really fine meat, often give it to a special friend of theirs or keep it for themselves, and give you the meat of a deer which is not so good. Then again, if the butcher is not your friend he more than likely will take off several sirloin steaks and a rib roast or two from your deer carcass for himself figuring you will never know the difference. You won't either unless you check what you get back from him against the illustration. The illustration gives you the proportions of all cuts you should get back. The same butcher who would return your wallet if you lost it and he found it will think nothing of taking your best sirloins and rib roasts.

To the best of my knowledge all information and illustrations published in books on deer hunting and outdoor magazines on how to cut up a deer properly are entirely incorrect. The average outdoor writer tells you to cut up the deer into chuck or shoulder roasts, chops, saddle or ribs, haunch, brisket, etc. Such descriptions and methods result in just one thing, that is, your venison is poorly cut up and much of the best parts cut, so that they cannot be used properly. If you tell a butcher to cut up your venison, by one of these methods, he knows at once that you know nothing about meat or how to cut it up and much of the best meat he will keep for himself, knowing you will never know the difference. Be sure to leave the sirloin tip on the round unless your deer is very large. On average deer and on antelope this piece is small and must be left on and included with your round steak or roasts to make them top quality.

Do not cut the tenderloin or filet mignon from your deer. It must remain as part of your steaks, chops or rib roasts.

JACK PINE SAVAGE VENISON STEAK

The old jack pine savage knew his deer meat. "Frying meat," on a deer meant rib steaks, porterhouse steaks, T-bone steaks, club steaks and sirloin steaks. If deer were plentiful the club steaks and sirloin steaks were stewed or roasted. You never caught any of them trying to fry any round steaks. The round went all for roasts and stews as it should. Venison round steaks tend to be tough and dry even in a young deer. If an old jack pine savage served you a round steak you knew for sure he did not like you.

The following is the old way and the best way to cook venison steak. First remove all the fat and fibers. By this I mean every speck of them. Deer fat is not good to eat and spoils the taste of the meat giving it a goat-like flavor. If you have ever tackled a mountain goat you know what I mean. Cut your steaks thin, not more than a half inch thick. Venison is not like beef, the thicker you cut a venison steak the poorer it is for eating. Make a formula enough to cover the steaks of ½ vinegar and ½ water, a tablespoon of salt for every quart of water and eight bay leaves and 8 whole cloves if you have them. Leave the steaks stand in this liquid 24 hours. Remove and drain off the liquid and rinse lightly in cold water and dry with a cloth. If taken from an old or large buck give the steak a good pounding all over with the edge of a saucer to soften up the fibers so they will absorb the butter while being cooked. Now pepper and salt to taste. Melt a generous amount of beef suet in a frying pan. Have your heat at about medium. Sear both sides of the steaks then fry them until done turning them frequently. Remove and brush both sides of the steak with butter to "finish" them. Steaks must have a butter taste to be good but must be fried in beef suet. Butter will burn when hot enough for frying. Do not cook venison steaks rare as they are usually tough this way. Cook them medium well done. This way they are the most tender. If you cook them very well done they tend to be dry and tough. Always serve venison on a heated plate. Venison cools rapidly and is tallowy when cool. Do not use lard, modern shortenings, margarine or oils to fry venison steaks.

Deer flesh is not like beef. No matter what a deer feeds on his flesh tastes about the same. I have eaten a large number of corn-fed deer and found them only slightly better than other deer.

PEMICAN

Pemican originated by the Indians is basically dried meat such as deer, buffalo, rabbit, squirrel, antelope, or beef broken up into small pieces and dried over a low fire. Dried fruit and herbs are added to the meat and it then is mixed with just enough of the fat of the animal to form it into solid blocks. The different Indian tribes added different things to pemican to flavor it. Some added dried wild grapes and cherries, others corn and still others beans and herbs.

Cut lean meat into thin ribbon strips and dry in the sun, over a low fire or in a low oven with the door open. Hang the meat over the rods of your oven rack never use a pan. When the meat is dry, pound it into a powder or put it through a food grinder. For each pound of meat, mix 2 tbs. of sugar and 2 oz. of dried fruit or herbs, to this add 5 ounces of suet and stir in well, form into solid blocks and store in cans or glass jars.

Pemican properly made is one of the finest foods that you can take into the wilderness or for a survival food in case of atomic bombing. Pemican keeps indefinitely. Today in our wonderful atomic age pemican is part of the survival ration of the newest United States Air Corps jet bombers.

A man exerting himself hard like you have to do in the wilderness craves fatty food and good pemican goes very well. You can make good pemican from grocery store dried beef or from jerky that you can make yourself. If you use jerky, pound it up into a powder. A hammer and a good solid block of hard wood will do this for you.

Chili powder that you can buy in any grocery store provides much the same seasoning for pemican as used by many of the Indian tribes. You take a good sized piece of pemican and place it in a pot of boiling water. Add a good level teaspoon or so of chili powder and you have an excellent wilderness or survival meal. If you have a few dried beans with you, soak them in water overnight and add them to the pemican and chili. You will have an excellent chili con carne.

HOW TO MAKE JERKY

Jerky is made up of meat that has been smoked and slow roasted until all moisture is out of it.

In case of an atomic bomb attack it would be very important to know how to make jerky, as it would be the only way left to preserve meat for long periods of time. With electricity knocked out electric freezers become useless. With the gas lines blown up gas ranges would be worthless. With the railroads blown up coal could not be moved in for cooking.

If you kill game in the wilderness it is very difficult to keep the meat during warm or mild weather. The only successful way to keep fresh meat in the wilderness besides making Pemican of it is to cut up into pieces about one half inch thick, one inch wide and 10 or 12 inches long. Build a log tower about three feet square and open at the top. This is quickly done simply by cutting up small logs and sharpening them on one end and driving them into the ground close together. If no trees are available simply dig a three foot square hole about three feet deep into the ground. Dig a narrow ditch from the side down into the bottom of the hole so that it has an oxygen supply when a fire is built in the hole. Build a small slow fire in the bottom of the hole or log tower. Put green lengths of small branches say about one inch thick over the open end. Lay the strips of meat over the pieces of wood. Cover over the top of the hole or tower with pieces of wood or anything available. Leave just enough of an opening so that the fire will not go out. Keep a slow smoldering fire going for about 12 hours. Drop in small pieces of wood to keep the fire going. If there are aspen trees in the area put the leaves from them into the smoldering fire. They give the meat a good flavor. If hickory, mesquite or maple wood is available use it for the fire.

The mesquite tree of the Southwest is as good or better than hickory, for smoking meat and fish. They grow in dry areas and have thin needle-like leaves. This one is in full foliage.

Meat made into jerky will last practically indefinitely. To eat it soak it in water for four or five hours. If possible boil it into a stew. If you have no vegetables, wild grape leaves, dandelion leaves, violet leaves, aspen leaves, laurel leaves or the bark from small pine trees boiled with the jerky is excellent.

HOW TO BUY WIENERS

For centuries wieners have been made as follows: The manure and partly digested food in the intestines of small animals such as sheep is removed. The intestines are then washed. They then are stuffed with wiener meat and roasted. This method produces a fairly good tasting wiener. The objections to such wieners are three. They curve in cooking and do not fit well into hot dog buns. They are hard to bite through as the intestine becomes tough when roasted. They take on the flavor of the intestine which sometimes is very objectionable.

The Dupont company brought about the first great improvement in wiener making in over two thousand years. Dupont's developed a cellophane tubing that wiener meat is stuffed into, shaped and roasted in. The cellophane tubing is then removed and you have a so-called skinless wiener. Actually the wiener is not skinless as roasting the wiener meat against the cellophane forms a thin tender natural meat skin on the wiener. The so-called skinless wiener has three distinct advantages. First, it has no objectionable odor from intestines. Second, it cooks straight and does not curve making it fit perfectly in hot dog buns. Thirdly, it bites off easily.

Skinless wieners are, of course, lower in cost as intestines are more expensive than cellophane. Many of the intestines used here in America have to be imported from sheep raising countries.

If you want really fine eating wieners buy the skinless ones.

BELGIAN WIENERS

This is a rare, really fine recipe. Be sure to try it the first chance you get.

Buy a pound of a good brand of skinless wieners. Get a French frying pan, with a wire screen mesh pan inside of it. Do not get a French frying pan with the inside pan perforated metal as they stop the grease movement and will not French fry well at all. Put good rendered beef suet in the French fryer. Bring the temperature up to 380 degrees. This is good and hot but not smoking hot.

Make the following batter. Take one cup of flour and add three-fourths of a cup of milk and mix in well. Then add one fourth teaspoon of salt, ⅛ teaspoon of nutmeg, one teaspoon of onion powder or grate an onion 1½ inches in diameter and use instead of the onion powder. Add one egg that you have beaten so that the white and yolk are mixed together well. Then add two level teaspoons of mustard and two level teaspoons of baking powder. Mix together well.

Take a skinless wiener and stick a meat skewer into the end or a large nail or piece of wire will work just as well. Dip the wiener well into the batter, then put it into the beef grease by carefully pushing it off the skewer, nail, or wire. Fry until a nice light brown. Usually takes about 2½ minutes. Remove and place on a paper to drain. Serve while warm. If you like catsup, brush the outside with catsup. If you like a lot of mustard, brush mustard on the outside. Wieners prepared this way make very fine eating.

HOLLAND WIENERS

Wieners are one of the world's fine foods when prepared properly. They have always been a great favorite of mine.

The early Hollanders brought with them a method for cooking wieners that I never have seen equaled and it is very simple and easy to do.

Take a cloth and dip it in salad oil and rub over each wiener. Put your oven at 500 degrees or broil. Leave the oven door open about a third. Place the wieners on a pan in the oven or broiling rack and broil for 2½ minutes, then turn and broil them another 2½ minutes. Remove them and serve them quickly on bread or buns with pickles, onion, mustard or catsup, whatever you prefer. The broiling gives the wieners a fresh, crisp taste that just cannot be beat. You will never go back to fried wieners or boiled wieners after once trying this method.

HOW TO COOK BOLOGNA

Bologna was invented in the town of Bologna, Italy in 1463 by a man named Anthony Garcia.

Bologna making rapidly spread to nearly every country in the world. Today you can buy good bologna almost everywhere. The really important thing that has been sadly forgotten completely through the centuries is the Garcia method of cooking bolgona.

Today the bologna makers tell you to simply put the ring of bologna into boiling water and heat it until warm and then serve. If you want strong tasting, greasy, bologna that you go around belching all day long this is the way to prepare it.

If you want mild, fine tasting bologna with no bad after effects cook it like the man who invented it intended it to be cooked. Use the original Garcia recipe. Bolgona so cooked is one of the world's really great delicacies. Here is Garcia's recipe:

Take your ring of bologna and with a fork jab holes into the bologna about one fourth of an inch apart on both sides of the bologna. Contrary to today's beliefs that the casing be left intact it was originally intended and rightly so to only hold the ground meat together. It was not intended to seal it up tightly leaving the bad taste of the fats dominate the taste of all the meat.

Fat has the ability to pick up and hold strong undesirable odors. You must remove the majority of the fat from the bologna to get rid of these odors.

Now place the bologna in a pan with enough boiling water to nicely cover it. Add seven level teaspoons of honey. If you have no honey add seven level teaspoons of sugar. Boil the bologna for 20 minutes. This will remove nearly all of the quick melting undesirable fat with its strong odors from the bologna and the honey or sugar will cleanse the meat giving it a clean good taste, but not a sweet taste.

Cooking bologna in unsweetened water is like trying to cure or smoke a ham without sugar or sweetening. It never was intended to be done without sweetening. The proof is the pudding, just try the Garcia method.

The early Italian immigrants brought this recipe with them and today their descendants are still using it.

Fish and Sea Foods

FISH ANTONY

Antony Van Leeuwenhoek was born in Delft, Holland in 1632. He spent nearly all of his ninety years on this earth in this same town. He was a linen merchant selling raw linen to the Irish for bleaching and also a surveyor. He also served as a deputy or chamberlain to the sheriffs of Delft for over fifty years.

In spite of all these occupations he found time to perfect the art of grinding and polishing bits of glass into lenses. Some of the lenses he made into microscopes. While he did not make the first crude microscope he made the first microscope of modern workable design and he is hence generally credited with making the first microscope. Some of his microscopes magnified one hundred and fifty times and more.

He discovered the first algae in water and the first microbes. In less than 200 years after Columbus visited America, Van Leeuwenhoek discovered the new worlds of life that exist in even a drop of water. His first glimpse of this new world was in 1674.

Van Leeuwenhoek was a great fisherman and fish eater. As you might imagine of a man with such a creative mind he was curious and creative in many, many ways. He was one of the first to raise garden peas in Holland.

Peas originated in Northwest India, Afghanistan and the mountains and plateau of Ethiopia. Peas were at first grown only for their dry seeds. The varieties known until about 1,000 years ago had smaller, and darker colored seeds than our garden types of today. In history there is nothing written about green peas as we know them today until the Norman conquest of England. In the 12th Century among other foods noted by the Normans was "green peas for Lent" stored at the famous old Barking Nunnery. In 1536 green garden type peas were described in detail in France but were scarce and fantastic prices were paid for them. They were actually worth their weight in silver. In 1696 Madame de Maintenon of the Royal Court in France wrote "This subject of peas continues to absorb all others. Some ladies even after having supped at the Royal Table, and well supped too, returning to their homes, at the risk of suffering indigestion, will again, eat peas before going to bed. It is both a fashion and a madness."

When you eat a can of peas today, just remember that not long ago they were actually worth their weight in silver and food prices are now not so bad after all.

Van Leeuwenhoek by raising green peas alone in his time, created quite a sensation with his neighbors.

He invented the following recipe and it became the sensation of the time. It is indeed a classic one and one of the finest methods of preparing fish ever invented.

Take a pound and a half of cleaned fish. Fish such as crappies, bluegills, sheephead, bass, stream trout, bullheads, walleyed pike, northern pike, haddock, are all excellent for the purpose. Place the fish in a pot with about a quart and a half of water. Add three tablespoons of vinegar and one level teaspoon of salt. Boil from 5 to 10 minutes depending upon the kind and size of the fish until it is well done and beginning to be flaky. Remove from the pot and drain well on paper.

Make a white sauce flavored with mushrooms. Today simply take one can of Campbell's mushroom soup and put it in a pot and add one half cup of whole milk. Stir over a medium heat until smooth. Add one number 1 can of canned peas. Fresh boiled peas as used in the original recipe are exactly the same. Add one heaping tablespoon of butter. Mix all together well. Now take a fork and remove all of the meat from the boiled fish taking out all of the bones. Put the fish meat into the sauce and stir over a medium heat until all is mixed well together. Salt to taste. Take hot toast and spread it with a mixture of half and half soft butter and grated onion. Serve the fish and sauce on squares of the toast.

This is a fabulous recipe, be sure to try it at once. Everyone gets tired of eating fried fish or baked fish and a recipe like this is a welcome change to the whole family. This recipe beats any of these modern tuna hot dishes by a wide, wide, margin. Tuna fish as you probably know is one of the poorest eating fish in the world. A carp tastes like a trout compared to it. They are so strong and oily that there are few people who can keep them down. Canned tuna has most of the objectionable oil removed or you would never eat it at all.

HOW TO MAKE CAVIAR

The making of caviar is generally thought to be of Russian origin. This is not true. The Mongolians were the first to make caviar and Genghis Khan, the mightiest ruler the world has ever produced, brought caviar making to Europe with his conquering warriors seven hundred years ago. Genghis Khan also brought buckwheat flour and pancakes to Europe.

In Minnesota the making of caviar was one of its earliest food industries. The Mississippi River in Minnesota used to be literally full of sturgeon. Sturgeon are still quite plentiful around Winona, Minnesota today. They are still offered for sale at Winona by commercial river fishermen.

Sturgeon eggs are one of the few fish eggs that are dark gray in color. They are never black as often stated by misinformed writers. Because of this unusual color for fish eggs, they became the fish eggs most sought after for caviar making. Actually sturgeon eggs taste no differently than bluegill, crappie, perch, walleye, or northern pike eggs prepared in the same manner.

Caviar was originally prepared in China from carp eggs. The carp is really a goldfish and is the only fish besides sturgeon that have gray colored eggs. They are a somewhat lighter gray than sturgeon eggs. Beyond a doubt carp eggs make by far the finest tasting caviar. The flesh of carp no matter how it is prepared is very poor eating and few people care for it at all. Although the first carp were brought to this country from Germany and people tend to call carp German carp this is not the correct name at all for these fish. All of the carp that were originally stocked in Germany came from China.

Caviar was first made from carp eggs.

Bringing carp to North America and stocking them here has damaged our game fishing in all the parts where they now exist. Carp root up the weed growth, eat fish spawn and worst of all when they are the dominant feed fish in any area, fish that eat carp minnows for the greater part of their diet die from paralysis very quickly. If a human eats raw carp flesh for a week he will also die. Ranch mink fed on raw carp also die very rapidly.

Here is the original and best caviar recipe:

Take one gallon of water. Add 2½ cups of salt. See if an egg will float in the solution. If it will not, add more salt until the egg will float. Add 1/6 of an ounce of sodium nitrate. (Get from your druggist, it cost practically nothing.) Add 1/32 of an ounce of sodium nitrite. (Get from your druggist, it costs practically nothing.)

Add one level teaspoon of powdered ginger. Add one level teaspoon of dry mustard. Wet mustard will do if you do not have the dry. Stir well. Then take the carp egg sack and cut it open and squeeze out the eggs into the solution. Leave stand at room temperature for five days. Then strain out the carp eggs and place them in glass jars and keep them under refrigeration or frozen until used. If you have no refrigeration put the eggs in mason jars and put on mason caps. Sterilize them as described elsewhere in this book and store in a dark place until used.

Caviar is used in this country as a cracker or bread spread or a spread for cheese. If you like salty food it is delicious. I like it very much on cheese. In Europe it is mostly used in salads or simply eaten separately by itself or mixed with one fourth its bulk in finely chopped onions plus one level tablespoon of lemon juice for every 4 ounces of caviar. I like this latter recipe very well also.

CLAM SHELLS SAINT JAMES

In France this recipe is called coquilles Saint Jacques. It is a very, very, ancient recipe and a very, very good one. The recipe was made by Saint James the apostle of Christ and was brought to France by early traders. It has always been a recipe that all really fine cooks used, yet it is not too difficult to make. Gather some large fresh water or salt water clam shells. Boil them well, then clean them if necessary with a stiff brush. Take a pound of fish preferably fillets. It can be from such fish as crappies, bass, bluegills, perch, walleyes, trout, catfish, or bullheads. If you use salt water fish codfish or halibut work very well. Put the fish into a pot and cover with enough water to boil them. Put in the water one-eighth teaspoon of mace and one-eighth teaspoon of thyme, one onion about an inch and a half in diameter or one clove of garlic if you prefer garlic and a level tablespoon of finely chopped parsley. Boil until the fish are well cooked but do not overcook. The boiling depends on the kind and size of the fish. Remove the fish from the water and strain the water into a pot and put them in a refrigerator to cool. Take two heaping tablespoons of butter and melt in a frying pan. Add 1½ heaping tablespoons of flour. Mix until smooth and creamy. Remove from the stove. Add one half cup of the water you boiled the fish in. Be sure the water is cold, and salt and pepper to taste. Mix together until smooth and creamy. Add four level tablespoons of grated cheese to the sauce and gently boil until the cheese is melted and incorporated well into the sauce. Remove from the stove. Now cut the fish into small pieces not more than one fourth of an inch in diameter. Mix the fish well into the sauce. Take one tablespoon of finely chopped parsley and mix it into the sauce. Now fill the clam shells with the mixture. Cover the surface fairly thick with cracker crumbs. Put small pieces of thinly sliced butter over the cracker crumbs. Place the shells onto a tray and put into your oven at 375 degrees and leave for a few minutes until slightly brown on top. Check them often so they do not get too brown. Remove and serve. You can use lobster, clams, scallops instead of fish also.

SQUID CHAPTAL

Jean Antoine Chaptal was born in 1756 and died in 1832. He was a French chemist and invented the processes we use today for making cement, alum, and saltpeter. He also created a great many of our present day food recipes. Here is his original recipe for preparing squid. Squid are plentiful along the North, Central and South American coasts. North American people do not know how to prepare them and hence are missing a wonderfully delicious, different food. In Italy, France, Spain and Portugal squid are widely eaten and considered a great delicacy. You can buy squid at grocery stores in most large towns or your grocer can get them for you. When you are near the ocean you can buy them from fishermen who use them for bait. The fish that they catch using them for bait is rarely as good eating as the squid.

Take two pounds or more of squid and remove the eyes, the ink sack and the stomach. Put the squid into boiling water, add the following to the water. One level teaspoon of salt, ¼ level teaspoon of black pepper, three bay or laurel leaves, one diced onion about two inches in diameter. Boil slowly for about 2½ hours. Remove and drain. Slice the squid into round slices about ¼ of an inch thick.

Make the following Antoineaise sauce and cover each piece with a ¼ inch layer of it and serve at once.

Antoineaise sauce was also invented by Chaptal and is made as follows. Take one envelope of unflavored gelatine and soften it in three tablespoons of cold water for five minutes. When softened warm the water until it boils dissolving the gelatine. Boil for one minute. Leave cool. Now add four or five drops of beet juice or red coloring to make it red and four drops of almond flavoring and stir into a cup of mayonnaise. Antoineaise sauce in itself is fabulous and is excellent on all fish, shrimp, lobster, tuna, salmon, turtle meat, oysters and clams.

HOW TO PREPARE FRESH WATER SHRIMP OR CRAYFISH

The large salt water shrimp, as we all know, is much sought after for food. The meat from their tails is the part that is eaten. I enjoy salt water shrimp either fried or boiled and served as a cocktail or as a main course. They are even excellent when dipped in soy sauce as served in Japan. I have eaten salt water shrimp, I believe from all the oceans including the small Belgian shrimp that is considered to be the finest flavored in the world. I have found, however, that the common fresh water crayfish, common in lakes, ponds, streams and ditches all over North America, are superior for eating purposes by a good margin. My grandmother learned how good fresh water shrimp were from the Sioux Indians. I seined wash tubs full of them for her at all seasons except when the ice formed in winter.

Locate some Crayfish, or fresh water "crabs" as they are sometimes known, in a lake, pond, stream or ditch and seine them out with a minnow seine. Take them home alive in a pail or wash tub. Fill the tub or pail with fresh water when you get them home, and throw in a handful of salt in the water. Leave them in the salty water for ten minutes. Heat a large kettle of boiling water and add a little salt and pepper to it. When the water is boiling, drop the Crayfish alive into the water. It kills them almost instantly, much quicker, in fact, than any packing plant kills chickens. Let them boil 3 minutes after they turn a beautiful red color just like a cooked lobster. Remove them from the water and let them cool. When they are cool, shuck the skin from the tails and you will have the finest "shrimp meat" that I know of. No salt water shrimp equals its clean, crisp solid flavor and texture. You can serve this meat from the tails cold or hot and with any sauce that may suit your fancy.

ROZE FISH CROQUETTE

In 1776 a man in Paris, France named Roze made the first CARTE, meaning card in French, listing the prices of individual foods served in a restaurant. He also made the first menu ever used. Roze was not only an accomplished restaurant manager but an outstanding cook. His fish croquettes are one of the world's great recipes. Simple ingredients and easy to make and very different wonderful eating. Here is the original recipe: Take one pound of fish preferably fish fillets. They can be from crappies, bass, walleyed pike, bluegills, catfish, bullheads, perch or trout. If you want to use ocean fish, cod or halibut are excellent.

Place the fish into a pot and cover them with just enough water to boil them in. Boil the fish in the water until cooked. This time will vary depending on the kind and size of the fish. Remove the fish from the water. Remove any skin on the fillets. Take a fork and break the fish flesh up into small pieces and mash it with your fork. Take one-third of a day old or older loaf of white bread and crumble it up well. Take an onion about one and a half inches in diameter and cut it up into little pieces. Mix this with the crumpled bread. Mix in the mashed fish. Add one egg, one level teaspoon of mustard, one tablespoon of soft butter, one-eighth teaspoon of nutmeg and salt and pepper to taste. Now mix all together in a bowl. When all are mixed make round balls from the mixture about 1½ inches in diameter. Beat the whites of two eggs stiff with an egg beater. Roll the balls into the stiff egg whites, then into cracker crumbs. Fry in a French fryer in beef grease same as described for making French fried potatoes. Remove and lay on paper to drain.

For Americans serve with homemade tartar sauce or tomato and horse-radish or shrimp sauce. For Europeans serve with homemade mayonnaise. This recipe came to Minnesota with the French fur traders and is the treasured secret of many an old cook.

MORMON TROUT

On July 22, 1847 Orson Pratt and George A. Smith with seven other men rode into the valley of Salt Lake City to look it over as a possible area for

Monument to Brigham Young in the center of Salt Lake City.

Monument of the spot where Brigham Young said, "This is the place," as he first looked over the valley of Salt Lake City, Utah.

a settlement. On July 23 the advance party of the Mormon group whom they were scouting for arrived and plowed the first land in the valley. The ground was so dry and hard that three plows were broken. They had to divert a stream to flow over the ground to soften the land enough so that it could be plowed.

On July 24th Brigham Young entered the valley, he was with the vanguard or rear of the group. All of the group decided that this was a good place for a settlement. The first winter little food was available. The Mormons lived on the roots of the Sego lily that still grows wild in the hills around Salt Lake, dandelion roots and leaves, mule deer, prairie dogs, oxen and trout.

The Sego lily still grows wild in the hills. Its root is not bad eating.

A new state called Desert meaning Land of the Honey Bee was formed and a petition sent to Congress to recognize it. Congress turned down the petition but created the Utah Territory and made Brigham Young governor of the territory in 1852.

The food in today's Salt Lake City is far from anything special. The old recipes are completely forgotten. The original Mormons did not believe in smoking or drinking. Today there are Jack Mormons who do smoke and drink but are of the Mormon faith and the old true Mormons who still do not smoke or drink. No Mormon is ever allowed to go on relief. The Mormons take care of their own and always have.

The town of Salt Lake City has very wide streets. It is said that they were laid out by Brigham Young so that he could walk down the streets abreast with all of his 34 wives at one time. He maintained five separate

Front of the Lion house in Salt Lake City.

Side view of the Lion house, Salt Lake City.

large houses. The most famous of which are the Lion House and Beehive House which are right near the large present day Mormon Temple. These homes are extremely well built, Brigham Young himself was an architect. At the time they were built they were as luxurious as any homes in all of North America. Even today they are very beautiful and well worth going through.

The early Mormon method of preparing trout was a very good one. You can use it to prepare any kind of fish. It is a broiling method but unlike

Front of the Bee Hive house, Salt Lake City.

Side view of the Bee Hive house, Salt Lake City.

other fish broiling methods that invariably make fish taste strong this method leaves them tasting mild and delicious.

Great Salt Lake in the evening. It is a big salt puddle out in a semidesert area.

Here is the original recipe.

Take a suitable sized layer cake pan with a fairly high rim so nothing can run out of it. Put one fourth of an inch of water in the bottom of the pan and two level tablespoons of melted butter on top of the water. Place the trout in the pan. Sprinkle the entire trout with finely crushed sage leaves and salt and pepper to taste. Broil at 450 degrees for six minutes on one side then turn and sprinkle the other side with finely crushed sage leaves and salt and pepper to taste. Broil for six minutes. Remove and serve at once with just bread and butter. Keep the fish a good five inches away from the heat scource for the broiling. You will have to vary the broiling time somewhat depending upon the size of the fish. Makes a fine eating trout. Same method works exceptionally well on bullheads. Bullheads are a char and a close relative of the brook trout.

The water of Great Salt Lake is so saturated with salt that it floats you like a cork. You have to take a bath in fresh water when you get out as your body becomes encrusted with salt. Local residents never swim in the lake. Only an occasional tourist gives it a try just to say they have done it when they get back home.

FISH CHARLES DE LINNE

Charles De Linne was a Swedish nobleman born in 1701 and died in 1778. He was a great botanist and his works are still well used today. He also was a very famous vegetable and fish cook. Here is his original recipe for one of the finest fish meals you have ever eaten.

Clean two pounds or more of fish, removing their heads, scales and insides. In the case of bullheads and catfish remove their skins. Crappies, perch, black bass, stream trout, bullheads, catfish, walleyed pike, northern pike, sea trout, grouper, haddock, smelt are all excellent for this famous dish. If the fish are large cut the flesh up into pieces about six inches long and 1½ inches wide and not more than a half inch thick. Take a large sized covered cooking pot, and place a layer of fish or fish pieces in the bottom. Over them put 1 bay or laurel leaf, one clove of sliced garlic, one fourth teaspoon of salt and 1/16 teaspoon of black pepper, one onion about an inch in diameter sliced very thin. Keep repeating these layers as long as you have fish. Add one 15 ounce can of sliced beets, juice and all. Then cover the fish with a mixture of ¾ vinegar and one fourth water. Boil gently for about 10 to 15 minutes depending upon the size of the fish over a medium heat. Then carefully remove the fish and vegetables and put them into a large bowl, (not a platter) to cool. Pour about three level tablespoons of salad oil mixed with three level tablespoons of vinegar over the fish and vegetables. When cold serve as the main course of your meal with boiled potatoes mashed with butter and small pieces of a mild cheese. This is one of the finest meals you will ever have.

JOSIAH SNELLING FRIED FISH

I have been asked many times for a really good method to pan fry fish. I am here describing by far the best method that I have ever encountered any place in the world.

Most people who really enjoy pan fried fish agree that a lightly battered fish fried slowly in butter with lots of thin slices of almonds in the batter is by far the finest method. This method is called in the world's finest restaurants such names as fish fried almonde, or fish fried almondine, or poissons aux amandes. I always tell them I know a very much better recipe and after they try it they invariably agree.

Not too long ago, in 1824 a Colonel Josiah Snelling was in command of Fort Snelling, a small fort that he had completed on the Mississippi River on the point where the city of Minneapolis had its first start.

Colonel Snelling was a great eater and cook and a student of cooking. He found two things in the areas surrounding the fort that really interested him. One was a great abundance of really good eating fish such as walleyed pike, bream, and channel catfish. The other an Indian method of baking fish covered with ground black walnut meats, also plentiful in the area. It wasn't long before Colonel Snelling substituted black walnuts for almonds in Europe's best pan frying fish recipe. He really hit it as I have never eaten fish any place in the world that are as good. It gives the fried fish a wonderfully different fresh taste that no other pan frying method can give. Removes all fishy odor. People who detest fish like them this way.

Here is his recipe:

Make the batter as follows: Take the whites of two large eggs and put them into a deep bowl. Beat the white of eggs with an egg beater until stiff. Take a fourth cup of very fine cracker crumbs and three fourths of a cup of white flour and mix well together in a paper bag. Take a cup of black walnut meats and with a knife slice them up fairly small. Do not grate them. If you have an electric liquifier use it. Take your fish fillets and if over an inch thick slice the thick part in two. You do not want the fish too thick using this method. Now place the fish fillets into the paper bag with the flour and cracker crumb mixture and shake well and remove. Use a fork to hold the fish fillets and dip them into the stiff white of egg mixture. Then quickly dip the fillets into a bowl with the sliced black walnuts in it. Get plenty of the nut meats on all sides of the piece of fish.

Take a frying pan and melt a good piece of butter into it. Put two tablespoons of water into the melted butter or two level tablespoons of melted beef suet to keep it from turning too brown. These are real master chefs' tricks. Now place the fish in the pan and fry slowly at low heat until well done.

There is not a restaurant in the world that even comes close to frying fish equal to fish pan fried using this method.

In the Middle West and through most of the South you can get all the black walnuts you want by simply going out in the woods in the fall and gathering them. In other regions you will have to buy them in grocery stores. If your grocer does not stock them make him get them.

He can order them from many companies including Slocum Bergren Co., St. Louis Park, Minnesota. At present they retail for 35c for 3 ounces.

FISH MARIE ANTOINETTE

Marie Antoinette was an Austrian woman, daughter of Maria Theresa, Queen of Hungary and Bohemia. She became the wife of Louis XVI of France. She was executed in 1793, may her soul rest in peace.

Marie Antoinette was a woman who really enjoyed and knew fine cooking. This recipe was made by one of the many palace cooks she maintained and was her favorite.

This recipe is popular in Minnesota. Scandinavian, Belgium, German, and Austrian people are especially fond of this ancient, famous recipe.

The original recipe was for cooking trout but it works just as well if not even better for cooking crappies, bluegills, sunfish, perch, bullheads, walleyed pike, bass and even halibut.

Put two quarts of water into a pot. Add six bay leaves, a half cup of vinegar, a level teaspoon of salt, nine pepper berries, or a level teaspoon of black pepper. Bring to a boil.

Clean the fish as follows: In the case of trout just disembowel them and leave the head on and do not remove the skin. If you use bluegills, sunfish, perch, smelt, walleyed pike or bass, disembowel and remove the heads and remove the skin before boiling them. To do this simply hold the fish under a hot water faucet for about a minute or so. After a fish has been in boiling or hot water a minute or so its skin thickens and the mucous glue-like bond between the skin and the flesh loosens making it possible to pull off the skin from the flesh as easy as peeling the skin from a banana. Stick a fork into the fish so that you can hold it under the hot water faucet without any danger of burning your hand.

If you use bullheads skin them the usual way by making a cut around the base of the head and grasping a piece of the skin with a pliers and pulling it off toward the tail. Place the cleaned fish in the boiling water for six minutes. In the case of large walleyed pike or bass it will take up to 12 minutes or more to cook them. Remove the fish and lay them on paper to drain, if trout is used remove the skin. The skin comes off easily after boiling. Place the skinned fish on a plate.

Take 3 heaping tablespoons of butter and melt in a frying pan. Add ⅛ level teaspoon of paprika and ⅛ level teaspoon of ground all-spice to the butter and quickly pour over the fish. Regulate the amount of the butter sauce you make by the amount of fish you cook.

A fish cooked in this manner has very firm flesh and no fish odor at all. If you try this method just once you are apt to end up using it a great deal. A really unusual old recipe.

FISH TONGUES SCANDINAVIAN

The Scandinavian people both Norwegian and Swedish are great lovers of fish tongues, and consider them a great delicacy.

I have eaten them for years and like them very much; in fact they are much better eating than the flesh of most fish. The tongues from stream trout, salmon, catfish, bullheads, walleyed pike, bluegills are all very delicious and are very easy to prepare.

1. They can be boiled in lightly salted water from five to fifteen minutes depending upon the size of the tongue. Leave drain on paper and serve with mustard or a sauce made from catsup and horseradish.
2. They can be French fried. It takes just a few minutes to fry them. Drain and sprinkle lightly with powdered mustard.

HOW TO COOK FISH EGGS BY ST. PATRICK

One of the first things my grandmother taught me to cook was fish eggs. In early Minnesota fish eggs were one of the best and most popular foods. To me the eggs of fish are in most cases much better eating than the fish itself. Today, sorry to say few cooks know how to properly prepare fish eggs and sinfully throw away this wonderful food. Occasionally someone will try to fry fish eggs as they wrongly guess that it is the way that they should be prepared. There are worse things than fried fish eggs I suppose but I do not believe that I have ever happened onto anything as bad. Fish eggs are simply not for frying.

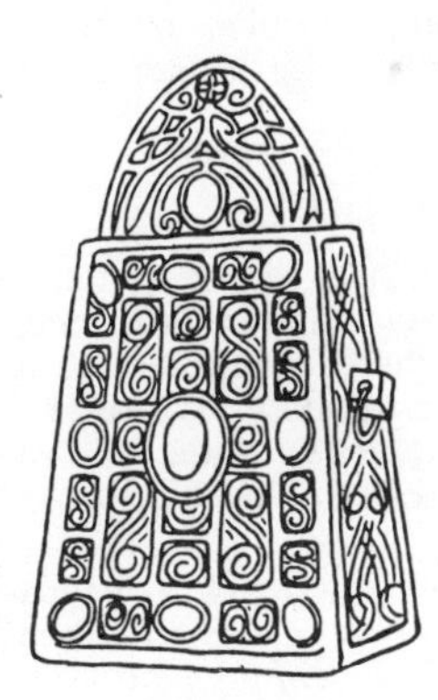

Shrine of St. Patrick's Bell National Museum, Dublin, Ireland

St. Patrick as history now proves was a Frenchman and came to Ireland through Scotland to bring the Irish Christianity. He was a fine great man and was truly loved by the Irish people.

Ireland was the home of such fish as the northern pike when St. Patrick arrived there and still is the home of this great fish today. Most record breaking northern pike have been caught in Ireland.

St. Patrick was a man who had to live off the land as he traveled. He was an excellent cook. He taught the Irish how to correctly prepare the eggs of the northern pike as well as that of other fish that they had. His method of preparing fish eggs is by far the best method. It produces wonderful, rare, food from the eggs of such fish as crappies, bluegills, perch, walleyed pike, northern pike, striped bass, bullheads, carp and catfish. Perch eggs are even far better than shad eggs which cost $3.50 to $4.50 a serving in restaurants. Here is the exact recipe:

Remove the eggs from the fish and cut the egg sack so that the eggs can be squeezed out of it. Squeeze the eggs into a pot of boiling water and boil them for about six minutes. Remove the eggs from the water by pouring the water through a strainer or cloth. Now place the eggs in a large bowl. Add an equal amount of cottage cheese and add about one level teaspoon of mustard for every cup of fish eggs you have in the bowl. Now mix the eggs, cottage cheese and mustard together well with a fork. Mix until the mixture is smooth and creamy. Add salt and pepper to taste. Spread heavily on buttered bread.

There were, of course, no potatoes in Ireland in St. Patrick's time but today fish eggs prepared in this manner and served with French fried potatoes make a fabulous meal.

King Donall Ua Laichlann of Ireland, was a great follower of St. Patrick and served fish eggs St. Patrick to his court at least twice a week. He had St. Patrick's iron bell put in a case of solid gold. Today it rests in the National Museum at Dublin.

French explorers and colonists came to Ireland very early and were very well thought of by the Irish people. Nearly all of them married and remained in Ireland. Those world famous beautiful black haired, gray and green eyed Irish colleens that Ireland is justly famous for are the result of the many early French and Irish marriages, and the famous Irish names of Patrick and Michael are not Irish at all but as French as a bottle of cognac.

FISH OLD MAXIM'S

This recipe is from the Old Maxim's restaurant of Paris, France and is one of the many great cooking tricks that made it famous.

Many fish have a strong fish odor and taste. This method of cooking them removes all strong fish odor or taste even on the strongest fish.

Take the fish and clean them well removing the skin as well as the scales. Sprinkle powdered ginger well over all parts of the fish inside and out. Put the fish on a platter and leave them stay in a cool place or your refrigerator for two hours. Then sprinkle cracker crumbs, or flour on them or dip them in a batter and fry them in butter. The ginger gives even the strongest fish a clean, fresh, mild taste.

HOW TO MAKE YOUR OWN FISH FRANCIS OR LUTFISK

The making of soda or lye fish originated in Italy at the beginning of the early Christian era. An early missionary Francis Amilo took this method of preparing fish up into central Europe where it spread into Norway and Sweden. Today only Norway, Sweden and Italy still make large quantities of soda or lye fish. In Norway and Sweden soda or lye prepared fish are called Lutfisk and it is served mostly at Christmas time, rarely at any other time of the year.

You can make your own lutfisk very easily and it is a truly delicious food. You can use most any good eating fresh or saltwater fish to make lutfisk. Scandinavian countries use codfish for lutfisk simply because it is inexpensive and plentiful.

The white codfish, spillanga is best and the yellow codfish or grasej is the poorest. The following fish make better lutfisk than codfish; bluegills, crappies, black bass, walleyed pike, northern pike, yellow perch, catfish, bullheads, stream trout, lake trout, sea trout, red snapper and striped bass.

Clean the fish removing the heads, scales or skin entrails and fins and split the fish into two pieces by cutting down the back bone. Place the pieces of fish in glass jars or pottery crocks. For each pound of fish use one cup of full strength washing soda. Take an enamel, cast iron, or stainless steel pot (not aluminum) and put the soda into it. Add enough boiling water to dissolve all of the soda and stir well with a wooden stick. Pour the soda mixture over the fish and add enough cold water to cover. If the fish float to the top put plates on them to keep them down. Leave for four days. Now remove the fish and scrub each piece with a vegetable brush if the fish are slimy. Now place the fish in cold water and soak for seven days. Change the water twice a day. If the fish get slimy, scrub off the slime with a vegetable brush. The fish are now ready to cook.

Remove the fish from the cool water and place in a clean white cloth such as an old dishcloth and tie the ends of the cloth together to form a sack. Place the sack in boiling salted to taste water for about one half minute, depending upon the size of the fish pieces. Do not cover the pot. Remove the sack and leave drain. When well drained untie the sack and place the fish pieces on plates for serving. Make one of the following sauces and pour it over the fish and serve. 1. Melted butter. 2. White sauce. 3. Cheese sauce. Serve with boiled or mashed potatoes.

You can keep uncooked lutfisk in cold water for long periods of time if you have the jars or crocks in a cool place.

You can, of course, dry fish and use them to make lutfisk. To dry fish do as follows. Fill crocks or jars with water and add salt until the water will absorb no more. Then place the cleaned fish pieces in the crocks and leave them stay there for four days. Remove and drain and leave dry in the sun under a screen to protect the fish from flies. Once dried the fish will keep for six months and more. To use soak in cold water for one week. Change the water five times during the week. Then prepare with washing soda as described. Three pounds of dried fish will expand to nine pounds when cooked and will serve twelve people with small appetites.

Lye is also used to make lutfisk. Lye however is very dangerous to use and to have around, especially if you have children. I advise using the washing soda instead because of the dangers connected with using lye. Lye is used as follows in place of the washing soda to make lutfisk.

Use one level teaspoon of pure lye to each four pounds of fish. Dissolve the lye in enough cold water to cover the fish well. Do not put lye in hot water or it is apt to explode and blind you. Let the fish stand in the lye solution for four days, keeping it in a cold place. Then pour off the lye solution and pour clear cool water over the fish. Soak the fish in this clear water for four days. Change the water each day. Then cook as before described.

PICKLING FISH

If fish are pickled properly it is one of the most delicious ways of eating them. Commercially available pickled fish in North America and imported pickled fish are of very poor quality. The makers produce them as cheaply as possible and with as little labor as possible. In most cases they make better cat food than human food. Pickling fish properly is both expensive and time consuming.

To get real pickled fish you must go to small towns along the coasts of such countries as Norway, Sweden, Finland, Denmark, Holland and Belgium. Here you must be invited into a home where the woman of the house makes her own pickled fish. The recipes in these countries for pickling fish are much the same. The recipe I give here is right from housewives from these countries. Nothing second hand about it, I got it myself. I have been pickling fish with this recipe for years and enjoy them very much.

Nearly any fish is good for pickling. Perch, sunfish, crappies, bass, bullheads, catfish, sheepshead, pickerel, northern pike, striped bass, buffalo fish, herring, salmon, trout, mackerel, lake trout are all good for pickling. Although herring is the most widely used fish for commercial pickling, it is one of the poorest pickled fish. It is widely used mainly because it is so inexpensive and plentiful.

Pickled fish made by the following recipe will keep for several weeks without refrigeration. If stored in a cool place of about 50 degrees or less they will keep for months.

In this recipe use ordinary distilled vinegar which contains 5 to 6 percent of acetic acid. Do not use fruit vinegars as the acetic acid content varies greatly and the fruit residue in the vinegar may give an off taste to the fish.

Clean and wash the fish well. If possible use fillets of the fish only, if not, trim off the thin belly flesh to the vent. Be sure to remove the dark streak along the backbone. This is the kidney. Remove the backbone. Cut the fish up into pieces one to two inches long. Pack the pieces loosely in a glass or pottery jar or crock. For every quart of fish in the jar add ⅝ of a cup of salt or a little over half a cup. Now cover the fish with undiluted ordinary distilled vinegar. Do not add any water. Stir so that as much of the salt as possible goes into the solution. Leave the fish in this solution from 4 to 8 days. The usual time is about 6 days. The time will vary with the freshness of the fish and the temperature of the days. An extra day will not hurt the fish so keep them in long enough.

Now remove the fish from the solution and place them in a container of cold clean water. Leave them in it for 8 hours. Remove the fish and give them a final quick rinse in clean water.

Now pack the pieces loosely in glass or pottery quart jars. Put a slice of lemon and a half slice of onion in each jar.

For every quart jar of fish prepare the following:

1 pint of distilled vinegar. If you do not like a sharp vinegar taste like that used in Europe use ½ pint of vinegar and ½ pint of water.

8 whole cloves.

8 bay or laurel leaves.

6 pieces of orange peel 1½ inches long and ¼ inch wide.

½ teaspoon of celery seed.

¼ teaspoon of dry mustard.
½ teaspoon coriander seed.
¼ teaspoon of black pepper.
⅛ teaspoon of paprika.
½ teaspoon of sugar.
1/3 of a clove of garlic.
¼ teaspoon of cinnamon.
6 cardamon seeds.
½ teaspoon dill seed.
½ teaspoon allspice.

Put the vinegar and all other ingredients in a pan and simmer them for 45 minutes. You must never forget this simmering. Spices are always at least a year old and more often three to five years old when you get them. They are dried to the point where unless they are simmered they will not give off their true flavors and odors. Now bring to a slow boil. Remove from the burner. Without delay take 1¾ teaspoons of gelatine such as Knox gelatine and dissolve it in a teaspoon full of cold water. Quickly add this to the vinegar and spice mixture and stir in well. Leave stand until lukewarm, then pour the mixture onto the fish in the jars. Leave stand in a cool place for three days. Now place in a refrigerator for one day and the fish is ready to eat. The fish should have an even golden brown coat from the spices. The gelatine clings to the fish as you eat it giving you the flavor of the spices with each bite. Pickled fish without gelatine is not pickled fish at all and is the secret of Scandinavian and lowland housewives. There is no fish in the world that can form its own gelatine as fish flesh does not contain ingredients that permit this.

If you like pickled fish in wine sauce use half the amount of vinegar to put the spices in. Then after the vinegar has the gelatine in it put in the same amount of white sauterne wine as you have vinegar and quickly pour onto the fish.

In making commercially pickled fish in wine sauce all North American and European makers have to do is to put in a drop of wine and they call the fish pickled in wine sauce. That is exactly what they do. Their wine sauce pickled fish is no more wine sauce pickled fish than the man in the moon.

To keep pickled fish indefinitely without refrigeration you must go to the drugstore and get vinegar with 15% acetic acid. This is merely 15% acetic acid in distilled water. Such vinegar stops bacterial growth. Use it instead of ordinary 5 to 6 percent vinegar to cook the spices, etc. in and to pour over the fish. Then when you want to eat the fish add two parts of water to the vinegar on them, leave stand for two days and they are ready to eat. This is the common European practice where pickled fish are kept during the summer months without refrigeration.

LIVER ESCOFFIER

Escoffier was one of the world's good cooks. He was born in France on October 28, 1846 and died February 12, 1935. He invented countless famous recipes. His greatest invention and discovery however beyond any doubt was that the livers of such fresh water fish as northern pike, perch, etc., made some of the world's finest most delicate tasting eating. Before this time people thought that the livers of fresh water fish would be fishy tasting and strong and did not eat them. Just the opposite turned out to be true. The livers of such fish as northern pike, perch, crappies, walleyed pike, lake trout, catfish, salmon, bluegills and bullheads have a delicate clean, very mild liver taste not fishy at all. These livers are not at all like beef or pork liver which are strong tasting and dry and not liked by most people. People who will not eat beef or pork liver are crazy about fresh water fish livers.

Here is his original recipe:

Take the fish liver and wash them well in water. Roll them lightly in flour and fry until done in butter. Salt and pepper to taste.

I have eaten fish livers prepared this way for over thirty years and they are just wonderful. I prefer them to the fish itself by far and you will, too, if you try them. They are one of the world's finest foods.

ITALIAN METHOD OF COOKING LOBSTER

In both Minneapolis and St. Paul there are large settlements of fine Italian people. I have not a few but a great many good friends among them. I always tell them they had to come to this country to learn how to cook spaghetti which always brings a laugh from them. This really is true as could be. The spaghetti as well as pizza pies, and ravioli in this country is by far better made and prepared than in Italy.

The Italians are excellent cooks; they have however one cooking trick that is an exceptionally rare one that all of us should use when we have the opportunity.

The Italians originated the pressure cooker and although they are good for cooking very few things they are absolutely necessary for cooking lobster. The first pressure cookers consisted of merely a section of steel pipe with a pipe welded over one end and a threaded cover on the other. Excess steam escaped through the threads which were not air tight. For lobster a pressure cooker is a necessity. Lobster or lobster tails are very expensive and when we get a chance to cook them they must be cooked as perfectly as possible.

To cook a lobster or lobster tail they put about a fourth inch of water in the pressure cooker, put the lobster or lobster tail in and pressure cook it for ten minutes. Take out the lobster and remove the meat. Served with salted melted butter, it is called Lobster American. Served with a sharp cheese sauce it is called Lobster Italiano which incidentally makes Lobster a la Newburg and Lobster Thermidore really taste very poorly in comparison. Served with mayonnaise it is called Lobster Francaise.

Lobsters have very strange flesh. If you broil or cook lobster in boiling water it causes the flesh to become tough and stringy and very unpalatable with a strong iodine taste, yet these are the methods used throughout North America. It is no wonder that most Americans do not like lobster. Lobster must be cooked in a pressure cooker in order to have the flesh tender and free from stringiness and unpleasant tastes.

FRESH WATER OYSTER STEW

The fresh water clams that are plentiful in lakes, rivers and ditches in many parts of North America have the same exact delicate flavor as salt water oysters.

In lakes you can easily catch them by walking along in the shallow water of a quiet sandy shore in the morning and following their trails. They leave a trail in the sand like a line marked in with a stick. When you come to the end of the trail simply dig down and you will find them shallowly buried. Gather a good pail full and take them home and put them in a large can filled with fresh water. The best place is in a bathtub if you have one. Cover them well with fresh cold water. Leave them in the water for two days. This will empty their intestines. Now place them in a pail of hot water one at a time. The hot water opens them. As soon as they open, cut out the oyster with your knife and put them in a pot.

From here on in there are two methods. One to use if you eat the oysters and one to use if you just like them for flavoring.

First we will describe the method to use if you eat the oysters.

Place the oysters in a pressure cooker and add ¾ of a cup of water. Cook them for 15 minutes. This makes them nice and tender. You should now have a quart of oysters and juice. Remove the oysters with a skimmer. Strain the juice to keep out any sand and add both to 1 quart of hot milk, ¼ cup of butter, ½ level teaspoon of salt and 1/7 level teaspoon of pepper. Serve hot at once.

The second method is for those who do not care to eat the oysters but just want them to flavor the stew.

Take the oysters, add ¾ cup of water and put in a pot and cook until the oysters are plump and the edges begin to curl a little. Remove the oysters with a strainer and add to a quart of hot milk, ¼ cup of butter, ½ level teaspoon of salt and 1/7 level teaspoon of pepper. Add the oyster juice but strain it to keep out any sand. Serve hot at once.

BALLARD BURGER

Seattle's restaurants, with the exception of a very few sea food restaurants, are nothing at all to brag about. Most of them sell atmosphere, not food and at very high prices.

Crawford's on Puget Sound, Seattle, Washington.

The three best seafood restaurants are Crawford's, Ivars, and the Wharf. Ivar also runs a restaurant called the Captain's Table uptown which serves about the same food as Ivar's down on the pier. If you are a raw oyster eater the large Kallivar oysters at Oceanhouse Restaurant have the best flavor. They go under several different names—just ask for the largest oysters that they have.

Ivar's Restaurant on pier 54 Seattle, Washington. Note the outside fish bar where you can buy cooked sea food to take home or to eat outside of the main restaurant.

Side view of Ivar's Restaurant showing how it is built out on pier 54 right over the water on Puget Sound.

The three seafood restaurants are all about the same. The clam chowder is bad at all of them as it is nothing but a mixture of tomato paste, flour, clams

You can buy some fried oysters, fish, or shrimp at Ivar's outside food bar and eat them on the dock rail as this Seattle resident is doing.

and a few vegetables. They must have been thinking about a stew when they developed these recipes. Other seafoods they serve are good if you know what to order at the right time of the year otherwise they can be very bad. Never order salmon or halibut in the winter. They have been frozen since

The Wharf Restaurant is on the Sound where all of the fishermen who go to Alaska to fish, dock their boats when they are at their Seattle home base. Many of them like to eat here.

Looking out on the Sound from a table at the Wharf Restaurant, Seattle. These boats dock here but fish Alaskan waters for salmon. You can rent one of these boats for $15.00 per person for 7 hours to troll for salmon in Puget Sound. You will average about a salmon an hour.

the fisherman quit fishing early in the fall. Salmon is a very fat fish. All the pink or orange color you see in salmon flesh is fat. It makes it impossible to freeze them without entirely changing the taste and texture of the fish. Even if you freeze the salmon in water as is now being tried they still lose flavor and texture.

Ivar's the Captain's Table is in downtown Seattle. Ivar's on pier 54 I found had better food.

Halibut cheeks are the best part of a halibut and are the only part of a halibut a good commerical fisherman will eat. Fresh, they just cannot be beat; frozen, they are stringy and tasteless.

In the winter for a fish, order red snapper as they are getting them in fresh not frozen every day. Never order King crab at all at anytime. It has a tough, stringy, sweet flesh that is always poor quality. When ordering crab on the west coast always order Dungeness crab. It is top quality and very delicious and tender.

At various towns on Puget Sound in the Seattle area, a number of types of oysters are grown. Some of the varieties have been brought in from Japan.

The smallest ones are from Olympia and are called Olympia oysters. These tiny oysters are only about as large as a quarter. They bring $5.75 a pint wholesale. Because of their small size some people think that it is smart to eat them. Actually they are the poorest quality of oyster grown anyplace in the world and have practically no taste at all. If you order them it just shows your stupidity about oysters.

Ocean House Restaurant in Seattle, Washington. It is very small but has very good large oysters for the raw oyster eater.

Best place to buy pastries in Seattle is on 5th street near the Olympic Hotel. They are not as good as New Orleans pastry by a long ways but are good.

The Seattle World's Fair is ancient history but the space needle remains in operation. The Olympic Hotel has leased it for twenty years and operates a restaurant in it.

Quilcene oysters are medium sized and have good taste and texture.

Kallivar oysters are the largest found in the area and for the man who really knows oysters these are by far the best. They have excellent taste and texture.

The real food delicacy from Seattle you will not find in any restaurants. It is the Ballard Burger. One section of Seattle is settled mostly by Scandinavians. Most of them are in the fishing and lumbering business. A lot of really good food comes from this area.

Here is the original recipe for the Ballard Burger.

Take a hamburger bun and butter it lightly on both sides. Add the condiments you prefer such as mayonnaise, catsup or mustard and the relish you prefer such as dill pickles, onion, cole slaw etc.

Fry a nice thin beef hamburger to fit the bun. In the same pan fry sufficient oysters to cover the same bun. Do not put any batter on the oysters. Place the hamburger on the bun and the oysters on top of the hamburger. You have to eat a Ballard Burger to understand how really good they are.

HANGTOWN FRY

In the eighteen hundreds San Francisco was quite a town. The Barbary Coast which was a section of saloons and houses of prostitution, was known the world over as second only to similar areas in Rio and Hong Kong. It catered to sailors who came to haul California's grain to Europe. In places like Little Egypt and many others on the Barbary Coast if a sailor walked into a saloon and didn't see three or four nude women lounging around he got mad and went to a more up to date spot. As time went on the reformers hung so many of the Barbary Coast's citizens that San Francisco gained the name of Hang Town.

In 1853 a man named Parker opened a saloon called Parker's Bank Exchange in the Montgomery Block, a famous building built by General Halleck. Parker invented and served a dish called Hangtown Fry. Its fame spread all over San Francisco and the surrounding areas. A few drinks and a Hangtown Fry was and is considered a gentlemen's evening.

The original Hangtown Fry was made like this. This recipe is for two healthy people. At today's prices it costs 46c a serving to make.

12 small fresh oysters or 12 canned oysters.

Eight eggs.

One onion about two inches in diameter.

One clove of garlic.

Six ounces of ham or a half can of Spam or similar product.

Celery salt.

Hot pepper sauce or Tobasco sauce.

Take a large bowl and break eight eggs into the bowl. Take one onion about two inches in diameter and grate into the bowl. Add six ounces of finely chopped up ham or Spam. Mix well together. Dip 12 oysters into cracker crumbs and add the oysters to the mixture. Take a large frying pan and put a heaping tablespoon of butter into it and melt it. Add the egg mixture, being sure to spread out the oysters so that they are evenly spaced out in the mixture. On a slow heat fry until the eggs are done on both sides. Remove and place on a plate. Salt all over with celery salt. Take hot pepper sauce or Tobasco sauce and put six drops on a plate. Take your finger and dip it into the sauce and rub a little on one side of each oyster. Serve at once. This is the finest of eating for those who like seafood.

Today the real Hangtown Fry is no longer to be found in San Francisco or anywhere else. It still is on the menus but when you get it you get nothing but an egg omelet with oysters and a couple of pieces of bacon across the top. The real Hangtown Fry is too slow to make and too expensive for our modern day restaurants.

Duncan Nicol took over the Parker's Bank Exchange Saloon from Parker and Nicols invented the Pisco Punch, the best drink that ever came from California. It was made as follows:

Two jiggers of Pisco, 2 jiggers of white grape juice, 2 teaspoonfuls of pineapple juice, 1 teaspoon full of Pernod.

Pisco was a brandy imported from Peru, in those days made from grapes grown on volcanic soil. It had a very mild, slightly sweet flavor. Christian Brothers Brandy made in Napa Valley, California today by the monks is as good as Peru Pisco or even much better in most cases and makes the finest Pisco Punch.

Thomas W. Knox wrote this about Pisco Punch:

"The second glass was sufficient, and I felt that I could face small-pox, all the fevers known to the faculty, and the Asiatic cholera, if need be."

Rudyard Kipling wrote this about Pisco Punch:

"I have a theory it is compounded of the shavings of cherubs' wings, the glory of a tropical dawn, the red clouds of sunset, and fragments of the lost epics of dead masters."

Today if you want a real Pisco Punch or Hangtown Fry the only way you will get them is to make them for yourself in your home.

One thing about Pisco Punch to remember is that it has no alcohol or liquor taste whatsoever. Don't let it fool you, two is enough for anyone. In fact Duncan Nicol only allowed two at a time to a customer. Even when John Mackay Multi-Millionaire and the richest man in North America at the time, came into his saloon and had two Pisco Punches he left the saloon and walked around the block and re-entered the saloon so that he could qualify as a new customer and have two more Pisco Punches.

OYSTERS A LA ROCKEFELLER

Antoine's was founded by Frenchman Antoine Alciatore in 1862. In 1860 he ran a boarding house at the Lacoul Home, 714 St. Peter Street. He left the restaurant to his son Jules, who in turn left it to his son Roy L. Alciatore who is at the restaurant at present with his brother Paul.

Antoine Alciatore the original owner made a specialty of snails Bourgnignonne which was popular in New Orleans restaurants during the 1850's and later. When Jules took over the business the taste for snails in New Orleans in any form had subsided. Jules in 1889 adapted the snail recipe to the gulf oysters. He called them Oysters Rockefeller simply because Rockefeller was a very prominent rich man at this time. Very similar recipes were already in use some as far west as in Colorado.

Antoine's waiters are supposed to remember your order and not write it down. This may have worked well at one time. On my last trip there in September, 1962, the waiter I had forgot part of my order entirely and never did get it to me.

Among other things I had potatoes au gratin and onion soup. In my opinion the potatoes au gratin were not too good. There was not as much good cheese on them as I like. The onion soup had more salt in than I like. I had oysters Rockefeller and they were good. I ordered sole but the waiter told me it was not sole but flounder. I ordered it anyway as I like both sole and flounder. I had a Gateau Moka or cake with Coffee Flavored Butter

Outside of Antoine's Restaurant in New Orleans. Built originally as a home by James Ramsay. The building was bought by Antoine Alciatore in 1868 from a family called Wiltenberger.

Frosting for dessert. The frosting was not a butter frosting and I was very disappointed with it.

Oysters Rockefeller is not a difficult recipe to copy and with waiters and cooks shifting around from one restaurant to the other they all know how to prepare recipes. None of the New Orlean's restaurants copied Antoine's recipe of Oysters Rockefeller. They developed recipes of their own for Oysters Rockefeller which they felt were far better. In my opinion Oysters Rockefeller made at Galatoires is by far the best version in New Orleans and Oysters Rockefeller made by Al Melke at the Cafe Exceptionale in Minneapolis beats any oysters Rockefeller in New Orleans.

Oysters Rockefeller is not a dish that you care to eat too often. You tire of this very rapidly. Many people do not like them at all. There are a number of ways to serve oysters in a similar manner which appeals to most people much more than oysters Rockefeller. You must know the truth about this recipe however as people often talk about it.

Inner dining room of Antoine's, you eat here if you are not wearing a jacket.

First dining room of Antoine's Restaurant in New Orleans, you eat in this room only if you have on your suit jacket.

Here is the basic recipe of Oysters Rockefeller and it has never been published correctly before.

The walls of the inner room at Antoine's are covered for the most part with framed cartoons.

If you are in an area where you can get oysters in the shell use one half of the shell to cook the oysters and sauce in. The natural shells lend a certain amount of atmosphere to this dish. Fresh frozen canned oysters that are available at most grocery stores are actually, however, just as good. If you use the fresh frozen oysters use little aluminum dishes or small pyrex glass dishes to cook them in.

If you use oysters in the shell remove the oysters from the shells. Scrub the shells well, then boil the shells for five minutes to be sure that any sand and sea growths have been removed from them. Uncleaned oyster shells have a bad odor.

In restaurants they fill metal pie pans with rock salt or clean coarse gravel, and cook the dish on the salt or gravel. The theory of this is that the coarse salt or gravel lets the heat come up from the bottom. This, of course, is not at all true. Actually the oysters cook better if you just put them in the half shells or in small pans in an oven on a cookie pan. The pie pans filled with rock salt or gravel, of course, give very good atmosphere to the dish but they do nothing for it.

Now prepare the following amount of oyster sauce for 4 persons, 6 oysters each or 24 oysters.

½ cup of butter.

½ cup of flour.

1 cup of boiled potatoes dried that is with the water poured off of them and then left over the heat until they steam dry. The potatoes must be dry.

¼ cup of cooked spinach run through a food mill or blender. Can be canned. It must be drained of all surplus liquid, this is important.

¼ cup of green onions, tops and all run through a blender or meat grinder. If you cannot get young green onions, large onions will do.

¼ cup of cooked leaf lettuce run through a food mill or blender. It must be drained of all surplus liquid, this is important.

¼ Cup of celery run through a meat grinder or blender.

2 level tablespoons of chopped up or blender cut parsley.

2 cloves of fresh garlic grated or run through a blender or one level teaspoon of powdered garlic.

½ level teaspoon of salt.

¼ level teaspoon of black pepper or ⅛ teaspoon of cayenne pepper.

1 level teaspoon of anise flavoring.

Take and heat the ½ cup of butter in a frying pan. Put the ½ cup of flour into a cup of cold water and mix them well together until not lumpy. Then add to the melted butter. Stir in well but do not brown. Over a very low heat leave cook until it forms a stiff paste. Now add one cup of the dried boiled potatoes and mix in well. Remove from the stove. Add the spinach, onions, leaf lettuce, celery, parsley, garlic, salt, pepper and anise flavoring. Stir in well. A mixer helps to mix everything together. If you have a blender this does a fine job and is what is used at restaurants. You will have to put about three level tablespoons of melted butter into the bottom of the blender to get it to mix this heavy mixture.

Take your oysters and wash them well in fresh water then put them on paper towels and really dry them. The oysters must be dried or it spoils the whole dish. When the oysters are well dried place one in a half shell or aluminum or pyrex glass dish and place on a cookie sheet. Put a half inch of the sauce over each oyster. Place the oysters in an oven at 500 degrees and broil for four minutes. Remember broil do not bake. The sauce should be just a trifle brown on top.

There are probably more completely incorrect recipes written about oysters Rockefeller than any other recipe.

Anchovies are often given as an ingredient in some recipes. This is an ingredient that ruins the recipe entirely. You do not want the sauce or the oysters to taste at all fishy.

Tarragon leaves and chervil are sometimes foolishly put into the recipe by some stupid writer who is not a cook at all but tries to be impressive. Tarragon and chervil are nothing but anise flavors and are not used. True anise is the flavor used. Still other would-be cooking authorities say absinthe must be used. Absinthe itself is a bitter acid with no flavor and has to have anise put with it so that it can be used in liquors.

Shallots are sometimes specified instead of onions. Shallots are just an onion and are not used at all. Regular onions are used.

The ones who are the worst are those who tell you to put the liquid from the oysters into the butter and flour instead of water. This ruins the recipe completely as you do not want an oyster taste in the sauce at all.

Still others say to use a butter and flour mixture without potatoes. This again spoils the whole recipe. You need the potatoes to kill the flour taste.

Some say to use white pepper instead of black or cayenne pepper. This too is entirely incorrect.

OYSTERS A LA ROCKEFELLER GALATOIRE'S

Galatoire's is a small New Orleans restaurant. The inside of it looks like an old barber shop. Old barber shop type mirrors line the walls and the old woodwork is painted white.

Galatoire's takes no reservations for anyone not even presidents and never advertises. They figure if you are in New Orleans and do not know about Galatoire's you have no business in New Orleans. If you want a table

Inside view of Galatoire's Restaurant. It looks like the inside of an old barber shop.

for lunch get there by 11:30 A.M. If you want a table for dinner be there by 6:15 P.M. If you do not get there early you simply have to wait in line for a table.

In my opinion Galatoire's serves the best food in New Orleans. It is far from the best restaurant in North America but it is the best in New Orleans.

Galatoire's was founded by Jean Galatoire, a Frenchman in 1905. Today it is run by the third generation Rene and Gabe Galatoire and Mrs. Yvonne Wynne their cousin. The restaurant remains the same as it was in 1905. Galatoire's closes every Monday but is open on Sunday. A few years back a fire badly damaged some of the interior of the restaurant. Some of the patrons asked Galatoire's if they would leave out the barber shop type mirrors when they repaired the damage as they felt like they were going to get a hair cut instead of food when they sat down to eat. The Galatoire's definitely refused to do this, the restaurant was restored exactly as it was before.

Here is the recipe of Jean Galatoire's for Oyster's Rockefeller. It is entirely different than the recipe of Antoine's. Jean Galatoire wanted a brighter green sauce as he felt it was more appetizing. Antoine's is a medium grayish green. This recipe is enough for 4 persons for 24 oysters or six each.
½ cup of cooked broccoli grated or minced or blender pureed. The broccoli is an important ingredient in this recipe. Keeps the sauce a bright green.
½ cup of parsley minced or finely chopped not pureed.

This again is a critical ingredient of this recipe. The parsley helps to keep the sauce a bright green.

1 cup of young green onions tops and all minced or blender pureed. Do not use whole large onions.

Galatoire's Restaurant, New Orleans. It is very small and you have to get there early to get a table. They do not take reservations. Jean Galatoire's bought out Victor's Restaurant run by Victor Bero. The building was built in 1831. Note the lyre in the balcony railing.

¼ cup of minced or blender pureed cooked spinach.
¼ cup of celery stalks including all the leaves minced or blender pureed.
½ cup of cooked leaf lettuce.
3 level tablespoons of melted butter.
2 cloves of garlic minced.
½ teaspoon of salt.
⅛ teaspoon of cayenne pepper.
1 teaspoon anise flavoring. This is a critical ingredient in this recipe. Gives quite a strong anise flavor. Tarragon or absinthe is not used.
½ cup of bread crumbs.

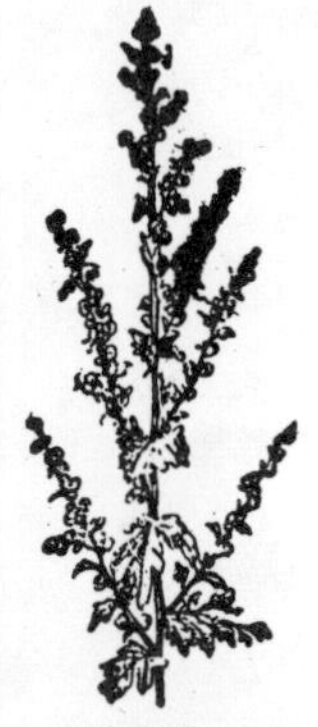
Absinthe.

The popular notion that absinthe liquor was made of worm wood is entirely untrue. All absinthe liquors were made from the acid from the absinthe plant and flavored with anise. Absinthe itself has no flavor at all but a very bitter acid taste. Absinthique is the acid that was taken out of the plant to make absinthe liquor. Absinthme is the disease caused by this acid. In 1915, France forbad the growing of the absinthe plant and the making of absinthe liquor. This is all on record in the NOUVEAU PETIT LA ROUSSE ILLUSTRE FRENCH DICTIONARY. Any anise flavor liquor tastes exactly like the old absinthe liquors as it was the only flavoring ever used in them.

Galatoire's use pie pans filled with rock salt and half an oyster shell with with an oyster in it and about a half inch of sauce over each oyster. The pie pans filled with rock salt are simply used for atmosphere. The oysters cook just as well if not better in little aluminum or pyrex glass dishes on a cookie tray.

Wash all oysters carefully in fresh water. Place the oysters on a paper towel and dry them thoroughly. The oysters must be dry. You can use oysters in the shell or fresh frozen canned oysters.

William Bordelon 4610 Pauger Street, New Orleans in my opinion is by far the best waiter in New Orleans and one of the three best in North America. At present, he is working at Galatoire's. He not only is an outstanding waiter but an excellent chef and will not serve food that is not prepared just right.

Make the sauce as follows:

Into a large bowl put the broccoli, parsley, onions, spinach, celery, lettuce, garlic, salt, pepper, anise and about three level tablespoons of melted butter. Be sure that all the water has been well drained from the broccoli, spinach, lettuce, etc. You must not have any excessive liquid of any kind. Stir together very well. If you have a blender put the whole mixture into the blender and blend. If you use a blender add the melted butter first as a blender needs a little liquid to get started.

An oyster bar is a marble top bar like this one shown in the photograph. The men behind the bar have oysters right out of the ocean stacked behind the bar resting on crushed ice. They open the oysters and throw away one half shell. They place the oyster in the remaining half shell on top of the marble bar. You eat the oysters now right out of the half shell with or without sauce. Photograph taken in the famous Felix Oyster Bar in New Orleans.

Now put a raw oyster into each shell or aluminum or pyrex dish and put about one half inch of the sauce over it. Sprinkle the top of the sauce heavily with bread crumbs. This is important for this recipe. For oysters Rockefeller at Antoine's they do not do this.

Place in an oven at about 400 degrees and broil for about four or five minutes or until the bread crumbs begin to brown. Do not bake. You must broil this dish. Remove and serve.

You will note that oysters Rockefeller Galatorie's is nothing at all like oysters Rockefeller as served at Antoine's.

A good waiter who really understands food and will not serve food unless it is prepared just right is very hard to find anyplace in North America. At present Galatoire's has New Orlean's most accomplished waiter. He is William Bordelon. Mr. Bordelon is not only a waiter but an excellent chef in his own right. If you can get him as your waiter you are going to get food perfectly prepared and perfectly served. As you enter Galatoire's ask if you can have him as your waiter. It will be a meal that you will remember. He is hard to get but well worth a try.

If you want to eat oysters raw or cooked or with tomato sauces or sauce of your own go to Felix's, Max's or the Pearl Oyster bars. They are not too fancy but the oysters are the best and the prices very reasonable.

OYSTERS CHRISTIAN HERTER

After eating Oysters Rockefeller a few times I felt that a better way to serve oysters should be created using a general anise base flavoring. This is the recipe and if you try it I know that you will agree that this recipe is much, much, better.

Felix's Oyster Bar, New Orleans.

Use oysters in the shell or fresh frozen canned oysters. Wash oysters carefully in fresh water and dry them carefully in paper towels. The oysters must be perfectly dry. Place each oyster in a cleaned half shell or in a small aluminum or pyrex glass dish on a cookie tray. Forget about the rock salt in a pie pan.

Make the following sauce:

¼ can of cooked spinach well drained or freshly cooked spinach well drained.
1 cup of mashed boiled potatoes. Be sure that they are dry before mashing them. Pour off the water they are boiled in and then leave them steam over the heat until dry before you mash them.
1 cup of canned or fresh cooked green lima beans well mashed or blended.
¼ cup of chopped parsley or dried parsley.
¼ cup of soft butter.
¼ cup of grated or blender cut large fresh onion not green onions.
2 cloves of minced garlic or one level teaspoon of powdered garlic.

4 ounce can of pimentoes minced or grated, liquid in can and all must be used.
1 level teaspoon of salt.
½ level teaspoon of black pepper.
1 level teaspoon of anise flavoring.

Fresh oysters being loaded into an oyster bar in New Orleans early in the morning.

Take all the ingredients and mix them together well in a bowl or mixer or blender. The main thing is to get them blended together. Gives you a pinkish green mixture, that looks far more appetizing on oysters than a green mixture that looks like chopped up sea weed.

Place a half inch of this sauce over each oyster. Sprinkle well with bread crumbs. Place the oysters in an oven at 400 degrees and broil, not bake, from four to five minutes or just until the bread crumbs begin to brown a little. This is really a fine way to eat oysters.

SALMON GUSTAVUS IV

Gustavus Adolphus was King of Sweden. He was born in 1778 and died in 1837. Swedish people are great fish cooks and Gustavus was no exception. In Minnesota, a famous college at St. Peter, Minnesota, bears his name.

Gustavus made a salmon dish that is excellent and especially a great warm weather favorite.

Take a pound can of pink salmon. Drain, and pour the flesh into a large bowl. Pick out all of the bones, the skin, and all of the dark brown areas under the skin. Take a strong fork and break up the flesh and mash it into as small pieces as possible. Use your fingers to tear apart any chunks that are too much for your fork. Add eight ounces of home made mayonnaise, and mix well into the salmon. Add twelve ounces of cottage cheese, medium or small curd, and mix it in very well with the salmon and mayonnaise. Salt and pepper to taste. Serve as an hors d'oeuvres or as a main dish with baked potatoes and butter.

If you desire to make a smaller portion buy a smaller can of salmon and reduce the other proportions accordingly.

SALMON QUEEN ASTRID

Queen Astrid of Belgium was a Swedish woman, daughter of Princess Ingeborg of Sweden. Her husband was King Leopold the II.

Queen Astrid was undoubtedly one of the most brilliant and kindly women ever born on this earth. She was only Queen of Belgium for a short time before she was killed in an automobile accident at the tender age of thirty. She establishd fine maternity hospitals and helped the Belgian people more than any Queen ever has before or since her time.

Queen Astrid was also a real housewife and a cook's cook. One of her favorite creations was Salmon Queen Astrid. Be sure to try it at your first opportunity.

Take a standard sized can of pink salmon. No need to spend your money buying red salmon as red salmon is red simply because the flesh has more fat in it. Any more fat in fish flesh than necessary is not desirable. Empty the salmon into a bowl and remove the skin and heavy bones. Place the salmon in a Foley Food Mill and grind it through into a bowl. Queen Astrid used a Passe Vite which is a Belgian made food mill of heavier construction than a Foley Food Mill but difficult to buy in this country. Incidentally a good food mill is a necessity around the kitchen. It will do jobs even the expensive electric powered food blenders will not do. You need not add water or juice to a food mill in order to pass through food. In most electric mixers you have to add some liquid to make them work. Now take one onion one and a half inches in diameter and grate it into the salmon. Add one fourth teaspoon of ground nutmeg to cleanse the fish. Mix together well. Form roughly into a good size ball for each serving. If the salmon is too dry to stick together well mix in a little mayonnaise to make it stick together properly. Cover the ball of salmon generously with mayonnaise that you made yourself. This recipe can be used as a main dish or as an Hors D'Oeuvres. The mayonnaise recipe to use is in this book. Salmon Queen Astrid is a great recipe worthy of a very fine Queen.

The Swedish and Belgian people in Minnesota often make this recipe using walleyed pike, crappies, smelts, bluegills or catfish as the fish. I even like it better with these fish then when made with salmon. I like salmon but I like these other fish even more. It is one of the greatest delicacies I have ever eaten when made with one of these fresh water fish. Nothing any where near as good is served in the highest priced restaurants anywhere in the world.

You simply clean the fish well. Then boil them in water with four bay leaves to remove all fishy odors. It does not take long to boil fish. The time depends on the size of the fish but watch this carefully. Remove the fish and pick the flesh from the bones leaving the skin with the bones. Leave cool. Then pass the flesh through the food mill, add one fourth level teaspoon of nutmeg and just enough mayonnaise so that you can form the flesh into a rough ball. Cover the top generously with your own mayonnaise.

CLARENCE BIRDSEYE SALMON, LAKE TROUT OR BULLHEADS

Around 1918 a young man named Clarence Birdseye left New York to go to Labrador to buy silver fox skins. He was only 26 years old but had already been a whalehunter, a biologist and a government worker.

When he got to Labrador young Birdseye noticed that his Eskimo companions before leaving their winter camps put their caribou, seal and bird meat down into the ground deep enough so that it was in permanent frost. Months later when they needed food they could dig up the stored meat and it was in pretty good condition.

Birdseye made $6,000 on silver fox fur the first year, which in those days was a real fortune.

Birdseye went back to New York and married. He then went up to Hudson Bay to live.

He had fresh cabbage sent to him and froze it in water. He found that when it was thawed out and cooked that it tasted fairly well. He came back to the United States in 1922, rented a small building and put frozen fish on the market. He soon added some frozen vegetables to his line.

In 1927, just five years later he sold out his share of the frozen food business for one million dollars.

Clarence Birdseye was a very intelligent man. He knew frozen foods the hard way from right out in the wilderness. He knew they were salable but he also knew that many frozen foods are not nearly as good as fresh foods or in many cases canned foods. He was afraid that the novelty of frozen foods would wear off and in some cases it definitely has.

A beautiful brook trout like this one deserves the best of attention in cooking. Its cousin, the bullhead, who is also a char tastes just the same when prepared with the same recipe.

Here is a method of his for preparing fish that have fat in their flesh such as salmon, lake trout, brook trout, rainbow trout, brown trout, or bullheads. This is a wonderful recipe and produces delicious fish. Fish so prepared are usually called the Salmon Fuma around New York or, salt, smoked fish other places. Such fish are selling from $2.00 to $3.50 a pound. Much too expensive for most of us. Here is how to make them at low cost:

Take one gallon of water. Add one-sixth of an ounce of sodium nitrate and 1 thirty-second of an ounce of sodium nitrite. Get these chemicals from your druggist, they cost practically nothing.

Add 2½ cups of salt. Mix together well.

See if an egg will float in the solution. If not add salt until it will float. Add five teaspoons of liquid smoke, available at Herter's.

Take the salmon, trout, or bullheads and skin them. Split them down the backbone. Put them into the solution and leave them in it for four full days. Remove the fish and slice into very thin slices only about a sixteenth of an inch thick. Serve with crackers. If you like fish, this is just wonderful eating. The world's most expensive restaurants serve fish prepared in this manner. It is a great luxury. If you have no salmon, trout or bullheads in your area go down to your grocer and get some frozen fresh salmon if he has it and prepare with this recipe.

ABALONE SERRA

San Diego was originally an area of grass covered rolling hills without brush or trees. The climate is just what most people prefer—in the seventies the year around with only about five or six days of rain—not unbearably hot and dusty five or six months of the year like such areas as Phoenix and Scottsdale, Arizona and in Palm Springs, California or Albuquerque, New Mexico.

San Diego was discovered by Portuguese Juan Rodrigues Cabrillo. He was a boat captain working for Spain. He sailed into the San Diego area on September 28, 1542. Juan claimed the land for his Spanish employers and called the bay San Miguel Bay. Spain, however, showed no interest at all in the land, if they had, Spain would be the most powerful country in the world today. It just shows that everyone makes big mistakes. In 1602 an explorer named Viscaino spent some time in the area. In 1769 the Russians who owned Alaska decided that they should have warm weather ports on the North American west coast. They thought it best to begin by taking San Diego first and working up North from there to meet their Alaskan holdings.

Spain became worried about the Russian plan and decided to establish missions and towns along the west coast. Father Junipero Serra, a 60 year old priest in Mexico, volunteered to start the missions and towns. He established missions from San Diego to Sonoma, 40 miles north of San Francisco.

When Mexico revolted, or rather overthrew Spanish rule, they took possession of San Diego in 1834. In 1846 the United States took the land from Mexico. This left an old festering wound between Mexico and the United States. Today it is one of the main reasons many Mexicans dislike the United States. They want California and part of Texas back, and in this changing world, who knows, they may get them back sooner than what you might think.

In 1866 while the United States was plundering the South after the War Between the States a shrewd merchant named Alonzo Horton came to San Diego and bought a thousand acres of the best land for 26 cents an acre. Today much of this land has sold for a million dollars an acre and more. Today's traffic problems in San Diego have been pretty much solved. They have much less of a traffic problem than such places as Phoenix, Arizona.

Father Serra was an extremely brilliant man. He could do everything well and could teach others how to do it. He was a stone mason, a foundry man, carpenter, woodcarver, tannery expert, dyeing and weaving technician and above all one of the greatest cooks who ever lived. He knew European, Spanish and Mexican cooking as well as any man who inhabited this earth. When Father Serra died, really fine cooking in California from San Diego to way above San Francisco died with him.

San Diego today has a great many atmospheric restaurants but the cooking, for the most part is indifferent and far from what it should be. San Diego is a navy town and you rarely find a navy town where people try too hard with food.

There are no shrimp in the area as the sea bottom is much too rocky. The shrimp they serve are mostly Mexican. There are no salmon, or sea trout. Crab meat is King from Alaska which is the poorest eating of all crabs. The local fish available are ones like sculpin, the porcupine fish, with spines all over its body. White sea bass, these are called a variety of names such as tutuava and many others. There are barracuda, tuna, cod and lots of sharks. Shark is sold as grayfish and under several other names. Small cod are sold as catfish. Unless you go to very reliable places, you are apt to get served most any fish in spite of what you order. When you see something like bottom fish on a menu never order it as you never can be sure of what you get. Scallops are sometimes stamped from shark fins. Abalone have become scarce

The best place in San Diego to buy smoked bonito. It is located on a pier off G street, right next to Tom Lai's Restaurant.

in California and can only be taken in limited numbers in certain seasons. Most of them are imported from Mexico. They are alright if you get them while they are fairly fresh but terrible if they are not. Fresh water trout such as rainbows are all bought from fish farms where they are fed on dog food. The flesh does not have the color or texture of fresh water trout at all.

There are halibut taken in the San Diego area and they are called "chicken halibut" because they are small and rarely weigh up to 35 pounds. Halibut cheeks are the best part of a halibut. On even a 35 pound halibut, they are very small. Halibut cheeks are sometimes made from shark flesh. The only large halibut cheeks come from Alaska and a few from the northeast coast.

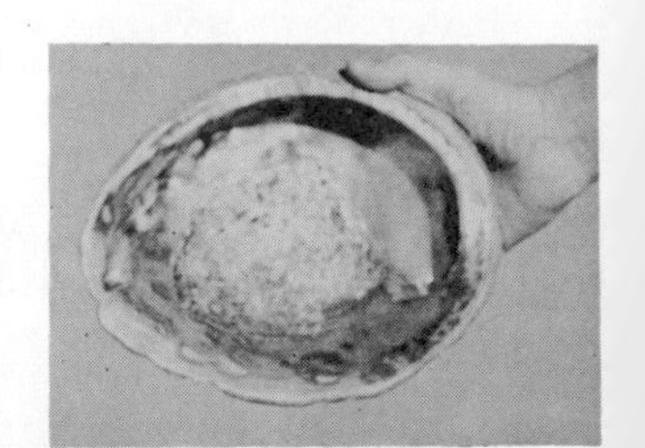

The shell of the abalone is very beautiful and makes a fine serving dish for bread, crackers etc.

Of the local fish smoked, bonito are the best. Remove the bones and break up the flesh in small bite-sized pieces. Roll the pieces in good mayonnaise and serve. Some restaurants in San Diego should get wise and start getting in walleyed pike from Canada so they could offer a top quality fish.

Father Serra served abalone as follows.

Take the well pounded abalone, salt and pepper to taste. Fry in butter or olive oil until well done. Use no batter under any circumstances. Take a cooked pimento, a canned one works very well and chop it up very finely on top of the abalone.

In today's San Diego most of the cooks have abalone confused with pancakes. They dip the abalone in batter and then fry it. The result is a greasy fish flavored pancake that tastes nothing like abalone at all.

One of Anthony's Fish Grotto Restaurants in San Diego.

Catherine Ghio started Anthony's Fish Grotto's, fish restaurants on July 18, 1946 in San Diego. Her sons, Tod and Anthony, and son-in-law, Roy Weber run them. Some of their food is good, some is not, but it runs about as good as you will find in the San Diego area.

Tom Lai's, is a restaurant down the pier at the foot of G street. Nothing too special but about what you will get in the area.

On Shelter Island is the Bali Hai Restaurant. The location is beautiful. The outside of the restaurant and the outside grounds are imitation South Sea Island atmosphere. The food is about the usual for American's, so-called Polynesian and Cantonese food which is actually not Polynesian or Cantonese at all. There were no tomatoes, green peppers, cornstarch, beef, pineapples etc. in the South Sea Islands or the province of Canton, China. There were not even any peas to get pea pods from. Tomatoes, green peppers, corn and pineapple all originated in Central and South America and the Indians entirely developed their uses in cooking. They only very

Tom Lai's Restaurant will bring back memories to many a former navy man.

recently have ever been used in China or the South Seas. Curried foods often appear on Polynesian menus. Curry powder is just a mixture of spices as made in India and Africa. It varies greatly, really, depending

Dining area of Bali Hai Restaurant San Diego.

The view from the ground of the Bali Hai Restaurant in San Diego is very good.

upon what the cook has on hand at the moment. Curries served in the United States, the South Seas and Hong Kong contain such items as red pepper which originated in Mexico. Recipes like this are simply made up for American tourists.

Never underestimate the Chinese people. The Koreans and Japanese are also pure Chinese. The people who originally inhabited Japan are nearly extinct and look much like our Navajo Indians. The average Chinese I. Q. is higher than that of Europeans or in other words the people who most of us decended from. The Chinese are fabulous businessmen. In Hong Kong, Honolulu, the South Sea Islands and in American, Polynesian and Canton restaurants, they serve Americans what they will eat. In most cases it is American food prepared with American originated recipes with Polynesian or Cantonese names.

Visiting Tijuana, Mexico while in San Diego is a poor waste of time. There is nothing to see on the way down and nothing to see when you get there. It does not pay at all to buy liquor there. It is of poor and questionable quality. If you drink it while in California you must pay the California tax on it. If you plan to take it out of California you have

Bullfighting is far less dangerous than prize fighting. Note the dulled rounded points on this bull's horns. Note also that its neck muscles at the base of the neck have all been cut so he cannot move or raise his head rapidly enough to hurt anyone.

to sign a lengthy statement to this effect. If you get caught with an open bottle in California that you promised not to drink in California you are in real trouble.

The bull fights are second rate tawdry affairs. The tips of the bull's horns are usually filed off so he cannot hurt the bullfighter. The bulls are often fed food that will constipate them greatly slowing down their ability to move about at all. Bull fighting is actually one of the safest ways of making a living in the world if you can stay sober. Less bullfighters are killed percentage wise than professional prize fighters in the United

States. Bullfighters simply never take any chances at all. No bullfighter has ever fought a bull unless its neck muscles have been completely cut by a man on a safely padded horse using a special cross shaped spear that completely destroys the muscles. The spear is carefully made so it not only cuts the neck and shoulder muscles but cuts them in two directions so that the wounds cannot close. The bull not only slowly bleeds to death but the mangled muscles prevent the bull from even being able to keep his head firm enough to hurt anything. He just cannot move his head from side to side and hit the bullfighter. If by pure accident the bull hits the bullfighter, if he is not drunk, all he has to do is to grab the bull's horns and the bull cannot hurt him. The bull's neck with its cut muscles has no strength left in it. The bull has to react the same as you would with the muscles at the back of your neck and shoulders completely mangled and cut. Bullfighters are paid simply on how well they can act and make the cruel torture of a fine animal appear like a fight.

In Mexico City on a rainy day when the area was slippery I have watched a bull hit a bullfighter solidly nine times in a row. The bull never even scratched or bruised the man he simply grabbed its horns and hung on its crippled weak neck.

SCANDINAVIAN METHOD OF PREPARING SARDINES

I never cared at all for sardines until I had eaten them prepared by Scandinavian friends.

There are three kinds of sardines:

1. Those canned in America and canned in soya bean oil, mustard, or tomato sauce.
2. Those canned in Norway or Denmark in silt sardine oil which is simply a very cheap fish oil.
3. Those canned in Norway or Denmark in olive oil.

Of these three general kinds of sardines the number 2 or Norway or Denmark sardines canned in silt sardine oil are absolutely worthless and unfit for either human or animal consumption. Silt sardine oil is just a cheap, rank, fish oil next to impossible to digest and with a strong undesirable flavor that pollutes anything you put it on. If you do not believe how bad this oil really is try feeding it to a husky sled dog who normally lives on a fish diet. These dogs will not even touch it.

Sardines packed in silt sardine oil are responsible for driving people away from all kinds of sardines. After they try sardines canned in silt sardine oil it ruins forever all desire to eat anything with the name of sardine connected with it.

Sardines types 1 and 3 or American sardines canned in soya bean oil, mustard or tomato sauce and Norway or Denmark sardines canned in olive oil, are all excellent but must be prepared with this simple Scandinavian trick to be really good.

Remove the sardines from the can and place them in a soup bowl. Take full strength vinegar and pour enough in the bowl to cover the sardines. Leave stand a half hour or more, then remove the sardines from the vinegar and serve. This vinegar treatment gives sardines a clean, fresh, delicious taste and makes them easy to digest. Be sure to try it.

SHRIMP REMOULADE NEW ORLEANS AND SHRIMP REMOULADE FRENCH

New Orleans is a town with a few good restaurants and a few original food recipes. If you do not know the places to go and the things to order it is not a good town in which to eat. There are more Italians than French in New Orleans. You have to go a long ways to find Italian food like they serve it in New Orleans. It is the worst that I have ever eaten and I have eaten

Commander's Palace Restaurant in the old plantation home area of New Orleans is an old home converted into a restaurant. It is not in the French Quarter. In my opinion the food is not up to Galatoire's.

Okra is one of New Orleans' most widely used vegetables. It is used as a soup thickener and also served separately as a vegetable. African slaves brought over the first okra seeds from Africa by stuffing them in their ears. Most of the slaves were brought over completely naked and it was about the only way they could bring seeds along. They brought over watermelon seeds in the same manner.

Dan's Pier 600 on Bourbon Street in the French Quarter. The most famous by far of all New Orleans' jazzy spots. Frenchman Jumbo Al Hirt played there in January, 1963.

The building on Bourbon Street, New Orleans where jazz was first played. The whole street jumps with jazz every night including Sunday.

Italian food not only in Italy but all over the world. More completely untrue magazine articles and cook book recipes have been written about New Orleans' food, than the food in any city of the world.

New Orleans was a French colony in 1717 founded by Jean Baptiste Le Moyne, Sieur de Bienville, who was a good cook in his own right. It was owned by Spain from 1762 to 1803. Then in 1803 Napoleon took it back. Napoleon's biggest mistake was not Waterloo where the Belgians, English and Germans defeated him. In 1803 he sold the whole Louisiana Territory including New Orleans to the United States for fifteen million dollars or 4c an acre. This was the greatest bargain the world has ever seen. The Louisiana Territory includes all or part of seventeen states. If Napoleon would have had vision enough to keep the Louisiana Territory, France would, today, be the most powerful nation in the world.

New Orleans is about sixty-five percent Catholic but this does not keep the city from being naughty, or even slowing it down a bit. The oldest con-

Bourbon Street bars show their offerings on their fronts. Some are pretty exotic.

vent and cathedral in North America is in New Orleans. Drunkeness is not a crime in New Orleans unless you get disorderly. Liquor can be bought every hour of everyday including Sunday. Legal prostitution was closed in 1917.

Now the girls are scattered out a bit instead of being concentrated in the red light district of Basin street.

Bourbon street, where Dixie Land jazz originated is lined with bars. Girls, in nothing but "G" strings, dance on stages in the bars or sometimes on the bars themselves. They usually finish their dance with nothing on at all. At one time the city required that the dancers wear not less than three inches of fringe on their pelvis even when they finished their act. This was considered a very strict ordinance. If the Bourbon street crowd, go into a bar and look up from their drink and do not see, among other things, a couple of well-formed breasts flopping about, the drink doesn't taste just right and they move to another bar.

Bourbon Street, New Orleans is a blend of fine old lace iron work and nude women.

People, in general, in New Orleans are very interested in food. You can talk to an oil station attendant while he puts gasoline into your car and soon he will pull out of his pocket a shrimp sauce recipe of his own and read it to you in detail. Everywhere you go you will run into individual recipes. Cook book writers, magazine writers and even some new people in New Orleans will falsely tell you that New Orleans' cooking is a mixture of French and Spanish. Nothing could be further from the truth. New Orleans was settled by the French and occupied by the Spanish for a time. The families intermarried somewhat and these mixtures were called Creoles. In French the word Creole means foreigner, in general. If you refer to a Creole from Martinique, like Napoleon's first wife, it means a foreigner with African blood. The cooking remained, however, mostly French mixed with the recipes of local cooks, plus

Broussard Restaurant and patio in the French Quarter. It was built on the site of the old Jefferson Academy.

Indian cooking of corn bread, black-eyed peas and beans. The French like the Italians of today took to Indian cooking and Indian corn bread very well. In Italy at present so much corn bread is used that many of the Italians think that they originated corn bread, nothing could be more untrue.

The word "Remoulade" means twice ground in old French, and comes from the word remouler. The original Remoulade sauce came from a Benedictine monk in France by the name of Andre Laboure. Benedictine liquor has nothing to do with the Catholic Church nor any Catholic institutions. Its manufacture and sale has nothing at all to do with any Christian church or religious group. The original Remoulade sauce recipe was as follows:

Take two large sardines like those from a can of Maine canned sardines or any small canned fish. One ounce of capers. Capers are just a prickly wild bush related to mustard whose flower buds are pickled because they are plentiful. Any small green bud of most any bush will give you about the same or a better taste. The small green buds of dandelions are even far superior in taste to capers. A cup of chopped parsley, one fourth cup of finely grated onions, one grated clove of garlic, one half level teaspoon of salt, one fourth level teaspoon of pepper. One level teaspoon of mustard, two level tablespoons of vinegar or lemon juice. Make a sauce as follows: Put two level tablespoons of butter into a frying pan and melt, add two tablespoons of flour and stir in until the flour and butter are well mixed and the flour slightly brown. Add just enough cold water to form a smooth creamy, medium gravy. Add three level tablespoons of olive oil. Now add all of the other ingredients into the frying pan over a low heat stirring continually and cook until just barely done.

Serve over shrimp, cold fish, rice, or rabbit meat. This recipe today has almost been forgotten in Europe and is never served in North America. You will note that the use of flour and butter to form a gravy or sauce or so-called brown roux, which is so popular in New Orleans' present day cooking, is very ancient in origin.

Arnaud's Restaurant in New Orleans. They serve the best onion soup in New Orleans, but in my opinion their shrimp sauce has too much horseradish and red pepper in it. The buildings were built in 1833 by a Victor Seghers.

Remoulade sauce as made in New Orleans today is not at all like the original French Remoulade sauce. It was first made by an early New Orleans French cook by the name of Adolphe Pierre Broussard. The ingredients in it such as tomato paste, cayenne pepper, pimentoes and paprika, etc., did not even exist in Europe at the time the original Remoulade sauce was made in France. It still, however, is pure French cooking with real imagination and a wonderfully different and delicious sauce. Today in New Orleans this Remoulade sauce can no longer be found in restaurants as it takes too long to make. The closest Remoulade sauce available in today's New Orleans is the one served at Galatoire's. Sauce Arnaud which is a version of Remoulade sauce and served at Arnaud's in New Orleans in my opinion has far too much horseradish and cayenne pepper in it and I do not like it at all.

Here is the original recipe:

4 tablespoons of horseradish mustard, French's horseradish mustard is just right.

½ cup of white vinegar with six drops of anise flavoring. Tarragon vinegar is not used. Tarragon vinegar is actually just a vinegar with an anise flavor derived from tarragon leaves. Pure anise flavoring is better.

5 level tablespoons of tomato puree. This is a critical ingredient.

1 level tablespoon of paprika.

¼ level teaspoon of cayenne pepper.

1 level teaspoon of salt.

1 whole large garlic or one half teaspoon of pure garlic powder.

Patio of Broussard's Restaurant. Note the statue of Napoleon in the rear. Mayor Nicholas Girod erected and furnished a house at 514 Chartres while Napoleon was on his second exile on St. Helena. Mayor Girod hired Dominique You, Jean Lafitte's top pirate lieutenant, to go to St. Helena and rescue Napoleon and bring him to New Orleans. Dominique You had a ship provisioned and manned by a select crew. The day they were ready to sail the news arrived that Napoleon had died of cancer on May 5 in his fifty third year. If he had lived another few years, he undoubtedly would have become Emperor of North America.

½ cup pureed onions. They can be green onions or whole large onions. In the case of green onions use the tops and all.

¼ cup of finely chopped parsley. If you cannot get the fresh parsley, the dried will work very well.

¼ cup of cooked finely grated or blended pureed pimentoes. This is a very critical ingredient of the recipe. Buy the canned ones for this. They work perfectly.

½ cup of salad oil. It can be olive oil or any good salad oil.

½ cup of pureed celery. You can grate the celery real fine or put it through a blender.

A New Orleans French Quarter restaurant patio. They are small in size. This is the complete patio. The French call such places COUR the word Patio is Spanish. Today, however, the most widely used name is patio. The word Creole frequently heard in New Orleans is from the Spanish word CRIOLLO, meaning to bring up. It means French or Spanish or mixed French and Spanish people in Louisiana.

First mix the salad oil, vinegar, horseradish mustard, anise, paprika, cayenne pepper, salt, parsley and pimento in a bowl. Then add the celery, onions and garlic. If you have a blender put in only half of the vinegar and salad oil to start with. Use the other half to puree the celery and onions in your blender, then add the remainder.

Store the finished sauce in glass jars in your refrigerator.

To serve, line a small salad bowl with fresh lettuce. Then put shrimp, crayfish tails, boiled fish pieces, or cooked cauliflower on the lettuce. Drench well with the Remoulade sauce. Boiled pieces of any fish such as black bass, crappies, perch, trout, bullheads, bluegills, walleyed pike and lake trout are all

French Quarter, New Orleans. The only place in North America where authentic old Southern plantation wagons are still being used as taxies.

wonderful with this sauce. My favorite fish with this sauce is bream or bluegills.

There is never any gums, tragathan or any other form of gum used in Remoulade sauce, or any catsup or other such ingredients.

WHEN TO CLEAN A FISH

There is no argument as to when to clean a fish from anyone who has any knowledge at all about fish flesh.

A fish should be stunned and cleaned immediately after being stunned. It then should be eaten or put under refrigeration until eaten. The exceptions, of course, are salted, lyed, or vinegared fish where salt, lye or vinegar is used instead of refrigeration.

There are two reasons why this is absolutely necessary. You stun the fish while it is alive with a blow on the head. This is done for humanitarian reasons only. Quickly cut off the fish's head immediately after it is stunned. This allows the blood to flow out of the fish. If the blood of the fish is left in the fish, as is true when you clean a dead fish, the blood gives the flesh of the fish a very poor taste. Fish flesh is no different in this respect from steer or pig flesh. You would not think of eating a steer or pig which had not been bled. No meat packer will allow unbled meat in his packing plant.

Secondly fish flesh, because of its make-up, deteriorates very rapidly. *Over 200 Times Faster Than Beef Or Pork.* An uncleaned fish deteriorates much more rapidly than a cleaned one. When a fish is dead and uncleaned, in a matter of minutes, not hours, its flesh becomes soft from deterioration. Deterioration is just a nice word for rotting and rotting as everyone knows changes the taste of anything very rapidly.

There are three ways to keep the fish flesh fresh.

1. If you are boat or pier fishing or wading a lake shore, keep your fish alive on a stringer or in a live net until you go home. If you put them on a stringer, string them by running the stringer through the heavy part of both lips. This keeps the fish from drowning. If you string them through the gills this keeps their mouths open too much, and strange as it may seem, they often will drown. Clean your fish at home before they are dead. If you live too far from home to make this practical, clean them before you leave for home.

2. If you are stream fishing from shore or surf fishing, if possible, clean the fish as you catch them. In the case of trout, clean them and then place them in your creel packed in wet grass or any kind of wet vegetation you can secure. When you rest, place your creel in the water, do not set it on the ground as flies and ground insects enter it rapidly on the ground. Wash your creel out everytime you go out on a fishing trip. If flies or insects have laid any eggs in the creel, these will thus be destroyed. In the case of surf fishing take along several gunny sacks with you and wet them and wrap your cleaned fish in them while you are fishing and also use the wet sacks for taking them home. Sea weed will also work fairly well. The evaporation of the water will keep the fish in pretty good shape for quite a period.

Do not leave fresh or salt-water fish after they are dead uncleaned for even a minute. I read a ridiculous statement in a fishing encyclopedia stating that all fresh-water fish will keep better and longer if not slit, or in other words uncleaned. Do not listen to such hog wash. It is absolutely untrue and shows only that the author did his fishing over a desk, not over water.

3. If you are fishing in a boat and have an ice chest, clean the fish as soon as they are caught and put them in the ice chest. This latter method assures you of the best eating fish.

HOW TO SCALE A FISH

There has been more strictly "hoey" written about fish scaling and more worthless gadgets made for scaling fish than for any other job I have ever known. The quickest and easiest way to scale fish has been in use for over three hundred years in the low countries, France, and the Scandinavian countries.

Take an ordinary spoon such as you use everyday at meal time; use a tablespoon for small fish and a soup spoon on large fish. Hold the spoon as the illustration shows.

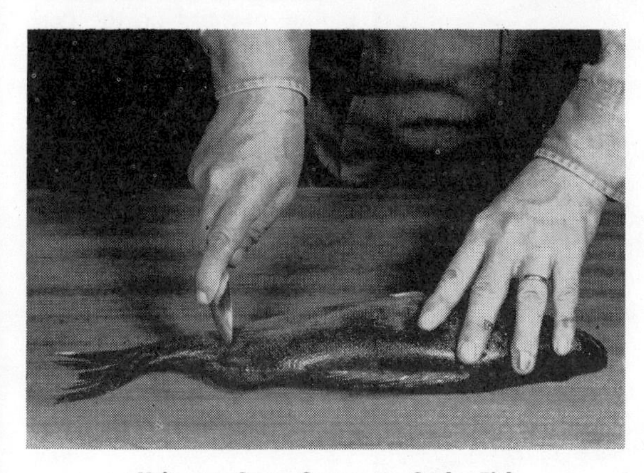

Using a Soup Spoon to Scale Fish

Scrape the scales off with the edge of the spoon by scraping them against the grain. If the scales are exceptionally hard to get off and some bunches of them tend to remain on the fish, scrape cross wise, or in other words, down, on these bunches and they will come off. Because of the shape of a spoon, it catches most of the scales and prevents them from flying about.

ALWAYS BE SURE THAT THE FISH HAS NOT DRIED OUT BEFORE YOU ATTEMPT TO SCALE IT.

A dried out fish is difficult to scale and should be soaked in water until the scales are softened, before attempting to scale it.

Most fish such as crappies, bream, northern pike, muskies, etc., scale very easily. Such fish as walleyed pike scale very hard.

TRUE FILLETING A FISH

Cutting Off the Fish's Head

1. Scale the fish as before instructed, with a spoon.

2. Cut off the fish's head.

3. Starting at the front of the fish right next to the back bone, cut down into the flesh until you strike the belly ribs of the fish, then run this cut backward until the beginning of the fin fil-

let area. Now go back to the beginning of the cut and by pulling outward on the flesh and cutting toward the belly, work the fillet off down to the belly bones.

Commencing to Cut The Fillet

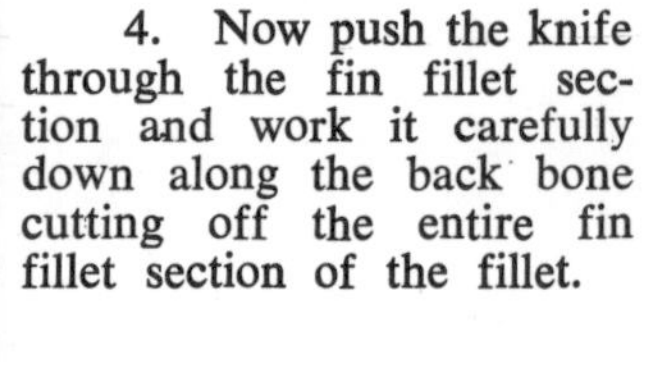

4. Now push the knife through the fin fillet section and work it carefully down along the back bone cutting off the entire fin fillet section of the fillet.

Push The Knife Through Fin Fillet Section

5. Now take your knife and cut off the fillet as the illustration shows.

Work The Knife Down to The End

Cutting Off The Fillet

6. Do the same on the other side of the fish. As you will note the fish does not have to be gutted.

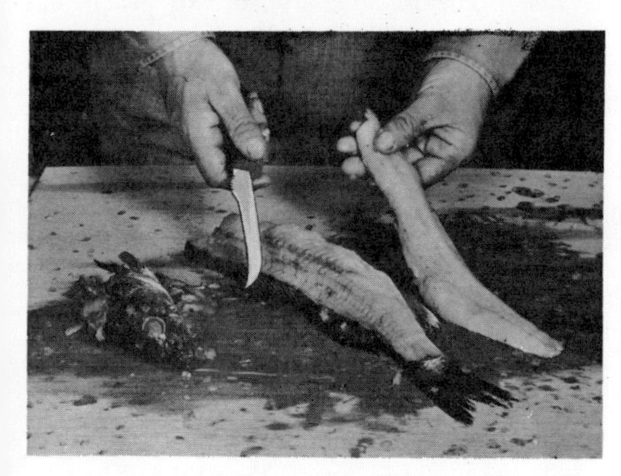

The Fillet Cut Off

If possible throw the waste, consisting of the head, and frame of the fish into the stream, lake or ocean it came from. The waste will furnish food for fish and also food for smaller water insects and animals that fish feed on. You are wasting nothing as this fish waste will produce good fish flesh for its weight.

MAKING A SPLIT FISH

A Split Fish

Splitting a fish is a simple procedure. Proceed as follows:

1. Scale the fish with a spoon.
2. Cut off the fish's head.
3. Slit the belly of the fish and remove the entrails.
4. Start at the front of the fish next to the backbone and make a deep slit all along the back bone of the fish right to the tail. Then go back and deepen the slit until it cuts all the way through the fish.

5. Do the same on the other side of the fish.

You will note by the illustration that all you have removed from the fish is the back bone and the fins, and of course the head. All the belly bones and poor belly flesh is on the split halves.

Splitting fish was originated in Europe for making cheap lyed fish and dried fish. By the time the fish were lye cured the belly bones were softened and the taste of the fish so changed that it made little difference what part of the fish you ate.

North Americans, because of years of fish market memories, nearly all make split fish of the fish they catch and call it "filleting fish" or "steaking fish." Both names are as far as you can get from the truth.

COLOR OF FISH FLESH

Most fish flesh is white when prime. Exceptions for example, are salmon, and trout. Their flesh when prime is various shades of peach and pink. The color in trout and salmon flesh is caused by the fat in the flesh.

INDIAN METHOD OF COOKING SMALL FISH

In some areas the only fish you can catch run small, yet you must eat them to supplement your diet or in some cases in order to survive.

For example you may be able to catch trout 5 to 7 inches long or perch 4 to 5 inches long, sunfish or crappies 3 to 4 inches long. Such fish are too small to fillet well and too bony to make a decent bite for an outdoorman if not filleted.

My grandmother taught me this trick and I have used it on practically every variety of fresh-water fish through the years except northern pike, pickerel, and muskellunge. These latter three are so full of fine forked bones in small sizes that they are very difficult to eat no matter how you prepare them.

Take the small fish and scale and clean them. Drop them into a kettle of boiling water. Leave them in for a few minutes. Just long enough so the flesh starts to come away from the bones. Then remove the fish from the boiling water. Now pick the meat off from the bones. You will find this very easy to do. Salt and pepper the flesh and place it in a pan of sizzling hot grease and brown it slightly. Remove from the grease and leave drain a few minutes. Then serve.

You can wolf down such fish, like fried potatoes. A batch of little fish that would ordinarily drive a hungry man crazy trying to get a few satisfying mouthfuls becomes a good wholesome filling meal.

Although this method is ideal for small fish it is also very good for large ones. Be sure to try it.

INDIAN METHOD OF SKINNING FISH

The North American Indians, with the exceptions of the Navajos and Cheyennes who will not eat fish, have always been great fish eaters. Fish they desired to skin or skin and scale at the same time they simply beheaded and dressed or filleted and put the fish or fillets in boiling water for a minute or so. They then took the fish out of the boiling water and pulled off its skin and scales. After a fish or fillet has been in boiling water a minute or so its skin thickens and the mucous glue-like bond between the skin and flesh loosens making it possible to peel the skin off the flesh as easy as peeling the skin off a banana. If you like the skinless, mild tasting fish this method is by far the best to use to skin fish. If mildness is important to you it is by far superior to skinning a fish than by any of the mechanical devices on the market. The hot water not only thickens the skin and loosens its mucus bond to the flesh, but it dissolves the bond and fat between the skin and flesh which contains most of the strong odors of the fish.

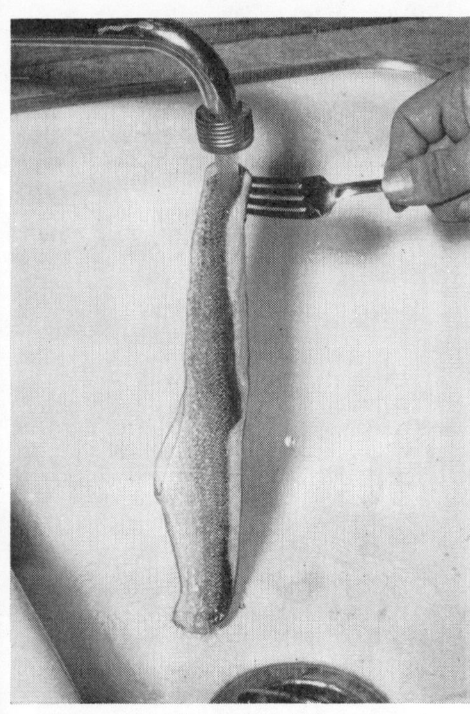
Fillet Held Under Hot Water Faucet

To use this old Indian method in modern day practices proceed as follows:

FOR SKINNING FILLETS OF FISH

If you have a hot water faucet in your home let the water run until it is as hot as possible, the hotter the better. Take and run a fork into the thick end of your fillet as the illustration shows. Run it just into the flesh, not through the skin. Leave the hot water run on the skin of the fillet for 45 seconds. Test the skin and see if it will come off easily. If it does not, leave it under the hot water for another 15 seconds. This will make the skin so it can be easily peeled off on most fish. On fish with extra heavy or tough skins it may take 15 to 30 seconds longer. If you do not have a hot water faucet in your home simply place the fillet in a vessel of hot water that is nearly boiling or just boiling slightly. Use the same time schedule as specified for using hot water from the faucet.

FOR SKINNING WHOLE FISH

Use the same procedures as described for skinning fillets. Prepare the fish as follows: Behead the fish, remove all entrails, then slit the fish down the belly to the back tail and from the front top of the fish back to the tail on each side of the back fins. These slits make it easier to get the skin off without tearing.

KEEPING OF FISH OR FILLETS THAT HAVE BEEN HOT WATER SKINNED

Fish or fillets hot water skinned of course keep much longer than ordinary fish flesh as the outside of the flesh is sterilized. They freeze very well or keep in your refrigerator very well after being hot water skinned. It is the same keeping principle as blanching vegetables before freezing them in your deep freeze.

I remember my grandmother boiling haunches of venison a minute to make them keep and boiling fish before salting them down in a barrel for the winter. It is all the same old principle and nothing new.

HOW TO SKIN AND CLEAN CATFISH AND BULLHEADS

Catfish and bullheads are two of the most widely eaten fish in the United States. In the South the catfish is preferred over all other fish and justly so. They make wonderful eating.

I well remember before the passage of food regulation laws that every railroad diner throughout the United States served bullheads under the name of brook trout. They did this when brook trout were also available to them at the same prices. People simply preferred a "bullhead brook trout" to a real one.

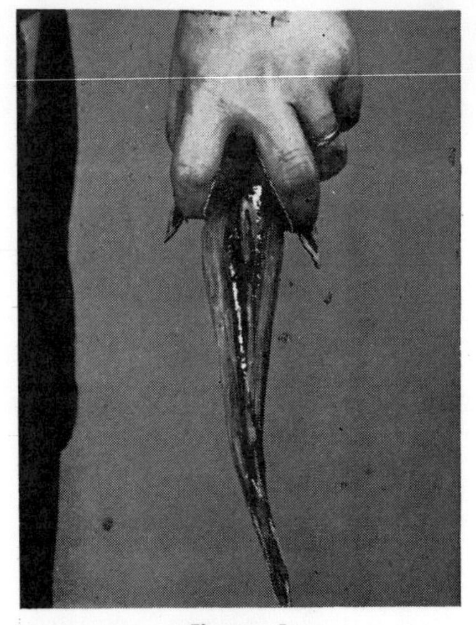

Figure 1.

You cannot learn to skin and clean a bullhead or catfish by cleaning just one fish. You must clean at least a half dozen to get the actual feel of it so you do it properly.

First stun the fish with a light blow on the head with a wooden billet.

Now grasp the fish over the back of the head with your left hand, placing your first and second fingers up against the pectoral fins or "front side fins" as the illustration shows in Figure 1. Keep your fingers away from the hard gill covers as they will hurt or cut your fingers.

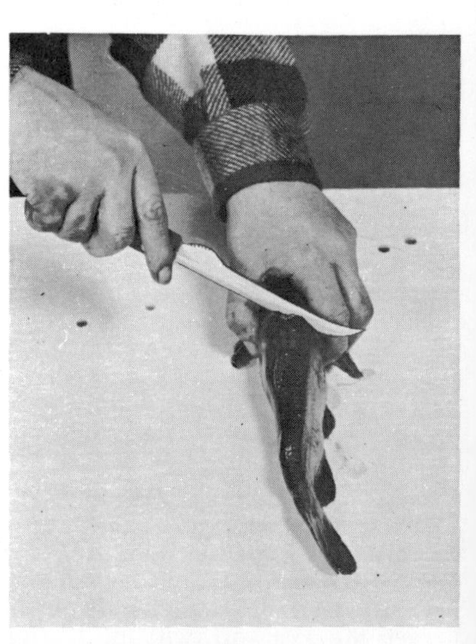

Figure 2.

Take your sharp fillet knife and make a cut across the back of the fish directly above the gills as shown in Figure 2. This is about half way between the head and dorsal or back fin. Then run the cut down the side of each of the gills to the beginning of the belly area. Takes only a second with practice.

Figure 3.

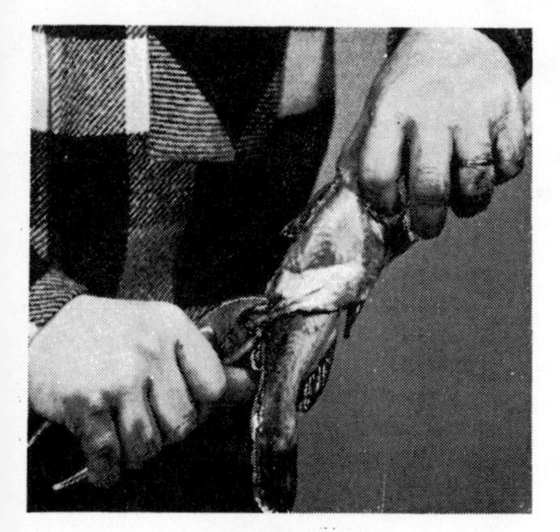

Figure 4.

Now hold the fish tightly with the first and second fingers of your left hand as shown in Figure 3. Hold it so your fingers are not in contact with the hard gill covers so they will not get hurt. Then take a pliers and grasp the skin just below the cut directly in front of the dorsal or back fin. Now pull the skin straight back down toward the tail. If the skin does not pull evenly off the two sides take your pliers and grasp the skin on the sides and pull it back toward the tail to get it started evenly.

Figure 5.

After you have pulled the skin about half way off the body or less (Figure 4) get a new grip on it with your pliers. Grip the skin as close to where it is just leaving the flesh as possible. The closer you grip the skin to the flesh the easier it will pull off without ripping or breaking the skin.

Now pull the skin completely off from the fish as shown in Figure 5. You can now lay aside the pliers.

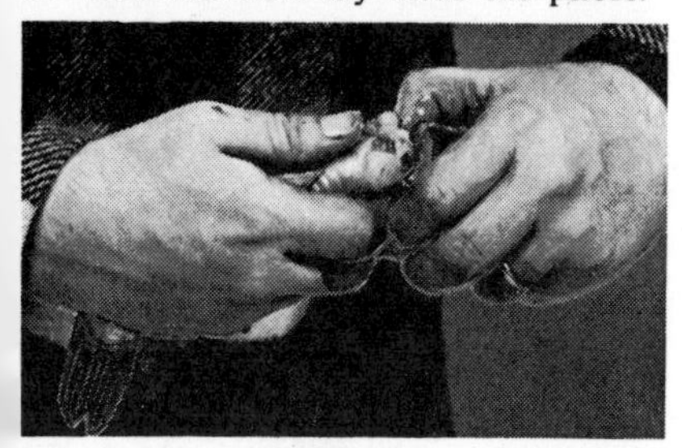

Figure 6.

Now grasp the fish as the illustration shows in Figure 6. Be sure as you grasp the body of the fish with your right hand that you press the dorsal or "back fin" down with your right hand so it does not hurt you. With your left hand grasp the fish just above its hard gill covers so they cannot hurt you. Break the head from the body as you would break a small stick. You will find that actually you do not break the backbone but you merely unhook it. After you have done six or seven fish you will get the knack of it.

You will find that most of the intestines and body organs of the fish will come out as you pull the head from the body after you have broken or "unhooked" the backbone. What few body organs remain in the fish can be quickly removed with a stroke or two of your fingers.

On real large fish it is sometimes better to cut the head from the body after the backbone is broken rather than just tear it off.

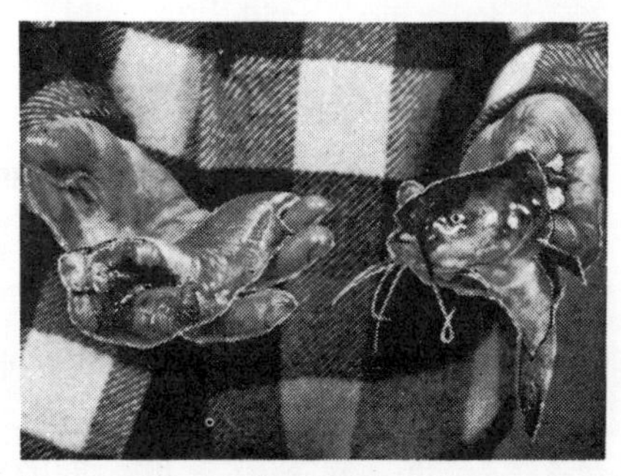

Figure 7.

Eggs

FRIED EGGS MENDEL

Mendel was an Austrian monk born in 1822 and died in 1884. He was a very, very brilliant man. During his lifetime he discovered and proved the laws of heredity in the plant world. Without his great work in the plant world it would not be possible for us to have any of the highly developed hybrid vegetables and grains that we have today.

Besides his great work in botany Mendel spent a great deal of time in developing ways to prepare basic foods so that they would taste better.

His fried eggs Mendel is the finest way of frying eggs I have ever tasted. Be sure to try it on your family. The recipe was brought into Minnesota by the early Austrian immigrants. It is a treasured recipe handed down only to daughters and sons and never given to anyone outside of the family.

Here is the original recipe:

Put two level teaspoons of butter into a frying pan and two level teaspoons of water. Melt the butter at medium heat. Crack a large egg into the butter. Cook as you desire either on one side or both. Watch your heat closely. If the white of the egg begins to bubble turn down the heat to low. Cooking eggs with too much heat ruins them. When done take a heaping teaspoon of cottage cheese and spread it out on top of the egg. Take a knife or the end of your spatula and chop the cheese down into the egg. Leave the cheese on top of the egg until the cheese is about half melted. Takes only a short time for this. Remove the egg with a spatula and serve with toast. If you like onions add one half teaspoon of chopped onions to the cheese before you put it onto the egg.

You just will not believe how good an egg prepared this way is until you try it.

BOILED EGGS MENDEL

Boil your egg to the softness or hardness you desired. An egg boiled six minutes is usually preferred by most people. Remove the shell from the egg and place the egg in a soup dish and mash well and salt and pepper. Add one heaping teaspoon of cottage cheese to the egg and mix it in well. If you like onions add one half teaspoon of chopped onions. Serve with toast.

Although the ingredients are the same for Fried Eggs Mendel the taste is entirely different. The cheese does not melt in making the Boiled Eggs Mendel as it does in making Fried Eggs Mendel.

I have made both Fried and Boiled Eggs Mendel out in the Western states for local hunting friends. They have been used to eating eggs in bacon grease for generations but today are cooking eggs Mendel whenever possible. These are truly great recipes.

HOW TO BOIL AN EGG

Sounds simple but with today's modern refrigerators it is a trick. In order to make a six minute egg for example you have to put the egg into boiling water and boil it for six minutes. You cannot put the egg into cold water and gradually bring it to a boil and boil it for six minutes. If you did this the egg will be too well done. If you take an egg out of your refrigerator and put it into the boiling water it will often crack at once and let out much of the yolk spoiling the egg. The calcium that makes up the egg shell is like pottery or glass. If cold it will often crack when put into boiling water. The trick is to remove the egg from the refrigerator and let it stand in a glass of warm water for 10 minutes or longer before putting it into the boiling water. Use a spoon to gradually lower the egg into the boiling water. The older the eggs the more easily they crack.

EGGS KING LOUIS IX

King Louis IX of France was undoubtedly one of the greatest Kings who ever lived. He would wear no ermine or scarlet or gilded stirrups or spurs in an era when everyone else who was a king did. He spent no money on parties and was very temperate in his eating and drinking. He treated everyone as equals and spent his life helping the poor in his country and fighting in the crusades. He was loved by his people regardless of their stations in life. He was the first man to bring lemons, oranges and limes to France. He died of the plague on his last crusade in the year 1270.

Lemons originated in Northern Burma east of the Himalayas and in Eastern India. The Arabs planted lemon seeds in Persia and Palestine. King Louis IX brought back to France lemon, lime and also orange seeds from his crusades. By the middle of the 13th century all of these fruits were well known in Italy as well as in France.

Columbus on his second voyage to the New World stopped at the island of Gomera, one of the Canary Islands, and stayed there from October 5 to October 13, 1493 and gathered orange, lemon, and lime seeds and the seeds of many vegetables. He brought all of these seeds to the New World.

King Louis IX brought back from the crusades a rare cooking secret for preparing eggs. Here is the original recipe:

Take two eggs and break them into a bowl. Add one teaspoon of lemon juice, one onion about one inch in diameter, grated or one-half level teaspoon of onion powder. Mix them well together until the mixture is a thin watery liquid. The lemon juice will completely dissolve both the white and the yellow of the egg, turning them into a non-albumous watery liquid. Place a small amount of butter in your frying pan. Put in the egg, lemon, and onion mixture. Cook over a medium to low heat until the mixture bubbles slightly and is done. The mixture will not fry like an omelette but will remain almost like a thin custard in consistency. Beat the mixture up with a fork slightly. Spread on buttered toast. The mixture spreads like butter. Your family will greatly appreciate this very different egg dish.

Served on small bread squares it makes a very different and rare hors d'oeuvres. Used instead of mayonnaise on salads it is delicious and has practically no calories. Used to dip French fried potatoes, boiled or broiled lobster, fish or shrimp in, it is delicious and non fattening. For putting on baked potatoes in their jackets or skins, it is very different and fine tasting.

If you like Worcestershire, or soy sauce add a half level tablespoon of either to the egg, lemon, and onion mixture before you cook it. Add small pieces of finely chopped spam, cooked shrimp, fish or similar products to vary the eggs from time to time.

As you probably know the famous Caesar Salad is based on this secret of lemon juice from King Louis IX being able to completely dissolve an egg.

HOW TO POACH AN EGG BY ST. FRANCIS

In 1212 Saint Francis went to the Holy Land. When he came back he taught his followers a simple way to prepare poached eggs for a meal. This is still the best known method to poach an egg.

Take a one quart cooking pot and fill it three-fourths full of water. Put it on your stove and bring to a boil. Add 1½ level tablespoons of vinegar and turn the flame to medium. Carefully crack an egg and put it into a small drinking glass. Stir a good whirlpool into the water with a tablespoon, then carefully pour the egg into the center of the whirlpool from the drinking glass. The egg will settle evenly on the bottom of the pan. Gently simmer the egg for 5 minutes if you want it with a soft center or 7 minutes if you want it with a cooked center. Then remove the pot from the stove and pour off all of the water. The poached egg will remain in the bottom of the pan. Lift the egg from the bottom of the pan with a spoon. Salt and pepper to taste. Serve with toast. The egg will not taste of the vinegar at all. The vinegar just keeps the egg from breaking apart as it is cooked in the water.

EGGS ODYSSEY

Celery came from a wild celery called smallage that originated in the Mediterranean lands. It was believed by the ancient Greeks and Romans to be a very good medicine for nervous tension and also a good flavoring for foods. It was not eaten as a food itself until 1623 in France. The Greek Homer, when he wrote his Odyssey 850 years before Christ came to this earth, mentions celery in it. Our present day word celery comes from the French word celeri which in turn came from a Greek word.

Celery is a fabulous vegetable and herb and is not completely understood by most American cooks. It is usually served here in salads or soups or raw. In Europe it is rarely served raw, usually being cooked and served as a hot vegetable. Boiled and drained celery served with an Antoine Van Dyck cheese sauce is a vegetable dish hard to equal but rarely seen in this country.

Eggs Odyssey is an ancient Greek dish from before the time of Christ. Here is how to prepare it. Fry or soft boil your eggs to taste. Sprinkle them well with ground celery seed. In the case of the soft boiled eggs mash the eggs before sprinkling them with the ground celery seed. Ground celery seed is hard to get these days although it is one of the world's finest herbs. Use celery salt if you cannot get the ground celery seed. Celery salt is ground celery seed mixed with salt. Serve the eggs with toast. The celery seed gives the eggs a fresh, clean, different taste that nothing else does. According to the ancient Greeks this dish will not only quiet your nerves but will help to make your wife pregnant. All I know for sure is that it really makes a fine meal.

Parsley which belongs of course to the celery family was also widely used by the ancient Greeks and Romans for medicine, flavoring foods and for garnishing. As a medicine it was eaten boiled and drained to prevent drunkenness.

OMELETTE

An omelette seems like a simple thing but is really one of the most difficult to make if it is to be fluffy and really good tasting. You would never guess the secrets to making a good omelette.

Melt some butter in a frying pan, then turn down the heat to low or medium low. Break 3 or more eggs in a mixing bowl. Do not add any salt as the salt breaks down the albumen content and spoils the omelette. This is the first secret. Now beat the eggs with an egg beater or pastry whip and this is important, without a second's pause in the beating pour the eggs into your frying pan. The second secret is to get them in as quickly as possible so they begin to heat before they can separate even slightly. Cook slowly. Turn if desired. Salt and pepper to taste when served. Sprinkle with chopped onions if you like onions.

Soups and Sauces

THE WORD MADRILENE USED IN COOKING IS STRICTLY A PHONY

A great many of the words used to describe recipes in French cooking mean nothing at all. Many of the words are strictly phony conjured up to simply give a very ordinary recipe a fancy name to falsely try to impress people.

A typical example is the word Madrilene often used on French menus and in recipe books describing a soup or some other recipe. Madrilene in French means in the style of Madrid, Spain and usually but not always such recipes have tomato in them. The whole thing is just pure "hokum." The recipes are not in the style of Madrid at all. If anything they are pure American Indian. The Indians were the first people to make soup with tomatoes in it as tomatoes originated in Central America. There were no tomatoes in Europe until they were brought back from the Americas and the recipes on how to use tomatoes were brought back with them.

CHEESE SOUP BOULANGER

In 1765 a Frenchman named Boulanger opened an eating place on Rue des Poulies in Paris, France. He featured two soups at this place, one a cheese soup, one a beef broth soup, with pearled barley, and with fresh red rose petals sprinkled on top. He called the place RESTAURANT, meaning, "to restore", in French. He meant a place to restore your strength. The name caught on, so to speak, and soon there were restaurants in every country of the world.

Both of the special soups he served were excellent and have never been bettered by any modern day cook. The cheese soup, however, is the really outstanding one. Here is the original recipe:

Take eight level tablespoons of butter and melt in a frying pan at medium heat. Add five level tablespoons of flour. Mix until smooth and creamy. Remove from the stove. Add two cups of cold water, salt and pepper and mix together until smooth and creamy. Take two cups of diced celery and boil until done. Usually around 20 minutes. Drain and leave stand. Take two egg yolks and mix well into one-fourth cup of milk. Mix into the sauce and leave cook slowly for ten minutes. Grate one-half pound of cheese, sharp cheddar cheese is good for this purpose although it can be any good cheese. Add the cheese to the sauce and slowly cook over a medium flame until the cheese is thoroughly melted and blended into the sauce. Now mix in the two cups of cooked celery and serve. This is a marvelous soup. The egg yolks keep the ingredients from separating and it is smooth and delicious as can be. This soup was one of the first to be served in early Minnesota restaurants.

CONSOMME ROYALE

Consomme Royale is one of the finest most different soups that I have ever eaten either here or in Europe. I have never seen anyone who did not like it. It is very easy to make like most good foods are. Be sure to try it. This soup is right at home in a cabin or a castle. Consomme Royale is the most popular soup at the Cafe Exceptionale in Minneapolis, Minnesota. The Cafe Exceptionale, in the Holiday Magazine North American Restaurant Survey, usually rates second or near the top. I do not agree at all on the selections this survey makes on restaurants, but the Cafe Exceptionale is in my opinion one of the ten best restaurants in North America. Their chef, Al Melke, is one of the world's outstanding cooks and bakers.

Consomme Royale came from the French bull cooks in early Northern Minnesota, Wisconsin and Michigan lumber camps. Nothing sissy about this soup.

Every so often some women's group tries to get the nude bronze statue in front of Charlie's Cafe Exceptionale removed but it still remains and really is a work of art.

Here is the recipe for 2 quarts as you want to make enough so everyone can have all they want.

Take one cup of dry macaroni and cook it. When cooked drain and then pour cold water over it and leave stand.

Put 2 quarts of water in the soup kettle. Put in a standard size can of mixed peas and carrots or 1 box of frozen mixed peas and carrots. Add 8 bouillon cubes or 2 heaping spoonfuls of B. V. or Bovril. Add 1½ level teaspoons of ground cinnamon (Actually cinnamon is imported pine bark.) Bring to a boil and boil for 2 minutes. If you used frozen vegetables boil until vegetables are cooked.

Now put in the cooked macaroni and remove from the stove. Salt and pepper to taste.

Do not let the cinnamon fool you, it blends with the bouillon giving the soup a taste of neither cinnamon nor bouillon. This is a wonderfully different tasting soup that gives you strength without bulk. Make some soon.

IRISH CONSOMME

The early Irish immigrants came into Minnesota and brought with them their well known mulligan stews. Irish mulligan stews are wonderful eating and are as widely used and popular today as they were a decade ago.

The Irish recipe I put down here is also well known but no longer under its own name. It is now known as Consomme Neopolitan, not Irish Consomme. It is served at such fine places as the Cafe Exceptionale, in my opinion, one of the ten best restaurants in North America.

Here is the real recipe just as it came from Ireland. It has a taste and bouquet that is different and very, very good. Serving is for 4 people.

Take a quart of hot water. Add 4 bouillon cubes, ¼ level teaspoon of cinnamon. Take one-half teaspoon of orange pekoe tea and put it in 5 or 6 teaspoons of hot water. Leave the tea in the hot water for 5 minutes, stirring it frequently, then drain out the tea leaves and put the liquid into the consomme. Heat and stir.

Cook one cup of broken up thin spaghetti. Pour cold water over it to remove the excess starch, and dump into the hot consomme and serve.

The tea and the consomme blend together and produce a very different fine flavor that taste neither of tea nor consomme.

SOUP DUPONT

Created by famed Arthur Dupont of Carniere, Belgium this is one of the world's finest and most original soups ever made. You will find nothing to equal it at the most expensive restaurants in the world. Here is the original recipe:

Take a soup pot of about three quart size. Put two quarts of water into the pot. Add a pound of soup bones with some meat on them or a pound of stewing beef. Put in one chopped up onion about three inches in diameter. Boil for three hours or until the meat is tender. Add one level tablespoon of basil, and one level tablespoon of parsley, one-half teaspoon of black pepper, and one level teaspoon of salt. Boil a few minutes until the spices are well blended into the soup. Now add two cups of finely cut up cooked egg noodles and one and a half ounces of blue or Roquefort cheese. Heat only until the cheese is well melted into the soup. Serve at once. This is one of the most exotic soups you have ever tasted and one everyone likes. It does not taste like the roquefort or blue cheese but has a very different taste all of its own.

ORIGINAL EUROPEAN SPAGHETTI AND TOMATO SAUCE

As previously mentioned the tomato originated in Central America. There were no tomatoes of any kind found in any other part of the world. The Indians of Mexico and Central America were the first to make spaghetti with tomato sauce. Cortez brought back tomato seeds to his native Spain as well as methods for making spaghetti with tomato sauce and ravioli. The Italians preferred spaghetti served with a butter sauce or other such sauces and for the most part still do. Some Italians finally used mixtures of tomato and spices on spaghetti but this they learned from the Spanish. Today, as always, in Italy, spaghetti with a tomato sauce is usually a pretty sad affair. The ones that use it mix up tomatoes, spices, onions and garlic in a nice sloppy mess that is neither good cooking nor good eating. Olive oil for one thing is wonderful for salads but when cooked in sauces it gives off an odor and taste that is far from delicate or desirable. If you want to stink up a kitchen nicely sometime try frying chicken in olive oil. It is about as bad as trying to fry using saffron oil.

The first use of tomato sauce on spaghetti in a good European recipe was neither Spanish nor Italian but German. This recipe remains today as the best tomato recipe ever devised for spaghetti. It was almost immediately copied in Italy and is used where really good spaghetti is served, not the tourist traps where they can get by with a sloppy tomato and olive oil sauce. Cooking such sauces for four hours or four weeks doesn't make it good. Throwing in a few anchovies or mushrooms into a blob of tomato sauce does not do anything for such sauces although it makes them perhaps sound better on a menu.

Otto K. Warner owner of a small restaurant in Strasbourg, Germany at the edge of the Alps Mountains across from Italy made the first and best European tomato sauce for spaghetti. The Germans, Austrians, Hollanders and Belgians are the great noodle and dumpling makers of Europe and they are also in many areas great users of spaghetti. Here is the original recipe.

Melt a level tablespoon of good lard in a frying pan and add ¼ cup of water. Add a 6 oz. can by weight of tomato paste no more, ¼ level teaspoon of crumbled oregano, 2 bay leaves or laurel leaves, 1 clove of garlic or ½ level teaspoon of powdered garlic, 1 inch square of onion or ½ level teaspoon of powdered onion, ¼ level teaspoon of ground nutmeg, ¼ level teaspoon of black pepper, ½ level teaspoon of salt and ½ level teaspoon of horseradish mustard. Stir well until all ingredients are mixed into the water and melted lard. Take one pound of good average quality hamburger. Crumble it up and put it into the pan. Stir the hamburger in the pan while it cooks so that it cooks in small tiny pieces. As soon as the meat is done remove and put over the cooked spaghetti. In cooking spaghetti do not overcook it. Boil the spaghetti in water to which add at least one level teaspoon of celery salt (not ordinary table salt) just until it is tender, no more. Then drain and blanch by putting the spaghetti in cold water about five seconds to slightly harden the outside skin of the spaghetti and to wash out any gluey free starch on the spaghetti. If you like mushrooms in spaghetti sauce mix about a 4 oz. can of drained mushroom stems and pieces into the sauce as the meat cooks. If you like cheese on spaghetti sauce sprinkle Parmesan cheese or grated Swiss cheese over the sauce. The grated Swiss cheese really adds the best flavor.

This spaghetti sauce contains no olive oil that when cooked gives off an objectionable taste and odor. It contains no anchovies. Anchovies are fine in certain salads, spreads and sandwiches but in spaghetti sauce they mix about as well as General Grant at a picnic in Richmond, Virginia.

This sauce is so good that you can put it just on a plain piece of bread and make a memorable meal.

SPAGHETTI DUPONT

This is the most fabulous recipe for preparing spaghetti that has ever been devised and is one of the few really original recipes of the past 100 years.

Arthur Dupont of Carnieres, Belgium, one of the most original cooks who ever lived, created Spaghetti Dupont.

Roquefort cheese as you know was invented in Roquefort, France by the sorceress Jehanne Muret. She created it by putting blue molded stale bread into sheep's milk and a little of the lining of a sheep's stomach. In this country Roquefort or blue cheese is made in the same way but cow's milk is used in place of the sheep's milk. Using the cow's milk instead of the sheep's milk actually improves the cheese rather than subtracts from it.

European cooks rarely use Roquefort cheese in salad dressings of any kind. They use it mostly simply as an after dinner dessert strange as it may seem. Roquefort cheese used in salad dressings was invented in France by Charles Derrault in 1701.

Here is the original Arthur Dupont recipe:

Take an 8 ounce package of egg noodles and boil in water until done according to the instructions on the package. Drain off the hot water. Fill the pan with cold water and then drain off the cold water. This takes away any loose starch on the noodles. Now place in a heaping tablespoon of butter in the bottom of the pot you cooked the noodles in, and add one ounce of crumbled Roquefort cheese to the noodles. You can buy Roquefort or blue cheese in one ounce foil packages at most grocery stores. Add ¼ level teaspoon of black pepper and salt to taste. Put a low heat under the pot. Stir the noodles, butter and Roquefort or blue cheese evenly until the butter is distributed all over the noodles and the cheese is melted and evenly distributed all over the noodles. Serve as the main dish while hot.

What will surprise you is that the noodles will have no Roquefort or blue cheese taste at all but an entirely different taste unlike anything that you have ever tasted. This is really fine cookery art not to be confused with the presentation type of cooking found in most high priced restaurants. In places like Maxim's in Paris which is supposed to be a good restaurant, most of the cooking there is poor and very unoriginal. They try to impress people in such places by using expensive cognac, old wines and champagne in their cooking and by burning expensive liquors over food. This is nothing but cheap "hokus pocus" and shows lack of ability to originate really good food recipes or even to follow good recipes.

This Spaghetti Dupont is preferred by most people to so-called Italian Spaghettis of any kind by several country miles.

SOUP ESCOFFIER

Escoffier the great French cook invented this soup made from tomatoes that is beyond a doubt the finest tomato base soup ever made. Here is the original recipe:

Take 10½ ounce standard can of Heinz tomato soup. You can make your own condensed tomato soup, with fresh tomatoes and cornstarch but this is not at all necessary. I specify Heinz tomato soup over others because it contains more tomato puree than other tomato soups.

Empty the can into a soup pot, add the same can full of water. Add one level tablespoon of brown sugar and one level teaspoon of curry powder. Stir well and heat until good and hot. Serve this soup alone just as it is or if you desire with some macaroni in it or with crackers or croutons.

This soup has an entirely different delicious taste and a beautiful aroma. It is a really great family soup that children and adults take to immediately, yet it is a soup that you can serve to snooty guests and completely baffle them. They never have tasted a soup as different and good as this one and cannot guess how it is made.

SOUP GODEFRY

The Duke of Godefry was born in 1061 and died in the year of 1100. He lived at the town of Bouillon, Belgium which is on the La Semois River. His castle is still there and is one of the most beautiful old castles left in the world. The trout fishing is excellent at Bouillon and fresh trout can be had any day at the restaurants. The Duke of Godefry was one of the most intelligent and finest men who ever inhabited this earth. He was a great Christian and Chief of the first crusade to Jerusalem. He became the first European King of Jerusalem. If he had received the support that he was promised and deserved from other European countries Jerusalem including both the Arabs and the Hebrews and the Middle East in general would today all have become Christian.

The Duke of Godefry in his castle at Bouillon invented a clear, delicious soup made as follows. This soup ever since has been known the world over as Bouillon. Boil beef bones in a large kettle of water for two hours. Keep all scum skimmed off the soup the instant it appears. Remove the beef bones then put in a medium sized piece of fresh beef and boil it for another hour. Again keep all scum skimmed off from the soup the instant it appears. If you leave the skum on the soup it will make the soup cloudy. Remove the meat and let the soup settle out until it is clear. Then carefully drain off the clear soup, season to taste, heat it and serve. Bouillon prepared in this manner is one of the world's greatest soups. As long as this world lasts, cooks will be forever grateful for this fabulous discovery.

The Duke of Godefry as Chief of the first crusade journeyed down through Europe and into the Middle East. He saw vegetables and spices that he had never seen before. For example such common vegetables as carrots and celery had never gotten to Central and Northern Europe and were entirely new to him. The use of grain flour mixed with water to make spaghetti and dumplings was also unknown in Central and Northern Europe at this time and was a great surprise to the crusaders.

The Duke of Godefry made the following soup which to me will always be one of the world's great recipes.

Take four quarts of water and put into a large soup pot. Add two cups of chopped celery. Two cups of sliced carrots. One small cabbage cut up into four pieces. One chopped up leek or onion about two inches in diameter. One half pound of hamburger broken up into as small a pieces as possible. Remove the red peppers from mixed pickling spices and add three level tablespoons. Add one level tablespoon of salt. Boil until the vegetables are tender stirring frequently. Add water to keep the water level the same at all times. Now add two cups of cooked and blanched egg noodles that have been broken up into small half inch long pieces. Remove and serve.

Somehow I can always eat another bowl of this delicious soup no matter how well filled I am.

SOUP BOURBON OR PORK SAUSAGE SOUP

Count Robert Clermont, sixth son of King Louis the IX of France, founded the House of Bourbon. His father died in 1270. Count Clermont will forever be remembered by everyone who drinks bourbon whisky as Count Clermont invented the process by which it is made. Bourbon was originally made from a mash made from grape seeds. After being distilled it was run through three feet of charcoal to filter and clean it. Today by law in the United States it has to be made from a mash containing mostly corn. Corn makes excellent bourbon but not any where near as good as when made of a grape seed mash. Bourbon was first made in the United States by Reverend Elijah Craig in 1789.

The Duke of Clermont had a cook named Andre Pollet. Andre Pollet invented Soup Bourbon. During the entire life of the Duke of Clermont he had Soup Bourbon served every Sunday, Tuesday, and Thursday. Soup Bourbon can be served as a soup or as a stew for the main dish of a meal. It is a soup that everyone likes. It is entirely different and no one can tell how it is made from looking at it or eating it.

Here is the original recipe.

Take a large soup pot and put three quarts of water into it. Add one level teaspoon of salt and one fourth level teaspoon of black pepper. Take one head of cauliflower not more than six inches in diameter or two packages of frozen cauliflower. Cut them up into squares about an inch thick and put into the pot. Take five large stalks of celery and cut the stalks up into about half inch squares and add. Cut up the leaves of the celery stalks as fine as possible and add. If you have parsley add three level tablespoons chopped up fine. The parsley however is not absolutely necessary. Take two green onions and slice them up into quarter inch pieces and add to the pot. If you do not have green onions use a two inch square of a large onion. Boil the mixture for about an hour. Now take four smoked pork sausages about five inches long and three fourths of an inch in diameter or their equivalent in smaller or larger smoked pork sausages. Cut the sausages up crosswise into one half inch long pieces and put them into the mixture. Take three eggs and break them into a soup bowl. Take a fork and mix them together until they are well blended together. Add the eggs to the mixture by dribbling them in and stirring the soup well at the same time. Boil for fifteen minutes more. The eggs form into tiny noodle like pieces in the soup giving the appearance of having added noodles or cheese to the soup. No one knows what the eggs in the soup really are. Serve this soup with buttered bread slices. Bourbon soup is one of the world's greatest food discoveries. It is wonderfully delicious and different. This soup on your menu will bring you justified praise every time you serve it.

JEAN'S VELVET CREAM SOUP OR JEAN'S SOUPE DE CREME VELOUR

Jean Lafitte was born in 1780 and lived to 1826. He and his brother Pierre did some pirating in the Gulf of Mexico and maintained their headquarters in New Orleans. The Lafitte brothers are revered today as the real saviors of Louisiana. When none of the major nations would trade with Louisiana the Lafitte brothers supplied the territory with trade goods that they needed to exist. The Lafitte brothers, allying with Andrew Jackson against the British troops, saved the United States as we today know it, at a very critical time, from English rule and occupation. Jean Lafitte was a handsome, very intelligent man with a flair for nice clothes, good food and attractive women. He was a very good cook in his own right and many of his recipes are still used in New Orleans today. His brother Pierre was also a handsome man but cross-eyed. Some stupid hyprocrite at one time put Pierre in jail in

New Orleans but his jailers released him and he walked out of his cell into the alley between the Catholic cathedral and the building he was jailed in. This alley has ever since been called pirate's alley.

The cell in the building next to the cathedral in New Orleans where Pierre Lafitte was kept a prisoner for a short time. The jailer conveniently left the lock of the cell open and Pierre escaped and ran down the alley between his cell and the cathedral. The alley has ever since been called Pirate's Alley.

Jean Lafitte's Velvet Cream Soup is my favorite of his recipes and it shows great genius as he was not at all familiar with any of the ingredients until they were brought to his attention.

His Jean's Velvet Cream Soup is my favorite of his recipes and it shows great genius as he was not at all familiar with any of the ingredients until he came to New Orleans.

Here is the original recipe.

Take one buttercup squash about eight or nine inches in diameter or two acorn squash medium sized. Put the squash into a pot with about three quarts of water and boil for one hour. Remove the squash and with a spoon remove the pulp of the squash and place it in a mixing bowl. Mash the pulp up into a fine paste. Put the mashed pulp back into the water the squash was cooked in and mix it in well. Add one level table-

Pattern shop of Lafitte's father on Bourbon street in New Orleans. It was used as a wood pattern making shop for making woodmaking patterns to cast cast iron, marine and industrial pieces. It was rented by the Lafittes and was also used as their meeting place. The building was never bought by the Lafittes. No cast iron grille work patterns were made as it was cheaper to have such work done in Europe.

spoon of salt, one sixteenth teaspoon of red pepper, one small can, juice and all of canned pimentoes or a large cut up red sweet pepper. In the case you use a fresh red sweet pepper boil the soup for twenty minutes to cook the pepper. Cut up the pimentoes in about half inch pieces. Bring to a boil and remove from the stove. Add one level teaspoon of almond extract stir in well and serve. If the soup is too thick add hot water to thin it out to the desired consistency.

MAKING THE ORIGINAL ONION SOUP WITH A 400 YEAR OLD RECIPE FROM LEGUME AVAILABLE IN THE WOODS

Like many other things in this world that are taken for granted and are not true, original onion soup contains no onions at all. The history of the original onion soup goes back as far as history does. It was and is Europe's most popular soup. The recipe we list here is 400 years old, actually, it is much older, but we have never been able to locate any written records of it beyond that time. Authentic onion soup is the finest of all soups and is very much at home at a king's palace or in a wilderness cabin. The recipe I describe here was taken by me from the kitchen of the Royal Palace in Brussels, Belgium. The recipe however, is the same throughout Europe.

First we must go into some historical facts. What we call the onion today is a comparatively new vegetable. Today's onions originated in the areas of Persia, Afghanistan and India. Such onions have been cultivated for only a little more than 4,000 years. Most of these onions have a sharp, eye watering, pungent odor distinctly their own.

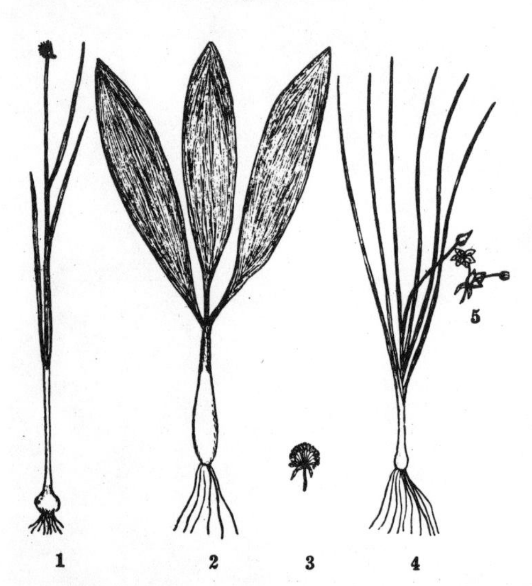

1. Wild Garlic. 2. Wild Leek. 3. Flower of Wild Leek. 4. Wild Onion. 5. Flower of Wild Onion.

The leek was found throughout Europe and North America from the beginning of history. The leek is a vegetable which has a white onion-like root. Its leaves are not like an onion at all, being of single thickness, not hollow and double like the leaves of onions. The leek has a soft, light pungent odor disstinctly different from that of an onion, yet if you did not have an onion on hand to compare it with, you might mistake it for an onion-like odor. The odor of leeks will not make your eyes water. The wild leek is commonly called a wild onion although it definitely is not an onion. In the state of Virginia, it is often called the "rank", a word brought over by early English settlers. It is eaten raw and also used in soups by many Virginians. The leek is so well liked in Wales in the British Isles, that it is their official flower. The leek, which originated in prehistoric times throughout continental Europe, Norway, Sweden, England, Scotland and Ireland, was and is a basic ingredient for any good soup in all these areas. Leeks add a bouquet and taste to soups that no other vegetable can equal.

In France, home of traditionally good cooking, the leek is called "poireau." Poireau soup has always been the most popular and most widely used soup in France. American tourists when in France liked poireau soup very much, but because of its aroma being somewhat similar to that of an onion, called it onion soup and the myth of the popularity of onion soup was created in Europe.

First when onions were imported into Europe, not too many centuries back, a soup was made from them in France. It has never become a popular soup in France or any other part of Europe. It has never even gained a fraction of the popularity of leek soup.

Wild leeks are found in the wooded areas of nearly all the United States and Canada. They are easily recognized. You can gather them anytime of the year except when the ground is frozen. If there are none in your area, order some leek seed from the Gurney Seed Company, Yankton, South Dakota or some other reliable company and plant the seed in rich soil early in the spring. If your soil is sandy, or clay soil, order some Chemical Soil Loosener. It can be bought from most all seed companies. It will keep the soil loose and allow it to hold water. Leeks will do well and in a few months' time are big enough to use for soup. They do not have to be full grown before using them for soup. You can leave leeks in the ground during winter, they never freeze out, even in Alaska. Domestic leeks have the same wonderful flavor of wild leeks. Today's domestic leeks are of a narrow leaf European strain.

The recipe for leek soup or the original soup is as follows: Go to any lengths necessary to make it, as it is the finest soup ever devised and will give you a reputation for good cooking like nothing else will. Once you or your guests have eaten it, you and they will be satisfied with no other.

LEEK SOUP, EUROPE'S MOST POPULAR SOUP

For eight servings:

4 quarts of fresh cold water.

Add 2 to 2½ pounds of beef, venison, or elk meat. If venison or elk meat remove all fat from it. It must be meat with some bone in it.

Add one level tablespoon of salt. Cover and bring to a slow rolling boil, not a wild boil. In about ten to fifteen minutes or when a gray white scum comes to the surface of the water, take a strainer and remove it. If you have no strainer, use a piece of bread to remove the scum.

Take a medium to large complete celery stalk and cut it into small pieces, leaves and all and add. Be sure to put in the leaves, as they have the best celery flavor. Add three laurel leaves, which are trade named bay leaves in North America. Add three whole cloves. Now take 36 wild leeks and cut off the bottom where the leaves start to go away from the stems. Now cut these sections in little pieces and add to the soup. If you are using large domestic leeks, say a half inch in diameter or larger, use only 6 leeks instead of the 36 wild ones.

Cut up one medium sized carrot and add it to the soup. Now cut up 2 pounds of potatoes in small cubes and add to the soup. Simmer the soup just at boiling for about 2 to 3 hours. Do not bring it to a rolling boil, as much of the good aroma will leave the soup if you boil it too hard. Now take 36 more wild leeks and cut off the bottoms where the leaves start to go away from the stems. Cut them up into half inch sections. If you have domestic leeks a half inch in diameter or larger, 6 will be enough. Now take a pan, not a frying pan, and melt enough butter in it to cover the bottom of the pan about a sixteenth of an inch or more. Do not heat the butter until it is brown, keep it yellow. Now add the cut up leeks to the butter. Cover the pan and fry them in the butter for ten minutes. Now add one cup of the soup stock and a pinch of black pepper. Now turn down your heat and barely simmer the soup stock and the fried leeks for about 25 minutes. Now take your main kettle of soup and remove the meat. Run the soup through a food mill or press it through a sieve. Now put the passed soup on the fire. Then add your butter fried leeks and soup stock mixture to the main soup mixture. Heat slowly for ten minutes. It is now ready to serve. Let the individuals add pepper and salt to taste.

The meat you have taken from the kettle serve separately. You will find it deliciously flavored with a real leek aroma. Let the individuals add pepper and salt to the meat to taste.

SOUP GAZPACHO

Gazpacho soup is very different delicious soup. Strange as it may seem it is served cold. This may make it sound unappealing to you but once you have tried it you will want it real often during hot and warm weather.

Gazpacho soup was invented by a poor Andalusia farmer in Spain named Xavier Fernandez in 1861. It is not an old recipe as practically all of the ingredients were unknown in Spain until a short time ago. The ingredients are nearly all from North America. Mr. Fernandez was visited by his friend Juan Diagre one evening. When the time came to serve his friend a meal he had to apologize to him because he had no wood to warm his vegetable soup. The two good friends ate the soup cold and both liked it very well.

Its fame soon spread all over Spain. Andalusia is in the southern part of Spain and is excessively hot in the summer and is not blessed with very much coal or wood for cooking purposes. Today Gazpacho soup is highly esteemed throughout Spain by all people rich and poor. Spain's best restaurants all serve it. I particularly enjoy Gazpacho soup at Botin's in the old section of Madrid and at the Cafe Mediterraneo along the port of Barcelona. In Seville it is very widely eaten and is as popular in comparison with chili, in the Southwestern part of the United States.

Here is the original recipe:

Take a large mixing bowl or pot. Cut up three cloves of garlic real fine and place in the bowl. Take 4½ pounds of fresh tomatoes or two kilograms. This is about 9 medium sized tomatoes. Place them in boiling water for a few minutes then remove and peel them and put them into the bowl. If you have no fresh tomatoes use 5, one pound cans of canned tomatoes and their juice. Works just as well. Peel one medium sized cucumber and grate it into the bowl. Take two medium sized green peppers and grate them into the bowl, seeds and all. Take one onion about two inches in diameter and grate into the bowl. Take a food mill and put the mixture in the bowl through it. If you have no food mill take a piece off of the end of an old broom or a similar piece of wood and mash all of the vegetables together well.

In a cup put in three level teaspoons of ground cumin spice. Cumin is also spelled cummin. It is a dwarf plant of the carrot family native to Egypt and Syria and cultivated for its aromatic seed. If your grocer does not have it he can get it for you. It is also the most essential ingredient in making chili so it is handy around the kitchen. Put 1 level tablespoon of salt in the cup, 1 level tablespoon cayenne pepper, 4 level tablespoons of olive oil or a good salad oil and 4 level tablespoons of vinegar. Mix the ingredients together well, in the cup; then mix them well into the vegetable mixture in the bowl. Take a cup of finely crumbled up dried white bread and mix it in the ingredients in the bowl. Now add ½ gallon or two liters of cold water to the bowl and mix it in well. Leave the mixing bowl stand in a cool place from 4 to 5 hours. Now pour the soup through a good strainer removing most of the solids. Some will always come through the strainer. Serve in regular soup dishes. At the table have bowls of onions cut up into small ¼ inch squares, tomatoes cut up into small ¼ inch squares, peeled cucumber cut up into small ¼ inch squares, a bowl of pieces of white bread cut up into squares and left to dry out, or small crackers. Leave the people add these to the soup as desired. This famous cold soup served on any hot day or at a barbeque will make your dinner a memorable one that will never be forgotten by your guests. You can use this soup to replace a salad at summer meals also. Although it is not at all the custom, I like this soup best eaten with crackers spread with Roquefort cheese or blue cheese.

Gazpacho soup never contains flour, ice cubes, tomato juice, cooked rice or noodles. One prominent American food editor says to omit cucumbers in making this soup because some people are allergic to cucumbers. This statement could be likened to a recipe for roast beef where the beef was omitted.

SALMON SOUP OSCAR

In Minnesota when you talk of Oscar as you well might know people know you are talking of King Oscar of Norway and Sweden. A goodly portion of Minnesota's population is Scandinavian.

King Oscar II was born in 1829 and died in 1907. He invented this soup himself and many Scandinavian immigrants brought the recipe to Minnesota. This soup is far better in taste than Bouillabaisse Marseillaise, a French fish base soup, although the French soup is very good also.

The ingredients are as follows:
1 pound can of pink salmon.
2 quarts of cold water.
2 level teaspoons of salt.
1 pound can of tomatoes.
½ cup of chopped onion.
4 whole bay leaves.
2 cups of celery leaves.
12 peppercorns or a level teaspoon of black pepper.
1 half teaspoon of almond oil or almond flavoring.

Take the can of pink salmon and drain it. Put the drained flesh into a large soup pot. Remove all the bones and skin and all of the dark meat areas under the skin. Break up the salmon into small pieces with your fingers. Add two quarts of cold water, 1 pound can of tomatoes, 2 level teaspoons of salt, ½ cup of chopped onion, 4 whole bay leaves, 2 cups of celery pieces, 12 peppercorns or a level teaspoon of black pepper. Boil lightly for 30 minutes. Leave cool for 10 minutes. Stir in one-half teaspoon of almond flavoring and serve immediately. This soup is very different and very, very good. Just with bread and butter alone it makes a fine meal.

BUCKINGHAM PALACE BROWN BEEF GRAVY

This recipe was brought to England from the continent by Prince Albert. It came to America first, to New England then to the Middle West by the John Shelley family who once worked in Buckingham Palace.

Making really good beef gravy, easy to digest and free from all lumps and paste tastes is very hard to do. The usual methods advocated in American cook books and ladies magazines to make beef gravy are very poor to say the least.

I will give you this old beef gravy recipe for 4 people. Use it with a beef roast or beef ribs for 4 people.

Put a heaping tablespoon of butter into a frying pan and melt with a medium heat until it just starts to brown. Remove the frying pan from the stove. Add one level tablespoon of flour. Mix the flour in well with the melted butter. It will make a thin paste. Now add a half cup of cold water and mix well until the flour and butter and water are nice and smoothly mixed. Put the pan back on the stove over medium heat. Stir until it begins to thicken.

This only takes a minute or so. Now add all the juice from your beef roast or beef ribs and salt and pepper to taste. Scrape every bit of juice and leavings from your roasting or broiling pan. These scrapings add good flavor and if you have enough of them they give your gravy the desired medium brown color. In cooking a roast you have to have some water in the bottom of the pan to keep it from drying out. Be sure to include every bit of it as it is fine beef stock. Mix and stir until the gravy comes to a slow rolling boil. If your pan leavings were not brown enough to give the gravy a good medium brown color add a few drops of Kitchen Bouquet to give it the desired color.

You will note this gravy recipe is entirely different than any other. The gravy comes out smooth free of all lumps every time. This is because you mix cold water with the butter and flour mixture and mix the flour in well. Cold water eliminates all chance of lumps forming in your flour. This gravy tastes rich and smooth because you have a butter base. No meat stock or drippings alone will give you the smooth, rich, taste of this famous gravy. You do not mix in the flour directly into the meat dripping, or meat stock. Mixing in the flour directly into the meat drippings or stock causes the gravy to have a pasty, gluey taste.

Be sure to try this famous recipe. Makes anything you put it on taste really delicious. This gravy digests very easily and will not upset the most delicate stomach.

RED EYE GRAVY

Red Eye Gravy is well known in the South but little known in the East, Middle West and West anymore. This gravy got its name from Andrew Jackson, American General and 7th President of the United States. He was born in 1767 and died in 1845. Andrew Jackson was a rugged, common, hard working man and minced few fancy words with anyone. While he was a general he sat down one day to have his noon meal. He called his cook over to tell him what to prepare. The cook had been drinking white mule or southern moonshine corn whiskey the night before and his eyes were as red as fire. General Jackson told the cook to bring him home country ham with gravy as red as his eyes. Some men nearby heard the general and ham gravy became red eye gravy from that day on.

Red eye gravy is very easy to make and very good. I like it especially well on boiled potatoes. Take a large frying pan, put a good heaping tablespoon of good lard into the pan and melt it. When melted put in slices of ham and fry them until well done. Add one cup of water and one crushed up clove. Bring to a boil and simmer for five minutes. Remove the ham and serve some gravy with the ham. Pour some of the gravy over a freshly boiled potato and mash the potato up with the gravy so that they are well mixed together. This is very fine eating.

BECHAMEL SAUCE

I have written up the facts on Bechamel sauce mainly so that when someone writes or talks about Bechamel sauce you know what they are talking about. Almost invariably persons who write or talk about Bechamel sauces actually have no idea at all what they are talking about. They copy the recipe from a cook book, the author of which, likewise did not know the true recipe either and just made bad guesses. Even the so-called finest cook books do not have the true Bechamel sauce recipes.

Bechamel sauce was invented by Duke Philippe De Mornay, Governor of Saumur, Lord of the Plessis Marly. He was a great protestant writer and was called the protestant pope. Mornay was the leader of the Hugenots. He was born in 1549 and died in 1623. He also invented Mornay Sauce, Sauce Chasseur, Sauce Lyonnaise and Sauce Porto.

Some cook books credit Bechamel, the French financier of the 12th century with inventing Bechamel sauce but this is entirely untrue. Bechamel the financier was strictly a money man and knew nothing about food and cared less.

Everyone, as the centuries went by, wanted to "get into the act", so to speak, and many famous cooks tried to pretend that they either invented Bechamel sauce or at least knew the original recipe. Escoffier, in his cook book, tried to give the idea that he knew how to make Bechamel sauce which he definitely did not. Escoffier was a very good cook but actually knew little of the history of cooking and tried to bluff his way through cooking more than anything else. His Bechamel sauce was terrible. Alexandre Dumas, who was a poor cook and knew little about cooking, in his book, Dictionary of the Cuisine, never bothered to write the truth about cooking but simply wrote what he thought would make a book that would sell. His Bechamel recipe was entirely different from that of Escoffier and Escoffier's different from everyone else's. The Bechamel sauce recipe in the Gourmet Cook Book of our present day is just some writer's dream.

Louis de Bechamel was maitre d hotel, or in other words, in charge of food and service for King Louis XIV. Louis XIV was born in 1638. He was King from 1643 to 1715. Louis de Bechamel, of course, wanted to give himself as much favorable publicity as he could in order to hold his job. He just had to look important. He named the basic white sauce of Mornay, Bechamel sauce.

The original Bechamel sauce invented by Mornay is as follows:

Put five level tablespoons of butter into a pan and melt over low heat. Do not brown. Remove the pan from heat. Add five level tablespoons of flour and stir in well with the butter but do not brown. Add one and three quarters cups of cold milk. Remember, cold milk. Warm milk will make the mixture lumpy. Put back on stove over medium heat. Stir well and bring to a slow boil until mixture thickens, salt and pepper to taste and then quickly remove from heat. This is also sometimes called a white roux.

To make a brown Bechamel sauce, make just the same but leave the butter brown lightly before adding the flour. This is also sometimes called a Brun-Roux.

These basic Bechamel sauces are the general basis for many sauces and souffles. Bechamel sauce in itself, is not used alone at all as some cooks would try to make you believe. Bechamel sauce contains no cream, chicken stock, veal stock, onion, thyme or nutmeg, etc.

SAUCE CHASSEUR ORIGINAL RECIPE BY MORNAY

Sauce Chasseur means Hunter's Sauce in French. Used on beef, pork, venison, squirrels, rabbits, quail, pheasants, etc.

Take five level tablespoons of butter and melt them in a pan until light brown. Remove the pan from the stove. Add five level tablespoons of flour and stir well. Add ½ cup of cold water that you have boiled beef in or beef consomme. Add one level teaspoon of onion powder or one finely grated piece of onion an inch square. One half cup of mushroom stems and pieces. Put back on stove over medium heat. Stir well and simmer until mixture thickens. Salt and pepper to taste. Add ¼ cup of port wine and ¼ cup of white wine and heat over a low flame and stir. As soon as the wine is warm and mixed in well remove from heat.

Sauce Chasseur contains no tomato sauce, no parsley or taragon.

SAUCE MORNAY ORIGINAL RECIPE BY MORNAY

Use on pork, pheasant, chicken, vegetables, macaroni, fish, etc.

Put five level tablespoons of butter into a pan and melt over low heat. Do not brown. Remove the pan from the heat. Add five level tablespoons of flour and stir in well with butter but do not brown. Add one and a fourth cups of cold milk and a level teaspoon of onion powder or a one inch square of onion grated. Warm milk will make the mixture lumpy. Put back on the stove over low heat. Stir well and simmer until mixture thickens. Salt and pepper to taste. Now, add one cup of grated sharp yellow cheese such as cheddar. Stir in the cheese until it is melted. Stir continually as you add the grated cheese otherwise cheese will go to the bottom of the pan and stick. Do not use any white cheese or mild cheese. Stir in two tablespoons of cream, ¼ teaspoon of ground nutmeg, ½ teaspoon of celery salt.

Mornay sauce contains no egg yolks, Parmesan or Swiss cheese. Recipes that call for them are entirely incorrect.

SAUCE LYONNAISE ORIGINAL RECIPE BY MORNAY

Take five level tablespoons of butter and melt in a pan over low heat. Remove the pan from the stove. Add five level tablespoons of flour and stir in well. Add 1¼ cups of cold milk and stir in well. Add one level teaspoon of powdered onion or a one inch square of onion finely grated. Put back over medium heat. Stir and simmer until the sauce thickens. Add salt and pepper to taste. Add one half cup of cold, white, dry wine. Warm and stir in the wine, then remove at once.

PETER'S SAFFRON

The strangest spice in the world is the miraculous saffron. It is the gold colored pollen and stigma from purple crocus flowers although it can mean the gold colored pollen from any flower. It contains enzymes and complex chemicals that man will never even begin to understand. This tiny golden dust contains the power of creating life itself. It is a food millions of times more powerful than even such foods as milk and honey.

Peter, one of Christ's Apostles, used saffron in soups, porridges, and in gravies. The saffron he used was the gold colored pollen from wild flowers.

The use of saffron today is limited almost exclusively to Spain.

Today a pound of pure crocus saffron is worth from $2,000 to $5,000 dollars. At grocery stores, when you can find it, a small amount of it costs 50c.

Just a pinch or two of it stirred into potato salad, dressing, chicken gravy, chicken soup, gives them a beautiful gold color and a very different delicious taste.

You do not have to buy saffron at all to get this wonderful saffron taste and color. Watch the flowers about you wherever you live. When lilies, tulips, crocuses or any other flower are full of a gold colored pollen in their center pull out the part and dry it. It will make you the finest of saffron. Even in the desert cactus pollen makes excellent saffron.

HOW TO MAKE AUTHENTIC MAYONNAISE

Mayonnaise cannot be bought in grocery stores. The concoctions they sell labeled mayonnaise are not even remotely similar to real mayonnaise.

If you want mayonnaise you must make it yourself and do not consider yourself a good cook unless you make your own mayonnaise.

There is only one authentic recipe for mayonnaise and that is the original one. Mayonnaise was invented in the resort town of Fort Mahon on the Somme River in northern France. This is a small town of about 700 people, most of them excellent cooks. When first invented it was called Mahonnaise. This sauce got its present name of mayonnaise purely by accident through a printing error in an early cook book.

Here is the original recipe brought to Minnesota by early French immigrant cooks right from Fort Mahon. It produces a mayonnaise beyond comparison in all respects. Using this famous recipe, mayonnaise is very easy to make and you never will have a failure with one exception. If you are a woman do not attempt to make mayonnaise during menstruating time as the mayonnaise will simply not blend together at all well. This is not superstition but a well established fact well known to all women cooks. With all the vast knowledge that we think we have we are still like lost children in a great woods. There are countless facts in everyday living that will always remain a complete mystery.

Put a large flat plate in the refrigerator a few hours to cool it. Be sure that it is one with as large a flat in the center as possible. Remove the plate from the refrigerator. Take two cool eggs from the refrigerator and remove the yolks and put them onto the plate. Do not break the yolks. Add one heaping teaspoon of prepared mustard such as French's. Now take a table fork and place the tines flat on the bottom of the plate. Now move the fork in a circle as large as the flat area of the plate will allow. Keep the fork tines flat on the bottom of the plate while doing this. Make 10 turns about every 5 seconds. This is fairly fast. This is called "turning." Never beat the ingredients in making mayonnaise or your results will not be mayonnaise.

Carefully "turn" the egg yolks and mustard until they are blended together. Add ¼ level teaspoon of salt and ⅛ level teaspoon of white pepper. Turn them in well. Take one and a half cups of salad oil. Slowly drip it into the egg and mustard mixture drop by drop and turn it in so there is no surplus oil in the mixture at any time. If you flood the mixture with oil it will curdle. Carefully turn in the oil until it is all well turned in. Now add one tablespoon of vinegar and one tablespoon of lemon juice. Turn them in well. Take ¼ cup of soft butter and turn it into the mixture.

In making mayonnaise have all of your ingredients handy so that you can keep turning almost continually from the time you start to make it until the mayonnaise is finished. If you can keep turning without any stops so much the better.

Your arm will be good and tired from turning but you now have real mayonnaise that is wonderful to eat no matter what you put it on.

You will note that real mayonnaise contains no sugar, no boiled egg yolks, no corn starch, no gelatine, no cream or other ingredients like the many concoctions that falsely call themselves mayonnaise.

P.S. Some cook book writers in writing up mayonnaise mistook Port Mahon for Fort Mahon and made up a purely fictional story that mayonnaise was invented by the chef of the Duc de Richelieu, great nephew of the Cardinal Richelieu. The Duc de Richelieu captured the Port of Mahon in 1757. The Port of Mahon is on the island of Minorca in the Balearic Island group off the coast of Spain. Mayonnaise was invented and widely used in France long before 1757.

ANTI-PASTO

Anti-Pasto means "before dinner" in Italian and in Italy is served as "before the meal" appetizer as well as to replace vegetables or salad or in some cases as the main meal. In American grocery stores Anti-Pasto usually comes in small glass jars of a few ounces and sells at terrifically high prices such as $1.25 for four ounces.

Anti-Pasto is a recent Italian recipe as the main ingredients in it came from the Indians of North and Central America. For example tomatoes first came to Italy in 1550 but it took to the 18th century before they learned how to use them and ate them extensively.

In 1703 in Rome there lived a man named Anthony Oliver. He had a small restaurant and also served wines and liquors. He had the habit of pouring a glass of wine for himself taking a sip then waiting on customers, then going back and taking another sip and keeping this up until the wine was gone.

Oliver had a pet cat that frequented his place of business. The cat had a great fondness for wine or brandy and when Oliver was not drinking from his glass the cat was. The cat often became so drunk that it would pass out in some of the customers' laps. Some of the customers loudly complained to Oliver about his drunken cat but Oliver never did anything about it.

One morning Oliver was eating a dish of cooked vegetables and fish. His pet cat had been drinking rather heavily. It jumped up on his table, lost its balance and knocked over a bottle of oil and vinegar, spilling some of both on Oliver's plate. Oliver put the cat outside to sober up. He came back and mixed the oil and vinegar with his boiled vegetables and fish and ate them. He found that they tasted delicious with the oil and vinegar and added his new found recipe to the things he served. It soon became popular all over Italy and Anti-Pasto was born.

Anti-Pasto served today makes a marvelous Hors-d'-Oeuvre, a very different salad, a very different vegetable, or a main dish on a hot day that is hard to beat. Here is a modern day adaption of the original Oliver recipe. At present prices it costs about $2.25 to make this recipe. It will serve 10 people as the main dish.

Take one cup of vinegar and two-thirds cup of olive oil or salad oil (makes no difference which one) and the contents of two 6 ounce cans by weight of tomato paste. These are the small cans. Put them in a bowl. Add one level teaspoon of black pepper and one level teaspoon of salt. Stir together until they are mixed as well as possible. Heat over a medium heat until hot, then remove and leave cool.

Take a large pan or pot. Into it add the following. Do not mix them up.

One 3½ ounce jar of small pickled onions, juice and all or take four onions about two inches in diameter. Make them into onion rings and boil them in water until done and add them.

One 4 ounce can of pimentos sliced in large pieces. Add the juice from the can also.

One 8 ounce by weight can of cut green beans drained.

One 8 ounce by weight can of cut waxed beans drained.

One 2 ounce jar of stuffed olives. Add the juice from the jar also.

One pound can by weight of carrots sliced crosswise.

One 4 ounce can of stems and pieces of mushrooms.

One pint of dill pickles sliced thin, crosswise.

One 6 ounce can of chunk tuna. Drain off the oil and add. On commercial Anti-Pasto they use large sardines like American sardines as they are cheaper than tuna or similar fish. These you can use in place of tuna or similar fish if you desire.

Now pour the mixture of salad oil, vinegar and tomato paste over the items in the large pan or bowl. Mix only until they are well covered with the oil, vinegar and tomato paste. Do not over mix as it tends to mash and break them up too much.

Although it is not at all necessary if you want to make your Anti-Pasto fancier add one cup of cooked drained celery, one cup of cooked drained cauliflower, another can of drained tuna or similar fish. Increase the salad oil to 1 cup and vinegar to one and a fourth cups.

The important thing in making Anti-Pasto is the oil, vinegar, and tomato paste. These must be mixed well together before being added.

Actually you can add any vegetables to your Anti-Pasto such as boiled radishes, boiled green peppers, whole kernel corn, small cooked beets, boiled sliced potatoes, cooked peas, cooked sweet pea pods, cooked lima beans, cooked Brussels sprouts, cooked asparagus, cooked parsnips, cooked turnips and cooked okra.

For fish in your Anti-Pasto the flesh of any of these fish is even much better than tuna, boiled crappies, bullheads, catfish, bluegills, stream trout, bass, sheepshead, northern pike, walleyed pike, striped bass or perch.

AVONNAISE

This is the only new sauce invented since mayonnaise was invented and since Careme invented Hollandaise sauce. Avonnaise was invented by famed Belgian cook, Berthe E. Gramme. Use this sauce on fruit salads, lettuce salads, and on baked potatoes instead of sour cream sauce, on roast beef instead of gravy or Bernaise sauce, on hamburgers use lettuce, pickles and avonnaise.

Here is the original recipe.

Take one cup of homemade mayonnaise and place it in a bowl. Take a ripe avocado and peel and remove the stone. Cut the flesh into small pieces and put into the bowl. Take a fork and mash the avocado pieces into the mayonnaise until the mixture is smooth. Once you have tried this sauce you will be using it often.

CHEESE SAUCE ANTOINE VAN DYCK

Antoine Van Dyck was a great artist as we all know. He was born in Antwerp, Belgium in 1599 and died in 1641. He was thorough about everything he did. This recipe that he used is a basic one but has never been surpassed by anyone.

Take two heaping tablespoons of butter and melt in your frying pan with medium heat. Add 1½ heaping teaspoons of flour and stir and mix into the butter until smooth and creamy. Remove from the stove and add one-half cup of cold water. Stir the cold water in well until thoroughly mixed. Never use warm water. Salt and pepper to taste.

Put back onto the stove over a medium heat. Grate a cup of sharp cheese such as McLaren's or a sharp aged cheddar. Add to the sauce and slowly stir and cook until the cheese is melted and well mixed in. Serve on good toast cut up into one inch squares. For my part this makes a really fine meal. Today this recipe is served as a gravy on baked potatoes and it really is a sensation served this way. It is also served on lobster and is far superior to Newburg sauce on lobster.

ROQUEFORT DRESSING PERRAULT

Roquefort cheese was invented by the sorceress Jehanne Muret in the year 10 Before Christ. She lived in the prehistoric cave dweller caves of Combalou mountain near the small town of Roquefort, France, department or province Aveyron. There are two towns named Roquefort in France. The one in Aveyron is the town we are interested in as it is the cheese making town, the other Roquefort is not a cheese making town. The early prehistoric cave dwellers of Combalou Mountain caught and tamed the first wild sheep in this area. The blood of these wild sheep is still in the flocks at Roquefort today. Some writers wrongly write that Roquefort cheese was invented by a young shepherd boy who was eating a sandwich made of sour sheep milk curds on bread on Combalou Mountain. He saw a pretty girl walking down below him walking along a mountain path.

He laid down his sandwich and went down and romanced a bit with the girl. When he came back to his flock he had naturally forgotten all about his sandwich. Four days later he stumbled onto the sandwich. The milk curd had fine blue lines in it and had hardened greatly. He ate the aged sandwich and found the taste delicious and different. By leaving milk curd on bread in the same area he was able to have the same delicious sandwiches every few days. This is a lovely legend but has no truth in it at all. Jehanne Muret discovered how to make Roquefort cheese by mixing blue molded bread, molded in the prehistoric caves with sheep's milk. She, like Zoroaster, sorcerer of early times had a religious following. It was said she could predict the sex of unborn children by looking into a woman's face and make charms that would attract any desired man to a woman. One thing that she certainly could do and well was to make a magically delicious cheese from sheep's milk and bread left to mold in her ancient cave.

Pline L'Ancien, Roman naturalist, wrote a series of 37 Natural History books. They are the most valuable Natural History books ever written and have never even come close to being equaled. In book 11 of these books he describes Roquefort cheese and states that it came from the other side of the Alps. He was killed 79 years after Christ at an eruption of Mount Vesuvius. At the time he was commander of the Roman fleet at Misne. He went to Pompei and Herculanum to study the lava flow and was choked to death by the fumes.

Charlemagne, one of the greatest of rulers, lived in the 8th century. He never ate any meal including breakfast without having Roquefort cheese on the table. In early Christian times the priests were given Roquefort cheese by the people for saying masses.

In 1666 the French Government gave the town of Roquefort the exclusive right to call their sheep's milk cheese Roquefort. On July 26, 1925 the French Government decreed that Roquefort cheese must be made entirely of sheep's milk. Today there are 700,000 sheep around the town of Roquefort. Roquefort cheese is made in the caves or "cabnes" or "cabanieres" as they are called by the local people. Up until 1882 Roquefort cheese was made by many small companies in Roquefort in their homes but today it is made by one large group. The sheep's milk is treated with penicillium glaucum, a fungus found in miscroscopic mushrooms in the prehistoric caves of the area. It forms readily on stale bread. This fungus gives the cheese its blue lines and fine flavor.

In North America Roquefort type cheese is made from cow's milk and is called bleu or blue cheese. Actually it is better than Roquefort type cheese made from sheep's milk.

Charles Perrault was born in Paris, France, in 1628. This man undoubtedly has entertained more children than any man who ever lived. Perrault was an accomplished writer and wrote history books. He loved children and took the time to write such great classics as Red Riding Hood, Cinderella, Tom Thumb, Puss and Boots and many, many, others. He wrote these books at no profit to himself but to provide good clean children's books. A pretty great man, much greater than most of the Nobel Prize winners we have today and much, much greater than most kings and presidents.

Charles Perrault had a brother who was both an architect and a doctor. Both brothers were very creative. Between them they created Roquefort salad dressing. It never, strange as it may seem, became very popular in France or Europe but became very popular in North America. Here is the original recipe and it is the only Roquefort salad dressing that is really great.

Take three ounces of Roquefort or blue cheese and put it in a fairly good sized glass or pottery crock. Add two tablespoons of whipping cream or whole milk and mash the milk or cream well into the cheese with a fork until the mixture becomes a paste. Add one fourth level teaspoon of salt, one level teaspoon of cerferuil, one fourth level teaspoon of tarragon, one fourth level teaspoon of black pepper. If you have no cerferuil or tarragon add ¼ level teaspoon of anise flavoring. Cerferuil and tarragon are simply plants with anise flavoring. Mix all the ingredients together well. Now stirring the mixture all of the time add two level tablespoons of vinegar. If you do not stir well, as you mix in the vinegar, the vinegar will tend to give the cream or milk an off taste. Tarragon is simply the dried leaves of one of the aster flower families, known as dragon flowers. The word comes from the Greek word Drakon meaning dragon. Cerferuil is the small dried leaves of a herb native to Europe. Tarragon you can usually get in some grocery stores but cerferuil is impossible to get in North America, yet it is a very necessary spice for fine cooking.

Put the dressing on your salad, then take a small amount of Roquefort cheese and break it up into small pieces and scatter them on top of the salad. You must have these small pieces of Roquefort cheese on the salad to give just the right taste to the dressing. This is a salad dressing for special occasions.

INDIAN MEAT AND FISH SAUCE

This is the oldest known North American sauce and one of the very best. It is very simple to make and just wonderful tasting.

Take one level teaspoon of horseradish to two ounces of catsup. Stir well and leave set for four hours. Then stir again and it is ready to use.

Use on meats of all kinds, fish, shrimp, and lobster. It just cannot be beat. Brings out the flavor of meat, fish, or sea food perfectly.

The original recipe called for drained tomato pulp with native spices but catsup makes it just as well.

Today somewhat similar sauces are called shrimp sauce. None of them however begin to equal this simple marvelous recipe.

Both tomatoes and horseradish were originally found only in the Americas and this sauce was popular in America long before any Europeans touched our shores.

BEARNAISE SAUCE

This was invented by Chef Jules Colette from Bearn, France. He worked at the restaurant Pavillon Henri V at Saint-German-en-Laye in Paris, France for a time. He had however perfected the recipe long before he came to work at this restaurant. Every chef at the restaurant tried to claim the recipe as his own.

Bearnaise sauce is best served on hamburgers. Cover both sides of the hamburger bun heavily with Bearnaise sauce. Put lettuce on the hamburger and tomato, and dill pickle slices on it too if you like them. The Bearnaise sauce makes a hamburger a fabulously different dish. In France Bearnaise sauce is served with roast beef or with such fish as halibut. You dip your pieces of roast beef into the Bearnaise sauce instead of in gravy. It is really good and a welcome change every so often for anyone.

Served with fish instead of tartar sauce Bearnaise sauce is very good. It is excellent with fried fish or with cold fish like salmon or tuna. It makes a wonderful cracker dip. Every good cook should be able to make a good Bearnaise sauce. Here is the original recipe.

Take a small sauce pan or frying pan. Put into it one level teaspoon of grated green onions or shallots or one level teaspoon of onion powder, one fourth teaspoon of white pepper, one level teaspoon of salt, two level teaspoons of dried tarragon leaves, rub the leaves well before adding them and remove any stem pieces, 2 drops of oil of anise and four level tablespoons of vinegar. Heat over a low flame until about one third of the vinegar goes off in steam. Stir well while this is going on then remove the pan from the heat and leave cool a little. Take five egg yolks and beat them together well in a bowl with a fork. Add the five beaten egg yolks gradually to the mixture in the pan stirring constantly and vigorously. Put the pan back on the stove over a very low fire and gradually add about six ounces of melted butter, stirring it in well. Do not let the sauce more than simmer. Be sure that the butter is just liquid and warm, not too hot as it is added. Stir the butter in well until the sauce is as thick as heavy cream. The egg yolks cooking cause the sauce to thicken. Remove the sauce just as soon as it thickens well and leave it cool slightly. Serve it just slightly warm or even cold. Never serve it hot.

When Jules Collette invented Bearnaise sauce he never gave the true recipe to anyone. If someone asked for the recipe he would give them one but never the right one and always a different recipe to every one that asked him for it. He took the secret of Bearnaise sauce to his deathbed and then gave it to his daughter Louise. Even the great chef Escoffier never was able to make a decent Bearnaise sauce. He made it so poorly that he usually just put some tarragon into mayonnaise and served it as Bearnaise sauce. Most of today's chefs do the same thing. Actually Bearnaise sauce is not made like mayonnaise nor does it taste or look like mayonnaise.

Bearnaise sauce never contains wine, chervil, tarragon vinegar, nor cayenne pepper. It never is strained through a cloth or sieve as this changes the texture of the sauce entirely.

JACQUES PIERRE DRESSING

Today it seems all chefs make up their own versions of French dressings, thousand island dressing, Roquefort dressing, etc., and you never know what you may get when you order it. In most cases it is usually nothing to brag about. Here is a dressing created by Berthe E. Gramme, Belgian, one of the world's greatest and most creative cooks from a family or rather generations of famous cooks. This is a dressing that is centuries ahead in the cooking world.

The avocado originated in Guatemala and in Mexico. The avocado was widely used by the Aztecs and other natives centuries before the Spaniards came to North America.

A corn meal pancake, avocado, and coffee are today thought of as a very fine meal by natives of Mexico and Central America and it certainly is as far as I am concerned, especially with chocolate syrup on the corn pancake.

The English name avocado comes from the Spanish interpretation of the original Aztec word Ahuacatl. The avocado is just one of the many great things to thank the Aztecs for developing. Here is the recipe for the finest salad dressing ever made.

Take one very ripe avocado. Peel and remove the stone. Cut off the flesh into small pieces and put it in a bowl and mash it very well to the consistency of smooth custard. Add three tablespoons of good salad oil. Add four level tablespoons of white vinegar. One level teaspoon of finely cut up or grated onion. Salt and pepper to taste. Put in a refrigerator and cool. Serve cool on head lettuce or leaf lettuce salads.

LAFAYETTE SAUCE

Lafayette was born in 1757 and died in 1834. As we all know he was a French general who fought with us during the Revolutionary War. Without his help General George Washington repeatedly said that it would not have been possible to win the war. Lafayette was a great personal friend of George Washington and his cook Frances.

Lafayette was a sensitive, warm man with a terrifically brilliant mind. Besides his great military aid to us he helped individual American friends of his in every way possible. Through one of his gracious acts we were able to print the first Bible in America. He gave 400 dollars in 1785 to Matthew Carey, an Irish immigrant to start him up in business publishing the Pennsylvania Herald and to print the first Bibles in North America.

Lafayette was a great lover of good food and an outstanding cook in his own right. The foods that impressed him most in America, of course, were foods not found in Europe, such as tomatoes, etc. Lafayette using his vast knowledge of French sauces and combining this with what he found in America invented a sauce that is far superior to any ever made. Several imitations of it have been attempted commercially under various names but they are nothing like the real thing, although they sell for about 35c for a 4½ or 5 ounce bottle.

Put the following ingredients into a gallon jug or jar. An old gallon vinegar jug is excellent. The items have been adapted for modern buying but change the recipe in no way.

Take nine or ten quarts of apples either green or ripe. Peel them and slice them into a seven or eight quart cooking pot. Cover them just to the top with brown vinegar.

Add one can of tomato puree or four large tomatoes, add one sliced onion about four inches in diameter. Add the following to the sliced apples: Two level tablespoons of ground spice. Two level tablespoons of ground nutmeg. One level tablespoon of ground cinnamon. Four level tablespoons of powdered coffee or four cups of black coffee boiled down as much as possible. Bring to a boil and slowly boil for two hours. As the water in the vinegar evaporates add half vinegar and half water to replace the vinegar. Stir frequently as apples burn easily and also tend to stick to the bottom of the pan. Remove and run through a food mill and add about 12 cups of the puree to the jug or jar.

Now add two level tablespoons of powdered garlic. Six level tablespoons of salt. Two level teaspoons of ground red pepper. One level teaspoon of sugar. Two level tablespoons of ground cloves. Six ounces of orange marmalade or a half of a can of frozen orange juice. One level teaspoon of spearmint flavoring.

Shake up well and add just enough vinegar to fill the jug or jar. You will need very little vinegar to do this. The thicker the sauce the better. It should be nearly as thick as catsup. This is not a thin watery sauce.

Do not use tragacanth in this sauce as imitations often do. Tragacanth is nothing but gum from East European trees. The gum swells up in water and acts as a cheap filler.

Use this sauce for the same purposes as Worcestershire sauce. It is somewhat thicker and simply delicious. You will be surprised how quickly your friends will notice and appreciate the rare taste of this fine sauce. Try it instead of catsup on hamburgers, makes a great difference.

ORIGINAL WORCESTERSHIRE SAUCE BY JOHN CRAFTON

This famous sauce was originated in Worcester, England by John L. Crafton a chemist in 1835 and is an adaptation of early French sauces. He wanted desperately to make his every day food taste better and he certainly succeeded. The sauce was first called Worcester sauce then changed to Worcestershire sauce by commercial companies who tried to vaguely copy the original sauce. The story that the recipe was brought out of India by the third Baron Sandys in 1837 is entirely untrue. Several other chemists at the time brought out similar sauces.

The original recipe is nothing at all like the present day commercial recipes. Commercial recipes for the most part are a black looking watery mixture of water, soy sauce, pepper and vinegar. They might be alright on chow mein or chop suey but hardly on anything else.

Real Worcestershire sauce is a light reddish brown in color, is not at all watery but quite a heavy bodied liquid. It contains very little water, has no soy sauce flavor at all although it does contain a limited amount of soy sauce.

Made by the original recipe it costs only about 75c a gallon to make. People really like it and your family will use a lot more of it than catsup if you have it available for them. Make up some for your church suppers also and put it on the table in old peanut butter jars with a spoon in it. It will create a real sensation whenever you serve it.

Worcestershire sauce is not at all difficult to make.

Take an old gallon vinegar jug or one gallon jar and put in the following:

Take one 15 ounce can of red kidney beans, (costs about 10c) drain and pass through a food mill. Commercial makers list tamarinds as a part of their recipe so that housewives will think that they cannot make their own as tamarinds are hard to find. Actually tamarinds are nothing but the pod from a tree in India that is nothing but poor cattle food and if eaten in any quantity is a severe laxative. One 6 ounce bottle of soy sauce.

1 level teaspoon of garlic powder, two State of Maine American sardines packed in soy bean oil. They come packed six sardines to a can and cost about 10c a can. Remove two sardines, put them into a small bowl of vinegar and wash them off. Remove and mash up with a fork and add. Commercial recipes say that they use anchovies to confuse housewives. Anchovies are actually nothing but a salt cured sardine.

Take about six or seven quarts of apples, either green or ripe. Peel them and slice them up and place them in about a six or eight quart cooking pot. Cover them just to the top with brown vinegar. Add one onion sliced up about three inches in diameter. Add the following to the sliced apples: Three level tablespoons of ground cloves, two level tablespoons of ground turmeric, two level tablespoons of ground nutmeg, three level tablespoons of ground allspice, three level tablespoons of powdered coffee or three cups of boiled down black coffee. Bring to a boil and slowly boil for two hours. As the water in the vinegar evaporates add half water and half vinegar to replace it. Stir frequently as apples burn easily, and also tend to stick to the bottom of the pan. Remove and run through a food mill and add eight cups of the puree to the jug or jar.

Now add: two level teaspoons of red ground pepper, four level tablespoons of corn syrup, six level tablespoons of salt, three level tablespoons of mustard, one level tablespoon of sugar.

Now fill the balance of the jug or jar up with vinegar. Shake up well and leave stand for 24 hours and it then is ready to use.

Worcestershire sauce is used for seasoning fish, meat, fowl, vegetables and vegetable juices. Here are just a few of the many ways that it can be used:

1. Poured directly over mashed boiled potatoes and mashed in. This is a popular Irish custom and very good. Be sure to try it.
2. Add three tablespoons to a glass of tomato juice.
3. In cooking pork chops sprinkle generously over the pork chops as you cook them. Gives them a clean, fresh flavor.

4. Beef stew. Add three tablespoons for about every quart of the stew.
5. Blend in two tablespoons into about each cup of brown gravy.
6. Sprinkle generously over turkey, chicken, duck, or goose dressing just as you serve them. It does wonders for dressings.
7. Sprinkle generously over beef hash just before serving.
8. Add one level tablespoon to each bowl of tomato soup just before serving.
9. Sprinkle generously on hamburger buns before putting in the hamburger.

HAMBURGER, HOT DOG, CONEY ISLAND AND CHIEN CHAUD SAUCE HERTER

I have been a great lover of hamburgers, hot dogs and coney islands all of my life. I will never forget the early days of the coney island in this country when you could get a steamed bun with a nice thin coney island weiner in it and an assortment of about a dozen sauces on the bun for 5c. I could polish off at least six of them before a meal and never bother my appetite a bit. They were delicious. They just do not make them that way anymore.

Hamburgers, I cannot get along without and even when I go to Africa on hunting trips I take along my own meat grinder so that I can make my own hamburgers right out in the field. They do not know how to make hamburgers in Africa and I am sure that I am the first man who ever made a hamburger in Africa.

I have tried every possible sauce, vegetable, cheese, etc. on both hamburgers and hot dogs. After a lifetime of testing and experimenting I have perfected the perfect hamburger and hot dog sauce. It is a simple sauce and does not sound like much but do not let it fool you. This sauce has an entirely different taste that brings out everything good in hamburgers and hot dogs. It can be used alone on them or with catsup, mustard, onions, lettuce, pickles and cheese if you prefer.

You must have a blender or food cutter to make this sauce. If you haven't one it is well worth the cost to buy one just for this purpose. It will pay for itself in no time at all.

Here is the recipe and remember a lifetime of experimenting has gone into it.

1 cup packed tight with sliced up dill pickles.
1 cup of sauerkraut.
1 onion about three inches in diameter.
1 large clove of garlic or one level teaspoon of powdered garlic.
¼ level teaspoon of black pepper or six drops of tobasco sauce. Use more or less as you desire.
No salt is needed as the pickles and sauerkraut are salty.

Put all of the ingredients into a blender or food cutter and if necessary add a little sauerkraut juice to get the blender started well. Do not add any more than necessary.

This sauce does not have a sauerkraut taste at all. It has a taste entirely of its own. Spread it liberally on the buns.

Strange as it may seem this sauce is also wonderful mixed with mashed potatoes, with salad, spread on fish and on peanut butter sandwiches. Always keep a quart jar full prepared ahead of time in the refrigerator.

A chien chaud is a hot dog in French Canada.

MUSTARD BORGIA BEST MUSTARD FOR HAMBURGERS, HAM ETC.

Mustard comes from the Brassicacae family the same as cabbage, brussels sprouts and cress. The varieties we use for greens and mustard condiment originated in northwest India. The white mustard and black mustard are grown for their seeds for condiment making only. The word mustard comes from the French word "moustarde" which in turn came from the Latin word "mustum" meaning "must." "Must" is the fresh juice or crushed pulp of grapes. In early Italy ground mustard seed was mixed with the juice of green unripened grapes instead of with vinegar to make a condiment. In England mustard was first called "Hedge Garlic."

The early Greeks and Romans used ground mustard seed mostly to flavor stews and to sprinkle on meat and fish. They called mustard "sinapis."

As early as 42 years after Christ a man named Columella in his writing called De re rustica described the same method for making mustard as is used today mainly softening the seeds in water, grinding them and mixing them with vinegar.

The French town of Dijon became a great center for European mustard making. Dijon mustard however is just another mustard from the early times right up until now and is nothing special. Today most of Dijon mustard contains a trace of horseradish. American made mustards are actually far better.

The Belgians, Hollanders, and the Germans made their mustard from a brown mustard seed right from early times up until now. Their mustards also are nothing at all special and today's American brown mustards are better.

The first cookbook that was made in France was Le Viandier by Taillevent, who was the cook for Charles VII of France. In this book he praises mustard very highly. Here is an actual passage from this book.

"One evening after a great battle with the English, Charles VII, with his three inseparable companions, Dunois, LaHire, and Xaintrailles, came to lodge in the little town of Sainte Menehould, of which only five or six houses remained standing, it having been put to the torch.

"The King and his suite were dying of hunger. There was nothing left in the ravaged countryside. Finally, four pig's feet and three chickens were procured. The King had no cook with him, and the wife of a poor toolmaker was entrusted with the preparation of the chickens. As for the pig's feet, they were simply laid on the grill.

"The good woman roasted the chickens, dipped them in beaten eggs, rolled them in bread crumbs with finest herbs, and covered them with a mustard sauce. The King and his companions left only bones.

"King Charles VII often afterward asked for chicken a la Sainte Menehould. Taillevent understood perfectly what he meant, and prepared it exactly as the toolmaker's wife had done."

This recipe is still popular today in some parts of France, the fine herbs used were powdered leeks or onions and cooked lettuce ground up real fine.

The finest mustard that the world has ever known, however, was invented by an Italian woman by the name of Lucrezia Borgia who was born in 1480 and died in 1519. This woman was a student of both chemistry and cooking. She made some great food discoveries. She would have been well remembered for them if she had not turned her knowledge of chemistry to poisons and got the bad habit of poisoning people she did not care too much for. Sadly today she is only remembered as a poisoner.

Lucrezia discovered early that in order to make mustard sauce less irritating some entirely different flavoring and material must be added to it. She tried literally thousands of different spices, flavors, and oils. She finally discovered that anise flavoring added to mustard gave it a clean, crisp, spice taste and takes away its raw irritating taste. Here is the original recipe. Use French's mustard as the mustard base.

To every six level tablespoons of mustard add one eighth level teaspoon of anise flavoring. You can get this at any grocery store. Stir it in well and leave stand for at least one hour before using.

This simple, wonderful recipe has been forgotten through the ages like the secret of Antonio Stradivari for making violins. Stradivari made some very good violins in his day. His secrets in making them were so simple that no one bothered to remember them including his relatives. He simply used a piece of wax like ambergris that he found walking along the seashore to make his violins sound well. He dissolved the ambergris which is just a substance from the intestine of a constipated whale in alcohol and painted it onto the wood of his violins to keep them from swelling and contracting with weather changes and cracking. He also added some of the ambergris to his resin varnish to make it more flexible.

All great things are simple.

SWEDISH FISH AND SHRIMP SAUCE

In Minnesota with a large portion of its population from Swedish and Norwegian extraction everyone is familiar with Scandinavian recipes.

Scandinavian cooking is wonderful and there are countless very outstanding Scandinavian recipes. This particular recipe however, I think is one of the very finest of all Scandinavian recipes. Here is its history:

John Baptiste Bernadotte was born in Pau, France in 1763. In 1810 he was adopted by the King of Sweden, Charles the XIII. In 1813 he fought against the French. In 1818 he became King of Sweden and received the name of Charles the XIV. He married Bernadine Eugenie Desiree Clary of Marseilles, France.

Charles the XIV of Sweden was a great lover of fish and sea food. He preferred Swedish cooking to all other. His own Swedish cook made a special recipe for him to use on cold shrimp and on hot or cold fish. This recipe is used throughout Scandinavia today as well as in many good American-Scandinavian restaurants. This is the original recipe and it just cannot be equaled for the purpose it is intended for.

Place one-half cup of white vinegar in a mixing bowl, add one and a half cups of olive oil or salad oil. Add two level tablespoons of grated onion. One level tablespoon of dried mustard or one and a half of wet mustard if you do not have the dry. One-eighth teaspoon of black pepper. Three level teaspoons of fresh dill heads chopped up as finely as possible. Mix together well. Whip a small amount of whipping cream and fold in four heaping tablespoons.

The sad part of this recipe is that it can only be made when fresh dill is available. To make this recipe the year round freeze fresh dill heads in water when they are in season and store them in your deep freeze if you are lucky enough to have one.

This sauce is expensive to make but better than any tartar sauce by a long margin.

NOTE: It contains no sugar.

Sandwiches

BLACK WATCH SCOTTISH HUNTER'S SANDWICH

As we all know sandwiches got their name in the 18th century from the Earl of Sandwich, an English nobleman. He popularized sandwiches. Sandwiches had been in use many centuries but without a definite name. The Earl of Sandwich was a great card player and rather than stop playing cards or leave the card table he simply had sandwiches brought to him instead of wasting his time going to meals.

One of the best and most different sandwiches was also developed in the 18th century in Scotland. This is the recipe as it was brought over by the early pioneers. It is a very different good recipe and one to try at the first opportunity.

Take two eggs and beat with one cup of milk to form a batter. This is enough for four sandwiches. Take two pieces of bread and dip them into the batter on both sides. Put small thin pieces of butter on one side of each piece of bread. Place a slice of cold chicken or ham on the buttered side of one of the slices. Add a slice of cheddar or similar cheese one-eighth inch thick onto the meat. Put the other slice of bread on top of the cheese. Put some butter in a frying pan and fry both sides until the bread is slightly brown on both sides. Now remove and put in a covered baking dish and bake in your oven at 400 degrees for about 15 minutes. The time depends on the type of cheese you use. The cheese must be melted before removing. If you have aluminum foil wrap the sandwich with it and bake. Do not try to fry the sandwich until the cheese melts because if you do the bread will be burned black. Cheese on bread should never be fried until melted. This hunter's sandwich is a delicious meal that will stay with you.

OYSTER LOAF SANDWICH

The oyster loaf sandwich is one of New Orleans' earliest and best foods.

Louisiana was named for Louis XIV or Louis Le Grand, as he was called. It was colonized at New Biloxi Fort on the gulf coast in 1699 by Canadians, Pierre Le Moyne, Sieur d'Iberville and his brother, Jean Baptiste Le Moyne, Sieur de Bienville. Pierre died shortly after the colonizing took place. Jean was ordered to move the colony up river. The French called the river Fleuve Saint Louis, the local Indians "great water" or misi sippi. Nouvelle Orleans was named for Louis Philippe duc d' Orleans the French regent at the time. The duke was well hated in France and the name Nouvelle was used as a pointed jab, the word Nouvelle in French is a feminine word and not

Softshell crab making pens on a Louisiana bayou. Crabs with hard shells are placed in these wooden boxes and lowered into the water just enough so that the crabs are slightly covered with water. When the crabs shed their hard shell, they are removed and sold before they can grow another hard shell. Their entire body and legs are soft and tender at this shell-shedding stage.

used with a masculine name, made him out as a complete fairy. Bienville called the town, Crescent City, because it was founded on a crescent of the river. Bienville picked the site in 1717 and in 1721 had Adrien de Pauger assistant King's engineer lay out the town in the shape of a square. The French speaking people immediately called the town the Vieux Carre which translates in English to "Old Square".

Bienville was a practical hard working man and he well knew that you have to keep people well fed to keep them happy. He taught the early colonists how to cook. Eighty of them were criminals shipped out of France for selling salt without paying a tax on it. Something like our old time bootleggers. He showed them all how to prepare turtles, oysters, crabs, alligator tail, catfish and such delicacies that were available.

One of the first and best foods Bienville taught the colonists to prepare was oyster loafs. Here is how they were originally made.

Take a pistolet or French roll about six or seven inches long. Slice it lengthwise. Sprinkle red dry wine over the cut surfaces of the roll. Take fresh oysters and roll them lightly in corn meal or flour. Deep fry them until they are just slightly brown. Cover one half of the roll with the fried oysters put the other half of the roll on top of the oysters and you have an oyster loaf sandwich that is wonderful eating.

As the years went by and tomatoes finally were discovered from the Indians and lettuce seed came over from Europe, sliced tomatoes and lettuce were also put on these sandwiches. Even mayonnaise, mustard and catsup are today used on this famous sandwich. No matter what you add to the fried oysters the red dry wine on the soft center bread of the roll is essential for the right taste. Today pieces of narrow three inch wide French bread is used to replace the hard rolls. The hard crusted French rolls are better though. The oyster loaf is still one of the most eaten foods in all of New Orleans.

BURRO SANDWICH

Aztec Princess Papantizin was Montezuma's sister and lived in a beautiful palace called Tlalteloleo in Mexico. In 1509 ten years before the murderers Hernando Cortez and his soldiers came to Mexico she appeared in court before Montezuma and King Netzahualpilli and the entire court of Aztec nobles and described in detail a vision which she had just had in which a child with wings and a cross on its head told her that ships would arrive with the sign of the cross on them and that these ships would bring

Aztec Princess Papantizin Tells Her Vision At The Aztec Court.

a knowledge of the true God with them. A complete record was made of what she said at the Aztec court and much concern developed about it.

At this time the Aztecs were killing about 20,000 people a year as sacrifices to their gods. They also were eating the victims. Do not frown upon this as the French, Hollanders, Danes, and Germans not too many centuries back were also cannibals all along their coastal areas. Meat was scarce and they ate each other to vary a tiresome menu of fish and mollusks.

Princess Papantizin was a talented woman and gave much to our present day culture. She originated the food known today as refried beans. Refried beans are today a basic Mexican as well as Texas, New Mexico, Arizona, and Southern California food. All of our edible beans that we eat today all originated in North and Central America and were developed entirely by the Indians.

In 1883 a man named Luke Short came to the Oriental Saloon at Tombstone, Arizona. The saloon was run by a law officer by the name of Wyatt Earp. Luke Short took a job at the Oriental Saloon as a card dealer. Luke Short was a farm boy from West Texas. He was a kind gentle man, well dressed and well mannered. He was however one of the fastest man who ever lived with a revolver but never used a gun unless absolutely forced to. Luke being from Texas liked refried beans and when he came to the Oriental Saloon in Arizona he soon had every restaurant in town making "Burro Sandwiches" as he called them. Here is the original recipe and they are very delicious.

Take a pound of dried pinto beans. If you cannot find any in your area get whatever dried beans that you can. If no dried beans are available use a can of cooked kidney beans. In the case of kidney beans of course skip the cooking of the beans. Soak the dried beans in water overnight. Next day place them in a pot with enough water to cover them. Add a half level teaspoon of salt and red pepper to taste, and one two inch in diameter onion chopped up. Boil until the beans are well done. Add water from time to time so that the beans are always just covered. Remove from the stove and drain off the liquid in a bowl and save it. Now take a potato masher and mash the beans. As you mash them add just enough of the liquid that the beans were boiled in to form a smooth paste of medium consistency. Now put enough bacon grease, lard or shortening into a good sized frying pan so that the pan's surface is just barely covered with the grease. Put the beans into the pan and fry them until they just begin to slightly brown. Stir them as they fry. Remove from the stove. Take two slices of bread; on one side of one slice lightly butter the bread. Take a spoon and coat the buttered side with about a fourth inch thick layer of the fried beans. Put grated onion on top of the beans and grated yellow cheese such as longhorn or a good medium or sharp cheddar cheese on top of the grated onion. Take a level teaspoon of chili powder and mix it with three level teaspoons of water. Sprinkle this sauce lightly onto the unbuttered slice of bread and place it on top of the bean covered slice.

This is a rare, fine sandwich and impossible to buy in any restaurant anymore. They still make a "burro" sandwich in some towns but they take short cuts in making them and they just are not what they should be.

SANDWICH DORA HAND

I do not wish the people who made and are making American so called "historical movies" for television and theaters any bad luck but if they would all drop dead it would be better for everyone. They have stupidly and purposely twisted American history with the sole purpose of falsely poisoning the public's mind and putting money into their own pockets without any regard for the good of the country. Although usually considered to be smart they are really a stupid lot as truth about American history is much more interesting than their untrue propaganda.

Dodge City, Kansas was just another western outpost until the Santa Fe railroad came in and it became a shipping point for buffalo hides and meat and Texas cattle. Cattle were shipped from the town for nearly fifteen years. Buffalo hides and meat were shipped until every single buffalo was killed. The cattle and the buffalo brought millions of dollars into Dodge City and quite naturally the town expanded and people from the East, Middle West and the South migrated into Dodge City. It was always a well-run town, a little wild at times but always under control. It never at anytime contained any more prostitutes, grafters, or tin horn sports per capita than are to be found in Hollywood today at anytime. Culturally it at all times was far ahead of present day Hollywood. Entertainment was excellent. Such stars as Eddie Foy liked Dodge City and played there as well as other Broadway stars. Light opera songs were heard nightly and well liked. Food and liquor in Dodge City were very good and it had a number of very excellent restaurants that offered Western beef, veal, buffalo, quail, wild doves, wild ducks, venison as well as pork, ham, chicken and turkey. Scotch and Irish whiskeys were available as well as the best of American whiskeys. You could always get the best American beers as well as the best of Irish and English beers. Ice chests were used and the beer was kept at the proper cool temperature. Contrell and Cochrane Stout Irish beer distributed by Ross of Belfast and Dublin, Ireland was a great favorite. Champagne was available.

The gunfighters were actually few and far between. All the ones of note were businessmen, cattlemen, saloon and restaurant owners, gamblers, law officers or bank robbers. Gunfighting was a side line to all of them. All of the ones of any note were blue-eyed. Most of them were ex-confederate soldiers and strongly pro-confederate and highly sensitive about any remarks against the confederacy. Many of them were related. Jessie James, the first of the gunfighters and his cousins, the Younger brothers, the Dalton brothers, and John Ringo are a typical example. Their blood lines all came from the Island of Britain. The Picts were the only true British people, like the Indians are the only true Americans. The French, Danes, Norwegians, Italians, and German types of people invaded and fought in Britain throughout the centuries. The Picts or true Britains were murdered off or enslaved the same as we did to the Indians. All of the invaders intermarried through the centuries and this mixture produced the present British race and most of the Scotch race. This hybrid race produced throw-offs that would gunfight. Very few people would gunfight under any circumstances as the odds were such that if you had any number of gunfights you were almost sure to get killed. Here are some of the facts on gunfighting. John Mclinn who rode with Quantrill and Jesse James was a good friend of mine as well as A. M. King, Wyatt Earp's old deputy. George Earp, cousin of Wyatt, is still alive at this writing. The Colt .45 caliber single action revolver is quite easy to shoot and a natural pointer. If you hit a man with the huge .45 caliber bullet he died in nearly all cases but rarely dropped when hit. In order to win a gunfight you had to shoot a man in the heart or head before he could shoot you. Hit anyplace else in the body a tough well muscled man would shoot you several times before he fell. Drawing fast was not much of an advantage at all. Shooting accurately was of much greater importance if you were to live through a gunfight. Drawing fast and shooting accurately enough to stop a man from shooting you, never went together too well. Such little things as a pistol sticking for a split second in its holster, being slightly off balance, not feeling just right, having a headache or a hangover or more than three drinks of whiskey, a too loose pistol cylinder, a worn sear, all meant sure death in gunfighting if you were up against a good opponent whose luck was running good. On top of this ammunition was poorly made in these days and it was not uncommon to have two shells that would not fire out of five.

The gunfighters stuffed newspaper into the ends of their holsters, rubbed graphite on the inside of their holsters, filed off the front sights to prevent the gun from sticking in its holster, bought new guns as soon as the cylinders or hammer became loose but still with all these precautions gunfighting remained a very poor gamble for both opponents.

Into Dodge City came lovely Dora Hand. A beautiful black haired, white skinned woman with gray-green eyes and fine manners. She immediately took a job in a dance hall as a singer. She had a marvelous voice and sang popular songs as well as light opera. Dodge City right down to a cowpuncher just in from the cattle trails liked Dora Hand's singing whether it was popular songs or opera. Dora became a great personal friend of James H. (Dog) Kelley, Mayor of Dodge City. They called Kelley, Dog Kelley, because he loved greyhound racing and raised fine greyhounds for racing. Dora kept strictly by herself or with another singer. She slept with no man and said she did not care to marry. These facts were well known in Dodge City and well respected. Dora Hand also went under the name of Fannie Keenan. Her real name was not known until long after her death. Her real name was Germaine Dupont and she came from New York City. Her wealthy parents trained her to be an opera singer and she had every sign and possibility of being one of the world's greatest. She fell in love with a young man named Marvin Ewest who worked as an accountant for a marine importing firm. Her parents did not approve of Marvin and her influencial father had him discharged from his job. Marvin had his neck broken when a heavy import box was accidentally knocked off the top of a pile by a stevedore as he left his office after being discharged. Germaine Dupont left New York one week later and headed for Dodge City. She never returned and never wrote to her parents. She, like Wyatt Earp, came to Dodge City to forget, after the death of a sweetheart.

Mayor Kelley had to go to Fort Dodge to be hospitalized. Before he left he asked Dora if she wanted to live in his small home behind the Green Front saloon until he got back. He did not want to leave the house empty while he was away. Dora said that she would stay in the house for him. She got another singer by the name of Ruth McGovern to live with her in Kelley's house.

Texan James W. (Spike) Kennedy had a long time grudge against Kelley. He had come into a place Kelley was running at one time and asked for a bottle of beer. When he got the beer he said, "You sure have to go a long ways to get beer like this, warm and flat." Kelley wasn't feeling too well and was irritable. He grabbed Kennedy by the collar and threw him out into the street. One thing led to another and soon Kennedy had developed a real bad grudge against Kelley. Kennedy was just a fair gunfighter. On the night Kelley left for the hospital Kennedy got to drinking a bit too much. He went over to Kelley's house and shot through the side of the house into the area where he knew Kelley's bed to be. Dora Hand was in the bed. The bullet mushroomed badly going through the wood of the house and struck her right in the center of her right breast and tore a large hole in her heart and back. She died instantly. Ruth McGovern ran screaming out of the house. Kennedy sobered up instantly. He knew that from that moment on he would be hunted like a dog and given no more quarter than a mad dog by anyone. Killing a woman for any reason was sure death in the early west and killing well respected Dora Hand, the most popular woman of the west, put a short number on any man's days. He didn't wait a second but got his horse and headed for Mexico.

Within minutes everyone in Dodge knew of Dora's death. Word went out in every direction to shoot Kennedy on sight. Wyatt Earp and Bat Masterson got together a posse and got Kennedy. Bat shot him in the arm shattering it completely. Kennedy had a wealthy father and was finally freed. He was killed shortly after this in a gunfight.

Dora Hand was a fine cultured woman. Some in Dodge thought she was married to a man named Hand which was not at all true. Some writers have said she was a prostitute which was entirely untrue also. She was used to good cooking. When she came to Dodge, Dog Kelley was running a restaurant among other things and she trained his cook for him. It is rightly said that you could get no better food anyplace in the United States than at Dodge.

Dora created a sandwich known in Dodge as Sandwich Dora Hand. It was very popular and was truthfully said to taste better after a cool beer than anything else in the world. Men would ride miles to get one. Here is the original recipe. Take two slices of bread or a hamburger bun. Butter the side of both pieces lightly. Take several fish and clean them. Catfish, bullheads, perch, crappies, or any good eating fish are excellent for this purpose. Fill a pot with water. Put two level tablespoons of vinegar in the water, a quarter teaspoon of black pepper and half teaspoon of salt. Put the fish in the pot and boil the fish until well done. Depending on the size of the fish this takes from three to about nine minutes. Remove the fish and let them drain on a paper. Place two level tablespoons of butter into a frying pan and melt it over a medium heat. Now place the fish on a plate and remove all the skin and bones. Mash up the fish well with your fork. Place the mashed up fish in your frying pan and fry it lightly until just slightly browned. As it fries keep mashing it up so that it is in small pieces. With a spoon take some of the fish and spread a thick layer over the butter side of one piece of the bread or bun. Press the fish well down into the bread or bun so that it stays well in place. Put thinly sliced dill pickle over the fish and thinly sliced onion over the dill pickles. Put a little mustard over the onions. Salt well and serve hot. Today a little tartar sauce goes well on this sandwich also.

I have eaten countless numbers of these Dora Hand sandwiches and always greatly enjoy them. This is a great food and should be as popular as a good hamburger. Be sure to try this famous sandwich at your first opportunity. Bend your head in a little prayer for Dora too; she was a fine woman.

POOR BOY SANDWICH

Probably the two most important things that were invented in New Orleans are the Poor Boy Sandwich and the expression O. K. now so widely used all over the world. The expression O.K. came from the New Orleans dock area. The French speaking people of New Orleans said, "Aux Quais", when anything arrived or departed properly from the docks or even from railroad stations. In French these words are pronounced O.K. Soon everyone used the expression for anything that was all right and O.K. spread from New Orleans to every corner of the world.

The Poor Boy sandwich was invented by the brothers, Clovis and Benjamin Martin. In 1919 the brothers had a restaurant in the French Market. In 1930 they started a restaurant on Chef highway. They invented a sandwich made as follows and called it the Poor Boy Sandwich.

Take a six or seven inch hard-crusted French roll or pistolet. Slice it lengthwise. On each side of the roll sprinkle a level teaspoon of French dressing made up of one fourth oil and three fourths vinegar lightly seasoned with onion, garlic, salt and pepper. Add leaf lettuce torn up into small pieces, thinly sliced tomatoes, cut up into small pieces and a few grated onions. Unless the lettuce and tomatoes are cut up into fairly small pieces they tend to pull out as you eat the sandwich spoiling the sandwich entirely. Add slices of thinly sliced beef with a little mustard on them and slices of thinly sliced cheddar

The corner on Chef Highway in New Orleans where the world famous Poor Boy sandwich was invented. There are no longer any restaurants on this corner.

Martin's present day restaurant on Chef Highway right across the corner from where the Poor Boy sandwich was invented.

cheese. This is the original Poor Boy Sandwich and it is a thing of beauty and a joy forever. John Gendusa, a baker friend of Clovis and Benjamin, made them a special real long loaf of French bread only about three inches wide. They sliced off pieces of this narrow French bread and used it in place of the French rolls. As time went by the Poor Boy Sandwich simply became a sandwich where you ordered anything that you wanted on it, depending upon how much money you wanted to spend on the sandwich. Butter, mayonnaise, salami, dill pickles, catsup, etc. The original Poor Boy Sandwich, however, has never been equaled.

SALOON SANDWICH OR TARTINE TAVERNE

The saloon sandwich will always rank among the top foods ever created in this world. It is a real symphony of good tastes.

A saloon sandwich is made as follows.

Get a good beef roast. Can be from any part of the animal, a shoulder roast, rump roast, rib roast or similar roast, all work very well. Place the roast in a covered pan, this is important. Put about one inch of water in the bottom of the pan. Add one onion about one inch square for a three pound roast, salt and pepper to taste, ¼ teaspoon of ground nutmeg. Cook the roast slowly at about 325 to 350 degrees for three to three and a half or four hours or until the roast is well done all the way through. This is a recipe that always has the meat well done. When done remove from the oven. Take two slices of rye bread, white bread, or a bun. Dip one side of each slice of the bread in the natural gravy or both sides of the bun. The words "au jus" in French simply means natural gravy of the meat without flour or cornstarch added and this is what you have here. Place a thin slice of roast beef without fat between two slices of bread or between the bun. Put a generous coat of mustard on the top side of the beef. Never use gravy with flour or cornstarch in it on the bread or bun. The sauce for the bread or bun must be the natural juices of the beef plus salt, pepper, onion, nutmeg and water nothing else. The saloon sandwich has a distinctive, fabulously hardy good taste all of its own.

The saloon sandwich is not at all a new comer. It was invented and served by Beauvillier's Restaurant, the first really modern type of restaurant founded in Paris, France in 1782. The restaurant ran for 15 years and brought a lot of honest happiness to many people. Other restaurants of the time such as Meot, Legacque, Very Freres, Henneveu and Baleine copied the food of Beauvillier's but never came even close to equaling it.

Mr. Beauvillier has the following selections on his menu every day all created by himself.

12 different kinds of soup.
24 different kinds of hor d' oeuvres.
20 different recipes of mutton.
15 different recipes of beef.
15 different recipes of veal.
30 different recipes for poultry and game birds and game animals.
24 different fish recipes.
50 different pastries and dessert recipes.

As is often the sad case when Mr. Beauvilliers died no one could take his place and his restaurant closed which was a grave catastrophy.

The saloon sandwich became very popular in Germany and in England. Immigrants brought the recipe to the United States. Saloons at this time furnished free food and the saloon sandwich at once became the most popular food item in saloons all over the states. It is still served in good saloons in much of America. There is many a man from ditch digger to millionaire that would not think of missing his noon day lunch of a saloon sandwich and a glass of beer. Actually there is nothing better.

MARGGRAF SANDWICH

In 1747 a German chemist named Marggraf discovered how to make sugar from sugar beets. He produced brown sugar, not white sugar. The first day that he produced the brown sugar he went down to a bakery shop and bought a loaf of fresh bread. He bought some butter from another small shop. Right in his work room he cut off a slice of bread, spread it well with butter and then covered the butter heavily with the brown sugar. He pressed the brown sugar down into the butter with his knife. One bite of this wonderful sandwich told him that he had indeed made a great discovery. He made Marggraf sandwiches for some favorite children of his in the neighborhood and all of them thought it was wonderful. I do not think that any child should be brought up without having plenty of Marggraf sandwiches. There just is nothing better tasting and nothing better for the health of a child. The combination of brown sugar, good butter and bread has never been beaten. This is a great adult sandwich too and a great one for wilderness trips. If you have not tried this famous sandwich do not let another day go by without trying one.

SANDWICH KOSSEL

Albrecht Kossel was a famous German chemist born in 1853 and died in 1927. In 1910 he was awarded the Nobel Prize for physiology and Medicine for his work on the chemistry of the human cell. Kossel was not only a great chemist but a very practical man who tried to improve on the living of everyday life. He often said that his greatest discovery and gift to mankind was the sandwich Kossel. It certainly has given real delight to countless thousands of people all over the world. Here is the original recipe.

Take a slice of good rye bread. Lightly butter the bread. Then spread a good medium heavy layer of mayonnaise on the bread and over this liverwurst sliced about one fourth of an inch thick. Use either as a sandwich or as a before-the-meal appetizer. This is one of my very favorite sandwiches and a very different real taste treat. The rye bread, mayonnaise and liverwurst blend together to give you a sandwich with amazingly good taste.

BURRITOS SANDWICH

In 1769 the Spaniard Gasper de Portola with a land expedition left San Diego in July and walked up the rolling hills of the coastline to the Indian town of "Yang-na" arriving there the first day of August. Father Juan Crespi who was with him renamed the Indian town, "Our Lady Queen of the Angels" because August 2nd was the religious day for, "Our Lady Queen of the Angels." In Spanish this was "Nuestra Senora la Reina de Los Angeles." The Indians picked the spot because there were a few fresh water springs there. Nothing was done on the site, however, until September 1781 when a few buildings were put up. A mission had been built a few miles to the east in 1771 called San Gabriel. In 1835 Los Angeles was made a city by the Congress of Mexico. When war broke out between the United States and Mexico, the people of Los Angeles fought among themselves in a civil war. The pro-Mexican factions against the pro-United States factions. Commodore Robert F. Stockton and Captain John C. Fremont raised the flag of the United States over Los Angeles on August 13, 1846. The Indians and inhabitants of Los Angeles wanted Mexican rule and chased out the United States occupation force. In 1847 the city was retaken by General S. W. Kearny, and Commodore Stockton. Mexico has, of course, never forgotten the loss of this tremendously rich area.

The climate of Los Angeles is very good with an average of 62 degrees a year. Today the only trouble with Los Angeles is that it has turned into a freeway jungle and is not at all the nice place to live that it was when the Indians had it.

Early California cooking was a mixture of European and Spanish, brought over by the Catholic Missionaries and mixed with Indian cooking with the Indian cookings always remaining the basis.

The taco of today which is a thin corn meal pancake folded over various mixtures of ground meat, beans, and cheese is a quite recent food. Taco in Spanish means "the butt of a billiard cue." Cheese was unknown to the Mexicans until the Europeans arrived. There were no goats, sheep, or cattle in North, Central or South America to get milk from to make any cheese.

Father Juan Crespi got European wheat growing in the Los Angeles area and started cattle, goats, and sheep. The brothers and priests taught the people cheese making as there was no other way to preserve the milk. The day of the milkman had not yet arrived. The Spaniards, as well as other settlers, tired of the fried corn meal pancakes of Mexico—most people do.

As soon as the first white flour was ground at the missions, Father Crespi made up a sandwich of his own and called it the "burrito." It was an immediate success and still is found in many areas of the Southwest. Los Angeles has never produced a recipe since, anywhere near as good.

Here is the original recipe.

Take a mixing bowl. Put in one fourth of a cup of fine corn meal and 1 cup of white flour. One level teaspoon of salt. Add enough cold water to form a heavy whipping cream consistency. Then stir in two level tablespoons of shortening, preferably bacon fat.

Farmer's market in Los Angeles.

In a large skillet with medium heat fry thin pancakes from the mixture, about seven or eight inches in diameter. When the pancakes are done, put the following in the center of each pancake and fold it over. Eat at once.

Two heaping tablespoons of ground meat such as hamburger, or venison fried in a frying pan and stirred so it keeps granulated and separate. Season the meat with salt and red cayenne pepper to taste. Two heaping tablespoons of chili prepared with the Mary Agreda recipe found in this book. One heaping tablespoon of grated or chopped up good strong yellow cheddar cheese. Roquefort cheese is also very good. The majority of Mexican people as well as other people, I find, definitely prefer burritos to tacos. They are awfully good eating.

Los Angeles today has its, "restaurant row," a street with many expensive restaurants. If you eat with your eyes the food is all right, presentation is very good but I always prefer to eat strictly with my mouth.

Farmer's Market used to serve good food but the last time I was there the roast beef was tough, the pastry frostings not made with butter, and the spaghetti sauce really indifferent. Nothing there to equal a good old burrito.

One of a number of restaurants in Disneyland. I still prefer bringing my own sandwiches.

Monorail at Disneyland.

Steamboat ride in Disneyland.

Castle in Disneyland is a scaled down version.

I have always been a great fan of Walt Disney films. His animal films and his cartoons, I have really enjoyed. Disneyland, however, to me is disappointing. It is a relatively small place—many state fairs are much larger. The motels surrounding Disneyland cover much more territory than Disneyland itself. The fantasy castle is a scaled down model and doesn't look like it does on film. The monorail is the same that gave you a rough ride at the Seattle World's Fair. I can't see why they call it a monorail as it actually rides on three rail surfaces. Much of the area is simply used for advertising adult products, such as shirts, etc. I wish they had someplace in it where you could see the good Disney animal films or cartoons. The kindest thing I could say about the food is that I wish I had brought along my own sandwiches. There are no pacifiers for small children and no penny suckers to quiet down older children. One place has a box of paper diapers which they sell one at a time. One good healthy child could use up the entire diaper supply in a day.

I went to Knott's Berry Farm. They have an imitation small mountain with an imitation mine in it. Some reptiles in one area. Moved in some western type buildings and built some western type buildings. There are no berries grown on the farm.

I am in favor of giving some land back to the Indians, they didn't do such a bad job with it at all.

SHUT YOUR MOUTH SANDWICH OR TARTINE FERMEZ VOTRE BOUCHE

In 1800 an Irishman, named John McDonogh, came to New Orleans from Baltimore. He went into business buying and selling farm produce and land. Within six short years he had amassed a very vast fortune. He never married but visited a Sister at the Ursuline Convent. He had gone with the girl before she had joined the order. It was said that he went with the daughter of Don Almonester, a Spanish nobleman, who lived in New Orleans. This is not true as Don Almonester was dead two years before John came to New Orleans. His daughter was only nine years old in 1806. She did go to school at the Ursuline Convent that John McDonogh frequently visited.

When John McDonogh died, he left three fourths of a million dollars to the city of New Orleans to build public schools and the same amount to Baltimore for public schools. Shrewd Frenchmen in New Orleans built 39 public schools from the interest of the fund before they finally used the fund itself to build a school.

John McDonogh had a great many slaves. In his will he gave them their freedom and each of them a ticket back to Africa. All of his slaves went back home shortly after his death. This certainly was fair thinking of a type rarely found in this world.

John loved children of all colors and any that stopped at any place in which he lived were always well fed. He believed that the best possible food for children and a food that quickly and well filled their stomachs was long French hard crusted rolls or pistolets. I certainly must agree that he was very close to the perfect answer. He made a sandwich that he called, "Shut Your Mouth Sandwich", and it is a great food invention. It is a far better food than you will find today in any New Orleans restaurant. Sad to say it is almost completely forgotten in New Orleans except by a few of the old French families. Here is the original recipe.

Take a long narrow hard crusted French roll or pistolet, about six to seven inches long. Cut off about a half to three fourths of an inch from one end. Poke your longest finger down into the cut off end, as far as it will go, making a hole in the soft bread in the center of the roll. Take a level teaspoon of salad dressing made up of ¼ oil and ¾ vinegar with onion, garlic, salt and pepper seasoning and pour it down the hole. Put mustard, grated onions and grated pickles to taste, down into the hole. Then put a small nicely fried or baked pork sausage down into the hole. Eat the sandwich from the open end so that the sausage and ingredients cannot escape but keep pushing back into the roll as you eat.

This is the way the "Shut Your Mouth Sandwich" was originally made. It can, however, have a roll of beef hamburger or weiner used instead of the pork sausage or even pieces of chicken. One day John McDonogh's cook ran completely out of meat for the sandwiches. She cut off the ends of the rolls as usual but simply poured honey and syrup down the holes on the rolls and the children wolved them down enjoying them almost as well as with meat. Most important of all the rolls filled them up well and rapidly.

I pray John McDonogh is in heaven. He was a truly, great, kind man.

SANDWICH HOLY NIGHT

In Salzburg, Austria a poor farm girl came to town to try her luck as a seamstress making dresses for the local ladies. She met a young man named Mohr who thought that she looked like a promising means of support if handled properly. He married her but when she became pregnant he deserted her for a more likely prospect. She had a son and named him Joseph after the Husband of Mary, the Mother of Jesus. She desired, of course, that the boy be baptized but no one wanted to associate themselves as baptism sponsors for this poor woman's child. Finally the public hangman of the area who was a devout Catholic offered to sponsor the child if the Mother would accept him as the sponsor. The poor distraught Mother was glad to get a sponsor at all for Joseph and readily accepted the kind hangman's offer.

As the boy grew up he proved to be exceptionally intelligent and a good worker. He supported his Mother by not only working for the various store keepers by day but by singing in the better taverns by night. Everyone thought very well of him. He told the local priests that he wanted to become a priest. He was obviously such an outstanding man that the Church agreed to educate him for the priesthood. He went through the seminary with flying colors.

The town of Oberndorf at Saint Nicholas Church needed a new priest as their priest died suddenly of a heart attack. Father Mohr was much too young for the job but he was sent there in the year 1818 on a temporary basis until a suitable older priest could be found. Oberndorf is on the banks of the river Salzach near Salzburg. In recent years the town became famous for making Mauser rifles.

On December 23, 1818 Father Mohr, as usual, tried the Church organ. He played fairly well himself and enjoyed playing a little each day. This day, however, the organ would not play at all. On examination, he found that a mouse had eaten several holes in the leather of the organ's bellows. He knew that the bellows could not be repaired by Christmas. Christmas Mass without music was unthinkable. He decided that the only thing to do was to write a song and have the children sing it to replace somehow—the usual organ music. Father Mohr knew the organist could play a guitar and he decided to ask him to accompany the children with him. Father Mohr went back to his room and within a few minutes and without any seeming effort at all he wrote Silent Night. The song flowed out onto his writing paper so quickly that it surprised him. He never wrote any music before this time or never again afterwards.

Later in the day Franz Gruber, the organist at Saint Nicholas Church, stopped by to check with Father Mohr on the music for the Christmas Mass. Gruber was 31 years old. He was a school teacher in the nearby town of Arnsdorf. Father Mohr told Herr Gruber that the organ was out of order. The only solution he explained was to have the children sing to replace some of the organ music with Gruber and himself accompanying them on guitars. He quickly went through the song he had written and gave Gruber the original copy. He told Gruber to polish up the music and improve on it as best he could. Gruber admitted that the song did not sound too bad and he agreed at once that he would do what he could to make it better.

On Christmas Eve after midnight Mass, Father Mohr and Herr Gruber and the children's choir marched down the main isle of the church to the altar. Father Mohr and Herr Gruber played their guitars while the children sang Silent Night. The congregation enjoyed the song but when it was over no one remembered it.

Father Mohr laid his guitar down on the communion rail and mingled with the congregation as they got up to leave.

A little girl tugged on Father Mohr's habit and asked, "Father who makes the moon go around?"

Father Mohr bowed down and replied. "The Virgin Mary of course. Drives it in a sleigh."

The little girl said, "I suppose Jesus sits in the front seat."

Everyone chuckled and this little bit of conversation was remembered and the song completely forgotten.

Father Mohr brought out a platter full of sandwiches for the children's choir and they all happily took one. Father Mohr's children sandwiches were the talk of the children world. The original recipe is as follows. Take a slice of white bread. Butter it lightly. Take a block of sweet cooking chocolate. Place a pot of water on the stove and boil it. Place a small pot in the boiling water and melt the chocolate in it. You must use solid sweet chocolate. Chocolate syrup will not work at all as it has a very undesirable sandy taste not suitable for these sandwiches at all. When barely melted spread a layer of the soft chocolate about one eighth of an inch thick on the bread. Over this spread a layer of red currant jelly one eighth of an inch thick. Now cut the bread in two and put one half of the bread on top of the other half so that there is a layer of chocolate in the center of the sandwich and on top of the sandwich. These sandwiches are incredibly good. During World War II food was very scarce in Austria. I have had Austrian's tell me that the only thing that they really missed during these years of privation were Holy Night Sandwiches.

Father Mohr was a deeply religious man but he liked to go down to the local taverns on occasion and have a few beers or a glass of wine with the river boatmen and the drinking element of the town. He often joined in their hearty singing of beer tavern songs which at times can get a little off color to say the least. It is remembered that he taught the men that if a stein or glass of beer looked like it was going to foam over as it was poured that all you had to do was to poke your finger down into the stein or glass and it would definitely not foam over. This is a very useful bit of knowledge at times and was deeply appreciated.

People being what they are, some of the older members of the Church did not take to Father Mohr at all. They wrote to the Bishop asking that he be removed and an older man put in his place. They forgot one of the prime teachings of Christ himself, "Judge not yet you be judged," and they forgot that the Great Christ Himself enjoyed a good glass of wine now and then and even miraculously created wine on occasion for friends. When it came time for him to be murdered he chose wine to be his own blood. I have always said that Heaven will never be over crowded with Christians. I have met thousands of people who called themselves Christians but only a handful who ever actually practiced Christ's teachings.

The Bishop removed Father Mohr at once.

A month later a repairman named Karl Mauracher from the town of Zillertal came and put new leather bellows in the organ. Herr Gruber was there to test the repaired organ. He played Silent Night. Karl Mauracher was impressed with the song and asked for a copy of it which Herr Gruber gladly gave him. Mauracher took the song back to Zillertal and had it published giving no credit at all to Father Mohr or Herr Gruber. This miraculous song quickly spread all over the world. Father Mohr and Herr Gruber were never given a penny for writing it although millions were made from the song. When they were old dying men they were finally acknowledged as the true creators of Silent Night, but were given none of the money that the song had earned. They both died as poor as church mice.

The people of Oberndorf finally built a chapel on the site of the old Saint Nicholas Church in memory of these two men. Herr Gruber's guitar was handed down in his family and today every Christmas Eve it is used to play Silent Night in the memorial chapel. Even the location of Father Mohr's grave is unknown.

If you ever sing this song in your home, church or on television send a donation to the Father Mohr, Memorial Chapel Statue Fund, Oberndorf, Austria. When they get enough they will put up a statue of Father Mohr, he certainly deserves one. Better yet make your donation the price of a six pack of good beer, he would understand this.

HOW TO MAKE A PEANUT BUTTER SANDWICH

Peanut butter is strictly American. Peanuts were first cultivated by the Indians. People in Europe have never taken very well to peanuts for food in any form.

I have always liked a good peanut butter sandwich but unless you make it yourself these days they are absolutely impossible to get. Most modern cooks have no idea how to prepare one. Peanut butter is very difficult to handle if not handled just so. Here is how you do it and it is a trick well worth knowing.

Take your slice of bread and butter it well with soft butter. Put it into your toaster and leave it for about 60 to 75 seconds depending upon your toaster or until the butter is well melted and soaked into the bread. Quickly remove the bread and while it is piping hot spread your peanut butter onto the bread. You will find that the melted butter will soften the peanut butter and make it flow onto the bread smoothly and evenly. As you know peanut butter is next to impossible to spread evenly as it comes from the jar. Now depending upon whether you like a sour or a sweet sandwich put sliced dill pickles or jelly onto the peanut butter. The pickles or jelly will keep the peanut butter from sticking to your mouth preventing you from getting its good nutty taste. Makes a really fine sandwich.

WELSH RABBIT

Wales the home of the Welsh people is a region that has produced some of the world's finest cooking. The Welsh are very ardent cooks and proud of their prowess in the kitchen. They are so conscious of good cooking that they chose the marvelous tasting leek as their national flower. In battle they wore a leek in their helmets as early as the sixth century. King Arthur and his Knights of the round table in the sixth century spent as much time studying food recipes as they did fighting. King Arthur himself was one of the best pudding cooks of his time.

Fine salmon come from the Dee and Wye Rivers of Wales. Duck prepared in ham curing solution and smoked is a delicacy of Carmarthenshire. Leek porridge in Carnarvon is simply wonderful eating. Spiced roast beef in Glamorgan is worth any amount of effort to prepare it correctly. Seaweed cooked and seasoned with nutmeg tastes somewhat like spinach and is a specialty of Pembroke. Near Swansea some of the first banana plants from India where bananas originated were grown and today bananas are still grown in the area.

The Welsh have an interesting food background as you can well see but to me the greatest of all Welsh food inventions is the famous Welsh Rabbit. Some fool cooking editors foolishly tried to change the name of Welsh Rabbit to Welsh Rarebit to make it sound fancier. They did not know of course the famous background of this dish or they never would have attempted it.

The Welsh Rabbit is the oldest known melted cheese recipe. It is a family recipe that goes a long way with a lot of hungry mouths. It is also however a recipe that the finest restaurants in the world list as one of their best dishes.

Mary Cameron who lived near Glamorgan made the first Welsh Rabbit in the 7th Century. The fame of it spread so that her name has been remembered through the ages even when Kings' names have been forgotten. In those days as now the Welsh were great lovers of wild rabbit. When a hunter returned empty handed after promising his wife a fat rabbit for supper it was indeed a sorry state of affairs. So it happened one day to Arthur Cameron husband of Mary. She saw Arthur coming over the fields with nothing to show for his hunting. She quickly cut up some strong yellow cheese in a pot near the fire, added some bacon drippings and a pint of ale. When Arthur arrived home she served him this wonderful sauce on freshly toasted bread. This recipe was so good that it was not long before it was used all over England, Scotland and Ireland.

The recipe was refined a bit as follows by the Tudor rulers but is basically Mary Cameron's recipe.

Here is the Tudor refinement. Makes 8 servings.

Take a double boiler. If you don't have one, get one as they are a necessity for many good recipes. Put three tablespoons of butter in the double boiler and melt them. Add one cup of beer and mix it in well with the butter. When the beer is warm stir in 1 pound of finely cut sharp strong cheddar cheese. Stir constantly with a fork until the cheese is melted. A later Welsh touch after America was discovered and paprika available, add ½ level teaspoon of paprika and ½ level teaspoon of dried mustard. If you do not have the dried mustard the wet will work very well. Stir in well. Salt and pepper to taste. Do not keep the mixture on the stove a minute more than necessary. Serve on one inch squares of buttered toast.

Welsh Rabbit never contains such things as Worcestershire sauce, eggs, cayenne pepper or curry powder. Such ingredients never were intended for a Welsh Rabbit and ruin it entirely.

THE FAMOUS WILDERNESS SANDWICH

The recipe for this sandwich goes way back to the time the first European people came to Minnesota, Wisconsin and Michigan. These sandwiches are still very popular today. They are a better sandwich for the deer hunter or wilderness cruiser than any made from bread. This wilderness sandwich actually is a perfectly balanced meal for the outdoorsman. It is an offspring of the French crepe suzette brought to North America by early French missionaries and settlers.

Take and fry a large pancake in a generous amount of bacon grease. Remove from the pan and cover the top generously with brown sugar. Break up pieces of cooked bacon and sprinkle over the brown sugar. Roll up in a tight roll and tie up the roll with a piece of ribbon or leather. Then wrap the pancake tightly in paper, leather or cloth and bind securely. Put in your pocket or pack.

The sugar gives you energy. The grease the pancake was cooked in and the bacon satisfies the craving for grease that all men have that exercise a great deal. The pancake itself gives you proteins to keep up your general strength.

You can go twice as far on one of these sandwiches than on three chocolate bars.

VEGAS SANDWICH

The town of Las Vegas, Nevada is a very new town. The first people came there in 1905. It was incorporated in 1912. The town was named after

Downtown Las Vegas.

Las Vegas never closes.

Right out in the middle of the desert at Las Vegas where even a jack rabbit used to have to pack his own lunch shows like this now abound.

Las Vegas in northern New Mexico. The words Las Vegas mean the "beam" or "support". These words do not mean "the meadows" as is sometimes

Hoover Dam near Las Vegas is a sight well worth seeing. It creates Lake Mead.

This is not a shoe store.

One of the well-known Casinos of Las Vegas.

This is not a place where you rent camels.

wrongly stated. Las Vegas is hardly a meadow. It is barren desert surrounded by distant barren mountains. Even a jack rabbit has to carry his lunch around Las Vegas. Mining gold, silver, lime, borax and gypsum are the main industries plus tourists.

Marrying is one of Las Vegas' growing industries. Photo shows the well-known Little Church of the West.

The Hoover Dam that supplies most of Los Angeles' electricity is only 29 miles away.

The first restaurant in Las Vegas was run by William Luther an ex-miner. He served a sandwich made as follows and called a Vegas.

Take two pieces of bread or a round hamburger bun. Butter two sides of the bread or two sides of the hamburger bun lightly.

Take a weiner and slice it up into thin slices and spread it carefully over one side of the bread or bun.

Take two slices of well fried bacon and cut or crumble them up and place over the sliced weiners.

Melt some strong cheddar cheese. Pour enough of it over the bacon and weiner to just nicely cover them. Salt and pepper to taste and serve at once.

Las Vegas has grown to be a large town with dozens of atmospheric restaurants but none of the food served will come close to being as good as a genuine Vegas.

This is not a photograph taken at some world's fair but the Landmark Restaurant and casino at Las Vegas.

GARLIC TOAST DUPONT

The word "garlic" comes from the Anglo-Saxon word garleac. Gar means spear or lance and leac means the vegetable leek. Homer wrote of garlic in the ninth century Before Christ. Garlic was introduced into China in the second century Before Christ. Garlic originated in the Mediterranean area. The first indication that garlic was in America was when Cortez found it in Mexico. This garlic must have been introduced to Central America earlier as garlic was not a native to North, South, or Central America.

The Romans disliked the strong, skunky, flavor and smell of garlic and would not eat it at all until recently. They fed it however to their slave laborers to make them strong and to their soldiers to give them courage. I imagine a good strong garlic breath would be enough to scare most enemies away for good. Most Americans do not care for garlic and rightly so. They do not know that the skunky odor of garlic must never be used alone but must be well blended with some other strong taste and smell. It is like making perfume where the skunky odor of civet is used to blend with flower oils to make fine smelling perfume. Garlic as well as onions, and leeks all belong to the lily family.

Making good garlic toast is quite a trick and few cooks know the secrets of doing it. Most so-called garlic toast is really a mess and not fit for man or beast. When made properly it is delicious with no skunky odor or taste at all. The late famed original cook Arthur Dupont from Carniere, Belgium invented garlic toast. Here is the original recipe:

Take four level tablespoons of butter and put them into a small frying pan. This is enough for four pieces of toast. Melt the butter just until it is barely done. Take a piece of white bread and holding it with your fingers, dip it into the butter on both sides so that both sides are evenly covered with butter. Place on a pan and shake garlic powder lightly over one side. Then shake celery salt lightly over the garlic powder. Place in your oven with your broiler heat on. Broil just until the butter begins to brown. Remove and turn over and again just broil until the butter begins to brown. Remove at once and serve.

Do not try to add the garlic powder and celery salt to the melted butter as they will simply sink into the butter and will not mix with it. Do not try to just spread butter on the bread rather than to melt it and put it on. The butter must be perfectly even on the bread and you cannot do this unless you melt the butter and dip the bread into it.

ARGENTINA MOCHA TOAST

This is a delicious method of toast making. Take slices of fresh bread and butter them well on one side. Sprinkle the buttered side heavily with powdered coffee or instant coffee, which is easier to get. Then sprinkle the toast well with sugar. Place the slices of toast on a flat pan and put in your oven at least six inches away from the flame or electric coils. Broil under medium heat just until the butter bubbles and becomes slightly brown. Remove quickly and serve with good coffee. Even beats pastry for breakfast, and is a very different dessert served after a dinner.

GERMAN TOAST

This recipe was brought to Minnesota by German settlers and immediately became very popular. Among good cooks it is even more popular today. To me it is one of the finest breakfasts you can have. Try it out on your family and you will find it a welcome change from modern day breakfasts.

Take slices of white bread and spread them well on one side with butter. Place them in a metal pan. Put your oven on at broil and leave open about one-third and put in the buttered bread. Leave it in until the butter bubbles well and shows signs of browning. Serve with a dish of maple or corn syrup. Dip the toast into the syrup and eat. This is a delicious, wonderful tasting food.

GREEK TOAST

The first record of cultivating wheat dates back to 2,289 years Before Christ in Chin-Nong, China.

The early Chinese and Egyptians made bread by simply mixing water, or milk and dried fruits together and cooking it. They knew nothing of how to use yeasts to raise bread.

The Greeks discovered how to mix yeast with flour and water, leave the mixture rise and than bake it. Fermenting beer was used as the yeast. The towns of Athens, Megare and Taba were the leading bread making towns. Bread making then went from Greece to Italy. In the year 365 the Italians brought bread baking to France. From France bread making was brought to Germany and Scandinavia and thence to England and Ireland.

Greek toast is a simple recipe and is widely used today throughout Europe and North America.

Take French bread or Vienna bread or for that matter any white bread you may prefer. Cut the bread into regular slices. Take one-half of a cup of butter that has been allowed to stand without refrigeration for at least five hours so that it is nice and soft. Squeeze the juice of one garlic glove into the butter. If you have powdered garlic put in one-fourth teaspoon instead. If you do not like garlic and many people do not, take an onion about one and a half inches in diameter and grate it into the butter. If you have powdered onion powder use a half of a teaspoon instead. Mix in well with the butter making the butter nice and creamy. Leave the butter stand for a half hour so it can absorb the flavor. Now spread the butter onto one side of the bread and sprinkle well with paprika. Take some oregano and pulverize it between your fingers. Remove any stems or hard pieces. Then sprinkle a small amount of oregano over the paprika. Place the bread on a pan and put into your oven at 350 degrees. Bake from 10 to 15 minutes so that the toast just begins to brown a little. Serve with any meal.

ST. ANTHONY SANDWICH OR SPREAD
THIS RECIPE IS OVER 7 CENTURIES OLD

Saint Anthony was an Italian and the patron Saint of stock farmers. He lived very simply but had the rare ability to create very different tasty foods from simple things. He developed the Saint Anthony sandwich and lived nearly entirely on it. His famous sandwich became well known throughout Europe centuries ago and came to Minnesota with the early immigrants from nearly all European countries. In all the passing centuries no chef has ever bettered this recipe for the finest hors d'oeuvres tray. Here is the original recipe:

Take a four ounce piece of Roquefort, blue cheese, or Treasure Cave Cheese. Place it in a bowl. Put in three tablespoons of white dry wine such as sauterne, Rhine wine, or Chablis. Add two level tablespoons of horseradish. Broil or fry crisp 6 thin slices of bacon. Crumble them up until fine and add. Mix together all the ingredients until they are smoothly blended. Now take a turnip. Peel off all the coarse outside fibers. Slice it in slices one-fourth of an inch thick. Place on a cookie tray and bake in your oven at 400 degrees until well done and just slightly crisp. Spread the cheese, horseradish and bacon blend onto the turnips and serve. This recipe is sometimes given using rutabagas instead of turnips. There were no rutabagas in existence at this time. The rutabaga is a cross between a cabbage and a turnip that came about in 1620.

SANDWICH SPREAD BOURBONNAIS

This recipe originated in the part of France that we got many of our well known superstitions from. Here originated the fear of the number "thirteen." That Wednesdays and Fridays were evil days. That when "thirteen" falls on a Wednesday or a Friday you should be very, very careful because the days are of great evil. That you should be married in May or November never in any other months. That if it rains on your wedding day you will have an unhappy marriage and if the sun shines brightly on your wedding day you will have a happy marriage. That if you do laundry during Holy Week or All Saints Week one of your family will die during the year. That if you drop a knife or fork you will have company that day. That if you dream of dark, dirty water someone you know well will die within two months. As you can well see this indeed is a land of superstitions and old folklore. Reminds me of Ireland which has much the same beliefs including that if you fall asleep in your bed with a full moon shining on your face you will develope a great nervousness.

This area of France besides giving us many superstitions has given us a great many wonderful recipes. This famous sandwich spread is one of them. Here is the original recipe and it makes my mouth water just to write it down.

Take equal amounts of olive butter and liverwurst sausage. Place them in a large bowl and mix them together well with a fork. When well mixed spread the mixture heavily onto a piece of lightly buttered rye or wholewheat bread. Olive butter is just ground up olives and can be bought very inexpensively at grocery stores as it is made from broken olives that they can sell in no other way.

This sandwich is fantastically delicious eating. Just try to imagine it with a cold bottle of beer or a room temperature glass of good wine.

PATE DE FOIE GRAS JOAN

Pate De Foie Gras was first made for Joan of Arc by one of her army cooks, Jean Baptiste Patrie who was from the goose rearing region of France.

Statue of Joan of Arc made in France from paintings made while she was alive.

Never underestimate the strength and courage of a woman that is really mad at you. This sturdy woman on May 8, 1492, not just badly defeated but completely routed the English forces under Sir John Talbot from the fortress dominating Orleans. Sir Talbot had stated not once but many times that this fortress was absolutely impregnable. On that eventful day it is said Joan's only food was a piece of bread spread with Pate De Foie Gras. Pate De Foie Gras is goose liver sausage mixed with the fruit of a special fungi called truffles or mushrooms. Actually goose liver tastes not a bit different than any other liver. It just happens that in parts of France that they raise a lot of geese and goose liver is plentiful. The goose liver sausage is mixed with truffles to flavor it. Truffles are an underground fungi of the genus tuber and have an edible black fruit. The flavor of truffles is about the same as that of the mushrooms raised here in North America commercially, in fact our mushrooms actually are much better tasting than truffles. To make a Pate De Foie Gras on some special occasion that is really much better than any made in France, proceed as follows:

Buy a liver sausage made by some reliable maker. Cut it open and place the contents in a bowl. Buy a can of stems and pieces of mushrooms. Open and drain off the liquid. Now take enough of the mushroom pieces to equal the bulk of the liver sausage. Run the pieces through a meat grinder or chop them up with a knife on a cutting board. Then mix them in well with the liver sausage. This mixture spread on crackers or bread is very rare and delicious eating. The mushrooms give the liver sausage an entirely different delicious taste.

PORTUGUESE RECIPE FROM BEFORE THE TIME OF CHRIST FOR AN ANCHOVY CRACKER AND BREAD SPREAD

The Portuguese people have been famous since long before the time of Christ for their preparation of anchovies. Anchovies are a small minnow like ocean fish. They are prepared by skinning them and preserving or canning them with salt and olive oil.

The Portuguese invented a cracker and bread spread over 19 centuries ago that is one of the finest and most different ever made. Its popularity spread all over the Middle East centuries ago. If you like fish or sea food you will really like this great delicacy. It is expensive to make but wonderful for a special occasion or holiday.

Take one 2 oz. can of fillets of anchovies from Portugal. Empty the entire contents of the can, olive oil and all into a glass mixing bowl. Add one 3 oz. package of cream cheese such as Philadelphia cream cheese. Add one level tablespoon of butter. Add one level teaspoon of prepared mustard such as French's. Take a table fork and mix this mixture well. Takes a little time as you have to break up the anchovies into small pieces with your fork so the small pieces mix in well with the cheese. Spread on crackers or bread. Very wonderful, different eating whether used as a main meal or a before dinner hors d'oeuvre.

Vegetables

HOW TO SEASON BOILED VEGETABLES

In June 8, 1784 on the street Du Bac in Paris, France a man named Marie Antonin Careme was born. He was one of fifteen children. His father was a poor workman and simply did not make enough money to fully bring up his children. As soon as the children were old enough to get a job which in those days was around eleven years old they had to leave home and support themselves entirely. When Marie Antonin became eleven his father took him to a small restaurant where he went to work washing dishes. He was a very ambitious boy and soon learned to cook. By the time he was in his twenties every king and ruler in Europe was trying to hire him. He became known as the King of Cooks. He rewrote the recipes of Gonthier d'Andernach who up to that time was considered the first man to make large advancements in fine cooking. He also added hundreds of new recipes of his own. Just a few examples of them are Hollandaise sauce, Strawberries Souvaroff, Ice Cream Souvaroff, sauce Nesselrode, Lyonnaise Potatoes, etc.

Here are his original instructions for boiling vegetables:

Beets—

For every quart of beets that you boil add four level teaspoons of basil and one level teaspoon of cinnamon to the water. When cooked, drain and serve slightly buttered or sprinkled with vinegar or with cheese sauce Antoine Van Dyck.

Green Beans—

For every quart of green beans that you boil add four level teaspoons of marporam and one diced onion two inches in diameter. When cooked, drain and serve slightly buttered, or with cheese sauce. (Antoine Van Dyck.)

Carrots—

For every quart of carrots that you boil add four level teaspoons of dill seed or four large complete heads of fresh dill. When cooked, drain and serve slightly buttered or with cheese sauce. (Antoine Van Dyck.)

Portrait d'Antonin Careme.

Peas—

For every quart of peas that you boil add two diced onions about two inches in diameter and two bay leaves. When cooked drain and remove the bay leaves and serve slightly buttered or with cheese sauce. (Antoine Van Dyck).

Early French, Luxembourg and Alsace Lorraine immigrants brought these recipes with them and have carefully taught them to each new generation.

CATTAIL SALAD

In the old days of Minnesota, of course, you had salad only when you could grow your own in the late spring and summer. In many of the wilderness parts of Minnesota this is still true today.

The Sioux Indians made salad from the ivory colored cattail shoots that came up in the early spring. The early pioneers were quick to copy this Indian custom and cattail salad became very popular in Minnesota.

To make a cattail salad go to some swamp early in the spring when the cattails are just beginning to send up their new shoots. Cut the shoots off that are anywhere from one inch to three inches long. Clean them so nothing but the solid ivory part remains. Cut the shoots up into small pieces. Salt to taste and add your favorite salad dressing. This makes a wonderful salad with a fine clean taste that you never will see bettered in the finest restaurant.

BEANS PAUL REVERE

Paul Revere, a Frenchman, was born in 1735 and died in 1818. His real name was Paul Rivoire, son of Apollos Rivoire. He was a silversmith by trade. His warning to early colonists that the British troops were coming made the United States possible more than any other act of one man. A defeat of the early colonists at the critical time would have undoubtedly meant a complete easy victory for Britain.

Paul Revere was a great craftsman and quite a sensitive type of man. He enjoyed food and was as creative with food as he was in silver design. His creations in both were conservative, not at all the fancy or the over done kind of things.

Before the discovery of the Americas, there were beans found in Europe but of very inferior varieties none of which we use in America today.

Lima beans were first cultivated in Guatemala. Their cultivation by the Indians spread up through Mexico and into the South and up into Virginia. The other beans we use today such as Navy or Pea bean, Red Kidney, Pinto, Great Northern, Marrow, Yellow Eye, all wax pod and green pod snap and stringless beans were all found in the Americas and not in Europe.

The Indians to a great extent lived on corn and beans. They, of course, invented succotash and this must have been a gift from God as succotash is one of the most scientific foods ever developed. Corn is high in starch but deficient in many needed vitamins. Beans have a terrifically high content of these necessary vitamins not found in corn. Hence succotash makes a wonderful balanced food that you could live on without any meat if necessary and still maintain good health.

The early New England colonists learned from the Indians how to cook beans and beans became a stable part of New England diet.

Boston or New England style baked beans soon became popular wherever there were colonists in the Americas.

Paul Revere evidently ate baked beans like the rest of the New Englanders for a great many years. He finally evidently got tired of them so developed a recipe of his own to give them a different and improved taste. He mixed the beans with chopped ham and mayonnaise. This makes either a wonderful main dish or an appetizer. I myself prefer it for a main dish. I have adapted this recipe to modern grocery buying with no change at all in the main result.

It costs at present grocery prices about 60 cents to produce this recipe and gives you 4 to 5 good sized servings. This is one of the best food buys I have ever seen and one of the best eating foods I have ever eaten.

Buy a one pound can of baked beans of some reliable brand. Put in a pot and add one tablespoon of liquid smoke to change the flavor of the beans. Heat until just nicely warm not boiling and remove from the stove. Chop into fine pieces one can of Mor, Spam or any such ground ham products. In my opinion none of these chopped ham products are good fried or used in stews or soups as they become flabby and spongelike when cooked. Used as in this recipe they are excellent. Mix one cup of mayonnaise with the chopped ham. Now mix the chopped ham into the warm, not hot, baked beans. Just serve with bread and butter. This is a meal too good for any king I have ever heard of.

SALAD WITH PICKLED FISH CHARDONNET

Hilaire Chardonnet was born in 1839 and died in 1924. He was a French chemist and physician. Without his work we would have no artificial fabrics today. He invented rayon and the basic processes for all artificial fabrics. Chardonnet was also much interested in foods and his Salad Chardonnet is a real food classic. I prefer it much over Caesar salad or salad Louie and other such salads. Here is the original salad recipe:

Take a head of lettuce that has been washed. Then break the head of lettuce into pieces and put them into a large salad mixing bowl. Take one pickled herring or the equivalent of herring pieces, wash it in water until it has no trace of the solution it was pickled in. This is important. Then cut it up into one fourth inch squares and add them to the lettuce and mix in well. If you have no pickled herring use a small can of tuna pieces. Drain all oil from the tuna pieces and put them in a bowl and cover them with vinegar. Leave for an hour stirring four or five times. Then drain off the vinegar and add the pieces to the lettuce. The pieces should not be more than one fourth inch square or thereabouts. Now take an onion about 1½ inches in diameter and cut it up into small pieces and add to the lettuce. Take six green olives and cut them up into small slices and add to the lettuce or add two level tablespoons of olive butter. Olive butter is just ground up olives that you can buy at most grocery stores. Mix all ingredients together well. Salt and pepper to taste. Take 5 tablespoons of olive oil and 3 tablespoons of vinegar. Mix them together well then mix them into the lettuce and other ingredients. Now take two hard boiled eggs and cut both yolk and white into small pieces not more than ¼ of an inch square or smaller. Scatter them on top of the other ingredients. Serve in individual bowls. This is a fabulous salad so good that it makes a whole meal in itself or of course is wonderful as the salad with a meal.

CAESAR SALAD

This famous salad is an excellent example of how cooks in so-called famous restaurants can really foul up an excellent recipe from pure ignorance of cooking.

Caesar salad was invented in about 1903 by Giacomo Junia, an Italian cook in Chicago, Illinois. Giacomo Junia was the cook in a small restaurant called The New York Cafe. He catered to American tastes as spaghetti and pizza in those days were little eaten by anyone including Italians. It is sometimes falsely stated that this salad was invented in Tia Juana, Mexico during the prohibition period and also in San Francisco. Nothing could be further from the truth. The only thing invented in Tia Juana were the finest methods ever produced to clip tourists.

Giacomo Junia called the salad Caesar Salad. He put a few pieces of Cos lettuce (romaine) in the salad to add a slightly bitter touch to it. Cos lettuce originated in Italy. Light green, dark green, and red spotted varieties were described in Italy in 1623. It had been widely grown in Italy from about the time Christ was born. Cos lettuce was common in Italy during the Middle Ages. It was and is cooked as a vegetable and never eaten alone as a salad as its taste is much too strong for a salad all by itself. A few pieces of Cos lettuce in Italy were occasionally added to other lettuce for salads. Cos lettuce was taken to France by Rabelais in 1537. At the end of the 16th century it still was rarely grown in France or Germany and when eaten it was cooked as a vegetable and rarely used in salads.

Giacomo called the salad Caesar Salad after Julius Caesar, the greatest Italian of all time.

Giacomo was not an exceptional cook but just a fair one. One thing that he tried to make with no success was mayonnaise for salads and for serving with fish. No matter how hard he tried he just could not make mayonnaise. He finally took the mayonnaise basic ingredients because he thought that the taste of them should be good on salad even if used separately, added some French fried bread for his French customers and some bacon to please his German customers and Caesar Salad was born. Junia never thought that the salad would be popular and was more surprised than anyone when people begin to ask for it. Many itinerant cooks learned how to make the salad and soon it was made all over North America and even in Europe. Junia left Chicago for San Francisco, California and shortly afterward died. Here is his original recipe which is unlike any of the fouled up Caesar Salad recipes that are pawned off on people today as Caesar Salad.

Take some white fresh bread and cut it up into about quarter inch or slightly larger cubes. Take your French fryer filled with rendered beef suet and heat to the same hot temperature as for frying French fried potatoes. French fry the bread cubes until they are just barely brown. Watch them carefully so that you do not over-fry them. Take about three dozen pieces of lettuce about two to two and a half inches square and French fry them just until they become very limp. This does not take long. Watch them carefully.

Take a large salad bowl. If you have leaf lettuce use it. If not, use two heads of head lettuce. Either leaf or head lettuce can be used to make this salad. Tear the lettuce up into small pieces. If you have Cos lettuce (romaine) tear up a cupful of pieces of it and add them to the other lettuce. This is not however at all necessary. Never use all Cos lettuce as many so-called Caesar salad recipes call for as Cos lettuce is not meant for complete salads. Never use olive oil to fry the bread pieces in. French fry them in rendered beef suet. Olive oil gives off a very objectionable odor and taste when used to fry such things as bread. Italians used olive oil in Italy mainly because at one time it was plentiful and cheap.

Today in Italy there is far more corn and soy bean oil used than olive oil. Do not try to fry bread cubes in a frying pan with butter. It does not work well unless you have at least one inch or more of butter in the pan. Fry four slices of bacon nice and crisp. Break them up into very small pieces and add them to the lettuce. Sprinkle the lettuce with ¼ level teaspoon of dried mustard, ¼ level teaspoon of black pepper, ½ level teaspoon of salt. Add the juice of a garlic clove or a fourth teaspoon of garlic powder. One-half cup of Swiss cheese grated up on the fine part of your grater. Never use Parmesan cheese as most cook book recipes today specify in Caesar Salad. This Parmesan cheese idea in a Caesar Salad was the idea of cooks who knew nothing about cooking but wanted to show off with a fancy named cheese in this salad. Grated Parmesan cheese is gritty. When used on spaghetti it is warmed and partially melted and softened by the spaghetti and is excellent. Put on a cold salad it is gritty and without taste and spoils the whole salad. Parmesan cheese is not a salad cheese and never is used as one in Italy. Now add 6 tablespoons of bottled olive or salad oil and the juice of two lemons or four level tablespoons of lemon juice and a half teaspoon of Worcestershire sauce.

Break two raw eggs into the bowl and mix well with the other ingredients. You will be very surprised to see that the lemon juice completely dissolves the egg white, as well as the yolk and makes the whole egg into a smooth liquid with the consistency of water, with no albumen or raw egg feel taste or smell at all. Put this dressing onto the salad proper, and lightly mix it in well. Just before serving, add the fried bread or croutons and toss them into the salad lightly. You want to mix the croutons in last so that they will not be soggy. Take the French fried lettuce now that it is cool and place it on top of each individual salad. If you put the raw eggs on the salad without mixing the lemon juice and oil with them first the salad is no good at all for man or beast.

Caesar Salad never contains such things as anchovies, sardines, or mixed vegetables. Caesar Salad is very good tasting. It is expensive to make but a real very different salad treat for a special occasion.

MAXIM'S FRESH CELERY

In 1893 Maxim's was a small Paris, France restaurant that served excellent creative food but had a hard time making things go.

Max Lebaudy and a group of friends went there one night for some late food. The party found the food imaginative and wonderful tasting. They washed the food down with 36 bottles of Champagne. They asked for light music with their eating; however, there was not even a piano in the restaurant at that time. The next day, though, Maxim's managed to purchase a piano for 240 golden francs and hired a male piano player for 5 gold francs a night. Those were the days you can see when the French franc was worth something.

Max Lebaudy and his party told their friends of the fabulous food at Maxim's and soon it became very fashionable to go there. By the year 1900 to dine at Maxim's was the desire of the elite of Europe. The salons were reserved for such people as the Prince of Wales, King Leopold of Belgium and the Hennessy's who made some pretty good cognac.

The War of 1914 like all wars changed all of Europe again and Maxim's was sold to Mr. Vaudable. His son Louis Vaudable now runs the restaurant and has managed to keep it quite popular. Today you will see all the great magnates of California, New York, and Texas, the Rockefellers, Vanderbilts, Maurice Chevalier, Doris Duke, Orson Wells, Ali Khan and such people at Maxim's in spite of the fact that the food is a far cry from what it used to be. Maxim's today smothers its food in presentation, and expensive ingredients that in many cases detract instead of add to their food. They need to go back and pick up some basic creative cookery.

The old Maxim's was full of creative food. Here is one of the simple creative recipes that made Maxim's the talk of Europe around 1900.

Celery as we know originated from the smallage plant in the Mediterranean area. The word "celery" comes from the French "celeri" which in turn came from a Greek word. Celery was for centuries only used as a medicine. In France and in Italy by the middle of the 17th century the small unmatured stalks and leaves were served with an oil dressing. This was the first use of celery as a food.

Take a fresh bunch of celery. Clean the stalks, cut off the leaves and cut the stalks up into pieces about three inches long. Take about a two quart bowl and fill it three fourths full of water. Add two level teaspoons of anise oil or anise liquid flavoring. You can get it at any grocery store. Fill the bowl with the cut up pieces of celery but be sure all of the celery pieces are covered by the liquid. Leave the bowl set in a cool place or your refrigerator from four to five hours. The celery will absorb all of the anise in this length of time and mix it with its own natural flavors and juices. Remove the celery from the water and serve while chilled.

The first bite of this famous celery surprises you and you do not quite know what to think as it has an entirely different taste. After the fourth or fifth bite however you simply cannot get enough of it. This is a really great recipe; try it as soon as possible.

CORN SERVED MOHAWK AS A VEGETABLE

The Mohawk Indians are descended from the Celts and are cousins to the Irish, Scotch, Bretons, and Welsh. This has always been a well known fact among Indians and early immigrants from Europe but only fairly recently recognized by anthropologists. Even the famous anthropologist, Dr. Jury now concedes this proven fact. The balance of Indians came from the Mongolians which makes them cousins to the Chinese.

The Mohawks had many interesting customs and were very fine cooks. Some of their recipes show great understanding of food and are far superior to many developed in recent North America.

The recipe I list here creates one of the finest foods I have ever eaten with a taste and aroma found in no other recipe. It makes some of the vegetables served at Maxim's, France's present day most famous restaurant, taste like they were prepared by an indifferent grade school girl.

Corn used as a vegetable is not too popular. It has a strong starchy taste that many people do not like. Prepared with this Mohawk recipe corn tastes entirely different and I have never found a person who was not fond of it. Here is the recipe:

Take a number 2 can of whole kernel corn. Open the can and put the contents into a small cooking pot. Cover with enough water to cover the corn. Boil for just a minute or two until the corn is good and hot. Drain off the water. Melt one heaping teaspoon of butter and mix it into the corn. Salt and pepper to taste using white pepper. Add one-fourth teaspoon of black walnut oil or flavoring and mix it in well. Black walnut oil or flavoring can be bought at most grocery stores or your grocer can get it for you. Serve while hot.

The Mohawks did not, of course, have canned whole kernel corn but simply cut the kernels off boiled corn. They had no salt or pepper, these are added for modern tastes. They used good animal fat instead of butter. They made their own black walnut oil by simply crushing black walnut meats.

Black walnut flavor and aroma is simply just what corn served as a vegetable needs. It is wonderful eating, not heavy and starchy but fresh and light. This was the recipe used by Kateria Tekakwitha, a Mohawk woman of great brilliance, who lived 300 years ago. She helped her people to adopt the good ways of the European immigrants and to ignore their bad ways.

SWEET CORN RETHWILL

Sweet corn, of course, originated in North America. There was no corn of any kind in Europe until early explorers brought back seed to Europe. European people with one exception never got to like sweet corn. Europeans use corn in limited quantities for feeding chickens and pigs. The only way they eat corn is in the form of cornstarch for puddings. There is practically no corn grown in any part of Europe. The exception is the Hungarian people. The Hungarians like sweet corn very much and grow quite a good deal of it. They cook it just the same as we do here. They do not, however, like popcorn. Popcorn is not liked anywhere in Europe, at the present writing.

The methods of cooking sweet corn we learned right from the Indians, and have not improved upon these methods in any way. The Indian methods were boiling in water, with and without sweetening, roasting with the husks on, roasting with husks on and covered with clay and lastly, boiling it in water, then cutting off the kernels making cream corn.

The secret in cooking sweet corn in using any method is to cook it as soon as possible after you pick it from the stalk. The corn on the stalk contains a good bit of sugar. This sugar gradually changes to starch after the cob is pulled from the stalk. Thus the quicker you cook the corn the sweeter and less starchy it tastes.

I like sweet corn very much and have eaten it cooked with all the usual recipes. Up until a time ago I believed I knew all the ways of cooking corn since I was six years old.

One August I took some leeks for planting to a neighbor, Mrs. Rethwill. I was surprised when she told me she had discovered a method of cooking sweet corn that I did not know and that was much better than any other method. I did not believe her at all until I had gone home and tried her recipe. Then I agreed entirely with her. Her recipe produced the best sweet corn I have ever eaten. Here is the recipe:

Remove the husks from the fresh sweet corn. Butter the corn lightly. Do not salt. Wrap each ear of corn tightly in aluminum foil. Heat your oven to 325 degrees. Put your corn into the oven and bake for 30 minutes. Serve the corn with the aluminum wrapper on the ears. Remove the aluminum wrappers only as you eat the corn. Salt and pepper to taste.

Sweet corn cooked in this manner tastes far better than by any other method. All the natural juices and sugars are left in it and are not boiled out as when cooked in water. When sweet corn is roasted in husks or in clay and husks juices and sugars are also mostly lost.

Save the aluminum foil and use it for cooking corn over and over again.

HUSH PUPPIES LA NOUVELLE ORLEANS

Hush Puppies today are widely eaten throughout the old South. The Carolinas, Georgia, Mississippi and Louisiana are favorite Hush Puppie areas. Hush Puppes were a great favorite of Jefferson Davis, President of the Confederacy, who died in New Orleans. They are very delicious and one of the finest foods that ever originated in North America.

Hush Puppies came to be in the town of Nouvelle, Orleans, shortly after 1727. A group of Ursuline Nuns sailed from France for New Orleans on February 22, 1727. They reached the mouth of the Mississippi River on July 23, 1727. The colonial officials of New Orleans sent a sloop and pirogues, which are actually narrow canoes, to meet the Nuns and to bring them up the river to New Orleans. It took a good ten days or more to go from the mouth of the Mississippi to upstream New Orleans. At five o'clock in the morning on August 6, 1727 some of the Nuns finally arrived at New Orleans. They immediately set up a school, orphanage, home for wayward girls, classes for Indian and African girls and they began work on a convent. By 1734 the new convent was completed.

Young women were sent over by Louis XIV as he fully realized that unless he got enough French women to New Orleans that the men would all have African and Indian children. When the girls arrived they were taken to the Ursuline Convent, taught how to sew and cook with the food available until a suitable marriage could be arranged. King Louis sent each girl with a dowry in a small chest and hence the girls were called "filles a la casette" or "casket girls".

New Orleans wasn't much in those days but the Nuns were smart and resourceful. They brought with them a complete knowledge of French cooking and they adapted it to the food available. Nearly all good New Orleans cooking is traceable to these Nuns in one way or another. They taught practically every wife and every early restaurant owner how to cook. Much of

The Ursuline Convent in New Orleans as it appears today. It was started in 1748.

the food was gotten from the Indians, local hunters and fishermen. Oysters, shrimp, red snapper, flounder, wild ducks, wild turkey, deer, rabbits, squirrels, frogs, turtles and wild geese were all very plentiful. In the spring of the year around about March depending upon the weather the shrimp leave the bayous and canals and go up on land. From the shrimp gathered from the land the Nuns created practically every shrimp recipe that is used in New Orleans today. They made Gumbo file from wild sassafras grass which they used to thicken soups. Corn meal was gotten from the Indians. The Nuns soon converted corn meal into a delicious food that they named Croquettes de Maise. The making of it spread rapidly into Mississippi, into Georgia and the Carolinas. The name Hush Puppies was given this food in Atlanta, Georgia by an African cook working in a hotel who gave a plate full to a howling puppie to keep him quiet. The name was cute and stuck.

Here is the original recipe:

Put into a large mixing bowl two cups of corn meal, 2 level teaspoons of double action baking powder, and one level teaspoon of salt. Take one onion three inches in diameter and chop it up real fine. Add the onion to the ingredients in the bowl. Take 2/3 of a cup of milk and mix one egg into it. Now mix the milk and egg into the other ingredients until you have a mixture that can be molded and will hold its shape. Mold the mixture into shapes about 3 or 4 inches long and about 1 inch in diameter. Fry them in real hot bacon grease, hot but not smoking, and have at least a fourth inch of grease in the pan or more. The bacon grease must be some that you have fried some fish in or at least a piece of fish so it has a slight fish odor. Fry until brown on both sides. Serve while they are hot with fresh butter.

Although it is not at all in the custom, I like Hush Puppies served with lots of real homemade mayonnaise. I like them too served with a good brown beef or pork gravy.

When I make them I use ammonia bicarbonate instead of the baking powder. This is dry powdered ammonia. It smells terrible but after the Hush

Ursuline Nuns arrive at New Orleans at 5 o'clock in the morning on August 6, 1727. This painting was made at the time of their arrival.

Puppies are cooked you can neither smell nor taste even a trace of the ammonia as it completely evaporates. It is available at drug stores. It gives them a better texture I think and with no acid or bitter taste that you cannot avoid when using baking powder.

The first pharmacist in North America was one of the New Orlean's Ursuline Nuns.

In 1814 General Andrew Jackson visited the Ursulines and asked them to pray for his victory as the British were threatening New Orleans.

In 1815 at the Battle of New Orleans the Ursuline Nuns treated the American wounded at the convent. General Jackson put his men behind cotton bales and earth mounds just outside of New Orleans. The British charged in tight formation and the squirrel hunters and pirates really flattened them. After the American victory General Jackson came to the convent and thanked the Nuns for their prayers.

The Ursuline Convent is the one place in New Orleans that you should visit if you go there. Skip a few of the bars on Bourbon street and walk through this great old historical building.

SEMINOLE CORN RELISH

Corn relish is very popular in America and used as a before-the-meal appetizer more than any other relish by far. Most of the finest restaurants in America use it on their hors d'oeuvres trays. However none of them serve as good a corn relish as given in this recipe. What they serve is bought ready made and of a far inferior quality.

The recipe for corn relish is a very, very old one.

Watermelon rind is an important part of the recipe. Watermelons of course all originated in central Africa. The ancient Egyptians were one of the first people to cultivate watermelons. Their cultivation spread to the warmer parts of Russia where watermelon was used to make beer and to the Middle East. In the 16th century watermelons were raised in the southern parts of Europe. Watermelon seeds were brought to America by the earliest European colonists. Watermelons were common in Massachusetts in 1629. The Florida Indians were growing huge quantities of watermelons by 1650. Father Marquette, French explorer of the Mississippi area, found Indians growing them in the area.

The Seminoles in Florida made a relish from watermelon rind, corn and red and green peppers. The settlers and hunters who visited the area all liked the relish very much and took the basic recipe back with them to all parts of America. Here is the original recipe modernized slightly for easy making at home with ingredients readily available. This relish should be made in the late summer when watermelons and red and green sweet peppers and corn are plentiful and inexpensive.

Take a large cooking pot and put the following into it:

1 No. 2 can of whole kernel corn. Do not drain.
1 cup of watermelon rind finely chopped up. (Remove the green outer skin from the rind and any red flesh on the inside of the rind.)
¾ cup of red sweet peppers finely chopped up.
½ cup of green sweet peppers finely chopped up.
1 onion 2 inches in diameter grated as fine as possible.
5 level teaspoons of corn starch.
1 level teaspoon of black pepper.
1 pinch of cayenne pepper.
2 level teaspoons of salt.
2 level teaspoons of sugar.
½ cup of white vinegar.
¼ level teaspoon of ground cinnamon.
1 level teaspoon of coriander seed. Add just enough water to barely cover the ingredients. Bring to a boil and boil for 10 minutes. Stir the corn starch in well while the mixture is boiling. Remove and keep what you want for immediate use in your refrigerator or in a cool place. Put the balance in Mason jars filling them within one half inch of the top. Screw down the lids completely then turn them back ¼ inch. Place the jars 2 inches apart in a shallow pan of warm water on the center rack of an oven preheated to 275 degrees. Do not permit the heat to fluctuate at all. Keep in the oven for one hour. Just as soon as you remove the jars from the oven place them on several layers of cloth on a table and tighten the lids down

tightly. When the jars cool tighten them down again. Do not leave jars cool in a draft.

If you have a pressure cooker use it to process the jars instead of the oven method.

DANISH LETTUCE FROM A RECIPE OVER 600 YEARS OLD

Many Danes came to early Minnesota. They were fine cooks and good pastry makers. They brought with them a 600 year old recipe for lettuce that the younger generations have very foolishly completely forgotten. It is a priceless recipe that gives you wonderful food with an entirely different delicious taste.

Centuries back when lettuce seeds were first brought into Europe lettuce was not eaten in salads at all but only as a cooked vegetable. As a cooked vegetable, leaf lettuce has a flavor like no other vegetable. It has a touch of the flavor of the tops grown by chicory roots stuck into sand. The Belgians and the English have always considered cooked chicory tops as one of the finest of cooked vegetables. It has a slight asparagus taste also. Cooked lettuce is not at all filling like carrots, peas, or corn but instead aids your digestion and keeps you from feeling stuffed. It is non fattening and very good for your blood. You can eat all you want of it. Cooked lettuce is a great delicacy and one of my favorite cooked vegetables with a meat and potato meal. This is one to surprise your friends with. They will never know what it is unless you tell them.

Here is the recipe just as Mrs. Iver Jensen long since gone used to make it. May her soul rest in peace, she was a great cook.

Take a large two or three quart kettle. Put in a heaping teaspoon of butter. Leave it melt. Add one fourth cup of water. Take one onion about two inches in diameter and dice it as finely as possible into the pan. Take eight large celery sticks from a good sized celery and cut them into as thin strips as possible and dice into the pan.

Now take and fill the pan full with leaf lettuce cut up into one inch lengths. Squeeze it together with your hand to pack it. Black Seeded Simpson Grand Rapids, and Salad Bowl are all good varieties for this. Leave come to a boil over fast heat, then leave simmer over medium heat for 20 minutes. Salt and pepper to taste. Serve as a vegetable.

The Danes often used to mix the cooked lettuce with mashed or boiled potatoes. It is delicious either way.

CABBAGE OR BRUSSELS SPROUTS CARTIER

Loose heading varieties of cabbage originated in Northwest Italy and Southeast France. The hard head varieties were developed in the Middle Ages in what now is known as Holland, Belgium, Germany and northern France. These people invaded Mediterranean lands a great number of times around 600 years Before Christ until the beginning of the Christian Era. They also invaded the British Isles in the fourth Century Before Christ. They brought cabbage seeds back from the Mediterranean area and cultivated them in their lands and also introduced them to the British Isles.

Just before the beginning of the Christian era the Italians invaded northern Europe as well as the British Isles. They brought new varieties of cabbage with them. These invasions not only mixed up the varieties of cabbage but mixed up Mediterranean and northern European people a great deal. The Roman nose of English people did not get there by accident but is a throwback to Italian occupation troops. The black haired French and German people also show the result of Latin blood.

The various names of cabbage in the different languages shows the common origin of languages. Note the similarity in the various names for cabbage. With the changing of a K for C or a C for a K which is normal change the words are much alike. Kopf, Kohl in German. Cabus and Caboche in French. Cabbage in English which came directly from the French caboche. Kappes, Kraut, Kapost from Tartar. Kopi from Hindu. Kaulion from Greek. Kale from Scotch. Kaal from Norwegian. Kohl from Swedish. Col from Spanish.

All of these languages originated in an area that now is India. On the edge of this area is Tibet where the people have authentic records showing that the area was the first to become land when the earth was formed. The oldest pyramids in the world are still there today. Makes you think a little.

Cabbage was first introduced to North America in 1541-42 by Jacques Cartier who planted it in Canada on his third trip to Canada.

Cabbage Cartier was made by a French cook in Quebec Canada named Henri Francois in 1881 and named after famous Jacques Cartier.

Either cabbage or Brussel sprouts may be used. Here is the original recipe. We will describe the recipe using cabbage.

Select two small heads of white cabbage. They must not be large heads as large heads of cabbage have an entirely different flavor than the small heads. Put the heads into boiling water and boil until done. Remove the heads from the water. Cut each head from the top to the bottom into four equal pieces. Place the pieces into a strainer and leave drain for twenty minutes. The draining of cabbage is all important. If you do not drain off every drop of the water the cabbage is no good at all. Any water on cooked cabbage entirely spoils its taste.

Now take about a three quart pot and put it on a medium flame. Put four level tablespoons of butter into the pot and melt. Add one teaspoon of curry powder and one fourth teaspoon of paprika. Mix the spices in well with the butter. Now put the well-drained cabbage pieces into the pot with the butter and spices and mix them about until they have soaked up all of the butter. Salt to taste. Serve as a vegetable.

The curry powder and paprika do something to cabbage or Brussels sprouts that nothing else even comes close to doing. This is one of the world's great recipes.

OLIVES FORUM OF THE TWELVE CAESARS

The Forum of The Twelve Caesars is a small restaurant in New York City that has received a great deal of national publicity. The food there for the most part is typical good French and Italian European cooking. It is a very fancy, plush place and the prices are very, very, high. I would not advise going there unless you have money to throw away on very elaborate atmosphere.

They serve olives however in the ancient Spanish fashion which is an excellent trick to know:

Take a jar of green olives either pitted or unpitted, stuffed or unstuffed. Pour off the liquid which is always a salt brine. Put the olives into a small bowl and pour about a teaspoon of olive oil on them or just enough to give each olive a light coating of olive oil. Roll the olives around until they are lightly coated with olive oil. Now sprinkle the olives lightly with powdered garlic. If you do not like garlic use dried onion powder. Leave them set about an hour before serving. Served in this manner they are very different and delicious.

Olives originated in the area from Syria to Greece. Olive growing then spread to Italy and into Spain. In Rome a favorite old saying was that a long and pleasant life depended on two fluids, "wine and olive oil." The Spaniards brought olives to Mexico and they came to California and Arizona from Mexico. Olives only until fairly recently were only grown to make olive oil. Olives fresh from the tree whether green or ripe are so bitter that no one could possibly eat them. They must be soaked in a strong solution of poisonous lye to remove their strong very bitter taste. They then are carefully washed in fresh water to remove the poisonous lye before they are pickled in a salt brine.

STUFFED PEPPERS COLUMBUS

Garden peppers are not related in any way to the Piper Nigrum vine from which we get our black and white pepper.

When Columbus came to America he found Indians of the West Indies growing hot as well as sweet pepper. This was of the greatest importance to him as he had come seeking a new route to India for spices and other products. There were not hot or sweet peppers of any kind in Europe or for that matter in any part of the world except the Americas. To Columbus this was a tremendous discovery. He took the hot and sweet peppers back to Spain with him as his greatest discovery in the new world. In 1493 a man named Peter Martyr wrote that Columbus had brought back to Spain a "pepper more pungent than that from Caucasus." American peppers were used in England in 1548 and in Germany, France, and Belgium in 1585. In the 17th century American peppers were taken to India and Southeastern Asia by the Portuguese.

All of the mild sweet kinds of American peppers are called pimiento in Spain while here in the United States only one variety of red thick fleshed sweet pepper is called pimiento.

The Hungarians grow a nonpungent red American pepper and call it paprika.

Cayenne pepper originally came from a red colored American hot pepper from Cayenne a coastal city in French Guiana, South America.

The sweet red peppers Columbus brought back to Spain were soon used to stuff olives, to mix in cheese and salads and to cook with meats. Columbus himself invented this famous recipe and to me it is really a great one.

Take medium-sized, green, sweet peppers and cut off the stem and top. Remove the seeds and veins. Rub the outside of the peppers with butter. Stuff them with the following mixture of ground beef. For every pound of ground beef used to stuff them mix the following into the beef carefully: one finely chopped onion, two inches in diameter, a two inch square of finely chopped strong yellow cheese such as today's sharp cheddar cheese, one half of a medium sized green pepper chopped up very fine and salt and pepper to taste. Stuff the sweet green peppers with this mixture. Place them in a baking pan and put about a fourth cup of water in the pan and put them into an oven at 350 degrees. Bake about one hour or until the green peppers are tender and the meat well done. Baking time may vary according to the exact size of the green peppers you use.

Serve as the main dish. This is a classic recipe and one you should use as often as possible while sweet green peppers are in season.

POTATOES AU GRATIN MARTEL

Charles Martel was the grandfather on his father's side of Charles the Great or Charlemagne. Charlemagne was born in Neustrie in 742 and died in the year 814. He was King of the Francs. Charlemagne was a truly really great man. He started the first schools in Europe. He defeated the Saracens at Potiers just 150 miles south of Paris or Europe would be Moslem today instead of Christian. In 792 he established the first protectorate around Christ's tomb in the Holy Land. In later years Joan of Arc carried his sword in battle. From his Martel blood he had great interest in food and growing new vegetables and farm crops. In his gardens at this early date he had such vegetables as cucumbers. Cucumbers originated in India. He also raised chicory and many other well known present day vegetables at this early time.

The Martels are still famous in Europe today. Martel cognac is a typical example. Ben J. Martel came to Minnesota and married a fine Swedish girl. They had a son whom they promptly named James Martel. James Martel is one of the world's finest cooks living or dead. The Martels have a restaurant just outside of St. Peter, Minnesota called the Holiday House. It is worth going hundreds of miles to eat there. It is a private restaurant but if you tell Jim that I sent you he is apt to let you in if they are not too busy. The prices are reasonable. You get wonderful atmosphere but you do not pay for it, just the food. The Martel restaurant is not the type of restaurant recommended by some self-styled authority who cannot even cook and sets himself up as an authority just to endorse products. We had a fine example of that in Minnesota where a recommended restaurant was found by the authorities to be selling sheepshead for walleyed pike. They simply used so much greasy, smelly batter on the fish that no one could tell what kind of fish it was.

James Martel is the head chef and is out in the kitchen all of the time. He really loves to cook. You can feel this when you watch him in the kitchen.

The Holiday House has good, really, aged, beef steaks, as are available anywhere in North America and far, far better than any to be found in Europe. European beef steaks are very much inferior to American. Martel's barbecued ribs are excellent as well as his walleyed pike and chicken.

The Martel's potatoes au Gratin are unequaled anywhere either on this continent or in Europe. Here is how they serve them. Try this out on your family or friends and see what a fuss they will make over them. Like all really fine recipes they are not hard to make.

Take enough potatoes to serve the number of people that you desire. Leave the skins on them and boil them until you can just barely run a fork through them. Have the water salted to taste. Remove the potatoes from the water and leave them cool just enough so that you can handle them. Then remove the skins. Now slice the potatoes into shoe string potatoes that are as fine as you can possibly get them. Slice them into a large bowl. For every serving of potatoes grate or chop up finely a half inch cube of onion.

Take two heaping tablespoons of butter and two heaping tablespoons of bacon drippings and melt in your frying pan with medium heat. Add three heaping tablespoons of flour and stir and mix up into the butter and bacon drippings until smooth and creamy. Remove from the stove and add one cup of cold water. Stir the cold water in well until thoroughly mixed. Never use warm water. Salt and pepper to taste. Put back onto the stove over a medium heat. You can now go to all the work of grinding up some medium sharp yellow cheese such as cheddar and mixing it with milk but this is not at all necessary. Take two cups of cheese Whiz which is simply a medium sharp cheese that has been beaten up well with milk, and add it slowly in small spoonfuls to the sauce. Slowly stir and cook the sauce until the cheese is melted and well mixed with the sauce. Now take individual or a large baking bowl or pyrex dishes and place about one-half inch of the sauce in the bottom of the bowl. Add potatoes and grated onion mixture to fill the bowl or casserole about three inches deep. Then place another layer of the sauce over the top of the potatoes. Sprinkle well with paprika. Place in your oven at 325 degrees and heat just long enough to just slightly brown the sauce around the edges of the bowl.

Serve piping hot. You will have the best au gratin potatoes possible to make. The secret of this famous recipe is the using of the bacon drippings in the sauce. The bacon drippings blend with the cheese and onions giving the sauce a delicious, very different flavor. You can cut the sauce recipe in half for a small sized family.

ANNE PHOEBE KEY METHOD OF CORRECTLY MASHING POTATOES

I believe that the worst prepared food that I have ever eaten is the mashed potatoes in such so-called modern foods as frozen dinners and other frozen foods that contain mashed potatoes. They have a grayish or tannish color to them, a soggy, starchy taste and a paste-like consistency. If this is supposed to be known as progress in food making and raising the so-called standards of our food, people who think this are losing their minds.

Mashed potatoes prepared properly are one of the best tasting foods known to mankind. Anne Phoebe Charlton Key was the sister of Francis Scott Key, the lawyer. He immortalized himself by immortalizing the famous English naval attack on Fort Henry through the song he wrote entitled "The Star Spangled Banner." Anne Key was a very beautiful woman. On January 7, 1806 she married Rodger Brooke Taney, a man who had gone to law school with her brother. Anne had seven fine children about as rapidly as possible and was a pretty busy woman. She found time, however, to vastly improve on the cooking methods of her time. I believe that her greatest contribution to good cooking was the method she devised for mashing potatoes. Here is her original method.

Peel your potatoes and boil them until well done. Remove and place in a bowl to mash them in. Add about one-fourth level teaspoon of baking powder per two cups of potatoes. Mash the potatoes, mixing in the baking powder well. Now add just sufficient milk or cream to give the potatoes the consistency you desire and mash them well. Place in a serving bowl and sprinkle the top of the potatoes quite heavily with paprika. The baking powder keeps the potatoes snowy white and fluffy. Even any left over mashed potatoes will be white and fluffy the next day. If you freeze the mashed potatoes made with this method they will still remain white and tasty.

HOW TO BOIL A POTATO

Sounds like the simplest thing to do but it is actually practically a lost art. Boiled potatoes form a large part of our today's diet, yet are rarely made so that they are as good to eat as they can be. I learned this method right from a Belgian born cook.

To boil potatoes properly first peel the potatoes. Cut them up in quarters and put them in boiling water. Salt to taste. When you can run a fork through the potatoes pour off the water, every drop. Now here is the real secret. Put the potatoes which are still in the cooking pot back onto the flame from 4 to 6 seconds or just long enough to puff off a little steam, drying off the potatoes well. Not enough to burn them at all. Then remove the potatoes from the pot. They are now dry and light and not at all soggy as they would be if you did not dry them out as described above. Now take a potato ricer. A potato ricer is an Italian invention based on the basic principles of a spaghetti machine. All the old European women who came to this country brought them with them or bought them when they got here. Today they are hard to find but can be bought at some hardware stores for 80c. They are worth their weight in gold if you enjoy eating.

Now put the boiled potatoes in the potato ricer and squeeze them through it. They come out light and fluffy, looking like well cooked rice. Now put butter or gravy on them. They are wonderful to eat. The gravy or butter mixes into them just right leaving them neither lumpy or a soggy mass, but light and really tasty. You will not find potatoes to equal them even at such fancy places as the Stork Club, Antoines, or the Cafe Exceptionale.

CONFEDERATE BAKED POTATOES

Getting a good baked potato these days is next to impossible. They are usually baked so they are too solid, too stringy, or too tough and bluish or gray in color. A good baked potato must be white, soft, and flaky right up to the skin.

For many years I used the old Indian method for baking potatoes as I found it to be far superior to the usual way of just putting them in an oven and baking them. The Indian method is to take a large metal pan, fill it with fine sand, bury your potatoes in the sand and place the pan in your oven. Bake for one hour at about 400 degrees.

This gives you a much flakier baked potato than just oven baking them. It keeps the skin from becoming hard causing the potato near the skin to become hard and over cooked.

A great many years back a group of ex-Confederate soldiers, refugees from the War between the States, came to Minnesota to start life over again. There was plenty of free homesteading land in Minnesota at the time. Their homes had been destroyed and burned during the fighting.

Among them was a John McLin, a wooden bridge builder by trade. The Confederate army had practically lived on potatoes and had learned by necessity how to make them as palatable as possible. This they certainly succeeded in doing. The potatoes baked by the McLins were entirely different and far superior to those baked by any method including sand or oven baked potatoes.

Here is exactly how it was done. This is a recipe to treasure and like all really important tricks in cooking is easy to do.

Go to your lumber yard and buy a dozen 60-penny nails. These are large nails as thick around as a lead pencil and about five inches long. The nails will be dirty and usually a little rusted. Take the nails and sandpaper them clean and wipe them off with paper. Paper cleans steel better than anything. Now wash them well in hot water and soap.

I am going to take the time here to tell you how to buy potatoes because unless you know how to buy them it is impossible to make good potatoes of any kind using any method.

Originally potatoes were, of course, taken from wild potatoes and cultivated by the Indians. They soon found that the red skinned potatoes were by far the best for baking, boiling or frying. Today these potatoes are known as Pontiac potatoes. Do not buy any other kind of potato but these. The white potatoes were promoted commercially by white men. They grow larger than the red skinned potatoes and hence are more profitable to grow. Some names for them are Russets, Idaho Bakers, etc. They have been promoted as a baking potato mainly. Actually they are good for nothing. When baked they are tough, stringy, and often turn gray or blue in color. When boiled they are mushy and for frying are very soggy. Remember the red skinned potato is your only baking potato as well as a boiling and frying potato. Don't let them fool you.

Take the potatoes and run a 60-penny nail lengthwise through each one leaving the nail protruding out of each end. Then take a sharp knife and cut a patch of skin off from the side of each potato about as big as a nickel. This patch lets off moisture from the potato when it first begins to bake preventing any toughness developing. After the potato bakes a short time this open patch seals over.

The nail puts heat right straight through the potato causing it to bake both from the outside and the center. Makes the potato as flaky as can be. Bake the potatoes about 50 minutes at 400 degrees.

Remove the potatoes from the oven and serve them with the nail in place as it keeps the potato at the right temperature until opened. Leave the person eating the potato cut down to the nail and remove it.

Potatoes baked in this manner are far superior to any baked in any other way. Be sure to try this method.

BELGIAN FRIED POTATOES OR POTATOES ORVAL

In Europe the best French fried potatoes by far are made in Belgium. There are two reasons for this. First the soil of Belgium is ideal for producing potatoes that French fry well and puff or souffle. Secondly, the Belgian cooks know how to cook French fried potatoes in beef suet and how to cook them twice so that they puff out or souffle the way that they should.

Belgian fried potatoes, however, are entirely different than French fried or any other types of potato. They are very delicious and once you eat them you will find yourself finding excuses to make them as much as possible. This recipe for Belgian fried potatoes is the one to use for example, on such occasions as when a mother-in-law visits you that has been critical of your cooking. Up until this book was printed this recipe has been the secret of professional cooks only at the finest restaurants in Europe. It has never appeared in written form before.

The recipe was invented by a monk named Vanderle at the monastery at Orval, Belgium. This monastery is famous for the cheese that it makes. Orval cheese is a pale golden cheese with a unique malty odor and a medium sharp taste. It is one of the finest cheeses made in the world. Lemke brick cheese made here in the United States is a copy of Orval cheese. It too is an excellent cheese and undoubtedly one of the world's really great cheeses. The story of how the monastery at Orval came to be built is worth knowing. In medieval times a queen had her castle by the lake at Orval. One day she went rowing on the lake in a small boat. Her wedding ring slipped off from her finger and fell into the lake. She rowed back to shore and prayed that she might be able to somehow get her ring back. She promised that if she did get her ring back that she would build a monastery at Orval. Her husband was a man with a very quick temper and she knew he would be very upset if he found out that she had lost her wedding ring. Several days later she again went rowing on the lake. A fish jumped into her boat and had her ring in its mouth. She took the ring and put the fish back into the lake. The queen immediately built the monastery. Today every cheese that is made at Orval has a fish with a ring in its mouth stamped on it.

Here is the recipe for Belgian Fried Potatoes or Potatoes Orval — This recipe is for 12 people. Cut it down to fit your needs.

Take 1 cup of boiling water, ½ cup of good lard, 1 cup of sifted flour and 4 eggs. Put the lard into 1 cup of boiling water and bring to a boil. Stir in the flour, mixing it in thoroughly. Remove from the stove and allow the mixture to completely cool. Now add the eggs, one at a time, beating the entire mixture well each time that you add an egg. Now mix in the same amount by bulk of mashed potatoes. Salt and pepper the potatoes to taste. Add only barely enough butter or milk to the potatoes to make them mash. Do not have them runny. Mix them in well. For about every cup of mashed potatoes you added, now mix in two level teaspoons of dried onion powder or two level tablespoons of grated or finely chopped onions. Mix them in well. Now take your French fryer with beef suet in it. Heat exactly the same as described for making French fried potatoes. Take a cookie dough press, put in a former for any plain shape about ¼ to ½ inch in diameter and extrude lengths about three inches long into the hot beef grease. French fry them as described for making French fried potatoes. These potatoes are hollow in the center when cooked. Serve them while hot. They are simply unbelievably good and no one can ever guess how they were made. This is a very rare recipe and one to try at the earliest possible moment. The mixture is very gluey texture before you French fry it and you get best results by using a cookie press as described. I have however been able to get good results by taking up a teaspoon of the mixture and dropping it carefully into the hot beef suet.

HOW TO MAKE POTATOES MADRID

When the Spaniards brought back potatoes from the Americas the first and best recipe they developed from potatoes was called potatoes Madrid. This recipe was the pride of the fabulous Spanish court cooks. Although nearly forgotten today it is one of the finest methods ever developed for serving potatoes.

The recipe is as follows:

Take three heaping teaspoons of butter and melt in a frying pan. Take three good sized shallots or fresh green onions and cut in small pieces. Place the pieces in the butter and carefully fry until they just barely begin to brown. Take three good sized potatoes, at least 5 or 6 inches long, and boil until done. Remove all water from them and mash immediately. Mix in one heaping teaspoon of butter and two teaspoons of fresh cream if you have it. In making mashed potatoes if you do not drain every drop of water from them and mash them immediately, they become hard and tasteless. Now mix the shallots and the butter they were fried in with the mashed potatoes. Salt and pepper to taste. Serve immediately. Potatoes served in this manner are worth a lot of effort to get. They make the finest of eating whether served with a meal in the finest restaurant or just with sliced bread.

BRABANT POTATOES

Brabant potatoes and Potatoes O'Brien are the favorite methods of serving potatoes in New Orleans.

Brabant Potatoes were invented by professional cook Robert M. Ducourtioux in 1889. Many cooks have claimed the honor of creating this famous recipe but Ducourtioux was the inventor. Here is the original recipe.

Ingredients.

3 boiled potatoes boiled with their skins on.
1 level tablespoon of fine chopped parsley.
1 level tablespoon of butter.
2 level tablespoons of rendered beef suet.
⅛ level teaspoon of celery salt.
1/16 level teaspoon of white pepper.
1 level teaspoon of white vinegar.

Remove the skins from the potatoes. Cut them into half inch squares. Put the 2 level tablespoons of rendered beef suet into a frying pan and melt over a medium heat. Put in the diced potatoes and fry them in the beef suet for about two minutes or until they are about half brown. Turn them all the while. Now remove the potatoes from the frying pan and pour out any remaining beef suet from the pan and wash the pan. Put the pan back over medium heat and put 1 level tablespoon of butter into the pan and melt. Put the diced potatoes back into the pan and lightly fry for just a few minutes until light brown in color. Now add the 1 level tablespoon of chopped parsley, and 1 teaspoon of white vinegar. Turn the potatoes and sprinkle with ⅛ level teaspoon of celery salt and 1/16 teaspoon of white pepper. Serve at once while good and hot.

Some present day cooks put a cheese sauce over the Brabant potatoes but this is to be frowned upon. Brabant potatoes if prepared correctly need no cheese sauce to make them extremely delicious. In fact the cheese sauce destroys their very delicate, delicious flavor. Do not make them "Au Gratin."

POTATOES O'BRIEN

Potatoes O'Brien and Potatoes Brabant are the favorite methods of preparing white potatoes in New Orleans.

Potatoes O'Brien were invented by John D. O'Brien, a professional cook in 1903. They took a long time to become popular but today are very popular in New Orleans. Here is the original recipe.

Ingredients.
6 medium sized potatoes.
¼ level teaspoon of salt.
One 4½ ounce can of pimentos or two fresh pimentos about 4 inches long boiled in salted water until done.
¼ teaspoon of onion juice.

Wash and pare the potatoes and cut them up into half inch squares. Dry the potato pieces well with a clean towel. French fry them in beef suet exactly as described for making French fried potatoes until they are a delicate brown in color. Do not French fry them twice, however, just once until done. Put them on a soft paper to drain and sprinkle them with ¼ level teaspoon of salt. Now put the potatoes into a frying pan with a little melted butter in it. Chop up the canned pimentos and add them or add the boiled fresh pimentos chopped up as fine as possible. Add ¼ teaspoon of onion juice. Over a medium heat cook until the pimentos are well warmed. Toss the potatoes and pimentos while they are in the frying pan frequently so that they will not burn. Do not press the potatoes or pimentos down onto the pan with a fork or a spatula.

Pimentos and potatoes with a little onion make a blend that is delicious and very different.

Today some cooks in New Orleans serve Potatoes O'Brien with a cheese sauce calling it Potatoes O'Brien Au Gratin. Potatoes O'Brien well prepared do not need a cheese sauce and such methods should be frowned upon.

SCALLOPED POTATOES JEFFERSON

Thomas Jefferson was born in 1743 and died in 1826. He was the third president of the United States. In 1785 he was minister to the court of Louis XVI of France. Although not commonly known Thomas Jefferson was even a better cook than he was a president. He knew Virginia cooking very well and when in France learned French cooking to perfection. He created a mixture of Virginia and French cooking that will still be used long after his statesmanship is forgotten. He spent days in his apartment in France on the Rue de Berri studying French cooking. He went at it carefully and thoroughly just as he had in writing the Declaration of Independence.

Thomas Jefferson brought saffron and many other spices to North America for the first time. In his garden at Monticello he grew asparagus, five kinds of endive, twelve varieties of greens, two types of celery, three types of cabbage and two kinds of peppers. This was indeed advance gardening for his time.

His greatest contribution to good cooking I believe was inventing scalloped potatoes. Here is the original recipe. Since his time the making of scalloped potatoes has degenerated into a very poor unpalatable product simply because cooks have taken short cuts on the original recipe.

Recipe for 8 servings:

Peel raw potatoes and slice four cupsful of them about one eighth of an inch thick. Dry the potatoes thoroughly between a clean towel. Take four heaping tablespoons of butter and melt it into your frying pan with medium heat. Add 3 heaping tablespoons of flour and stir and mix into the butter until smooth and creamy. Remove from the stove and add one cup of cold water. Stir the cold water in well until thoroughly mixed. Never use warm water. Add one eighth teaspoon of ground saffron and salt and pepper to taste. If the ground saffron is not available use the shredded. Simply grind up the shredded saffron by crumbling it between your fingers but use ¼ teaspoon instead of ⅛. If your local grocer does not have saffron you can buy it for 15 cents a box by writing to any large spice maker. Saffron is the dried center or stamen of a special crocus flower that grows in Spain. Before it was used for coloring and seasoning food. Way back in the thirteenth century it was used as a powder for women's faces to give them a suntanned look. Put back on the stove and bring to a slow boil stirring well all of the time. Then remove from the stove. Milk is never used in making scalloped potatoes. When milk is baked it becomes lumpy and gives the dish not only poor taste but a lumpy poor appearance. The butter in the original recipe lends all the dairy richness to the dish that is needed. Now take a baking dish and generously grease it with butter. Put in a layer of potatoes and scatter a few finely chopped onions over them and finely chopped green peppers and pieces of mushrooms. Then pour the sauce over the layer. Repeat until the dish is full.

Bake at 350 degrees for about 2 hours. Do not turn the potatoes with a spoon while cooking.

These are scalloped potatoes that simply cannot be equaled and a great delicacy.

For buying purposes you will need the following quantities of the following items the recipe calls for: one onion 2½ inches in diameter, one medium sized green pepper and one 8 ounce can of mushroom stems and pieces. If saffron becomes a problem to get, the golden yellow pollen from lilies, tulips, or a flower dried, works just as well.

POTATO PANCAKES

Potato pancakes are one of the earliest American foods and one of the best foods ever developed. Potatoes as you know originated in America. There were not any potatoes in Europe until they were brought in from America. The Indians made potato pancakes as well as corn pancakes so far back that it is difficult to find when they first made them. Early European immigrants to America would not eat potatoes in any form. It was many years until the immigrants realized what a wonderful food potatoes really were and began eating them.

The original Indian recipe for potato pancakes has changed very little throughout the centuries. We now add a few items the Indians did not have but they can be made without these additions and are excellent. The Indians ate potato pancakes with whatever fruit that was in season. This varied from such fruits as tomatoes, wild plums, grapes, and cherries. I much prefer them with tomato sauce. The potato pancake itself was nearly always flavored with wild leeks.

Here is the basic Indian recipe with cracker crumbs substituted for coarse ground seeds and onion substituted for leeks, chicken eggs substituted for wild bird eggs, and a little pepper and salt added.

Take three or four large potatoes and peel them. There is a theory that if you soak them in cold water overnight that it will remove some of the starch from the potatoes making them better. Soaking potatoes in cold water does nothing at all for them as any chemist will tell you. Now grate the potatoes. For every pint of grated potatoes proceed as follows: Take two eggs and place them in a bowl and beat them well, then mix them into the grated potatoes. Add four level tablespoons of cracker crumbs, one-half teaspoon of salt, one eighth teaspoon of pepper and half of a two inch in diameter onion well grated. Melt some butter in your frying pan. Drop in large spoonfuls into the frying pan. Flatten them out so that they make pancakes not more than one fourth of an inch thick. If potato pancakes are made thick they are not good at all. Turn and brown them slightly on both sides. If you add flour, milk and baking powder to the grated potatoes as modern recipes call for you only spoil the pancakes. Flour makes them pasty, baking powder does nothing for them and leaves a bitter taste, milk simply makes them gluey.

Today potato pancakes are usually served with apple sauce or catsup. To make apple sauce peel and core your apples. Cut them up into small pieces. Melt a heaping tablespoon of butter in a large covered pot. Place the apple pieces in the covered pot over slow heat with no water. Raise the heat up a little after the apples form some juice in the bottom of the pan. Then turn the heat up just so the apples just barely simmer. Add one-half cup of sugar for every quart of apple sauce and mix in well. Add ½ teaspoon of cinnamon for every quart of apple sauce and mix in well. As soon as the apples are soft and mushy remove them and simply mash them well with a spoon. Serve one heaping tablespoon of apple sauce for every potato pancake served.

TITTY SAUCE YAMS

In the old slave plantation days of Georgia, yams or sweet potatoes were very popular. The white potato was not popular in the South in slave days; in fact still has not gained a great deal of favor. Rice is even more popular than the white potato in most of the Old South today.

The African slave women were used in bringing up the plantation owners babies. If the mother could not nurse the baby or did not care to which was often the case, the African women nursed them. In Africa nursing women often put honey or honey mixed with water mixture on the tits of their breasts. This not only prevents the tits from becoming sore but makes a baby that is not feeding well; suckle long and often.

An African woman named Canary Richardson who was a cook on a Northeastern Georgia plantation made the following recipe based on the honey and water tit mixture. It is the greatest recipe ever made with the yam or sweet potato and one that will bring you instant compliments.

Boil sweet potatoes with the jackets on for 20 minutes in water with 1½ teaspoons of salt per quart. Remove and put them into an oven at 380 degrees and bake until done usually about 40 minutes. Never remove the jackets of sweet potatoes and try to boil them. This ruins them entirely. Take from the oven and remove the skins or jackets. Spoon them up into bite size portions and put in a shallow vegetable dish. Avoid breaking up the flesh as much as possible. Pour a generous amount of the following sauce over them at once and serve.

Take one half cup of water and place in a small pot and heat until good and warm. Add one fourth cup of honey to the water and stir in until well dissolved. Remove from the heat. Add one teaspoon of almond flavoring and one teaspoon of cherry flavoring. You can get these both at practically all grocery stores. Stir in and quickly pour over the bite size portions of yams. Put small pieces of butter over the yams.

INDIAN METHOD OF PLANTING TOMATOES

With all of our fancy hybrid tomato plants and commercial fertilizers we never have even come close to producing tomatoes as quickly or as large as those produced by the Indians centuries ago.

My grandmother raised tomatoes consistently that weighed two pounds each and in record time from seed saved from tomatoes from the year before.

Here is how it is done:

Raise or buy nice large tomato plants about 12 inches tall grown in individual pots.

Dig a hole in your garden about twenty inches deep. Put two inches of corn cobs or cornstalks into the bottom of the hole. Place three inches of manure over the cornstalks. Chicken manure or cow manure I believe works best. Well rotted horse manure is also good. The Indians used deer and buffalo manure or fish. Do not use commercial fertilizers with the exception of Milorganite which works. Now place four inches of dirt over the manure. Remove all the leaves from the sides of the tomato plants leaving only the main branches on top. Set the tomato plant on the dirt and cover the stem with dirt up to about three inches from the main branches. The corn cobs hold moisture and cause the manure to heat, warming the soil. It is like growing tomatoes in a hot house. When the tomato roots work down and hit the manure soaked soil the plants literally seem to jump up over night.

If you put manure on the roots or stems of tomato plants when you plant them it will kill the plant within a few days. The roots must work into the manure area by themselves and adapt themselves to the manured soil gradually.

THE TOMATO AND THE SKUNK

Tomatoes originated in North and South America. They were cultivated by the Indians. Today's strains are no better than the selected strains the Indians were growing a thousand years ago. Europeans never saw a tomato until the Indians showed them. They then thought they were poison and that only Indians could eat them and live. This belief persisted for a great many years. Finally the Europeans found that they could eat tomatoes and live so they sent seeds back to Europe. The Europeans living in Europe, liked tomatoes at once and tomatoes became an important item in Europe's diet.

Like so many things taken for granted Italian spaghetti is about as Italian as an Irish potato which in turn is about as Irish as corn on the cob or Hungarian Goulash which is not Hungarian at all. The Indians were making spaghetti with tomato sauce, baking potatoes, eating corn on the cob and making paprika stew or so-called Hungarian goulash thousands of years before any European even knew they existed.

The word paprika in Hungarian actually means "green pepper" not red pepper which paprika is made from today. The name Hungaria itself is an oriental name from the ten arrow tribe, a part of the orientals who conquered and ruled Hungaria under Attila and other orientals.

The tomato besides its very different, excellent taste has the power to dissipate odors like nothing else will not even the finest chlorophyll. This I learned from the Indians. If you or your dog are sprayed by a skunk the only way to remove this odor is to scrub and wash your skin or your dog with tomato pulp or juice. Skunk scent or odor laughs at chlorophyll, pine oil, alum compounds, and all other modern deodorants.

SALADE DE TOMATOES JEFFERSON

Thomas Jefferson, the famous statesman and very progressive Virginia farmer and cook, grew tomatoes in his farm as early as 1781, which was pretty early for tomatoes in American farm gardens. At this early date no one thought much of tomatoes. Jefferson was a great student of food and new French methods of preparing food as well as early Virginian. His Salade de Tomatoes is a fabulous recipe and one of the finest ways that I have ever seen for preparing tomatoes. It makes a very different delicious salad. Here is the original recipe:

Take four large tomatoes four inches in diameter or more if possible. Slice them into a large bowl. After each slice is made, salt it well. Leave the tomatoes stay one hour in the bowl. This is called "disgorging" the tomatoes. It removes much of the water and juice from them. Pour off the water and juice from the bottom of the bowl. Save this for drinking separately. Now cut two tomato slices into quarters and leave them in the bowl. Take one onion about three inches in diameter and cut it up into small quarter inch squares and place with the tomatoes. Take four level tablespoons full of olive oil or salad oil and pour them over the tomatoes. Now press the tomato pieces down slightly so that they are well packed and fill the bowl with vinegar so that the tomatoes are just barely covered. Leave them stand for 24 hours in a cool place or in your refrigerator. Serve in a deep salad bowl or soup bowl. Pepper to taste. Just try this recipe and you will be amazed how delicious tomatoes prepared in this manner are.

INDIAN METHOD OF PRESERVING TOMATOES

Tomatoes as you know are native to North and Central America only. The Indians cultivated selected varieties of them centuries before Europeans came to this continent. Cortez brought back tomato seeds and methods for preparing tomato dishes including spaghetti with tomato sauce and ravioli to his native Spain.

Nowadays you can buy fresh tomatoes nearly everywhere as well as canned tomatoes. We live in a land of the greatest luxuries the world has ever known. A few hydrogen or cobalt bombs could however, put us back to wilderness times in a matter of minutes. This Indian method of preserving tomatoes would then be of the highest value. This Indian method of preserving tomatoes was taught to Spaniards by Cortez. It is still widely used in Spain, Italy, and Sicily.

The Indian method of preserving tomatoes is as follows:

1. For preserving sliced tomatoes. The days must be hot or very warm. Slice the tomatoes fairly thin and place them on unpainted boards directly in the sun rays. Slant the board slightly so surplus liquids will run off. Salt them well. Have the boards up against your steps or the side of a building so the building will reflect the heat onto the sliced tomatoes. Cover the tomatoes with mosquito net to keep off the flies. When the tomatoes become shriveled and dry place them in sealed jars for keeping. To use in soup put them into the soup in their dried state. They will absorb moisture from the soup and become soft and tasty. To use in salads soak in water until soft, then mix in with your salad.

2. To make tomato paste proceed as follows:

Place the tomatoes in hot water for enough seconds so their skin loosens its hold on the flesh of the tomato. Then the skin can be easily removed with a knife. Now press the tomatoes through a sieve. Salt well. Place the puree in dishes and set them out in the hot sun. Be sure the dishes are up against your steps or house where the steps or house will reflect the sun's heat back onto the dishes. Cover the dishes with mosquito netting. Stir occasionally until dry. Then pound into powder and store in air tight jars.

Add the powdered tomato puree to soups or make tomato soups from it.

During tomato harvest time you always have too many tomatoes as they ripened so rapidly. Either of these methods will make it possible to use every tomato you raise and to store them for use in a very small space.

U. S. SENATE BEAN SOUP

In the Senate building in Washington D. C. is the Senate restaurant where all the senators eat. It is run by a commercial restaurant firm. The food there as a whole is nothing to brag about but the bean soup that they serve is excellent and the only reason many people eat there. Their bean soup is an exact copy of Bean Soup Jean Debruyn, a Belgian bean soup originated by Jean Debruyn. A Minnesota Senator Knutson was said by some to have invented this soup but this is not at all true. Mr. Debruyn's bean soup today in Belgium is more popular than ever and a real national Belgian dish. I like it very much. It certainly rates well up on the list of the world's finest soups. Mr. Debruyn was unquestionably one of the most far seeing and finest men that ever lived on this earth. He was a very godly man. In the days when the slave trade first began in Africa he did his best to arouse European public opinion to put a stop to it. He advocated leaving the Africans in Africa and not enslaving them in Africa or anyplace else. His pleas fell on deaf ears everywhere. He finally went to Africa with the thought that he might be able to stop the slave trade at its base. Europeans, Americans, Arabs and Africans were all in the slave trade. He talked and tried to reason with the slavers but all of them spurned him and plotted his quick murder. The Arabs wasted no time and quickly killed him. If people just would have listened to this righteous man look what troubles the world would have been spared. At this writing the slave trade still flourishes in Saudi Arabia. Great nations are too busy trying to gain material power and care for the so-called "needy" with surpluses that they do not want and are just happy to get rid of under the guise of charity. There is not a nation in the world that is doing one thing to stop the ungodly slavery that is still going on.

Jean Debruyn not only was a great man but a famous cook. He gave Belgium its famous bean soup. Here is the original recipe.

2 cups of beans soaked overnight in water.

2 quarts of water.

1 ham hock or ham bone with about a cup of meat left on it or one cup of ham cut up in one half inch squares. A cup of diced Spam will do it well too.

1 onion about 2½ inches in diameter diced.

¼ teaspoon of liquid smoke.

¼ cup of butter.

1 level teaspoon of salt.

Take a frying pan and melt the ¼ pound of butter over medium heat. Put in the diced onion and lightly brown the onions. Put the soaked beans into a large pot with two quarts of water. Add the butter and browned diced onions and the ham hock, ham bone, or cubed ham, salt, pepper, and liquid smoke. Boil gently until the beans are tender.

SOUP CAPISTRANO

Father Junipero Serra founded the Missions at San Juan Capistrano in 1776. A chapel was built that still remains intact today. It is the oldest building put up by Europeans in California. The chapel had to be made quite narrow as there were no large trees in the area to make longer beams across the roof. The altar was brought in from Barcelona, Spain. The

Statue of Father Junipero Serro on the mission grounds. His life really began at 60.

The original old Spanish made altar. Note that the church is very narrow. There were no large trees in the area to make longer roof beams.

pictures, statues, candlestick holders and decorations are all the original ones and are very well preserved.

A large stone church was started in 1797 and finished in 1806. In 1812 an earthquake shook down all the walls but a side arch. The side arch remains in place today. The bells of this church were saved and put in a specially built arch or campanero as souvenirs and remain there today.

A very few swallows have built mud bottle-like homes in the old arch. The swallows come to the mission on St. Joseph's Day, March 19th and stay until the later part of the summer. They are very scarce and you are lucky if you see a few flying about the mission toward evening. Today, the priests have put white doves on the grounds and they are the only birds you are actually apt to see.

The mission was really a complete town in itself. On the mission grounds the priests built a tannery for tanning hides, a dye shop, a weaving shop, a candle making shop, vats for making tallow, a mill for grinding grain and for extracting oil from olives, a metal forge and foundry for both forging and casting iron and a complete hospital and two kitchens and storehouses for food. They even built a calaboose or jail for locking up Indians who got drunk. They built a building or barracks for soldiers, as soldiers guarded the mission and went along with the padres on missionary work in the hostile areas.

The padres were well trained in practically all trades. They were expected to live in the wilderness entirely on their own as well as to build up small towns and missions with their own hands. The priests were the finest cooks, wine and cheese makers and farmers.

The country around Capistrano has large rolling hills covered with high grass. Some of the valleys have patches of brush and a few medium sized trees in them but native lumber was and is scarce. There were a few deer in the hills and some quail. The sea is only a short distance away but fishing has always been spotty. Some of the time good, some of the time nothing at all. As soon as it was possible, the padres brought in their own cattle, goats and sheep. They planted their own vegetables, grain and olive trees. Food at the mission of Capistrano was very good and many a traveler made it a point to stop at the mission around meal time and eat with the padres.

The kitchen was called the pozolera. On regular days for morning and evening "atole" was served. This was stew made from roasted grain, meat, fish, vegetables and olive oil flavored or flavored with the pollen from the flowers. "Pazole" was served at noon. This was stew with meat, beans, peas, vegetables, chick peas or garbanzos. Garbanzos originated in the Mediterrainean countries. The padres liked them very much and grew huge fields of them and sometimes used them in this stew.

The original bells from the large church at Capistrano now rest in this memorial arch.

Olives were also used as flavoring, as well as chili from Mexico and pollen from flowers. The Spanish priests were used to using the pollen of the saffron crocus of Spain for flavoring and knew that pollen of all flowers makes wonderful food flavoring.

Many special dishes were made at the mission and used on special church days. Soup Capistrano was a great favorite. Here is the recipe broken down so that you can make it easily at home.

All that is left of the main church at Capistrano. A very few swallows have mud nests in the structure The birds in the photograph are white doves that have been stocked on the grounds.

Take a five quart soup pot and add the following. A half pound of hamburger broken up into small pieces. The padres ground or pulverized meat so that everyone got an equal amount in their bowl. One 15½ ounce can of ripe olives. Chop them up in small pieces. Add the liquid they come in to the pot also. One 4 ounce can of canned pimentoes chopped up fine; add the liquid from the can also. One standard 15½ ounce can of baked beans. One standard 15½ ounce can of peas. One level teaspoon of liquid smoke.

If you have any flowers in bloom in your yard or house add a level teaspoon of yellow flower pollen. Salt and pepper to taste. Add two quarts of water and boil over medium heat until the meat is done.

VEGETABLE ESCOFFIER

Before Columbus came to America our beans such as navy, pea beans, red kidney, pinto, great northern, marrow, yellow eye, green and yellow snap beans, wax beans and lima beans were unknown in Europe or Asia. They were cultivated by the Indians and with corn formed the large part of their diet. Europeans however were quick to get bean seeds from the Indians and take them to Europe for planting. By 1700 all of our fine beans were well known in Europe as well as in Africa, India, and the Philippines.

The great French cook Escoffier, like most European people, was a great lover of American beans. He developed a recipe for using red kidney beans as a vegetable that is a classic. Here is the original recipe.

Take a pound can of red kidney beans. At this writing their cost is about 15c a can. Pour out the beans into a strainer. Run cold water

Lulu Belle Restaurant and bar in the wind blown desert town of Scottsdale, Arizona.

over them until all of the starchy water they came packed in is washed away. Then place the beans in a good sized glass or crockery bowl, add three level tablespoons of white onions cut up in about one fourth inch squares, 8 bay leaves, one fourth teaspoon of black pepper, one fourth teaspoon of salt, one level teaspoon of dried parsley leaves or chopped up fresh parsley, and one level tablespoon of salad oil. Mix well together. Now pour white vinegar into the bowl until the beans are just barely covered by the vinegar. Put the bowl in your refrigerator or in a cool place for two full days.

Remove and serve cold as a cold vegetable with your dinner. You can also use the beans as a relish just before the meal. Kidney beans prepared in this manner are simply delicious. They must set however for two full days before they develop the delicate proper flavor and aroma desired. Beans prepared in this exact manner are widely served throughout Europe.

The Lulu Belle Restaurant in Scottsdale, Arizona serves Vegetable Escoffier under the name of San Francisco Relish. They do a good job of it except that they should use the bay leaves.

PAELLA CARLOS VEGA

The Spanish dish Paella was invented in Valencia by Carlos Vega in 1840, a small restaurant owner. He invented it as a means of flavoring rice and this is actually the whole function of the recipe Paella. Today Paella is served all over Spain and is one of the most popular dishes in the world.

The lowlands of Valencia are easily flooded. Hence when rice seed came in from Asia, rice was almost immediately grown in Valencia's easily flooded lowlands. After Spain began to grow rice it became a very important part of the diet for all of Spain, almost as important as rice in the Chinese and Japanese diets. With the rice seed came orange seeds from China, and Valencia became the orange growing center of Europe and still is today. Valencia is the only town in all of Europe where the people in eating spoon toward the center of the table not toward their mouths. Hence Valencia is the only place in all of Europe where an American can eat his soup as we Americans do and still have good table manners.

Authentic Paella is an easy prepared simple delicious food. Food editors and cook book writers who have never been to Spain have managed as usual to louse up this wonderful recipe with a lot of stupid concoctions of their own that do not even make good sense.

Here is the original Carlos Vega Paella recipe.

Take two cups of green string beans. Remove the strings and open the pods and separate them into two lengthwise pieces. Put in a pot of cold water and boil until tender. Remove and place in a large covered cooking pot. Put ½ cup of olive oil or salad oil into a large frying pan. Take two onions about two inches in diameter and cut them up into long thin slices. Add two medium sized sweet pimento peppers cut up in long thin slices. If you have no fresh pimentos the canned ones are just as good. Use one small can of pimentos juice and all. Brown the onion and the pimentos lightly in the oil. Put one level teaspoon of paprika into the oil, and stir in well. To the covered cooking pot add one pound of good fish boned and cut up into about half inch squares. Walleyed pike, bluegills, crappies, catfish, halibut, haddock are all excellent. Put the oil and onions and pimentos into the pot. Add one clove of garlic, grated or cut up real fine, ½ level teaspoon of oregano, 2 level teaspoons of salt, ¼ level teaspoon of black pepper, ⅛ level teaspoon of saffron, 1½ cups of uncooked white rice, and ½ cup of chopped parsley. Then add about 3 cups of hot water. Cover the cooking pot and under a low heat cook for about 15 minutes or until the rice is cooked and has absorbed all of the liquid. Watch the pot carefully so that the rice or other ingredients do not burn. Remove and put on your serving plates right from the cooking pot.

Instead of fish which is the authentic Paella meat, you can use a pound of fresh or canned shrimp, lobster, oysters, eels, clams, turtle meat or snails. Your Paella will sound fancier but will not be a bit better than when made as it originally was with good fish. You can use a mixture of say ½ pound of shrimp and a half pound of oysters or any other sea food combination.

Real Paella never contains such things as celery, chicken or beef broth, peas, carrots or potatoes nor pieces of beef, pork or fowl meat.

If snails are available in your area prepare them for Paella as follows. Put them into a large bowl of cold water with three level tablespoons of salt and stir them around well for a minute. Then pour off the water. Now put them into a bowl with just enough water to cover them. Keep them in the water until their heads poke out of the shells. Any that do not poke their heads out throw away. Then put the snails into a pot of boiling water and boil for two hours. Remove and drain and throw away the snails. Use three cups of the liquid for your Paella water.

Carlos Vega also made a beautiful red cabbage colored Paella that I like very well. To do this just add pieces of red cabbage leaves about four inches square to the cooking pot. Just use the thin leaves of the cabbage not the hard stems. The stems will not cook fast enough. If you have no Saffron which is the golden yellow centers of crocus flowers use the pollen from lilies, tulips, roses, daisies or any other flower with golden covered pollen.

DIRTY RICE STUART

James Ewell Brown Stuart was born in Virginia on Feb. 6, 1833. He went to West Point in 1850 and became a Lieutenant in the United States Army. When Virginia decided .o become part of a new country the Confederate States of America, Stuart went to defend his state against attack. He was given a chicken Colonel's rank in the Confederate Army. In 1861 he was made a Brigadier General. He then was made a Major General and the commander of the Confederacy's cavalry which included artillery.

Stuart was killed in action at Yellow Tavern on May 10, 1864. He undoubtedly was one of the greatest military geniuses the world has ever seen. He had the almost unbelievable ability to take entirely untrained men and lead them into a complicated battle and give a perfect performance. Time after time Stuart made fools of the North's high ranking officers like McClellan. He even captured all of General Pope's secret staff documents in a carefully planned behind the lines raid. Stuart was never out maneuvered on equal terms. He finally was smothered with superior manpower and equipment. If Hitler would have had one Jeb Stuart in World War II he would have clobbered both us and England. Stuart's dish was stumbling and fumbling military men like Montgomery and Eisenhower.

Stuart moved fast and fed his men mostly on a rice ration when possible as it was easy to carry. His men cursed the "damn dirty rice" that Jeb rationed them and called him the "Chinese General" but there was never a man who served under him who would not gladly lay his life down for him.

The recipes varied from time to time but when the ingredients were at hand here is how it was made. Break it down into the proportion you desire for your own use.

4 pounds of raw white rice.
4 pounds of large whole onions.
¼ cup of bacon drippings.
2 pounds of hamburger. Actually any meat handy was used—sometimes beef, sometimes pork, chicken gizzards and livers, rabbits, squirrels, even horsemeat. The meat was cut up or powdered real fine so everyone got a taste.
18 green onions, tops and all cut up fine.
1 level teaspoon of red pepper or pepper to taste.
Three level tablespoons of salt or salt to taste.

8 strips of bacon fried crisp and broken up into small pieces.
1 cup of chopped up parsley.
9 cups of water.

Soak the rice overnight, changing and draining the water on it three times. Then cook the rice in water until just barely done. Chop up the large onions real fine and brown them in the bacon drippings. Put in the hamburger and cook until just barely done. Chop up the green onions real fine and the parsley and add the water, salt and pepper. Cook until the green onions are just barely done. Add the pieces of bacon. Pour over the cooked rice and leave stand until the moisture is absorbed. Stir slowly. Serves 30 to 40 people.

The French in Louisiana today add five cloves of minced garlic with the onions. They also put pieces of butter on the rice after it has absorbed the moisture of the mixture and brown at 350 degrees for 15 minutes in an oven. The Louisiana French like ground up chicken gizzards and livers instead of hamburger in the recipe. I like dirty rice with any kind of meat but prefer it with beef hamburger or squirrel hamburger.

THE MYTH ABOUT SO-CALLED WILD RICE

Rice is found in a wild state in North America and Asia. All rice is wild rice as it all comes originally from wild rice seed. All rice of all kinds is being cultivated today.

In North Amerca there are two native species. Northern wild rice which is an annual and Texas wild rice which is a perennial. There are three varieties of northern wild rice, one is found in the eastern part of the United States and is a very large plant. One is found in the north eastern part of the United States which is smaller and one in the middle west like in Minnesota and Wisconsin. The latter rice is also a large plant.

Long grain natural dark brown Asia wild rice or so-called Duck Marsh rice is far better than any of them and is being grown in this country.

Being brought up in Minnesota I am very familiar with so-called Minnesota wild rice. It is a long grained dark brown rice that when cooked tastes exactly like cooked barley. Blind folded you cannot tell the difference between it and cooked barley. It is the poorest eating rice in existence. Actually to me it tastes like mud from a pond and barley mixed together. No one ever ate it. Not one settler or Indian ever bothered with it at all as they knew it was no good for eating. We and the Indians hunted ducks in the rice beds as the wild ducks like to feed on it and that is about as far as it went. Drainage and pollution killed off most of the rice beds and when the rice began to become somewhat scarce some-one decided it was good to eat because it was scarce. Immediately so called Minnesota wild rice began to sell at nearly $2.00 or more a pound The Indians began gathering it and men went into the rice business and began planting it. Today they do a flourishing business on so-called Min-nesota wild rice and it is seeded and harvested like all other rice. The taste of Minnesota wild rice is so bad that in order to get it down you have to practically camouflage the flavor with other strong flavors. The Indians have never fallen for this modern "hokum" about Minnesota wild rice and still will not eat it if they can get other rice.

Natural dark brown long grain Duck Marsh rice is wonderful and far superior to polished white rice available at grocery stores. For stuffing ducks, pheasants, quail, doves, turkey, geese, squirrels and rabbit it beats anything. Served as a vegetable with game dinners it is wonderful. If you cannot secure it locally we keep some in our main display room and will ship to you. Price 47c a pound, put up in vermin proof cans. A fourth pound will stuff 2 mallards or pheasants or three teal.

RECIPE FOR STUFFING WITH DUCK MARSH NATURAL BROWN RICE

Take one cup of the rice and wash thoroughly in 5 or 6 waters and place in a 3 quart pot with a tight fitting cover. Add 3 cups of cold water and 4 bouillon cubes. Place over a moderate flame and bring to a vigorous boil. This should take 8 to 10 minutes. When steam and foam begin to escape, turn flame down lower and cook the rice until it is tender. This takes about 40 minutes. All the consomme should be absorbed, if not, pour off any surplus. For the last few minutes of cooking watch the rice carefully so it does not burn. Now take four slices of bacon and cut them up in about inch squares and fry in a pan until about half cooked. Add one tablespoon of butter and one medium sized sliced onion. Fry until the onions are about half done. Now add 3 bay leaves, (these are really nothing but laurel leaves) 1 level teaspoon of oregano, 1½ cups of chopped celery, 1 small can of mushroom stems and pieces and the cooked rice. Salt and pepper to taste and mix together well. Then stuff the birds. The dressing is actually better to eat than the birds and will form the main dish, and don't ever think it won't.

DUCK MARSH NATURAL BROWN RICE SERVED AS A VEGETABLE

Take one cup of the rice and wash thoroughly in 5 or 6 waters and place in a 3 quart pot with a tight fitting cover. Add 3 cups of cold water and 4 boullion cubes and one-fourth level teaspoon of cinnamon. Place over a moderate flame and bring to a vigorous boil. This should take 8 to 10 minutes. When the steam and foam begin to escape, turn the flame down lower and cook the rice until it is tender. This takes about 40 minutes. All the consomme should be absorbed, if not, pour off any surplus. Watch very carefully toward the end so the rice will not burn. Take one can of cream of mushroom soup, heat and mix with the rice lightly. Salt and pepper to taste.

SWEDISH METHOD OF PREPARING RUTABAGAS

(The only correct way ever invented to prepare them.)

The rutabaga is a very strange vegetable. It occurred from a rare accidental hybridization of a cabbage and a turnip in Switzerland. The Swiss botanist Caspar Bauhin described the rutabaga for the first time in 1620.

The rutabaga never became popular in Europe for a very long time after its chance discovery as it had too strong a flavor and the texture of it was coarse.

By 1800 the Swedish people were raising large quantities of potatoes which, of course, originated in America. The Swedish people not only liked potatoes very much but made wonderful flour from potatoes. They used this flour for breads, cakes, and for mixing with ground fish to make fish balls. When the Swedish people first tried eating boiled rutabagas they found them far too strong in flavor. Like other European people they did not care too much for them at all. They then tried mixing boiled mashed rutabagas with one third of mashed potatoes. To this they add one eighth teaspoon of nutmeg for two cups of the mixture and a one inch square of grated onion per two cups of the mixture. Mix in the onion and nutmeg well while the rutabagas and potatoes are hot and add butter to taste and season with salt and pepper. This they called "Stockholm Creamed Rutabagas." They are simply delicious. Served in this manner they are one of the finest vegetables you can serve with any meal. Be sure to try them without fail.

The name rutabaga comes from the Swedish word ROTABAGGE. So popular is the Swedish method of preparing rutabagas that in England and in Canada rutabagas are called "Swedes" or "Swede turnip." The French love them prepared in the Swedish manner and now call rutabagas, "navet de Suede" (Swede turnip) and "chou de Suede" (Swede cabbage).

BELGIAN SAUERKRAUT

This is the best 30c worth of food I have ever come across. Everyone is familiar with sauerkraut with pig's feet and with wieners and used as duck and goose stuffiing. Some people like sauerkraut these ways and some do not. I have never seen anyone, however, tnat did not like Belgian sauerkraut. It has a distinctly different taste that is not like sauerkraut at all. In fact you cannot taste the sauerkraut in it. The recipe comes from the same province in Belgium that invented such well known foods as Limburger cheese.

Put a generous amount of butter in a pot, not a frying pan and melt it. Cut up one medium sized onion in the pot and cook the onions until half done. Take one can of tomato puree and mix it in the pot. Add one can of water using the tomato puree can as the measure. Add 2 bay leaves, ½ level teaspoon of oregano and one-half level teaspoon of sweet basil. Cut up a medium sized potato in thin slices even thinner than you would for scalloped potatoes and cut them in fourths and add. Now add a standard pound can of sauerkraut. Mix all together well and cook on medium heat until the potatoes are done. Add just enough water as it cooks so the mixture will not burn. The amount is hard to say as it depends on how much juice came with the sauerkraut. Do not add any more than necessary.

HOW TO MAKE SHALLOTS FROM ONIONS

It used to be that every immigrant from every country in Europe knew how to raise shallots and make potatoes Madrid. Today the old ones are long since gone and few people in North America even know what a shallot is.

Strange as it may seem to you although a shallot is an onion type vegetable in its own right they can be made from red or yellow skinned onions. Here is how you make shallots from onions.

There are two ways to make shallots. The first method is as follows: If you raise your own onions, in the spring of the year you usually have some that have softened up so much that they are not edible. If not, go to the grocery store and buy some inexpensive red skinned onions about an inch to an inch and a half in diameter. If red skinned onions are not available buy the yellow skinned onions. Plant either your own softened up onions or the ones from the grocery store so that there is about one-half inch of soil over the top of them. These onions are two years old as it takes a year to raise sets and then a year to raise onions from the sets. The third year, replanted onions will come up as shallots.

The second method: Buy the largest red onion sets you can find. They must be at least an inch in diameter. If you cannot get large red skinned sets buy the yellow skinned ones. Cut each set from the top to within a quarter of an inch of the bottom into four equal sections. Be sure not to cut the sections free of each other, they must be held together at the base by about a quarter inch of the set. Plant each cut set in the ground so that the tip of each section sticks out a trifle.

In the fall remove the onions made into shallots from the ground and hang them in the sun to dry as you do onions. The onions made into shallots however will not look nor taste like onions. They will have the appearance of a garlic bulb and they will taste much milder and finer than an onion and digest better.

The word shallot comes from the Latin word ascalonia meaning a wild onion from Ascalon a port of old Palestine. The French crusaders landed at this port and brought back shallots to France. A shallot looks like a garlic bulb but tastes like a mild onion. They grow wild around cliffs near Ascalon.

SPINACH NESSELRODE

Count Karl Robert Nesselrode was born in 1780 and died in 1862. He was a Russian statesman. He was very interested in good food, in fact actually far more so than in being a good statesman. He traveled around Europe a great deal and always spent a good deal of his time with Europe's court cooks. Many famous cooks named dishes for him such as ice cream Nesselrode, sauce Nesselrode, etc.

He himself made this excellent recipe. I will adapt it here to present day means.

Take one box of frozen spinach or one quart of fresh spinach. Chop it up into as fine pieces as possible. Take one box of frozen broccoli spears or one quart of fresh broccoli spears. Chop them up into as small pieces as possible.

Put about two cups of water into a large pot and add a teaspoon of salt. Bring the water to a boil. Add the chopped broccoli and boil for six minutes. Add the chopped spinach and boil for four minutes. Mix the two together well. Remove and drain. While hot quickly mix in enough mayonnaise to just barely coat the pieces slightly.

People that ordinarily will not touch spinach in any form are very fond of spinach prepared in this manner. It makes a very, very, different vegetable to serve with any meal. Immigrants brought this famous recipe to Minnesota many years ago. It is also found today in many of the finest New York restaurants.

SPINACH MOTHER OF CHRIST

The Virgin Mary, Mother of Christ was very fond of spinach. This is as well a known fact in Nazareth today as it was 19 centuries ago. Her favorite music was that of the crude bagpipes of that time, and this also is a well-known fact.

Her recipe for preparing spinach spread with Christianity throughout Europe. On the eve of Christ's birth in the cave that was called a stable, Her only meal was spinach.

The early European immigrants from Germany, France, and Italy nearly all brought this recipe with them. This is a recipe for people who like a mild garlic flavor, it definitely is not for people who do not like some garlic.

This recipe cannot be made from canned spinach. Canned spinach in no way resembles fresh or frozen spinach and in my opinion is fit for neither man or beast.

Take six quarts of fresh spinach and carefully remove the heavy stems. If you use frozen spinach take two boxes. Boil the fresh spinach five minutes — no more. If you boil spinach too much it completely loses all of its original taste. If you use frozen spinach place it in boiling water. With a fork break up the frozen blocks as soon as possible. After the blocks are broken up and the spinach loose boil it for 1 to 2 minutes — no more or it is worthless. Take and put three heaping teaspoons of butter in a frying pan and melt it. Chop up four cloves of garlic and put them into the melted butter. Fry them with medium or low heat until slightly brown. Frying the garlic in butter entirely changes its odor and flavor making it quite mild. Take the drained spinach and mix in the butter and fried garlic. Salt and pepper to taste. Originally the spinach was then pestled to a puree. Today take your food mill and pass the spinach through it making it into a puree. Serve as a main dish with bread and butter or as a vegetable with a regular meal.

Today in Belgium and Germany a little nutmeg is sprinkled over the top of the puree. This however was not in the original recipe.

SUKIYAKI AND A WORD ABOUT FISHERMAN'S WHARF

Sukiyaki is a Japanese meat and vegetable dish and was created by order of Daimyo of Satsuma, Shimazu Takahisa at the castle of Kobubu, fifteen miles from Kagoshima in about 1540. The Daimyo of Satsuma was one of the six actual rulers of Japan at this time. Go-Nara-Tenno, 105th descendant of the Sun goddess, Amaterasu who was supposed to rule Japan at that time did not have any actual power at all.

The Japanese as we know them today were a tribe who settled in Japan from Asia. The original inhabitants of the islands were a race much like Eskimos. They are now nearly extinct, only a few of them being left in present day Japan. The ancient Japanese unlike the Chinese did not care for games of chance, considering it a form of theft and highly dishonorable. There were fewer thieves in Japan than any country in the world as they hated stealing and punished thieves with death. White was a color of mourning and black and purple colors of celebrating. They spoke a language of their own not Chinese and had their own alphabet and number system. For the most part they drank Cha, a tea made from crushed berries of a mountain bush. They did not drink tea like the Chinese. Japanese food in Ancient times as well as modern times, is nothing like Chinese food in any manner. The Japanese people have never cared for Chinese food of any kind. Chow Mein, which means fried noodles in Chinese, and Chop Suey which means fine mixture, in Chinese, no Japanese ancient or present would ever think of eating. Japanese women are the cleanest of any in the world. If they have enough water they will take a bath twice a day. That really is something. Many an American soldier who did duty in Japan has regretted ever since that he did not marry one.

The original Sukiyaki was made first with fish as the Japanese around 1540 would not eat meat or even fowl; as customs changed they used bear grease and bear meat, then later on with water buffalo, then India cattle and finally beef from European bison or buffalo which we have on our American farms today. Sukiyaki makes one of the finest meals I have ever eaten and everyone whom I have ever seen who tried it thought it wonderful. Although Sukiyaki contains quite a few onions, it has no onion taste at all. Neither will your breath smell of onions after eating it nor will you ever belch up any onion gas. The sauce that it is cooked in completely neutralizes the onions. This in itself is a real cooking trick.

Here are the ingredients you need for four hungry people:

Two cups of cooked fine egg noodles. Japanese today often use clear potato or corn starch noodles. These are much cheaper to make but not nearly as good as the old fine egg noodles.

One large, mild onion about four inches in diameter or two small onions about 2 inches in diameter. Slice the onions in circular slices about one-eighth of an inch thick, then cut these slices in two, down the center.

Two bunches of young, green onions, ten to a bunch. Cut off the roots and cut the white section in two-inch lengths. Cut the green tops into half-inch lengths. Be sure to use all the green tops.

One can of mushroom stems and pieces, 4 ounce drained weight size.

One 5-ounce can of water chestnuts.

Five medium sized radishes, sliced one-eighth inch thick. If you desire, use ten radishes sliced and leave out the water chestnuts, as they are quite expensive and not that important.

One 5¼ ounce can of bamboo sprouts.

Two cups of celery sliced lengthwise and cut up into pieces about ¼ of an inch square. Celery was not used in Sukiyaki to start with, as there was no celery in Japan. Bamboo sprouts were plentiful and cost nothing and were used. Actually bamboo shoots have no taste at all and the celery improves the Sukiyaki greatly. You can leave out the bamboo shoots altogether and just use 2¼ cups of finely diced celery and your result will be excellent. One two-inch square cake of soybean curd. This you do not need. Soy bean curd cake tastes like a sour piece of custard and looks like it and most people do not like it. Here again is an ingredient that was and is cheap in Japan and used simply because of this. You do not need anything to replace it at all, but if you want to be fancy and greatly improve on it, put in a two inch square or two of custard or one egg made into an omelette and cut up into one-half inch squares.

Eight beef chip steaks. These are very finely sliced beef. If you cannot get these, get one-half pound of round steak, or rib or sirloin steak sliced real thin. Make your butcher put it on his cold meat slicer and slice it as thinly as possible. Preferably not more than one thirty-second of an inch thick.

Now take 8 ounces of soy sauce and put it into an empty one-fifth of a quart liquor bottle. Add one level tablespoon of sugar to it and eight ounces of water. Shake well. Although there were originally no grapes of any kind in Japan a good modern day Japanese trick is to use 7 ounces of water and one ounce of grape juice instead of the 8 ounces of water with the soy sauce. It adds a great deal to your Sukiyaki.

Take a large frying pan and put four level tablespoons of beef suet into it and melt it. The Japanese are some of the world's finest cooks and soon found that beef suet was far better than lard or vegetable oils for cooking.

Put your meat into the beef suet and fry it until it is just barely done. Now put in all of the other ingredients except the cooked egg noodles. Now add enough of the soy sauce mixture so that it comes up to about one-fourth of an inch from the top of the mixture in the pan. Over a medium heat without a cover on the pan leave the mixture boil. Stir it quite frequently. Add soy sauce mixture if necessary. Cook just until the onion green tops and sliced onions are barely done. Do not overcook. The mixture will have absorbed each other's juices and the soy sauce mixture and most of the water will have boiled off in steam in the process. Just before removing the frying pan from the stove, take the cooked egg noodles and pick up a fork full at a time and mix them into the mixture lightly so that they stay in separate bunches. Let them warm in the mixture until they absorb some of the sauce and turn slightly brown in color from the sauce.

Remove and serve alone or with boiled rice as a side dish. Most Americans prefer it just served alone. If you serve with rice, be sure that you use enough of the special soy sauce in cooking the Sukiyaki so that you can pour a good bit of sauce over the rice. Do not just use plain soy sauce on rice as you do in Chinese cooking.

This will make you one of the finest meals that you will ever have in any country in the world.

If you ever get a chance to go to the Fisherman's Wharf in San Francisco which is an area of restaurants, take this advice. The Fisherman's Wharf in San Francisco is strictly phony atmosphere. There has been no commercial fishing in the whole San Francisco area for many, many, years and no fish come into Fisherman's Wharf. A few boats go out for crabs, but that is all. As you walk around the wharf, the mongers try to sell you what is known as a "Walk Around Cocktail." This is a

The Tokyo Sukiyaki Restaurant on Fisherman's Wharf is worth your while. It isn't often that you can find a good restaurant where you can sit down, really relax and eat.

Your waitress is also your cook at Tokyo Sukiyaki and prepares your food right at the table.

Fisherman's Wharf, San Francisco. Note the restaurant built out over the water. The sea gull would be better eating than some of the food served on the wharf.

"I would rather have a hamburger."

The best food available at Fisherman's Wharf is the sour, hard-crusted French bread. A good man can eat a loaf in three meals.

paper cup of small shrimp. All of these shrimp come from Mexico. If you go into one of the seafood restaurants you will find that the live lobsters are all from Maine, the large shrimp from Texas, the fish and abalone from Mexico, and the oysters from Louisiana or the east coast. The seafood is not bad, but no better than you can find in a good restaurant in your home town. In fact, as long as they have to import everything, they should have walleyed pike, shad roe, red snapper, sea turtle meat and catfish, which are some of the real delicacies in fish and sea foods.

There is a restaurant on Fisherman's Wharf that is very much worthwhile to go to however, and it is called Tokyo Sukiyaki. This is a very fine Japanese restaurant. Go there and have some Sukiyaki and you will have something to really tell your friends about when you go home. The Sukiyaki there is excellent, not as good as you can make at home, but very good. A beautiful Japanese girl right from Japan, and no phony, in true Japanese dress, will prepare your Sukiyaki just for you on a private little burner right at your table. You will find that she can just barely speak enough English to answer a few questions regarding preparation of your Sukiyaki. If you are a drinking man have a glass or two of warm sake before your meal and a bottle of Japanese Kirin rice beer after your meal.

TRUE FRENCH FRYING OF FISH AS TAUGHT IN THE "CORDON BLEU" SCHOOL OF COOKING IN PARIS, FRANCE

The Cordon Bleu cooking school in Paris, France is the most famous cooking school in the world. All the world's leading chefs from all countries attend and sponsor it.

Fish are cooked countless different ways in the various countries. I could easily write a book on the hundreds of good methods I have encountered. The method I describe here however is one of the very best. Using this method you can cook practically any fish, fresh or salt water, and it is delicious.

True French frying of fish is a very secret art, yet it is very, very simple and very inexpensive to do. You will not find how to do it in any of the cooking sections of North American women's magazines, nor in any cook book, North American or European. The real secret of French frying is a much more closely guarded one than any military secret! This is the method taught by the Cordon Bleu School and is known only to a limited number of male cooks.

Buy a French frying pot with screen pot to go inside of it. It must be a screen pot not a perforated metal pot. The perforated metal pot will not work at all as it stops the circulation of the grease. In the event you cannot purchase one locally, you will find them both in Sears Roebuck and Montgomery Ward catalogs. Go down to your butcher and buy four or five pounds of fresh beef suet, preferably off the back of a nice young carcass. Cut the suet in small pieces and put them in a large pot and render them slowly and uncovered. Use a low flame so they will not burn. When all the fat is out of the suet pour off the fat into your French frying pot through a strainer. Pour in enough to fill the pot up to the desired depth. If you have a surplus, simply pour it into a jar for future use. It will keep indefinitely without refrigeration.

You have already learned the most important thing in French frying whether it be fish, potatoes, or crustaceans. Use good beef fat to do your frying in.

Here are the reasons why:

Beef fat has a higher melting point than lard or commercial shortening. You can get it hotter without smoking.

Good beef fat is the only fat that gives no odors to things you fry in it. It is the only fat that does not penetrate food fried in it giving it a heavy greasy taste.

It is the only fat that gives you absolutely no after taste.

It does not penetrate foods like oils and give them a greasy taste and appearance. Beef fat has been used for centuries for deep frying by the best French cooks.

Beef fat fries foods so good and differently that they cannot be compared to anything else.

WHY YOU CANNOT USE THE FOLLOWING FOR FRENCH FRYING

Soybean Oil: It is fairly good for mixing with paints and for making linoleum but is much too strong and harsh for a frying oil.

Cotton Seed Oil: Fine for making plastics, but no qualities of a cooking oil.

Peanut Oil. This oil retains the poor digesting qualities of peanuts and also gives an off taste to foods fried in it.

Corn Oil. This oil is a heavy oil that simply does not have the qualities of a top frying oil. It is, however, an excellent oil for baking purposes. It is used to a great extent in making plastics.

Olive Oil. Has many good frying qualities and is the best on salads but is too greasy for fish frying.

Vegetable Shortenings. They are widely used in North America but give fish a greasy, heavy taste because they penetrate the flesh much too easily.

Margarine. This may seem strange to you but no self-respecting cook in Europe anywhere will use margarine for anything. I have been in a grocery store in Belgium and seen poor women come into the store and wait until everyone had left before buying a kilo of margarine as they did not have money enough to buy anything else but were ashamed to let anyone see them buy margarine. Margarine simply does not have frying qualities.

Lard. If lard is home rendered on a farm it has many good qualities. It is excellent for baking and pastries. Bought in a store it is nearly always worthless because if lard is taken off from a female hog during a fertile period, it has an offensive smell. If it is taken from an uncastrated male hog at the wrong time, its odor is also bad. Lard is the most sensitive fat known to man and absorbs and gives out odors more than any other fat. The poor smelling lard from one hog will taint thousands of pounds of good lard. At our packing plants all lard is mixed together. The French discovered the most important thing about lard and that was that it absorbed and held odors more than any other material in the world as before mentioned. The French perfume industry was created and is still maintained with lard. The French discovered that by placing the petals of fresh flowers on trays of lard that the lard took the perfume or smell of the flowers. The lard was then distilled and the scent recaptured in liquid form from the lard. This is still being done today in France.

If lard is used to French fry it takes the odor of the fish and penetrates it throughout the fish like nothing else will. This reason alone, bans it for French frying.

Safflower oil. It is a very poor salad oil and should never be used for French frying. It is one of the worst possible oils for frying meat or fish. It has an offensive odor that you cannot get out of the food that you fry in it or for that matter you can't get the odor out of your house or kitchen. The Safflower has been grown in India, Egypt and Europe for a great many centuries. In medieval Europe Safflower was grown for its pollen which was used as a yellow dye substitute for crocus pollen called saffron. Safflower pollen, however, was not sunfast and its use for dyes disappeared. Today a dark red powder made from drying and pulverizing its thistle like flowers is used to mix with talcum powder to make face powders that do not irritate the skin but they have a bad odor. The seeds of the Safflower are used to make oil for making paint whiter and that is what it should be used for and not a salad or cooking oil. It has less cholesterol than corn oil. There are about 700,000 acres of Safflower now grown by United States farmers. Brings a good price without government support.

Now getting back to our cooking, heat your beef grease from 380 to 390 degrees F. This is good and hot but is not smoking hot. Smoking hot is around 400 degrees F. Be sure you have at least three inches or more of beef grease in the pot. The more the better.

Take your fish fillets and dry them as much as possible in a towel. The dryer they are the better, as grease of any kind is lighter than water and penetrates anything too wet, very rapidly. Rub ½ level teaspoon of Monosodium Glutamate per pound into fillets. Monosodium Glutamate was originally a seaweed derivative invented by the Japanese and used by good Japanese and French cooks. It can be obtained at nearly all grocery stores or from International Minerals and Chemical Corp., Chicago, Ill. Salt and pepper fillets to taste. Leave fillets wrapped in a dry towel while you make your batter.

There are three French frying batters that are used with the Cordon Bleu method, all three are excellent. It is merely a matter of choice which you prefer.

MILK BATTER

Take a pint of fresh milk and place it in a bowl. Add a quarter tablespoon of salt to it and stir in the salt until it is dissolved. Place the dried fillets in the milk for twenty minutes then remove and roll lightly in white flour and French fry.

BEER BATTER

Take one half pound of white flour. Add 12 tablespoons of 6% beer to it, 1 tablespoon of salad oil. Mix all together thoroughly. Now take the whites of three eggs and beat them until they are stiff and carefully incorporate them with the mixture of flour, beer, salad oil. Roll and work the batter around the fillets and French fry.

EGG BATTER

Take one large egg and break it into a bowl. Take the juice of a half a lemon and mix it into the egg. Add a pinch of dried onion powder, this may now be purchased at most grocery stores in North America. Dip the fillets into this mixture and then roll them in a mixture of one-half white flour and one-half finely ground bread crumbs. Then French fry.

GRAMME FRENCH FRIED ONIONS

The Gramme family in Belgium discovered the first coal mines in Belgium, invented Europe's first electric dynamo, had a Bishop of Liege and gave us some fine writers. They also have always been good eaters and cooks through the centuries. This recipe for French fried onions dates back to the time onions were first brought up from India to Europe and is a rare cooking secret.

In this country restaurant cooks almost invariably make a batter of eggs, flour, oil, etc. to dip onions in for French frying. When the onions are fried with such batters they come out with a doughnut like heavy batter. They are very poor eating and not true French fried onions in any sense of the word.

First get a French frying pot with screen pot to go inside it. Be sure it is a screen pot, not one made of sheet metal with holes punched in it as such inner pots stop the circulation of the grease. It is absolutely necessary that the grease circulate freely for French frying. Render good beef suet as described in French frying fish and fill the pot about half full. Heat to around 380 to 390 degrees. This is good and hot but not smoking hot.

Take the whites of two large eggs and put them into a deep bowl. With an egg beater whip until stiff. Take a fourth cup of fine cracker crumbs and three fourths cup of white flour and mix together well in a clean paper bag. Take a large onion and cut it into slices about one fourth of an inch thick. Punch out the rings so they are all separate. Dose the onion rings in water so they are good and wet. Put the slices in the bag with the flour and cracker crumbs and shake well. Now take the slices with a fork and dip them well into the stiff egg whites. Then put the slices directly into the hot beef grease. Turn them once or twice to avoid puffing up the batter too much. Cook until nicely brown, then remove and place on a paper to drain. Salt and pepper to taste.

Onion rings fried in this manner are just wonderful eating, much better than you will get them at any North American restaurant.

MAKING FRENCH FRIED POTATOES

I have had so many letters since this book was published asking how to make French fried potatoes as they do in France and Europe in general that I have decided to add this recipe.

For potatoes themselves we have our own Indians to thank for them as well as such good foods as corn, bush beans, lima beans, parsnips, green peppers, red peppers, sweet potatoes, pumpkins, squash, tomatoes, vanilla and chocolate. None of these vegetables were known to Europeans until they were shown them by the Indians. The Indians had been cultivating selected wild strains of potatoes that equal or better our present day strains long before white men visited this continent. Fernand Cortez, Spaniard, who died in 1547 sent potatoes back to Spain for horse food. Sir Francis Drake, an Englishman who died in 1596 took potatoes back to England and Ireland. Potatoes soon were cultivated throughout Europe but were used to feed horses. A famine in Ireland forced people to eat them and potatoes became Ireland's most popular food.

In 1757 a French army chemist named Augustin Parmentier was taken prisoner by the Germans. His prison diet consisted mainly of potatoes. He became very fond of them. When he was released he decided that the French people must learn how good potatoes really were. The French people like all other Europeans disdained eating potatoes as they considered them only food for animals. Parmentier was a persistent man and finally secured an audience with Louis XV. He told Louis XV what a wonderful thing it would be for France if the people would realize what wonderful food potatoes were. He made some potato soup with cheese in it for the king and the king liked it very much. He became highly enthused with Parmentier's idea. The king wore a potato flower in his button hole as the emblem of the campaign. From then on the entire court was impressed with "this marvelous root" which they called Pomme de Terre or apple of the ground. French doctors including the famous doctor Diafoirus proclaimed potatoes poisonous. In spite of the doctors, potatoes almost overnight became France's most popular food. The grateful French people set aside a day each year to commemorate the anniversary of Augustin Parmentier's death and are still doing it today. In France today potato soup is still called Potage Parmentier.

The recipe for properly making French fried potatoes has never been published in this country nor in Europe. It has been a closely guarded European cook's secret and they simply do not bandy them about as it is so to speak their life blood.

Take your potatoes, peel them and cut lengthwise into sections about ½ inch thick. Dry the pieces by rubbing them around in a dish towel. Do not soak the pieces in ice water or salt and ice water as most recipes state. This will ruin them. The theory is that the ice water will remove some of the starch from the potatoes. Actually soaking the potatoes in water only makes them absorb more water and this in turn makes them absorb grease too readily when cooked. Heat your beef grease to about 400 degrees. Using beef grease is the real secret of making crisp, flaky, good tasting French fried potatoes. In France nothing but beef grease is ever used. Never use lard or vegetable shortening. Put the potato pieces in your French frying basket and put them down into the beef grease. Leave the pieces in until they are cooked and have a thin crisp skin formed on them, not a brown skin, just a thin pale colored skin. This takes from 7 to 10 minutes depending on the kind of potatoes you have. Then remove them from the grease and leave them drain for about 2 to 4 minutes or until your grease is again up to around 400 degrees. The grease cools down from cooking the potato pieces. Now place the potatoes back in the grease and leave them in it until they are slightly brown. Shake them about a bit as they brown. This takes a minute to a minute and a half, depending upon the kind of potatoes they are. Take them out and leave them drain on paper. Sprinkle them lightly with powdered mustard. If you like French fried potatoes these will really please you.

This recipe was discovered by Henri Armand Gourand, cook in Lille, France in the time of Louis XV. Louis XV was going through the area and a suitable meal for him was prepared by cook Gourand including French fried potatoes. Louis XV was late due to a heavy rain slowing down his coach and cook Gourand had to put his French fried potatoes back into the beef grease to warm them up. Lo and behold the potatoes came out crisper and flakier than ever before and thus the true French fried potato was born.

FRENCH FRIED SOUFFLE POTATOES

The French fried souffle potato was also discovered by Henri Armand, cook in Lille, France in the time of Louis XV. It is often mistakenly written that the souffle potato was discovered in the time of Louis XIV. This is not at all true.

The French fried souffle potato is a version of a regular French fried potato. Actually it is just like a long hollow potato chip and tastes about the same. There is no potato in the center of them at all — just air and the walls are the thickness of potato chips. Because they are much like a potato chip souffle, potatoes have gained little favor in Europe or in North America. People like potato chips with a cold snack or a hot dog, but not usually with a hot meal unless they are losing their mind. The only restaurants that serve souffle potatoes to any extent in North America are Antoine's and Galatoire's in New Orleans. They would please most of their customers much more if they served good French fried potatoes instead of the French fried souffle potatoes.

Here is the recipe for French Fried Souffle Potatoes:

Select some large baking size white potatoes. Peel them and cut them into lengthwise slices about five inches long, two inches wide and about as thick as a half dollar or from 1/16 to ⅛ of an inch thick. It is hard to get them all just the exact thickness. Dry the slices well in a clean towel. Do not put them in ice water or run cold water over them. Any cook who tells you to do this is a rank amateur. Have three French frying pans each properly filled with beef suet. Have the first French frying pan at about 225 degrees. The second at about 300 degrees and the third at about 425 degrees. Put enough potatoes slices in the bottom of the 225 degree French frying pan to cover the bottom, do not crowd. Cook from four to five minutes shaking gently or until the slices rise to the top and show slight signs of puffing around the edges. Remove the potatoes — put them in the second French frying pan at 300 degrees. Leave until they show more signs of puffing. Remove and put into the last French frying pan and fry until well puffed and brown. Remove and drain. Sprinkle with salt and a little dry mustard and serve.

These souffle potatoes look beautiful and pretentious but are not anything special for eating.

POTATOES CHRISTIAN HERTER

These potatoes were invented by Berthe Herter and there is just nothing like them nor any form of potatoes as good as they are. The only trouble with them is that they simply take too long to prepare. Use them only when you really want to put someone in his place who does not think too much of your cooking.

Make a suitable sized batch of mashed potatoes. Use the desired amount of milk or cream to give them the proper consistency and plenty of butter. Now for about every four cups of mashed potatoes add ¼ level teaspoon of ground nutmeg and a 4 oz. can or jar of pimentoes chopped up real fine or grated real fine. Add the liquid the pimentoes came packed in also. Mix well into the mashed potatoes and add salt and pepper to taste.

Make a batch of hollow French Fried souffle potatoes. When done, carefully cut a flap in one end of each souffle potato and with your little finger stuff each one with the mashed potato, pimento and nutmeg mixture. Keep them warm in an oven until served. This is going all out on potatoes but well worth the effort on real special occasions.

HOW TO KEEP BOILED POTATOES FROM TURNING GRAY OR BLACK OVERNIGHT

Many times you have a few boiled potatoes left over at supper time. There is never room in the refrigerator for items like this. If you take them out of the water they were boiled in they will quickly dry out in your refrigerator. If you put them in your refrigerator in the pot that they were boiled in the pot takes up much too much room. Just leave the extra boiled potatoes in the water that they were boiled in. Add one level teaspoon of lemon juice either fresh or bottled. The potatoes will stay nice and white and can be served the next day.

Desserts

BABA AU RHUM

It has been my experience in visiting with famous cooks that this is the favorite dessert of the large majority of them. It is one of those rare desserts like Creme de Menthe Gelatine that aids the digestion. It helps to relieve that over full feeling after a meal.

I have never seen an authentic Baba Au Rhum recipe in any American cook book although some of them do have recipes that they call by the same name.

Here is the history and recipe for this rare dessert:

Way back when Stanislas Leczinski was King of Russia his court baker made a yeast raised cake filled with dried fruits. The cake was made in the shape of a crown. The day before the cake was to be eaten it was soaked in a sauce made from malaga wine, a sweet fortified wine. King Leczinski made a visit to France with his baker and he had him make these cakes for the French court. After these cakes were soaked in the wine sauce for a day the dried fruits would fall out of them most of the time. The French called the cake a baba, meaning, falling over or dizzy. The cake never became popular in France.

In the 18th century a French cook named Savarin made a special cake and served it with a rum sauce. He called it Baba Savarin. The dessert became very popular but the people called it Baba Au Rhum and soon forgot about Savarin. Baba Au Rhum was brought to Minnesota by the French and is served at a number of Minneapolis and Saint Paul restaurants. It is also served in Faribault where the population is mostly French and German.

This is Savarin's original recipe:

FOR THE RUM SAUCE—

Take 1½ cups of white sugar. One cup of cold water. Boil for three minutes. Leave cool. When cool and not before, add one third of a cup of rum either brown or white, or two teaspoons of rum flavoring and mix in well and leave stand.

FOR THE BABA—

Take 1½ cups of sugar, two eggs, two tablespoons of heavy cream and ⅛ level teaspoon of salt. Mix together until smooth. Take one cup of sifted flour plus two heaping tablespoons of flour and a teaspoon and a half of baking powder. Mix them in well with the other ingredients. Add one teaspoon of vanilla. Now take one half cup of hot, not boiling milk and mix in well with the other ingredients. Now, immediately, just as soon as the hot milk is mixed in, pour into a cake pan that you have greased with butter. Have the oven at 360 degrees and bake for 30 minutes. If you delay in getting the batter into the oven after you have added the hot milk it will damage the Baba.

Remove the Baba from the oven and remove the Baba from the pan. Place the baba in a slightly larger pan. A covered pan if possible. Leave cool down until it is warm but not steaming. Now pour the rum sauce slowly over the Baba leaving it soak in well. Cover with wax paper, not aluminum foil or a pan cover. Leave stand overnight.

Take one-half pint of whipping cream, one-third cup of sugar and one and a half level teaspoons of almond flavoring. Whip together until stiff. Cut the Baba in squares and top with the whipped cream. There is just nothing like this.

BELGIAN CHEESE CAKE

Not many people like cheese cake as the only cheese cake they have ever seen is the so-called Lindy style or New York style of cheese cake. This type of cheese cake is a heavy, soggy cake, hard to digest that has nothing to recommend it and is nothing like a true cheese cake at all. Real cheese cake comes from the Holland, Belgium border area. It is a rare treat and once you have eaten it you simply must have it every so often. It is light, not at all heavy and soggy, and served as a dessert has a good digestive effect on your stomach. It is not hard to make.

Take one cup of cold water, ½ cup of sugar and 1½ packages of unflavored gelatin. Put in a double boiler. (A double boiler is simply a pan that fits down into a pan of water. Prevents the heat getting directly on the top pan.) Stir until the gelatin dissolves. Then take ½ cup of cold water and put 4 egg yolks in the water and mix well with your mixer or egg beater. Then add this to the hot mixture in the double boiler and stir in until it blends together well and thickens. Takes about 8 minutes. Now remove the double boiler from the fire.

Take four 3 oz. packages of Philadelphia cream cheese and 2½ tablespoons of lemon juice. Mix until creamy in your mixer or with an egg beater. Then with a large spoon blend in to the hot mixture well. Place in a refrigerator and cool until it thickens but is not completely set. This usually is about 45 minutes. Now take and crush enough graham crackers to fill a cup and mix with ¼ cup of sugar and 4 level tablespoons of soft butter. Take a cake pan and with soft butter grease it lightly on the bottom and the sides. Take half the graham cracker mixture and line the bottom of the pan and the sides if you desire. The butter makes it easy to line the pan with the graham cracker mixture.

Now take a half a pint of whipping cream and whip it. Then with a large spoon fold the whipped cream into the cake mixture. Take 4 egg whites and whip them until stiff and with a large spoon fold them into the cake mixture also.

Now pour the cake mixture into the cake pan. Take the other half of the graham cracker mix and cover the top of the cake as thickly as possible. Put the cake in your refrigerator for 3 to 4 hours and it is ready to serve. One cake will serve 12 to 15 people.

BELGIAN MOCHA CAKE FROSTING

There are a lot of good frostings for cakes. I just love to eat a great many of them but the finest cake frosting made in the world by far is Belgian Mocha cake frosting. It is very expensive to make, but you can find some special occasion as an excuse to make it. Many of the first missionaries in Minnesota were Belgian such as the well known Father Hennepin. The Belgian families who followed him brought with them their knowledge of fine candy and pastry making.

This recipe is for frosting a large cake. One of the many good points of this frosting is that it never hardens remaining as fresh as the day you put it on the cake, no matter how long you keep the cake. At Antoines in New Orleans or the Cafe Exceptionale in Minneapolis, the two highest rated restaurants in North America, you find nothing as good as this frosting on any of their pastries.

Take one cup of unsalted butter. You can usually obtain unsalted butter at your creamery, but if not use the salted butter. Whip the butter in your mixer or with an egg beater until creamy. Add 1 cup of powdered sugar to the butter and 2 egg yolks. Beat in your mixer or with an egg beater for about 5 minutes. Add 1 tablespoon of almond flavoring and 1½ tablespoons of real rum, not rum flavoring. Mix in with your mixer or egg beater. Now take one heaping teaspoon of powdered coffee and ½ teaspoon of cocoa and put them into a cup with 2 teaspoons of boiling water and mix well. Now add this to the main mixture and beat it in with your mixer or egg beater. Then add ½ cup of powdered sugar to the mixture and beat in well with your mixer or an egg beater. Spread the frosting thickly on your cake.

(The original recipe calls for evaporated strong coffee but this is nothing but today's powdered coffee. Nothing new about powdered coffee or tea after all. The Japanese have been using powdered tea for centuries and European cooks have known how to evaporate coffee nearly as long.)

FRENCH CANADIAN RECIPE FOR CREAM PUFFS

Modern recipes for cream puffs are nothing like the real recipe and difficult to put together. Cream puffs are very easy to make. This recipe is from a French lumber jack bull cook and is the easiest and best I have ever seen.

Ingredients: 1 cup of boiling water, ½ cup of good lard, 1 cup of sifted flour, 4 eggs.

Put the lard into the 1 cup of boiling water and bring to a boil. Stir in the flour, mixing it in thoroughly. Remove from the stove and allow the mixture to completely cool. Now add the eggs, one at a time, beating the entire mixture well each time you add an egg. Now take heaping soup spoons full of the mixture and drop them on a well greased pan or heavy cookie sheet. Make the drops circular in form and a little higher in the center than around the edges. Heat your oven to 400 degrees. Put them in and immediately reduce the heat to 350 degrees and bake for one hour. Take out and cool. Then cut a slit in one side and fill with whipping cream or pudding or even with ice cream. Dust the cream puff well with powdered sugar or give it a coating of chocolate sauce if you prefer.

WHIPPED CREAM FULBERT

Mr. Fulbert of Normandy, France was a very poor man who tanned cattle hides to try to make a living. He had a beautiful daughter named Arlette Fulbert. Arlette was not only very beautiful but very intelligent. The Duke of Normandy's son saw Arlette washing clothes in a stream and fell in love with her. Arlette also fell in love with the Duke's son. Very foolishly in those days because she was poor there could be no official marriage between them. Arlette in the year 1027 bore a son for the Duke's son and called him William. This son turned out to be one of the greatest men history has ever known. He was called William the Bastard by the English. This turned out to be the greatest name calling mistake ever made in the history of the world. It justly angered William to have his wonderful mother so unfairly discredited. He attacked England and in 1066 at Hastings, England completely routed and conquered all of England and became the King of England. Everyone at once was very glad to call him William the Conqueror. He married a French girl, daughter of Count Baudouin of Flanders and had six daughters and four sons. His son, William the Red ruled England from 1087 to 1100. William the Lion was King of Scotland from 1165 to 1214. William the Fourth left the English throne to his niece Victoria. Henry the First was William's descendant. Other descendants of William were a King of Spain, a King of Bavaria, a King of Portugal, and a King of Sicily. A pretty good showing for the daughter of a poor leather tanner. In parts of England today French is still the official legal language. There are two good morals to these facts. First, hold your tongue on name calling. Secondly, the best royalty came from common, real people like Arlette Fulbert.

Arlette Fulbert was an outstanding cook. In Normandy apples are the main crop. Apple cider is the main drink. Calvados is hard liquor distilled from cider. Cider champagne is also made there. Arlette had recipes for excellent apple butter, apple pastries, etc.

One of the outstanding things she invented was how to make whipped cream that would really stay nice and high even in warm weather. Here is this simple but effective recipe. Take your whipping cream and put it into a bowl. For very half pint of cream add the white of one egg. Sweeten to taste. Whip well. The white of the egg stiffens the cream and gives it a smooth airy taste that just cannot be duplicated.

HOW TO MAKE FRENCH, ITALIAN OR VIENNA BREAD

Many people prefer a bread like French, Italian, or Vienna bread that has a hard nutty crust and a soft center. Housewives nearly all over Europe bake this type of hard nutty tasting crusted bread. Many girls and women in North America would like to make this type of bread at home. It is absolutely impossible to do because they cannot buy high gluten European type flour at the grocery stores in North America and without this flour you cannot even come close to making French, Italian, or Vienna hard crusted breads.

Flour makers in North America do not want housewives to bake bread. They want all bread making to be done by bakers hence this flour is unavailable.

Magazine food editors and cook book authors do not know how to make hard crusted breads and go on printing stupid recipes calling for ordinary grocery store flour and none of these recipes will even come close to working. There is not a cook book in North America that has a French bread recipe that will work at all. First you must have a high gluten European type flour or there is no use trying to make hard crusted bread at all. We have a high gluten French Vienna flour for our own use and put some up in 5 pound sacks for our friends. If you want some order out a sack from Herter's, Waseca, Minnesota. It is very inexpensive.

Here are the ingredients for French, Italian, and Vienna bread.

10 cups of high gluten European flour sifted.
3 cups of lukewarm water.
1 level tablespoon of salt. (If you like your bread real salty use an additional teaspoon of salt.)
1 cake of yeast.
1 level tablespoon of shortening.

Soften one cake of yeast in ¼ cup of lukewarm water. Then add to balance of lukewarm water in a large mixing bowl or pan. An old dish washing pan works well. Add salt. Melt the shortening and mix into the luke warm not hot water. Then mix in gradually the high gluten flour. Mix well until the dough pulls away from the side of the bowl with just a little stickiness. Put the dough on a lightly floured board or counter top and knead for about 10 minutes or until the dough loses nearly all stickiness and the dough becomes very smooth and evenly textured and slightly elastic.

Lightly butter a large pot that you have a cover for. The cover must fit about level over the pot not high up like a roaster top. If you have no large pot use a dish pan and cover the top with aluminum foil. Place the dough in the pot or pan and put the cover or aluminum foil on and place the pot in a warm but not hot place or if none is handy just set any place so long as the room temperature is not below 73 degrees.

The dough gives off moisture as it ferments and this moisture must be kept in the air around the dough as it ferments. The air must be humid while the dough ferments or the bread will not be any good. Let me repeat, the air must be humid around the dough as it ferments, this is of the highest importance. The heat the dough ferments in is of little importance compared to the humidity of the air. The humidity in the air also prevents the dough from getting a crust on top while fermenting. Getting a crust on top while fermenting will also spoil the dough. Just putting a cloth over the dough and leaving it in a warm place to ferment is one sure way to make poor bread.

Now leave the dough ferment for one hour and fifty minutes. At this time it must be at least double in size. If it is not double in bulk leave rise until it is. Press two fingers down deep into the dough. If the holes remain, the dough has fermented well.

Now with your fists punch down the fermented dough. Again put the cover or aluminum foil over the bowl or pan of dough. Leave ferment for 45 minutes. Now again punch down the dough.

Again put the cover or aluminum foil over the bowl or pan of dough. In ten minutes remove the dough from the bowl; put it on your working table or counter top. Divide the dough into half loaf size pieces and put them back into the bowl or pan with a cover or alumium foil on it and leave for 15 to 20 minutes. Do not place them in the pan so that they will touch each other after fermenting. If it looks like they will, use two pans. Remove and shape each piece into a long cylindrical loaf with blunt not pointed ends; this is traditional. Round or oblong loafs however are just as good. Take a cookie sheet and sprinkle it evenly with corn meal. This prevents the bread from sticking to the sheet. Do not grease the sheet as the grease will burn and make your oven smoke. Cover the loaves loosely with aluminum foil. Leave the aluminum foil loose around the edges do not tuck it to the cookie sheet. Leave enough space between the foil and the loaves so that the loaves can double in size without touching the foil. If you put the foil tightly around the loaves they will not be able to ferment and double in size. If you have a metal or wooden box that is good and tight use it to put the cookie sheets with the loaves on them, in it. Be sure the box is not more than an inch or two deeper than the dough will be when it is double in size. A box like this is hard to find, you will probably have to make one. Place in a warm place for about 45 minutes or until the loaves are double the size they were when you divided the dough into pieces. From now on handle the loaves with great care. Do not press them in any way as it will make them fall. If you desire what is known as "wild breaks" in the bread do as follows. Take a sharp scissors and cut small diagonal slits across the top of the loaves about one fourth of an inch deep and about two inches long. Now brush the top and sides of the loaves with a pastry brush with lukewarm water. Put the loaves in the oven at 400 degrees for about 50 minutes or until a golden brown in color. The oven must be 400 degrees when the loaves are put in it. Remove, and with your pastry brush, brush the top and sides of the loaves with a mixture of one egg white and two level teaspoons of water. Now leave the bread cool before wrapping it for storage or for freezing. If you wrap the bread before it is cool the moisture in the bread is held in by the wrapping and will soften the crust. The crust on all French, Italian and Vienna breads softens a little after they have been left out for a day. To put them back to their original hardness put the loaves back in the oven at 400 degrees for just 8 minutes. This will harden the crust to its original hardness at once.

The recipes found in North America's so-called best cook books and magazines for making French, Italian, and Vienna bread are so full of hokum and stupidity that they are really laughable. One of the stupid things you will often find mentioned in these recipes is to put a pan of hot water in the oven while you are baking the bread. This does nothing for the bread at all.

If you desire a faintly sweet loaf, add one level tablespoon of honey to the basic mixture.

This bread is so good that if served with fresh butter and coffee it makes a wonderful meal just in itself.

With this recipe a child can make this bread perfectly every time.

WHY IT IS IMPOSSIBLE FOR MODERN WOMEN TO BAKE WELL

In some of the recipes in this book I have explained how the large flour companies and large shortening making companies have purposely made it impossible for women today to buy flour and shortening that they can bake well with. These large companies want you to either buy all of your bakery items from a baker or sell you mixes which carry a very, very, high profit. They have been so successful that today 99 and 99/100 of all bread, cake and rolls are bakery made.

Here is the truth about flour, in this country. This is not at all true of Europe; all flours are available there.

The flour companies only will sell you what is known as an "all purpose flour." This is the flour that is available through grocery stores.

This all-purpose flour is a very, very poor quality soft wheat flour with very little strength. In their small flour bags such as five and ten pound sizes they pack a very, very, poor quality flour that will not even make good gravy thickening. In their 50 to 100 pound sacks of flour they pack another soft, poor quality flour that is entirely different from what they put in their 5 and 10 pound sacks. It will not make decent bread or rolls or pancakes or anything else for that matter.

Here are the flours that you must have in order to do good baking. All of these flours have been purposely made impossible to buy from your grocer.

1. Bread Flour. This is a high quality, strong patent flour. Without it, it is absolutely impossible to make a good loaf of bread or flaky pastry of any kind.

2. Pastry Flour. You must have this to make good rolls, muffins, pie crust, or even good pancakes.

3. Cake Flour. This must be an extremely fine high grade flour. You must have this very fine honest cake flour and a special emulsified shortening that will hold sugar well to make a really good cake. You cannot buy either.

4. High Glutin Flour. To make French, Vienna, Italian or Bohemian bread or applestrudel you must have this flour. It is absolutely impossible for the modern woman to make these items without these flours.

With these flours a child can bake beautifully; without them no one can.

Food editors of magazines, television, and newspapers, and cook book editors for the most part only know how to take pictures. They do not know how to cook and they have all been taken in by this flour and shortening racket. They keep printing recipes with beautiful pictures that will not work. The flour and shortening companies run enough advertisements in the magazines on television and newspapers to control anything that the food editors might print; in fact can actually pick the ones they want for the jobs. The flour companies even carefully get out cook books of their own with recipes that they know will discourage women from baking. The people who control the newspapers, magazines and television go right along on this racket and have cold bloodedly practically destroyed the woman's right to be a good woman and wife and do her own baking. This may seem like a small trifle but it is not. A woman is a natural housewife, cook and baker. Give her idle time from lack of being allowed to bake and even divorces can result. The television moguls, of course, want her to watch their idiotic contest and quiz programs with silly, stupid masters of ceremonies who think acting silly makes them a comedian. If a teenage child acted as stupid and silly as these masters of ceremonies you would question their sanity. Yet this is what the real powers in television have forced onto America.

HOW TO MAKE PUFF PASTE OR FLAKY PASTRIES

This is one of the great baking secrets. You can write every magazine food editor in North America and ask for puff paste recipes and take the recipes for puff paste from any cook book. Try them all and none of them will work nor even come close to working.

The bakers do not want housewives making flaky pastries at home and neither do the flour makers and shortening makers. The material necessary to make flaky pastry cannot be bought in any grocery store in North America. Puff pastry or flaky pastry cannot be made by using butter or margarine for the shortening coat between the layers of dough; yet all without any exception call for butter or margarine for this purpose. You must have a special hydrogenized vegetable shortening known as French flaky pastry shortening or puff paste shortening.

There are two formulas for making puff paste or flaky pastry dough, both work very well. Use either one you desire but use Formula No. 1 first.

Pastry flour can be bought at Herter's, Waseca, Minnesota in 5 pound sacks. You have to have it for good pie crust and Danish pastry also.

Here are the ingredients:

Formula No. 1

6 cups of bread flour sifted. All-purpose flour that is available at grocery stores will not work.

2 cups of pastry flour sifted.

¾ cup of butter.

½ level tablespoon of cream of tartar.

1 level teaspoon salt.

2 whole eggs.

2 cups of cold water.

3¼ cups of flaky pastry shortening or puff paste.

Put the flour into the mixing bowl, add the salt and cream of tartar. With your finger tips work in the butter and the eggs and gradually add the ice water. Using the hands mix quickly and lightly making a dough with about the same consistency as butter. Mix until the dough is smooth and stiff. Then allow the dough to rest for about 15 minutes. If you do not allow the dough to rest as stated it will be no good at all.

Three way fold.

Four way fold.

Then take the dough and roll it out into an oblong shape on a lightly floured board or counter top to about ½ inch thick. Take your French flaky pastry shortening and cut it into sheets about ¼ inch thick and 2 inches wide and 1½ to 2 inches long. Place them on two thirds of the dough as the illustration shows. Make a three way fold as the illustration shows. This is called one roll. Brush off all flour. Leave the dough rest for thirty minutes in your refrigerator. If you do not leave the dough rest, you cannot make flaky pastry. The resting of the dough lets the gluten content of it relax which is absolutely necessary. Now place the dough on a lightly floured table or counter top with the side edges facing you and roll it out from the body making a long rectangle. Roll the dough out ¾ inch thick without any of the flaky pastry shortening breaking through.

If there is any question about how thin to roll it out, keep it a little thick. It is better to have the dough a little too thick than too thin. Give the dough another three way fold. Brush off all flour. Leave the dough rest in your refrigerator for another thirty minutes. Give the dough two more three way rolls making a total of four rolls. Rest the dough in the refrigerator 25 to 30 minutes between each fold. Roll on slightly floured table top or counter but be sure to brush off all flour when your roll is completed. If you leave on the flour it will toughen the dough making it heavy. After the last roll leave the dough rest in the refrigerator 25 to 30 minutes before making it up into shapes for horns, Napoleons, turn overs, etc. Use three way rolls only. After you have made five or ten batches, you can try a four way roll for the last roll only. Some like this four way roll but most pastry makers do not. In rolling out the dough remember to not roll it thinner than ¾ of an inch.

Ingredients:

Formula No. 2

6 cups of bread flour sifted. All-purpose flour that is available at grocery stores will not work.
2 cups of pastry flour sifted.
4 cups of French flaky pastry shortening or puff paste shortening.
1¼ level tablespoons of salt.
2 cups of cold water.

Put the flour in a large mixing bowl. Add the salt. Break up 2 cups of the flaky pastry shortening in small pieces and blend it into the flour with a pastry blender. Now mix well with your finger tips. Add the water gradually mixing in well with your hands or with an electric mixer. Mix until the dough is smooth and tough. Put the dough in your refrigerator for 15 minutes. Then remove and place on a lightly floured table or counter top. Roll it out about ½ inch thick leaving the center about ¾ of an inch thick. Shape the French flaky pastry shortening into a piece about one half inch thick and place in the center of the dough. Fold the laps of dough so that they meet and cover the shortening. Roll the dough into an oblong shape about one inch thick. Carefully brush off any flour. Give the dough a three way fold as illustration shows. Put the dough in your refrigerator for 25 minutes. Remove and roll the dough out about ¾ of an inch thick and without any of the flaky pastry shortening breaking through. It is the best to roll the dough out a little too thick rather than too thin. Give the dough a three way fold. Again put the dough into the refrigerator for at least 25 minutes. Then remove, roll out and give another 3 way fold and put back into the refrigerator for at least 25 minutes. Give the dough a total of five rolls resting it in the refrigerator at least 25 minutes between rolls. If you do not rest the dough between rolls the dough will be ruined. After the last roll allow the dough to relax in the refrigerator for 30 minutes or longer before making it up into horns, Napoleons, turnovers, etc.

Remember to not roll the dough out thinner than ¾ of an inch and to brush all flour from dough after every roll.

HOW TO USE PUFF PASTE OR FLAKY PASTRY DOUGH MAKING APPLE TURNOVERS

Roll out a piece of flaky pastry dough about one fourth of an inch thick on a table or counter top that is lightly floured. Cut with a knife into 5 or 6 inch squares. Wash the edges of the dough lightly with water to seal them. Put in the same apple filling as described for applestrudel or a filling of rhubarb, cherries, apricots, etc. Then fold the piece so that it forms a triangle. Brush off any flour as much as possible. Seal the top and bottom edges by pressing down on them with your fingers. Place on a buttered cookie sheet. Wash the tops with a mixture of one egg mixed with one tablespoon of water if you want an egg glaze on them. Cut a slit in the top with a sharp knife to allow the steam formed during baking of the filling to escape. Allow to rest for twenty minutes in the refrigerator before baking. Bake at 375 to 400 degrees for about 35 minutes or until a golden brown. Watch carefully as baking time will vary.

Turnovers may be made oblong by cutting the pieces of dough about 6″ x 4″ and then folding them so that they will be about 6″ x 2″.

A beautiful glaze can be given turnovers as follows: Bring to a boil ½ cup of corn syrup and ¼ cup of water. Allow to cool somewhat and brush over turnovers.

CREAM HORNS OR LADY LOCKS

Roll out a piece of flaky pastry dough about ¼ inch thick or slightly less on a lightly floured table top or counter. Cut it into strips 18″ x 1″. Brush off as much flour as possible. Wash the strips with a mixture of one egg mixed with 1 tablespoon of water if you want an egg glaze. Roll the strips spiral like on metal cones made for this type of pastry. If you do not have these small metal cones take heavy aluminum foil and wrap pieces of it in enough layers to form small cones. The cones should be about as long as an ice cream cone but about half of the diameter. Sprinkle granulated sugar into the washed egg if desired. Place in pans. Allow to rest in the refrigerator for 30 minutes or more. Then put into the oven and bake at 375 degrees for about 35 minutes or until a golden brown. Watch carefully. Remove and leave cool then fill with one of the following:

MARSHMALLOW FILLING

Beat together until light the following ingredients. Use an electric mixer or hand beater. (Cut recipe in half for a small batch).

5 1/3 cups of powdered sugar.
3½ level tablespoons unflavored gelatin softened in a little cold water then add a little boiling water to dissolve. Leave cool to lukewarm.
¾ cup clear corn syrup.
1½ cups of cold water.
Then add:
Vanilla or almond flavoring to suit your taste.

Put into a canvas pastry bag with a small star tube and fill the horns. If you have no pastry bag use a knife to fill the horns. You can sift powdered sugar on the horns if desired.

A beautiful glaze can be given the horns by brushing them with the following after they are done. Bring to a boil ½ cup of corn syrup and ¼ cup of water. Allow to cool somewhat and brush over the horns.

STABILIZED WHIPPED CREAM

2 cups of whipping cream.
¼ cup hot water about 160 degrees F.
½ level tablespoon unflavored gelatin.
3 level tablespoons granulated sugar.

Soften gelatin in a tablespoon of cold water then add to the hot water to dissolve. Leave cool to lukewarm. Stir this into the cream. Place in a refrigerator and leave for at least two hours. It can be kept at this stage in the refrigerator for several days. Remove from the refrigerator. Put into a bowl and whip. Add the sugar just before the cream is stiff enough. Add vanilla or almond flavor and whip it in. Fill the horns with a knife or spatula with this mixture.

NAPOLEONS

Roll out two pieces of flaky pastry dough about ¼ of an inch thick on a lightly floured table top or counter. Cut the rolled out pieces of dough into two pieces 18" x 26" inches. Place them on two lightly buttered cookie sheets or bun pans. Prick the surfaces of the dough with a table fork about an inch or so apart. Put the dough in a cool place or your refrigerator for 30 minutes. Then bake at 375 to 400 degrees until a light golden brown. Watch carefully. Usually takes about 25 to 35 minutes. Remove and leave cool. Cover the top of one piece of the flaky pastry about a half inch thick with a layer of custard cream. Place the other piece of flaky pastry on top of the custard cream with the bottom up.

This will give you a smooth level surface to ice on. Now give the top a good coat of icing and sprinkle it with chopped or sliced nuts. Cut the pieces into bars about 3½ x 1½ inches. Place a candied cherry in the center of each bar.

Make the custard cream for Napoleons as follows:

Mix together well.

12 level tablespoons of cornstarch.

¼ cup of milk.

Now add to the cornstarch mixture.

1 cup of whole eggs and mix in well.

Put 4 cups of milk in a large pot. 1¾ cups of granulated sugar, and 1 teaspoon of salt. Stir well and bring to a slow boil. When the milk mixture begins to boil add the starch mixture slowly and stir until thick. Then stir in six ounces of butter and vanilla or almond flavoring to suit. Remove and leave cool somewhat before spreading on the Napoleons but do not leave completely cool or the custard cream will not spread smoothly.

CAKE SHELLS

Roll out a piece of flaky pastry dough about ¼ of an inch thick. Place in a pie pan. Put in the refrigerator for 30 minutes. Bake at 375 to 400 degrees until a golden brown. Fill with a custard cream or other pie filling.

Flaky pastry dough makes a pie crust so flaky and different that people who see and taste it talk about it for weeks.

APPLE STRUDEL OR APPELSTRUDEL

The making of Apple Strudel is one of the great secrets of baking. Very few cooks in the world can make Apple Strudel or even come close to it. There is not a cook book published in the world that contains a recipe that will work. I wrote every magazine food editor in North America and none of them sent me a recipe that would work. Apple Strudel made with the real authentic recipe produces a pastry so thin that you can see through the layers. It is one of the most delicious and different of all desserts. The making of real Apple Strudel is relatively new; it is not an old dish. The ingredients to make it have not been made for many years. Apple Strudel was invented in the town of Aachen or Aix-la-Chapelle, Germany by a priest named Otto Miller in 1881. This famous town of Aachen or Aix-la-Chapelle, has the two names because it at different times has been ruled by French and German speaking people.

In America today, the flour makers and the bakers do not want the American housewife to bake at all. The flour companies sell a bunch of cake and biscuit mixes and this junk is supposed to satisfy women's natural instinct to be a good baker and cook. The ingredients, such as the proper flour for baking and proper shortenings cannot be bought by American housewives in their grocery stores. Do not blame the young girls and married women because they no longer bake, as it is absolutely impossible for them to buy the proper ingredients to bake with. Apple Strudel is a typical example. Without a good quality high gluten flour it is impossible to make it. Good quality high gluten flour can be bought by housewives anywhere in Europe but cannot be bought in North America.

In order to make Apple Strudel and French, Vienna, and Italian hard crust breads for our own use we bring in a barrel of high gluten flour. Many of our friends wanted some so we have it put up in 5 pound paper bags. You can send for 10 pounds of it if you want to. The cost is low.

Here is the original recipe. Cut down the amounts in half if you want to make just a small trial batch. Half of this recipe will make about six. Take a large mixing bowl and put in 10 cups of French Vienna high gluten flour. Make a well in the center. Add 3 cups of lukewarm water, one level tablespoon of salt, 6 eggs, 8 tablespoons of corn oil, 7 level tablespoons of sugar. Mix the dough well in your electric mixer until it is silky to the touch and very pliable. If you have no mixer, mix well in the bowl with your hands and a spoon. This dough is sticky and it is hard to mix but have patience. Then put the dough on a lightly floured table and knead for at least 15 minutes using both hands. Use the palms of your hands mostly in the kneading. Knead until the dough comes away fairly clean from your hands and is very pliable. Weigh the dough into one pound pieces and shape it into an oval or round loaf. Place the pound loaves into a dish of corn oil at room temperature for about 30 minutes. Now put a piece of plywood on the table 4′ x 4′ and give it a good coat of corn oil. If you do not coat it well the dough will stick to it. Do not try to use a pastry canvas as it will not work. Put a pound of dough in the center and with the palms of your hands press it out as thinly as possible. Brush some corn oil lightly over it. The dough will appear somewhat transparent. Leave it relax for forty minutes and again press it out as thinly as possible. Leave relax twenty minutes.

FILLING:

Take about 2 pounds of apples or about 12 small apples; peel and slice them up very thin. 2/3 cup of raisins, 2/3 cup of sugar, 4 level teaspoons of cinnamon, ¼ level teaspoon of salt. Mix all together well and sprinkle evenly over the stretched out dough and take your hands and spread the filling out in all the empty spaces if necessary.

Trim off any uneven edges of the dough. Now carefully roll up the thin dough. This is hard to do as the dough is soft and floppy and quite sticky. The roll will not look like much but do not get discouraged. At this stage it is not supposed to look like much. You should end up with a roll about 3 or 4 inches in diameter. Slide the roll onto a buttered cookie sheet. Brush with corn oil and sprinkle with powdered sugar. Bake in a hot oven of 400 degrees for from 35 to 45 minutes. Watch carefully as it bakes and remove when golden brown. Take a cup of corn syrup and ¼ cup of water and bring to a boil. Leave cool to lukewarm and brush over the top and sides to form a glaze. Save the left over corn oil from the bowl that you put the dough in and use the next time.

This is a rare dessert, one to use on a special occasion when you really want to show someone that you are a really finished baker. At church bake sales, everyone wants these extremely fine appelstrudels and they will make more money than any other baked item. You can use fresh peaches, plums, rhubarb, apricots, pears, gooseberries, or currants instead of the apples in the filling. All are excellent.

DOUGHNUTS GREGORY

Elias Gregory was a sea captain from Portland, Maine. His mother, Elizabeth Gregory was a famous local sea front cook and the originator of the doughnut.

In 1803 throughout New England, fried pastries such as fried cakes, Bismarks, long johns, crullers, beignets were widely made. Mrs. Gregory made up a dough recipe for deep frying that was very original yet typical of her background. It contained nutmeg and cinnamon which she was very familiar with as her son hauled these items as cargo regularly on his ship. The recipe also contained lemon rind. Lemons were the most important thing in a ship's stores in those days as fresh lemons or limes kept the crew from getting scurvy and colds on long voyages. Mrs. Gregory made the whole recipe with the idea of the pastry being one that could be taken aboard ship to sea and kept safely for long voyages without spoiling and that would help prevent scurvy and colds. They were intended to be eaten by dunking them in hot black tea or coffee aboard ship. Mrs. Gregory put hazel nuts or walnuts in the center of the pastry as she was afraid that they might not cook all the way through in the center. She called the pastry doughnuts which was exactly what they were. Her son Elias took fifteen hundred of them on board for a voyage. The crew as well as himself were very fond of them. No one on the voyage developed either scurvy or a cold. Elias Gregory was a wise captain and knew the value of a penny. When he docked at Portland again he went straight to the tinsmith. He had him make a cutter in a circular shape with a small hole in the center. He took the cutter to his Mother and had her make up some doughnuts with the center out eliminating the necessity of using expensive nuts in the center. They deep fried beautifully as, of course, the hole in the center prevented them from having a soggy center.

His crew down in the town taverns exulted the great goodness and medicinal qualities of doughnuts at sea and although on the next voyage the doughnuts had no nuts they still were highly praised by the crew. Soon doughnuts were the most popular pastry throughout America and still are today.

Here is Mrs. Gregory's original doughnut recipe. Although many have tried to improve on this recipe it still is the best doughnut recipe that the world has ever known. Have all the ingredients at room temperature including the milk.

Crack two eggs in a large mixing bowl and beat them up well with an egg beater. Add slowly, beating constantly one cup of sugar. Then stir in one cup of milk. Stir in 5 level tablespoons of melted butter. Melt the butter, then let it cool until it is just liquid before stirring it in. Sift well before measuring 4 cups of white flour. Add 4 level teaspoons of baking powder, ¼ level teaspoon of nutmeg and ¼ level teaspoon of cinnamon. One half level teaspoon of salt. Resift the flour and other ingredients. Stir in two level teaspoons of grated lemon rind into the flour mixture. Now stir the sifted ingredients with the egg mixture until they are well blended. Put about one-third of the mixture on a floured board and turn and knead slightly. Then roll out to one-fourth of an inch thick. Cut out the doughnuts with a doughnut cutter. Add the trimmings to half of the remaining dough and roll out and cut as before. Take the trimmings and mix with the remaining dough and cut into the machine without rolling it out. To fry, heat beef suet or any reliable vegetable oil to about 370 degrees. Put not more than three doughnuts into the fat at one time so as to not change the temperature of the fat. If a fat thermometer is not available drop a one inch piece of bread into the fat. If it is a golden brown in one minute the fat is about 370 degrees. You must keep the grease at an even temperature. If the grease is not hot enough the doughnuts will absorb the fat. If the fat is too hot they will brown too quickly before they have raised properly. Remove all small pieces of dough from the fat that come off from the doughnuts to avoid smoking. When the doughnuts are brown on one side, with a fork carefully turn them over on the other side to brown. Do not turn them more than once. Do not puncture the doughnuts with the fork. When cooked remove the doughnuts from the fat by putting a fork through the hole in the center. Lay them on paper towels to drain. When warm enough to handle place three or four in a paper sack with a half cup of powdered sugar and one level teaspoon of cinnamon and shake gently to sugar them. Remove and they are ready to serve.

Strange as it may seem doughnuts are still only made in North America at this writing in 1959. Europeans have never learned to make doughnuts.

BEIGNET OR RAISED DOUGHNUTS

The word beignet comes from the early Celtic word bigne meaning to raise. The Celtic tribes came from Indo Germany and today their descendents are the French, Belgians, Hollanders, Germans, etc. The Celtic language came from the India area.

The Beignet or French doughnut stand in New Orleans. After a hard night at the bars this is where everyone goes for a cup of dark roast coffee and raised doughnuts.

A beignet is a fried, raised piece of dough usually about two inches in diameter or two inches square. After being fried, they are sprinkled with sugar or coated with various icings. The real beignet is coated with a frosting of mocha but these are very hard to find. The recipe for this mocha frosting is on page 231.

The beignet recipe was first brought to North America by the Ursuline French Nuns who came to New Orleans. For many years the beignet was made in the shape of balls or squares and covered with mocha frosting. Finally, however, the beignet was cut in the shape of a doughnut and the raised doughnut was born. The first raised doughnuts, of course, were made in the Ursuline Convent in New Orleans. Today it is the custom in New Orleans to stop at the old French doughnut stand and have a cup of chicory flavored or dark roast coffee and raised doughnuts after a night about the town.

Raised doughnuts or beignet cannot be made anymore in your home as they require bread flour to make. The ordinary all purpose flour sold at grocery stores to prevent women from baking at home simply will not work. The large flour mills want you to buy from the bakers and not do your own baking. It is much easier for them to ship carloads of flour to bakers than try to sell the proper grades of flour for baking in grocery stores. If you have a good baker friend who will sell you some bread flour, which is not at all like all-purpose flour, you can make raised doughnuts at home.

Here is the original French recipe for Beignet or raised doughnuts.

Warm a large mixing bowl by putting it in an oven at low heat. Remove the bowl when warmed and put ½ cup of bread flour into the bowl. Break up one cake of yeast and spread it over the flour. Make a hollow in the center of the flour and yeast and put ½ cup of lukewarm milk and 1½ level level teaspoons of sugar into the hollow. Stir all the ingredients together until they are well blended. Now cover the bowl with a warm moist towel and place it in a box with a cover near a warm place for 20 minutes. The dough must rise in humid air hence the use of a covered box.

Take ½ cup of soft butter and beat until real soft and creamy. Add ½ cup of sugar to the creamed butter and blend until you have a creamy mixture. Then add to the mixture ½ level teaspoon of salt. 1 level teaspoon of grated lemon rind. 1½ tablespoons of lemon juice. 2 well beaten eggs. 1 teaspoon of almond extract. ½ cup of milk. Sift 4 cups of bread flour and stir in about a half a cup into the butter mixture then knead in the balance with your hands. Now add the raised bread, flour, milk, yeast and sugar that you left to rise and knead all together.

Now cover the mixture with a warm moist cloth and place in a covered box for from three to four hours or until it has doubled in bulk. Then pad into a sheet or sheets about one-half of an inch thick. Cut out the doughnut rings with a doughnut cutter. Place the doughnut rings on a lightly floured board. Put the little circles left from the rings also on the board. Place a moist warm cloth over them and leave rise until they have doubled in size.

Fry in deep fat, preferably beef suet or half beef suet and half a good cooking fat at about 370 degrees. This is hot enough to brown a cube of bread in one minute. Brown them on one side then turn them over and brown them on the other side. Leave drain on absorbent paper. Coat with a mocha frosting on one side when cool.

GLACE BLANCHE DUPONT

This is a recent invention and a great one made in 1942 by Blanche Dupont in Belgium. It is one of the greatest known cooking tricks.

Take one cup of corn syrup, mix with ½ cup of water. Put in a pot and bring to a boil. Leave cool until lukewarm.

Brush or pour over the top of fruit cakes. This mixture gives them a rich clear glass like glaze and brings out their color.

Brush or pour over doughnuts. It gives them a beautiful glaze and taste.

Mix ⅛ level teaspoon of ground cloves or a few drops of cherry flavoring into the mixture and brush on fried or baked ham and fried or cold Spam or other similar canned meats. Mix in a few drops of orange flavoring and brush over pieces of tame or wild ducks or geese it makes them really delicious. Put in a few drops of peppermint flavoring into the mixture and brush over the tops of brownie cookies. Makes them into a great delicacy instead of just another cookie.

Brush over the tops of apple turnovers, horns or lady locks just as it is. Pour over squash and sweet potatoes just as it is.

SPRITZ COOKIES BERNADOTTE

Charles Bernadotte was a Marshal of France. He was adopted by King Charles the XIII of Sweden and became Charles the XIV of Sweden in 1818.

Bernadotte loved the Swedish people and they loved him. Many of his friends came to visit in Sweden and stayed and married. French sailors for centuries have intermarried in Sweden and Swedish sailors through the centuries have gone to France for their wives. Those beautiful black haired Swedish women are the result of these many intermarriages.

Charles Bernadotte brought a great knowledge of French cooking to Sweden and blended it with the famous Swedish cooking. The Spritz cookies are a typical example. Charles Bernadotte had his cooks make French galettes, a small French waffle about four to five inches square. His cooks took the same dough and baked it as cookies and called them Spritz. Everyone liked these cookies very well.

Here is the original recipe and it makes a far different and better Spritz cookie than the so-called Spritz cookies of today and the ones passed off as Spritz cookies by magazine food editors.

1 cup of butter.

1 cup of sugar.

1½ teaspoons of almond extract.

1 teaspoon of vanilla.

¼ teaspoon of salt.

2½ cups of sifted flour.

1 egg.

¼ level teaspoon of powdered ammonia.

Take a mixing bowl and put in the butter, sugar, egg, almond and vanilla. Mix together well. Stir in the salt. Mix the dry ammonia well into the flour then mix in the flour. Never mix the dry ammonia directly into a wet mixture. Mix until smooth. Take a cooky press and put a star tube in it. Extrude the mixture into an ungreased baking sheet. Leave stand for 5 to 6 hours before baking. This is important. Bake in a moderately hot oven of about 360 degrees for about 8 to 12 minutes or until done. Pieces of nuts and fruits and colored sugar may be placed on the cookies before they are baked. The dry ammonia can be gotten at any drug store. It smells terrible but when the cookies are baked they have no ammonia smell at all. Without the ammonia they do not have a true spritz texture at all.

EGG NOG COLBERT

Nero in 60 A. D. was the first to serve snow mixed with crushed fruit. He had specially trained runners bring the snow from the Alps in insulated boxes. Marco Polo learned how to make ices and was the first to add cream to crushed ice. Charles the First of England at one time hired a Paris chef at an enormous salary, who had developed an ice cream. He made the chef promise to make his type of ice cream just for his court.

Ice cream, as we know it today, was invented in France during the reign of Louis the Fourteenth. His minister in 1664 was Jean Baptiste Colbert. Colbert publicized ice cream until it became widely used. He invented an egg nog that has never been even closely equaled and makes a Tom and Jerry taste poor and flat in comparison. Here is the recipe brought up to date. It was and is the treasured possession of many a French immigrant. The recipe makes four small drinks.

Take one and a half cups of milk and two egg yolks. Mix well together with a beater.

Add one cup of vanilla ice cream and mix with a beater until nice and creamy. Add one-fourth level teaspoon of cinnamon and one-fourth level teaspoon of nutmeg. Add four ounces of rum, either brown or white, white preferred as the white rum is much better quality than the dark. Mix together well so it is nice and smooth. Serve in small wine glasses.

WHERE TO BUY FRENCH PASTRY IN NEW ORLEANS

There are two very good pastry shops in New Orleans. One is Patisseries Aux Quatre Saisons at 505 Royal Street, run by K. Dingeldein, this is right across from the Royal Orleans Hotel in the French Quarter. They have both

Patisseries Aux Quartre Saisons. Four Seasons Pastry Shop.

French and German pastries of all kinds. There are tables and chairs in the shop and you can go in and pick out the pastries you want and sit down and have coffee and eat them. Their Napoleons are excellent. The custard cream filling is mixed with highly flavored fresh whipped cream. They open at nine o'clock in the morning and when I am in New Orleans I hold off breakfast until nine and have Napoleons for breakfast. They also have a room upstairs, for eating pastry that is beautiful, one of the finest places where food is served in New Orleans.

The second pastry shop is The Boyer French Pastry Shop on Benefit street. This shop is open only from October until May as Mr. Boyer spends the rest of the time in France. Boyer pastries are all French and are in my opinion the finest available in New Orleans. He keeps all the various frosting and coating ingredients made up on hand. If you want a special frosting or coating he will put it on the pastries while you wait.

The small buildings with the one slant roofs behind the large buildings were slave quarters. African waiters for pastry shops were kept in such quarters in the plantation days.

CHERRIES JUBILEE

This is a very nice easily made dessert. It is, however, usually made incorrectly more times than any dessert in the world. It was invented by French Basque cook Valentin Mondragon in 1709. It was copied from him by many cooks including Escoffier and foolishly changed slightly so that people would think that they invented it. The changes only ruined the original recipe and are a very, very, poor substitute.

Here is the original recipe brought up to date but unchanged.

Buy a one pound can of sour cherries. Pour the juice from the can into a measuring cup. Add enough water to make 1½ cups. Add ½ cup of honey or sugar and boil for 5 minutes. Then add 2 level tablespoons of arrowroot or 1 level tablespoon of cornstarch. Mix them in a little cold water before adding. Add to the syrup stirring in well and cook until slightly thickened. Leave cool, then stir in ½ level teaspoon of almond oil flavoring. Then stir the cherries into the mixture. The almond flavoring is the secret to Cherries Jubilee; without it they are nothing. Serve in small individual dishes.

Other cooks trying to make the recipe appear as their own added an ounce or so of brandy on top of each serving and lit the brandy to make a flaming dessert. All this does is to waste good brandy. Still others pour an ounce or so of Kirsch over the dessert and light it. Here again you ruin the dessert and waste the Kirsch. Kirsch is nothing but a mixture of alcohol, sugar and cherry flavoring. When the alcohol burns away you have nothing but sugar and cherry flavoring left. You already have the cherry flavoring blended with almond and you want no more cherry flavor and the dessert needs no more sugar.

Today using ¾ cup of clear corn syrup instead of the sugar makes a better, smoother Jubilee. In this case only boil the syrup with the water and cherry juice for one minute.

BANANAS ALEXANDER THE GREAT

The banana is second only to the potato as a world food. Bananas originated in India and were on this earth before man and spread with man as the human race spread over the globe.

The banana is a very strange plant. It actually is a gigantic herb or mushroom and not a tree at all. The part above the ground is a sprout ten to twenty feet high from an underground stem. Once the sprout has fruited it dies and another sprout will grow out from the underground stem.

These are not regular bananas but bananas that are quite hard and have to be fried or cooked to be eaten. They are called "plantain" in some areas. Note that they are more pointed at the ends than eating bananas and have a different curve.

The bananas that are shipped into the United States are the species M Acuminata and are a sweet banana that must always be eaten uncooked. The bananas that are good cooked are starch bananas like the dwarf or Cavendish variety and these are not imported into the United States or grown here at all. Cooks read foreign recipes for frying and baking bananas and believe these apply to sweet bananas which are available in the United States. Nothing could be further from the truth. Bananas available in the United States if fried or baked are simply terrible eating.

Alexander The Great was born in the year 356 Before Christ and died in the year 323 Before Christ. He was King of Mecedon. Alexander was one of the world's great military leaders and made great conquests in Italy, Africa, Syria, India and Persia. When he was only twelve years old he pushed his teacher Nectanebus into a pit and killed him. Maybe present day teenagers are not so bad after all. This man Alexander was pretty head strong even at an early age.

Alexander in his conquests in India saw the banana trees for the first time. Bananas were called "pala" in India and still are around Malabar. He had bananas prepared for him with the following recipe and it is I believe the finest banana recipe ever invented.

Take a bowl of fresh whole milk. Add one level tablespoon of honey. Stir the honey into the milk until it is dissolved. This takes quite a bit of stirring as honey does not dissolve easily. Then slice a banana into the honey flavored milk and eat at once. This recipe makes fabulously good eating.

You must remember that honey is a delicate very strange spice and not just a sweetener. It is made from the nectar secreted by plants. Honey actually never contains more than 11% Sucrose or cane sugar and on an average only contains about 2% of Sucrose or cane sugar, some honey none at all. Honey contains such things as vitamin B complex. Honey is often recommended by doctors for diabetics. It has good antiseptic properties and has been used in healing cuts, wounds, sore nipples and burns. It stimulates plant growth. Eaten at child birth it greatly prevents the development of disease in the mother. Mixed with milk it is the best food for premature babies. It often cures the symptoms of hay fever. It is the only material known in the world that when eaten by both dogs or man will stop falling hair. Honey absorbs and holds moisture very well. Used in baking cookies and cakes instead of sugar it keeps them moist much longer. All good ice cream is made with honey not sugar. Honey is a wonderful strange food not possible to make synthetically by man. Do not miss out on its many great uses.

CREME DE MENTHE GELATINE

After a meal a dessert that tends to settle your stomach and get you away from that too full feeling is what you want. Nothing does this like oil of mint flavored desserts.

In France, Belgium and in Germany this dessert is popular and practical. It is widely used in parts of Minnesota where immigrants brought in the recipe.

Here is the recipe:

Put a half cup of cold water into a large bowl. Take one envelope of Knox unflavored gelatine and sprinkle it onto the cold water. Stir it in with a spoon until it softens. Mix in one-third cup of sugar and ⅛ level teaspoon of salt. Pour in one cup of boiling water and stir until all are dissolved. Add green coloring until the mixture is a dark green. Add one teaspoon of peppermint, not spearmint flavoring. Stir in well. Pour into wine glasses and place in your refrigerator and chill. If you are watching your waist line serve just as it is. If you are not, top with chocolate syrup or chocolate flavored whipped cream.

HORS D'OEUVRES TURKISTAN

The prune although often thought to be of European origin originated in western Asia in the area south of the Caucasus Mountains to the Caspian Sea. Prunes came to Europe fairly recently by being introduced into Hungary from Turkistan late in the 15th century. They were introduced as a before the meal appetizer and were at first so expensive that you could actually buy good quality Turkish harem girls by the pound much cheaper than you could prunes. The rage of Europe became hors d'oeuvres Turkistan.

Here is the original recipe and I must say that it is a welcome change from the junk that you see on most hors d'oeuvre trays today.

Buy a package of good quality prunes. Boil them in water until barely done according to the instructions on the package. Drain the prunes and place them on a plate. Take a sharp pointed knife and make a slit lengthwise across the top of the prunes and remove the pit. Take a 3 oz. package of soft white cheese. Philadelphia cream cheese is excellent for the purpose. Place the cheese in a bowl. Add two level tablespoons of honey or sugar. Three level tablespoons of chopped walnuts and one-eighth teaspoon of anise liquid flavoring. Now with a fork mix everything together to form a smooth paste. Take the paste and stuff the prunes with it. Place the prunes on a plate and serve. They make fabulous eating.

HORS-D'OEUVRE PERIGNON

The famous French monk Dom Perignon, who was the cellarer of the Abbey of Hautvillars, France was born in 1639 and died in 1715. He invented champagne and sparkling wines. This was certainly a great invention and showed what a deep thinking, patient, creative inventor this man really was. However, even more important than this invention of champagne was his invention of the Hors-d'Oeuvre Perignon. In his lifetime of experimenting with wines, cognacs, champagnes, etc., he discovered the following great secret: Take a piece of bread or cracker and lightly butter it. Cover the top with a slice of light golden fairly sharp to sharp cheese. Make the slice about one sixteenth of an inch thick. Lemke brick cheese or sharp cheddar cheese is excellent for this sandwich. Sprinkle the cheese heavily with celery salt. It is very delicious. The celery salt does something to cheese that nothing else can. This is a wonderful sandwich on its own but served before serving wine, beer, liquors, or cocktails it makes them taste much better than they ever tasted before and much better than they really are. After eating one of these sandwiches no one can tell aged wine from unaged wine, or good beer from bad beer, or good liquor of any kind from bad liquor. They all taste very good like, the very best you have ever tasted every time.

Today in Europe unsuspecting wine or liquor buyers are given an Hors-d'Oeuvre Perignon before being allowed to sample the seller's products.

Hors-d'Oeuvre Perignon is a must for the smart hostess. Any liquor, wine or beer served after it will taste like the best ever made. Blessed be the Monk Perignon for such a great discovery.

MILLE LACS ICE CREAM

Mille Lacs Lake in Minnesota was named by the early French fur traders. Mille Lacs lake is surrounded by huge areas of hard maple trees. The Indians in the area make large quantities of maple syrup and sugar from the trees.

One of the favorite Indian dishes was and is to pour maple syrup over a ball of snow. It makes delicate delicious eating. The early French and Norwegian pioneers rightly thought it to be the most wonderful dessert they had ever tasted. There are no hard maple trees in Europe and hence no maple flavor. This new flavor they preferred above all others. Of late years the snow has given way to ice cream. Take a scoop of vanilla ice cream and pour maple syrup over it. Maple syrup does things to the taste of ice cream that no other flavor ever comes close to. Just try it and see what I mean. You do not need pure maple syrup. Maple syrup is like perfume oils. It is much better when diluted. Cane syrup is what is used to dilute it. The best mixture is 15% maple syrup and 85% cane syrup. Any of the well known brands are good such as Log Cabin or Oelerich's Old Manse.

Perfume oils themselves smell not nearly as well as when mixed with alcohol. Maple syrup has many times a better aroma, and taste when mixed with cane sugar.

Although it is not generally known Minnesota produces as much maple syrup as Vermont. The cigarette companies however buy it all up for cigarette tobacco flavoring leaving none for the syrup market any more.

MOUSSE COLTELLI

In 1686 an Italian named Francesco Procopio Dei Coltelli in Paris, France, opened a place of business selling coffee and desserts. He called his place CAFE meaning coffee in French and hence invented the first cafe. Soon cafes sprung up all over the world. His coffee never made him famous but one of his desserts called Mousse Coltelli did. This recipe was brought to Minnesota by both French and Italian immigrants. There are many Italians in Minnesota, one county of Minnesota is named Beltrami after the famous Italian early explorer of Minnesota. This Mousse Coltelli is a wonderful recipe and here is how it is made today:

Take one envelope of Knox unflavored gelatin and put it into a half cup of cold water, and mix in well. Put in a cup of warm strong coffee and mix in well. Add one teaspoon of vanilla. Now put in a cup of chocolate ice cream and one cup of vanilla ice cream. Mix them in well with an egg beater until the entire mixture begins to jell. Take two egg whites and place them in a bowl. Beat them stiff with an egg beater. Take a large spoon and fold the stiff egg whites into the mixture. Fold them in until they are well mixed. Pour into dessert glasses filling them three-fourths full. Take one-half pint of good whipping cream, add one third cup of sugar, and whip well. The original recipe, of course, called for honey instead of sugar as there was no sugar in France at this early date. Add two level teaspoons of almond extract and whip into the whipped cream. Top the dessert with the almond flavored whipped cream.

This dessert can be made and eaten in less than a half hour as it jells rapidly.

ORANGE MARIE

Marie de Hongrie once had a fine castle at Mariemont, Belgium. The remains of it are still there. One of her admirers presented her with a group of Indian slaves from South America and fresh oranges at the same time. The Indians wore huge South American ostrich plumes in beautiful high headdresses. The Queen and the villagers learned to love the Indians dearly and soon the Queen gave them their complete freedom. Today every year at the nearby town of Binche, Belgium the people celebrate the arrival of the Indians and oranges. Nearly every man in the town dresses up in an Indian costume with huge ostrich plume headdresses on their heads and they carry a basket of oranges to give to children on this festive day.

About thirty years ago a man named Andre Dupruis, a Cafe owner in Binche invented a wonderful orange drink and called it Orange Marie in fond memory of Marie de Hongrie. It is a fabulous, unbelieveable, different and delicious drink. One of the finest warm or cold weather drinks that I have ever tasted anywhere in the world. Here is a modern adaptation of it.

Take six level tablespoons of malted milk. (Phosphatine in Belgium)
1 can frozen orange juice.
3 empty orange juice cans of water.
3 empty orange juice cans of gingerale.

Put the ingredients into a glass water jug that you have a cap for and shake together well. See that the cap is tight and put into your refrigerator and leave stand for three days. The drink is no good at all until three days have passed. Remove from the refrigerator, shake well again and serve cold. It is the smoothest drink you have ever tasted.

If you use alcohol in your drinks add four ounces of vodka to the drink after the three days have passed and serve at once. Everyone who drinks it will marvel at its taste and never guess what the ingredients are.

There are drinks with orange juice bases served in America such as the Orange Julius but none of them can be compared to this famous drink. It is in a distinct class by itself.

PRUNES MAXIM'S

Prunes are a plum that originated in the area south of the Caucasus Mountains to the Caspian Sea. They are fairly large, have a dark blue colored skin, a high sugar content and dry perfectly without removing the pits. Prunes were first introduced into Europe to Hungary from Turkistan in the late 15th century. Prunes were brought to North America to the Maritime provinces of Canada by the French. Today prunes are our most widely grown plums by far. More than 200,000 tons a year are dried and shipped from California, Oregon, Washington and Idaho.

Stewed prunes are widely used for a breakfast fruit, or for a main dessert with other meals. They are not too tasty and are eaten more for their laxative effect than for their taste.

The original Maxim's restaurant in Paris, France discovered the secret on how to serve stewed prunes making them one of the most delicious and different fruit dishes possible to serve. Here is this well guarded secret. Be sure to try it.

Place cold stewed prunes in an individual portion fruit dish and barely cover them with the stewing water. Put four drops of almond flavoring or oil into each dish and stir gently with a spoon. The almond flavoring completely changes the flavor of the prunes giving them a delicious very different taste. People that would normally not touch a stewed prune simply cannot get enough of them when flavored with almond.

RHUBARB JUBILE FRANCIS JOSEPH

Rhubarb makes wonderful pies and sauces. Of late years however people have somewhat got out of the custom of rhubarb pies and sauces and it certainly is a shame.

The word "rhubarb" comes from the French word "Rhubarbe." Rhubarb originated in the eastern Mediterranean, Asia Minor, middle Asia and in China. The earliest records of the use of rhubarb date to 2700 years before Christ, in China. The Chinese have always used small quantities of rhubarb root in medicines. Rhubarb root contains a number of very powerful chemicals that violently disturb the stomach and intestines when eaten in any quantity. Rhubarb root has been used as a poison to kill both animals and humans for many centuries. The leaves of rhubarb also contain strong substances when if eaten will cause serious illness or death. They too have been used as a poison for humans for centuries. Only the stalks of Rhubarb are edible.

Rhubarb came to Europe through Italy. It was grown at Padua, Italy in about 1608. Rhubarb came to England in 1725. It came to North America from England to Maine in 1790. Rhubarb like apples never runs true to seed. Each seed you plant produces a different kind of rhubarb. You must use root pieces for planting in order to get the same variety.

Napoleon Bonaparte officially had only one son, the Duke of Reichstadt. His wife at the time was Marie Louise, daughter of Francis the second of Austria. Napoleon, of course, tended to be a little careless and had a number of other children from different women throughout Europe. His son the Duke of Reichstadt was born in 1811 and died in 1832. He spent nearly all of his life in Austria. He was a sickly lad but not so sick that he did not exercise some of the traits he had inherited from his father. He had a child with another man's wife. This child was Francis Joseph of Austria. He became Emperor of Austria in 1848. Francis Joseph was a man of great ill fortune. He had a daughter and a son. His son although married to a Belgian Princess committed suicide with his mistress, and his daughter amounted to nothing. Francis Joseph's wife was assassinated. Francis Joseph himself managed to find a nice looking mistress who would cook his favorite dishes. Among these were pork sausages fried with grated apples, a really fine dish too. The favorite dessert of Francis Joseph and a great court favorite was Rhubarb Jubile. It is a really fabulous dessert with a delicious, entirely different flavor. Here is the original recipe.

Use a large bowl. Put in one envelope of gelatine and ½ cup of cold water. Stir well until the gelatine is mixed well into the cold water. Add one third cup of sugar, ⅛ teaspoon of salt, three level teaspoons of cocoa and stir well being sure that the cocoa is well mixed in with no lumps.

Take two cups of cut up rhubarb stalks, add just enough water to cover them well and boil for 8 minutes. Remove from the stove. Take one cup of the liquid from the boiled rhubarb and add to the other ingredients in the bowl. Then take one cup of the cooked rhubarb pieces and add them to the other ingredients. Mix all ingredients well and place in a cool place or in your refrigerator to harden.

This is a wonderful dessert. Try it as soon as possible.

SWISS FROZEN STRAWBERRIES

In nearly every country in the world strawberries are considered the finest of desserts. I like strawberries very much and have eaten them in nearly every country in the world including the oblong shaped wild, all red and all white strawberries found in France, Germany, Belgium and Switzerland. These wild strawberries are supposed to have the best flavor and aroma of any in the world. I disagree with this as I have found North American strawberries to be far superior to them as to both flavor and aroma.

The Swiss people, however, have discovered the right way to freeze strawberries and their frozen strawberries are far superior to any frozen strawberries found in the world simply because they use an entirely different method to freeze them.

It is a very simple secret but one that really works magic on strawberries. Proceed as follows:

Pick your strawberries, clean them and slice them as you always do. Then mix in one pound of brown sugar to every 4 pounds of sliced strawberries. Leave them stand for ten minutes, then pack them in containers and freeze them. You need not quick freeze them. Quick freezing or sharp freezing is strictly advertising propaganda. Freezing them in your deep freeze works just as well as records at the University of Minnesota definitely prove.

The brown sugar is the secret. Unlike white sugar it preserves the natural red color of the strawberries and their fresh natural flavor and aroma. White sugar destroys the natural color of strawberries giving them a faded look and white sugar gives them an old taste instead of a fresh taste. Try it and you will see the great difference.

CREPE SUZETTE

The original Crepe Suzette was invented by Monsieur Joseph in 1897. He was in charge of the Restaurant Marivaux in Paris, France. There was a play at the Comedie Francaise at the time in which a maid, called Suzette, had to bring in some pancakes. The pancakes were made by the Restaurant Marivaux. Joseph named his pancake invention after Suzette the maid who it is said was more than a friend of his. Joseph came to London, England when Ritz left the Savoy. He replaced Ritz and introduced the Crepe Suzette to London Society at the Savoy.

There are many, many, cooks who have made Crepes Suzette since that time and have made them up as they saw fit or from lack of knowledge of the original recipe. The Crepe Suzette, however, first was made by Joseph. The original recipe for both Crepe Suzette Pancake mix and Crepe Suzette Syrup have been given to Herter's Inc., at Waseca, Minnesota and these products are now available from them at low cost. A little rice flour has been added to the original Crepe Suzette recipe which improves it.

The original recipe for Crepe Suzette contains no liquors of any kind. Today chefs actually not knowing how to make the real Crepe Suzette dump such expensive, fancy named liquors as Benedictine, Maraschino, Curacao, Cointreau, Grand Marnier, Golden rum, Kirsch etc., into the syrup for the crepes to make you think that they are fancy cooks and are really giving you something. Such liquors completely ruin the dish. Actually these liquors with the fancy sounding names are nothing much anyway. For example maraschino is just cherry flavoring, sugar and alcohol, curacao is nothing but orange oil, sugar and alcohol. It takes more skill to make good southern moonshine than these liquors with the fancy sounding names.

VANILLA, THE MAGIC LEMON YELLOW ORCHID

We are prone to believe that only European people were fortunate enough to be exposed to Christianity and a high culture, and that the Indians never had this great privilege. Nothing could be further from the truth.

Lemon yellow vanilla orchid growing wild in Mexico.

Joshua 10:13 in about 1451 years before Christ says that the sun stood still in heaven and did not go down for the space of one day. This caused Indian Mexico to become dark. Early Mexican history tells us of this long night. They tell of a comet that appeared at this time and then turned into the morning star.

In 1509, ten years before Hernando Cortez arrived in Mexico, Princess Papantizin told her brother Montezuma that the Spaniards were coming. This is a matter of official Aztec record. Not only Montezuma heard the Princess make this revelation but King Netzahualpilli of Texcoco plus dozens of Aztec nobles heard her. Princess Papantizin told how an Angel with a cross on its forehead told her that strangers were bringing the True God to them. She saw ships with banners and crosses on them coming to Mexico. She became a Christian in 1525 and in 1529 unfortunately died. Anyone who cares to study Indian religions will find that Christ's Mother appeared to Indians three times on this continent talking with them in great detail. Today the Indians are the most Christian people on these continents and conduct far less pagan rites than the present settlers. On the pure pagan rite of Christmas trees and Christmas cards without religious meaning more money is spent in America today than is donated by all of the people of America to all of its churches.

The Indians of course were the discoverers of both vanilla and chocolate. It took real scientific work of the highest sort to make and develop these discoveries. Vanilla comes from a beautiful lemon yellow orchid that was found only in Mexico. A small bee of a certain species is the only insect that can pollinate the flower. When it is pollinated it produces a fruit or bean. The fresh bean has no flavor or odor at all but when aged properly and carefully for up to six months time it can be made to develop the delicious true vanilla flavor.

The cacao tree produces a pod with seeds. The seeds dried and partly fermented produce cocoa and chocolate. The cacao trees grew wild in South America. The central American and Mexican Indians traded for the seeds and grew cacao trees throughout their lands countless centuries ago.

Hernando Cortez was served the standard Indian drink called "xoco-lot", pronounced chocolate, when he dined with the Aztec Indian Emperor Montezuma.

The Indians had discovered centuries before this time that chocolate drinks and chocolate candies had to have vanilla in them to mellow the coarse flavor of the chocolate so as to make it mellow and rich tasting. When Hernando Cortez went back to Europe he of course took both chocolate and vanilla back with him. If he had only realized it the chocolate and vanilla he took back to Europe with him was worth millions more than the gold he murdered for and stole from the Indians and took back to Europe.

Chocolate rapidly became the most widely eaten confection the world has ever known and the world's second most popular drink. Vanilla became the world's most widely used flavoring. North Americans alone consumed over 400 million gallons of vanilla ice cream in 1959.

Our modern chemical industry at this writing in 1959, has never been able to produce a good imitation vanilla. They have not even been able to discover enough about true vanilla flavor to be able to give a complete definition as to what it is. For more than 300 years after Cortez brought vanilla to Europe no one could even get the vanilla orchid to bear beans in any country but Mexico. Finally a Belgian scientist, Charles Morren found that only a tiny bee native to Mexico could pollinate the orchid. He finally developed a way to artificially pollinate the orchid and his method is still used today for raising vanilla orchids in such places as Madagascar.

The Indians used vanilla to flavor stewed fruit, fruit pies, and fresh fruit besides flavoring chocolate. Vanilla blends and mellows fruit flavors, yet never overshadows them. Hugh Morgan, apothecary to Queen Elizabeth I was the first to make puddings flavored entirely with vanilla.

The French are great users of vanilla. They put it in all good quality fruit preserves, fruit pastries, fruit gelatines, compotes, stewed fruit and fruit pies. Escoffier, a famous well known French chef, used vanilla more than any other flavoring. Vanilla increases the flavor of all fruits and their natural sweetness without inserting its own flavor at all.

Here are the best ways to use vanilla developed from over 1,000 years of use by American Indian chefs and the finest European chefs Europe has ever produced.

1. In chocolate mixed with milk drinks use one-half level teaspoon per cup and reduce usual amount of sugar used by one-third.

2. In plain milk drinks, one-half teaspoon of vanilla per cup and reduce usual amount of sugar used to one-third.

3. In serving fresh fruit, such as strawberries, raspberries, blackberries, loganberries, muskmelon, grapefruit, etc. Where you used one half cup of sugar normally use two tablespoons of sugar and two teaspoons of vanilla extract. Reducing the sugar also, of course, helps people greatly who are dieting.

4. In making fruit preserves, cut every cup of sugar normally used to two-thirds of a cup, and use one level teaspoon of vanilla to replace the one-third cup of sugar.

5. In making fruit pies, cut the sugar normally used one-third per cup and add one level teaspoon of vanilla per cup of sugar normally used.

6. In making caramel, butterscotch and chocolate puddings add two level teaspoons of vanilla for every four portions made.

7. In making chocolate cake, add two level teaspoons of vanilla per average size cake. One is far too little.

8. In making chocolate candy of any kind such as fudge, chocolate

bars, etc., use one level teaspoon of vanilla per two cups of the candy mixture.

9. In whipping cream, use about one level teaspoon of vanilla per 2 cups of whipped cream, regardless of what other flavor you add to the whipped cream. Cut down the amount of sugar you use one-third.

Imitations of vanilla are simply not vanilla at all. They sometimes contain such mixtures of things such as ethylvanillin, propylene, glycol, caramel flavoring, etc. These things have nothing to do with vanilla at all. Save on food items when you can but buy pure vanilla extract, there is no substitute made by man that even comes close to it.

PRALINES NEW ORLEANS AND FRENCH

In the French quarter of New Orleans are several buildings that in slave days were called the Quadroon Ballrooms. One was at Salle de Conde now Chartes and Madison streets. Salle Orleans was another although incorrectly denied by some writers. Quadroon balls or dances were held in a great many places, even in theatres. A quadroon in those days was a person with one fourth African blood and three fourths white blood. The quadroon girls were sent to these ballrooms. The sons of the white planters and the white planters themselves came to the Quadroon Ballrooms and danced and were entertained by the quadroon women. These quadroon women were beautiful, exotic and extremely intelligent. Their complexions were a pale ivory tan, their hair ranging in colors from black to blond and red and their eyes from brown to blue.

Interior of the home of the Duc de Praslin whose valet, Jean Dulac invented the praline candy.

These quadroon women were not created by accident but were the result of careful selected breeding. They contained the finest African blood plus the finest white blood. Their manners and bearing were impeccable.

In the slave days Africans were bred like animals to produce the best possible persons for a desired purpose. For plantation work large, tall, well-muscled African men and large tall muscular white men were selected to do the breeding. White college boys of the time mostly from the eastern states were especially in demand and paid well for a summer's work. For places like the Quadroon Ballrooms African women were bred to white men. The girls resulting from this intercourse were again carefully bred to white men.

Many of the young men who frequented the Quadroon Ballrooms fell in love with one of the quadroons. They often fought duels over the girls. A good place to fight a duel was the garden in the Catholic cathedral. There got to be so many duels fought in the cathedral garden that the archbishop finally had to ban dueling on church property.

The Quadroon Ballrooms were run very well. A favorite bit of food to munch on at the ballrooms between dances or before a drink was a praline.

The praline was originated by Jean Dulac the chef in charge of the kitchen for Gabriel De Choiseul, the Duc de Praslin near Orleans, France under Louis the XV. He was the secretary of marine and foreign affairs. He saved France from the disasters of the Seven Years War. The duke was a great man for bonbons and was always giving them out to his lady friends. One day in the middle of the afternoon the Duke ran out of conventional bonbons. His valet rushed into the kitchen and put together the following recipe so as to get some bonbons in a hurry.

Put four cups of brown sugar in a pot with ½ cup of milk or cream, 2 level tablespoons of butter, one teaspoon of cherry flavoring. Stir over a quick medium heat until the sugar dissolves in the milk, butter and flavoring. Bring this mixture quickly to the boiling point and boil for three minutes without stirring. Remove the syrup from the stove and stir in carefully one pound of almonds. Pour the candy onto a well greased pan in little puddles about

Site of the Orleans ballroom and theatre D'Orleans used for Quadroon parties. The site was bought by Thomy Lafton, a free African, in 1881 and he built the present building on the site. Today it houses a school for African girls run by African Catholic Nuns of the Holy Family Order.

two to three inches in diameter. Separate the nuts from each other with a fork and leave cool.

The quickly prepared bonbons were such a success that the duke gave them his name of Praslin. The name gradually became changed to Praline as in French Praslin is pronounced praline. The word praline did not come at all from the French Marshal Caesar du Plessis Pralin neither did such a man become the Duc de Choiseul. Many writers incorrectly state that this man

Garden in back of the Catholic Cathedral in New Orleans where duels were fought.

invented the praline which is not at all true. They also sometimes state that pralines are just almonds boiled in sugar water or sugared almonds which again is not at all true.

This recipe was brought to New Orleans by the Ursuline Nuns. Almonds were scarce so pecans were substituted for the almonds. Cheery flavoring gradually was left out because it was expensive. They are not pralines, however, with out it.

In Europe today the word praline has come to mean both the original praline candy as well as liquor-filled chocolate candies.

SOURDOUGH PANCAKES LA SALLE

Robert La Salle was born in 1643 and died in 1687. He explored the whole center section of North America. On April 9, 1682 he took legal possession of all of the land drained by the Mississippi river and its tributaries. This was the recognized legal method of possessing land at the time. At Fort Creve Coeur on the Illinois river which now is called Peoria his sourdough pancakes at one time were a very deluxe rare food item and, for me they still are.

Good sourdough pancakes are tender, but have a slightly chewy texture and an appetizing taste that pancakes made from many ready mixed pancake mixtures definitely lack. Everyone prefers them to most ready mix pancakes.

Here is the recipe:

Peel and cut up four good sized potatoes. The original recipe did not call for potatoes but simply fruit peels. Potatoes, however, work very well and are handy and produce a very uniform end result.

Boil the potatoes until well done. Remove the potatoes from the water and eat them. Add one tablespoon of salt to the water the potatoes were boiled in and stir in just enough flour to make a thin creamy batter. Now cover the pot with a dish cloth or something similar and tie a string around the pot and cloth to keep the cloth tightly in place. This will keep the flies or insects from getting into the pot. Leave in a warm place for from two to three days or until the batter is definitely sour. You can smell it to see when it is good and sour. The night before you are going to make the pancakes take out two cupfuls of the sour batter and place them in a large mixing bowl. Mix in one cup of flour and just enough water to make a medium batter. Cover the mixing bowl with a dish towel and tie a string around the bowl and towel to hold the towel in place. Leave stand overnight in a warm place. In the morning mix in the following to the batter: Two well beaten eggs, 1 level tablespoon of sugar, 2 tablespoons of melted butter and one level tablespoon of baking soda. Leave rise for a few minutes. Then take a spoon and drop the batter into a well greased hot frying pan. The pancakes should be about 4 inches in diameter. Now add more flour and water and a half teaspoon of salt to your starter until you again have a thin batter. Leave stand until you make sourdough pancakes again. I know of such batter starters that have been going for over two years.

KAHWAH, KAHUE, KAFFE, CAFE OR COFFEE

All of the above words mean coffee, a bean from a bush that people buy about 400 million pounds of a year.

Coffee was discovered in the year 291 by a well to do Arab farmer and land owner named Khalifah Al-Kulab in old Arabia. He noticed that when his goats ate the ripened bean like berries from certain bushes that they became frisky and did not want to bed down for the night. He chewed the sun ripened berries himself and found that they stimulated him. He boiled the berries in water and found that the brew also stimulated him. He took some of the dried beans to merchant friends of his and brewed coffee for them. Everyone seemed to like the brew. The Arabian people are shrewd merchants so Khalifab and his friends decided to roast the beans to destroy their fertility as they wanted to control coffee production to themselves. They found, however, that roasting the berries greatly improved their flavor.

The merchant group first sold their roasted coffee in Persia.

The story that Al-Kulab took the first coffee beans to a priest at a monastery is completely wrong. In the first place in 291 there were no monasteries Christian or otherwise in Arabia. There were also no Moslems as Mohammed did not have any success with his religion in Arabia until after 622. After Mohammed established his Moslem religion in Arabia he formed an Army to drive the Christians out of Europe. In 732 Charles Martell a Frenchman defeated Mohammed's army at Poitiers, France which kept Europe Christian instead of Moslem. The Arabs, however, remained in Spain until the 15th century when they were finally driven out of Spain. The Arabs brought coffee to France and Spain with their Armies. The French did not at first take to coffee but the Spaniards did.

By 1600, however, coffee was well known in France. An Armenian named Louis Pascal started one of the first coffee houses in Paris. He served coffee to his patrons from a portable coffee pot kept hot by an alcohol lamp.

An Austrian spy named Joseph Kolschitzky operated in 1680 in the Turkish lines as they tried to capture Vienna. The Austrians defeated the Turks. Kolschitzky gathered up all the sacks of coffee that the retreating Turks abandoned and started the first coffee house in Vienna. He called it the "Blue Bottle."

From 1680 to 1730 coffee drinking became very popular in England. At that time London consumed more coffee than any city in the world. The famous London Insurance group, Lloyd's of London, began in Lloyd's Coffee House which was a meeting place for sea captains, merchants, brokers, insurance men and gamblers.

The Belgians originated modern type coffee making in 1700 by using a linen bag or strainer to hold the ground coffee in. They suspended the bag at the top of a pot. Before this coffee was either made of finely ground coffee beans boiled in water or the beans themselves boiled in water.

In the 1800's the English learned the Belgian method. They called the can or pot to make coffee in "biggin".

Louis XII of France was so fond of good coffee that he raised his own in his own gardens in order to get it as fresh as possible.

Today the English, Scotch and Irish have gone over to tea drinking and the United States now drinks more coffee than any other nation.

I have drunk coffee nearly all over the world. As a whole coffee everywhere is very good. I like them all, including thick Turkish and Greek coffee, chicory flavored French coffee, robust Scandinavian coffee and delicate South American coffee. Methods of making coffee vary greatly from one country to another, but the method of making coffee is not of too great importance. Using individual French and Italian coffee filters produces no better coffee than that made in a clean cotton stocking like they do on Belgian farms and small towns.

The secret of really good coffee making is simply to use very soft water to make the coffee. The softer the better. Rain water and snow water produce the finest coffee in the world.

Soft lake and river water are good also. If no other soft water is available use artificially softened water. Soft water is very corrosive, something you probably did not know. It actually breaks down the coffee letting out its wonderful aroma and taste and destroys bad tasting coffee oil entirely. It is absolutely impossible to make good coffee from hard water.

Here is a chart that applies in general to all methods of brewing coffee. It is handy to have for hunting and fishing camps, resorts, family gatherings, or Church suppers.

Average servings	Amount of coffee	Amount of water
2	2 tbsp.	1½ cups
4	4 tbsp.	3 cups
6	6 tbsp.	4½ cups
8	8 tbsp.	6 cups
10	10 tbsp.	7½ cups
20	½ lb.	1 gal.
40	1 lb.	2 gal.
60	1½ lb.	3 gal.

Here are just a few of the many excellent methods of making coffee that are well known throughout the world. I have found that most everyone welcomes a change in the way that they usually make their coffee.

CAFE DIABLE OR DEVILED COFFEE

"Diable" means deviled in French. This coffee was invented by Joseph Bonaparte brother of Napoleon and King of Spain and Naples. After Waterloo when the Belgians, Germans, and English defeated Napoleon, Joseph went into exile in the United States. Here is the original recipe.

Take ground coffee in the amount you prefer and add one fourth the amount of coffee in chicory and one eighth level teaspoon of ground cinnamon for every cup you desire to make. If you have a filter type of coffee pot use it. If not just take a clean cotton or linen cloth and tie the coffee, chicory, and cinnamon in it and brew as you usually do. When the liquid is brewed pour into cups. Add one lump of sugar to each cup and one ounce of brandy. Drink at once.

Do not boil the brew with brandy in it or light the brandy in making this famous coffee. Boiling or lighting the brandy simply burns out or boils out the alcohol destroying completely the intended taste of this famous coffee.

BEER COFFEE

Originated in the flax growing areas of Belgium in 1891 by Paul Van Loh a restauranteur and minor painter.

Here is how it is made.

Put a cup of strong black coffee in a beer glass. Add two ounces of cognac. Put an inch of whipped cream on top of the coffee. Looks like a glass of dark bock beer and hence its name.

The Irish have bought their flax in Belgium for centuries to take back to Ireland for bleaching.

As the centuries went by, many of the Irish remained in Belgium and married. Today much of the flax country of Belgium is a mixture of half Irish and half Belgian. In some areas it is nearly solid Irish and they have been there so long that they can speak no Gaelic or English.

The drink was taken back to Ireland before 1900.

The Irish substituted Irish whiskey for the drink instead of cognac when they were out of cognac. The fable that this drink was invented by a chef named Joe Sheridan at the Shannon airport in 1938 is entirely untrue. The same goes for the food served at the Shannon airport, none of the recipes are Irish except the names and the food is not at all anything special. The Irish or Gaelic word Slainte meaning good health is, of course, pure French in origin.

COFFEE EMPRESS JOSEPHINE

Marie Josephine De Lapagerie was born in 1763 on the island of Martinique. She married Viscount de Beauharnais. He was guillotined and she was also nearly guillotined herself. In 1796 she married Napoleon Bonaparte. She became Empress of France in 1804. Napoleon divorced her in 1809.

The Empress Josephine was known in her time as one of the most beautiful women in the world. Coming from the island of Martinique she knew both French and island cooking very well. When she came to France she quickly learned European cooking. Her coffee Empress Josephine became popular all over Europe and still is. Here is the original recipe.

Make your coffee with your usual favorite method. Make cocoa with your usual favorite method. Make a mixture of one half hot coffee and one half hot cocoa. Top the cup of liquid with sweetened whipped cream flavored with almond flavoring.

This is a fabulous drink and one that will delight anyone you serve it to.

COFFEE ROYALE OR IRISH COFFEE

This famous coffee drink was invented in Dublin, Ireland by Pierre A. Lamont, a French brandy and wine salesman, in 1809.

The Irish have always had a great love for French brandy and cognac. Henessey cognac has always been the most respected drink in Ireland for fancy drinking, much preferred over Irish whiskey. The Irish however have a throat for strong drinks and have Henessey cognac made specially 120 proof for drinking in Ireland. No other country in the world buys Henessey more than 84 proof.

Pierre Lamont well knew the Irish taste for strong cognac but he himself could simply not drink their specially made strong cognac straight as they did. In drinking with his customers he put an ounce of 120 proof cognac into a cup of coffee, added two level teaspoons of honey and stirred the mixture well. He called it Coffee Royale. It made a beautifully smooth drink. It caught on somewhat in Ireland as an after Church drink on Sunday morning but never caught on for a serious week day drink. In other parts of the world Coffee Royale became very popular and remains so to this day.

Just a few passing notes regards coffee. The Austrians, Hollanders, Belgians, Swiss and French for the most part all use some chicory in making coffee to give it added flavor and bouquet.

Coffee expresso is simply coffee made in an expresso coffee making machine. You use finely powdered coffee and steam pressure to force soft water through the coffee to extract the flavor. The water contacts the coffee only for a short time and the coffee yield is smaller than with other methods. It is almost the direct opposite of percolator coffee.

CAFE BRULOT

The word brulot in French means a very spicy meat or genievre or gin or alcohol burned with sugar. The word has nothing to do with burning brandy or cognac.

In New Orleans a drink is served today called Cafe Brulot. It is of fairly recent origin and is simply a drink dreamed up to look fancy and clip the tourist for a fancy price. It is strictly a tourist trap drink and contains among other things orange, lemon, cloves, and, of course, flaming brandy. I suppose there are poorer drinks but they would be difficult to find.

There was a cafe Brulot drink that was invented in New Orleans but today it is completely forgotten and you cannot get one in New Orleans unless you tell the bartender how to make it. It was made by Dominique You, top lieutenant for Jean Lafitte the pirate, and this is a real man's drink and

Tomb of Dominique You in downtown New Orleans. His real name was Frederic Youx.

well worthy of it's name. Dominique You's real name was Frederic Youx. His men called him Captain Dominique because he was from Santo Domingo. Jean and Pierre Lafitte and Dominique You captured many different kinds of trade goods and sold them in New Orleans and vicinity. They frequently sold beautiful porcelain tableware, fine cutlery, and cooking utensils. They often had the demi-tasse coffee cups that had stem type bases which were popular at this time. They used them for drinking strong chicory flavored and dark roast coffee. All French people do not drink chicory flavored coffee then or now. Dominique You as well as Jean and Pierre Lafitte liked their cognac as well if not better than coffee.

The original old absinthe bar on the corner of Bourbon and Conti streets in the French Quarter of New Orleans. It was built in 1838 by Randall Curell. The old Absinthe House bar has an old wooden bar. At the right end of the bar is a marble water dipper. Water was dipped into glasses of absinthe with the idea that the dipping mixed well into the absinthe. The bar wás originally in the Old Absinthe House on Bourbon and Bienville street just a block away.

Dominique You, made up the following coffee for himself in a demi-tasse cup.

1 level teaspoon of sugar.

1½ ounces of cognac or brandy.

½ ounce of cinnamon spiced wine or dry vermouth.

1 ounce of strong coffee.

He called it Cafe Brulot meaning spiced coffee not at all a flaming coffee. No Frenchman in those days would be stupid enough to waste good cognac by burning it. The tourist had not as yet arrived in New Orleans.

The Absinthe House in the French Quarter of New Orleans. It now is a restaurant and bar.

Jean Anthelme Brillat Savarin born 1755 died 1825 wrote of Vin Lafite.

Dominique You was quite a romancer and is probably better known for the phrase he coined, which went like this, than for Cafe Brulot: LES BONBONS ACCEUIL-LIS, PRODUISENT LEUR EFFET, MAIS LA LIQUEUR TRAVAILLE PLUS VITA CET EFFET.

This translates to the simple words, "Candy is dandy but liquor is quicker."

Cafe Brulot became popular enough so that word of it got back to France. The Lafite brothers were French heroes and in France they changed the name to Vin Lafite or Lafite's wine.

In 1823 Brillat Savarin wrote of Vin Lafite in the second volume of his book, La Physiologie Du Gout Ou Meditations De Gastronomie Franscendante Aus Gastronomes Parisiens.

You can buy Cafe Brulot cup and saucers made of porcelain at the department stores Holmes and Maison Blanche in New Orleans for $1.00 a cup and saucer. Down in the French quarter tourist trap antique shops run by migrant New Yorkers they sell the same cups and saucers for $3.00 a set.

MING ICED OR HOT TEA

The tea that we know today was discovered in what we now call Indo China in the year 427. A tea bush of our present day tea is just another bush with leaves shaped like the blade of a spear.

A man named Chih Yunchien noticed that leaves that fell from these bushes and fell into little puddles of water after a time turned the water an orange color. What actually happened was that the leaves fermented in the rain water and in fermenting turned the water an orange color. He tasted the orange water but found it quite bitter and did not like it. He thought little of it. As in all periods of time the world had its share of alcoholics in Chil Yunchien's time. One of his own sons became a hopeless alcoholic. In desperation he went into the wilderness and gathered leaves from the bushes that he had noticed had produced leaves that colored water orange and bitter. He boiled the leaves in water but found that the leaves produced a green liquid with an almost soap like taste. This was the first green tea and today green tea is made from the dried fresh leaves of this same bush. He went back into the wilderness and gathered up leaves from the bushes that were lying in puddles of rainwater. These he took home and boiled in water. The water turned

orange and the world had its first black or orange tea. The secret was that the leaves when they were left in the water fermented and in fermenting developed a new flavor and color. Today all black or orange tea is simply green tea leaves fermented and then dried. Chih forced his son to drink all of the tea he could hold and when he could hold more he gave him more. Chih simply desired to keep his son full of a harmless bitter liquid that would stop his terrible craving for alcohol. The brew miraculously did stop his craving for alcohol and tea became known as a cure for alcoholics and for many years was used only for this purpose. It still is the best cure for alcoholism ever developed. A man full of tea has no desire for alcohol and it is very soothing to his stomach and nerves. Coffee has just the opposite effect on alcoholics; it does not decrease their desire for alcohol and badly upsets their nerves and stomach if more than ordinary amounts are consumed.

As the years went by the Chinese people thought that if tea was such a fine medicine it must have wonderful qualities for just everyone. They began to drink tea gradually but their tastes preferred the green tea, not the black tea, for the most part. As time passed the Chinese people added such things as honey, candied fruits, and orange juice to the tea and soon it became a tremendously popular drink.

In 1313 John of Marignolli, an Italian, visited the Great Khan who then ruled China as well as all of the area up to and including Armenia and Hungary. Tea was then a well established drink and was served at all meals. He found tea being served both hot and cold. The Ming dynasty carried over through the Khan and held sway in China from 1368 to 1644. Tea drinking both hot and cold became even more popular and became almost a part of their religion. Candied fruits were usually served in the tea. China is where all oranges came from and it was only natural that it became a custom to add three spoonfuls of orange juice to every serving of tea. On certain occasions a leaf of crushed mint was also added to the tea.

Tea made hot or cold with three tablespoons of orange juice in it per cup or glass and a leaf of crushed mint in it is unquestionably a rare, really fine drink and the only way to make really good tea. Be sure to try it with this century old recipe. There is nothing worse or as stupid as putting lemon juice in either hot or cold tea. This custom came into being when tea was served on early trading ships and a slice of lemon or lime was put on the cup or mug so that the men would take their lemon or lime ration to keep them from getting scurvy. Eating a raw piece of lemon or lime is not very appetizing and soon the sailors were squeezing the lemon or lime into their tea and drinking it. They did not care for the taste of the tea with the lemon or lime in it but it was less disagreeable than eating raw lemon or lime. On shore the sailors as a joke told people that the Chinese always used lemon in their tea and in spite of the bad taste people thought that they must learn to like tea with lemon in it if the Chinese did who were the world's experts on tea. Actually no Chinese person would ever think of ruining tea with lemon.

Today China, Japan, Ireland, Scotland, England and Russia are the tea drinking countries. It is a really great drink when properly prepared, very good for nerves and your stomach.

In Japan tea bushes called "yama-cha" (mountain tea) grew in the forest from ancient times. It was only 770 years ago, however, when a Japanese Buddhist priest brought the seed of the tea bush to Japan from the China mainland. All Japanese tea except Hokkaido comes from the bushes that grew from these seeds. In 1859 Japanese tea was first exported to the United States. Green tea is favored by most Japanese people.

How to Dress Game

HOW TO CLEAN A TURTLE

We will take a snapping turtle for an example.

Use reasonable care in handling a live snapping turtle. The safest way to handle a turtle is by its tail. Turn the turtle over on its back. Tease the turtle with a stick until he strikes the stick or sticks his head out. Then chop the turtle's head off with an axe. Do not use a knife. You can chop off his claws now or later, either method will work well. I usually prefer to chop off his claws at the same time I chop off the turtle's head.

If you have a large clean can or kettle fill it with water. Add one level tablespoon of salt per gallon of water. Put on a fire and bring to a boil. Put in the turtle and boil him for one-half hour. Now remove the turtle from the water and place it on its back. This boiling the turtle in water for a half hour makes the cleaning of the turtle much easier.

If you have no large kettle or can to boil the turtle in after you have chopped off its head leave the body lay in a cool place from

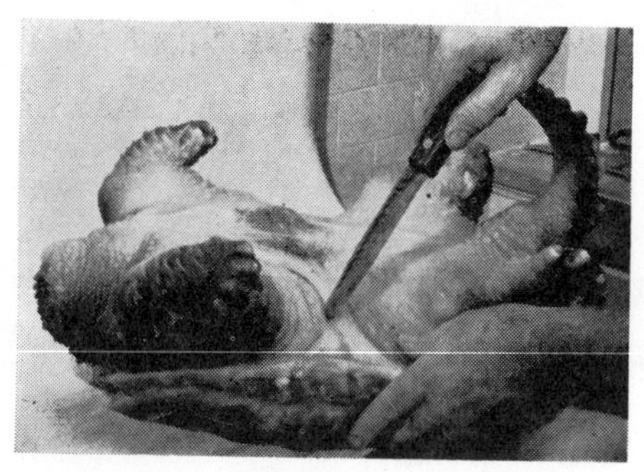

Figure 1.

Start Cutting the Belly Shell from the Turtle Here.

one to eight hours, depending upon the weather. The hotter the weather the less time it is necessary for it to be left before cleaning the body. The reason that it is necessary to leave the turtle's body alone for a time after chopping off its head if you do not boil the body is as follows: It takes quite a while after a turtle's head is chopped off before its heart stops beating and before its reflexes stop working. It is difficult to clean a turtle if its legs still react as if it were alive and hence it is better to wait until these reflexes have stopped.

Figure 2.

Removing the Belly Shell

Now to get on with the cleaning of the turtle. Have the turtle on its back. With your Bull Cook knife cut the belly or under shell from the turtle. This is done by finding the soft spots or gristle at each joining of the top and belly shells that holds the two shells together. Free the under shell of any skin holding it in place and cut the skin from the flesh so that you can remove and throw away the undershell. Skin out the four legs and locate the leg joints to the body and cut off the legs with the attached hams of the legs. Skin out the neck and the chunk of meat at the base of the tail. Cut off and discard the outer part from the vent back. You now have all of the turtle's meat that is edible. The entrails are not handled at all and are left intact in the top shell. Throw away the top shell and entrails. Remove all fat from the meat and wash it in mild salt water for a few minutes. Use about a tablespoon of salt per quart of water.

Turtle meat is very delicious and can be fried, baked, or roasted, or used in soup. It does not have a fish taste. It does however, have much the same stringy texture that frog legs have. If you like frog legs, you will like turtle meat.

When used in soup recipes you can substitute turtle meat for beef or pork.

Fry turtle meat in butter as you would beef.

All small, medium, and large turtles have very tender meat. In case you get an old extra large turtle just to make sure his meat will be real tender do the following:

Using this formula, ¾ water to ¼ vinegar make up enough liquid to cover the turtle meat. Add one tablespoon of salt to every quart of the liquid. Put the turtle meat in the liquid and leave stand over night. Then rinse well in clean, cold water and dry on an old dish towel. The meat is then ready to use.

FIELD DRESSING GAME BIRDS

If you really enjoy eating wild birds and want them at their best you must field dress them. When you shoot a pheasant, dove, partridge, quail, duck, goose, turkey or rail ninety percent of the time you put shot in their intestine. This immediately releases the manure juices and it doesn't take long before they give the bird a taste and odor that ruins it for fine eating.

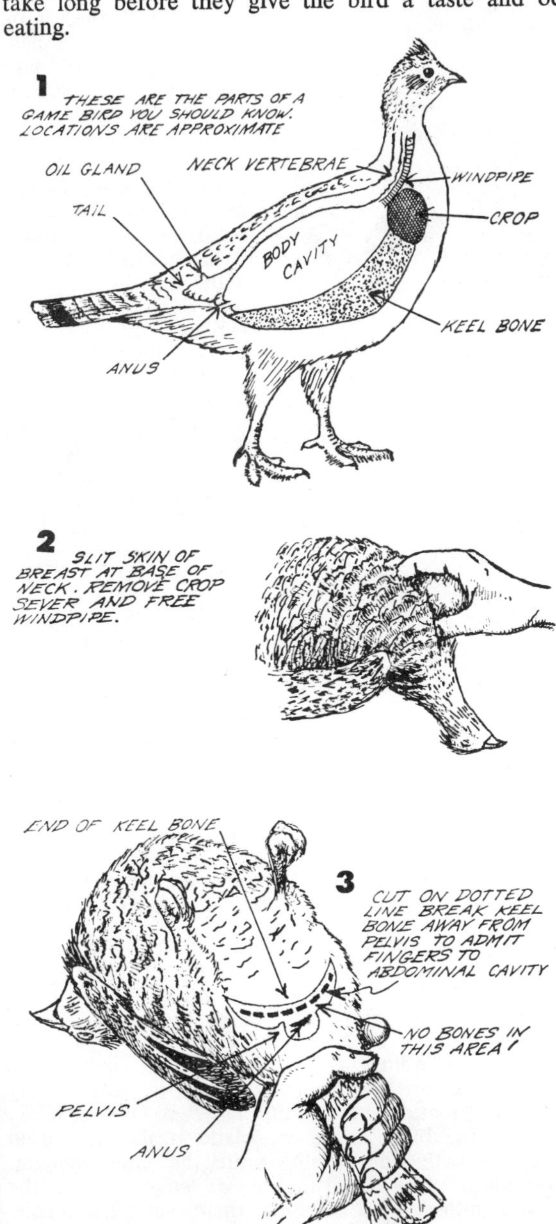

The crop of birds often contains wild food that if left in for any length of time will taint the whole breast.

Government law forbids the sale of poultry of any kind unless it is drawn immediately after death. This is done so the body heat can escape quickly without causing spoilage or tainting of the meat. The body heat of all game birds is over 100 degrees. How long does it take to spoil meat if you set it out in the sun in 100 degree weather? That is exactly what happens when you do not field dress a bird.

Field dressing also, of course, helps to remove blood from the flesh. Blood as we all know in meat spoils its flavor. If your butcher tried to sell you some meat that had not been bled you would not accept it. No wonder birds not field dressed have such strong and disagreeable tastes.

The illustration shows how to field dress game birds in general. In warm weather put a few leaves or dried grass or twigs in the body cavity to be sure it keeps well open so the body heat can escape as rapidly as possible.

Save the liver and heart of all game birds

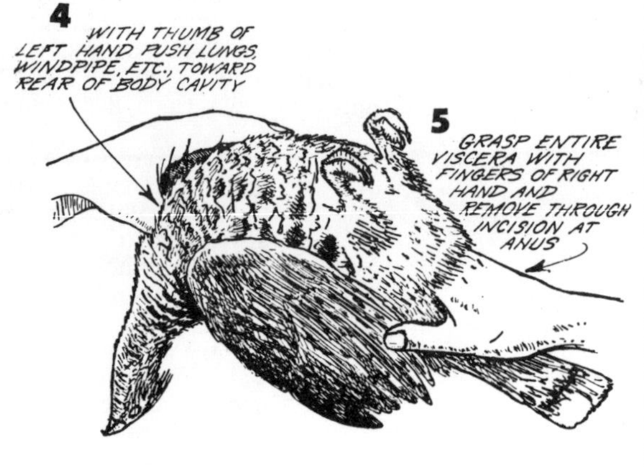

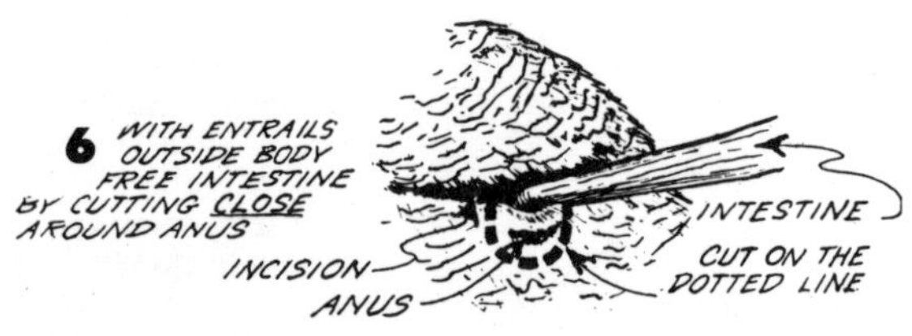

and the stomach if you want it for flavoring your gravy. You can simply stuff these organs back into the body cavity of the bird after you have cleaned it or carry along a little plastic sack and drop them into it and put the sack in your pocket.

Every so often some would be outdoorsman tries to tell me that such birds as quail, rails, and woodcock should be cooked with the innards left in. Such stupidity is almost unbelieveable. All of these fine birds are simply delicious eating when dressed properly and they stink as you can well imagine they would when they are left to spoil in their own body heat and flavored in their own manure. There ought to be a law against such goings on.

Game birds today are very expensive to shoot. They deserve being properly dressed so you can enjoy them properly.

THE CORRECT WAY TO SHARPEN A KNIFE

Never under any circumstances use a power grinder of any kind to sharpen a knife, as the heat generated will remove the temper from the edge of the blade.

If a knife is extremely dull and nicked, the first step in sharpening it is to roughly grind the edge sharp on a hand powered, fine grinding wheel or whetstone. Turn the stone very slowly and use not a little, but plenty of water on the stone. You must generate absolutely no heat on any part of the blade. The thin edge can quickly become very hot. If the edge of your blade turns blue from the grinding it has become too hot and is ruined. Hold the knife crosswise on the stone, moving it very slowly back and forth in a crosswise direction. Hold the knife so the grinding follows the established bevel of the blade or if the blade is flat, it should be held at a slight angle. Grind both sides of the knife the same amount. To judge the edge for sharpness, look carefully at its edge. Move the knife slightly. Flat areas will reflect light, making them very noticeable. Grind the flat areas a little more until they cannot be seen reflecting light.

A fine file can also be used to begin the sharpening on a very dull or nicked knife.

If the knife is not very dull or to finish sharpening it after rough grinding the edge, use a combination stone one side coarse grit and one side fine grit. Put kerosene or fine penetrating oil on the stone, never use any other oils as the stone will not function well with other oils. First, use the coarse side of the stone. Use straight even strokes, never use circular strokes. Move the knife toward its cutting edge as illustration shows. It does not take many strokes, sharpen each side of the edge the same amount.

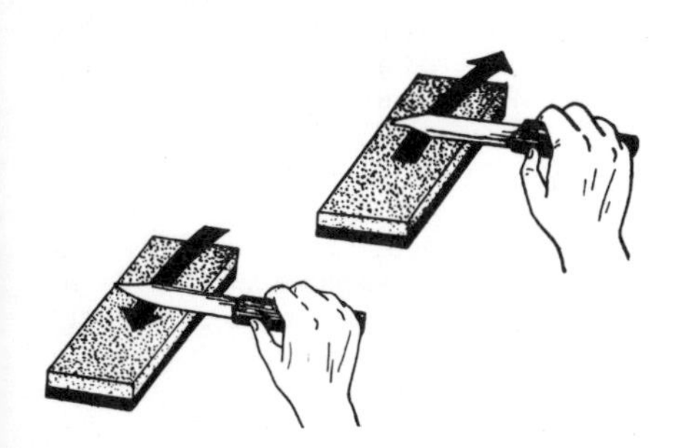

Hold the knife edge nearly flat, but at a slight angle. A slightly greater angle than when you rough ground it so the edge will be strong. If you hold the edge at the same angle as when you rough ground it the edge will be too thin and weak. If the blade has a wire edge or in other words one that bends back and forth, strop the edge on the heel of your hand or on an old belt and it will remove the wire edge. Now stroke the blade on the fine side of the oilstone and you will have a really sharp edge. It takes but a few strokes. If you want a super edge use a Washita stone to give a razor finish to the edge. A Washita stone is cut from natural rock, whereas oil stones are made from compressed powdered grits. Use kerosene only on the Washita stone. To remove scum from your oilstone or Washita stone use gasoline or ammonia.

DO NOT USE HOUSEHOLD TYPE KNIFE SHARPENERS ON A BULL COOK KNIFE AS THEY WILL RUIN THE EDGE OF THE KNIFE.

Wine, Beer and Liquor

FAMOUS MEN HAD THIS TO SAY ABOUT WINE

GEORGE WASHINGTON, President of the United States, quote, "My manner of living is plain and I do not mean to be put out of it. A glass of wine and a bit of mutton are always ready."

BENJAMIN FRANKLIN, discoverer of electricity quote, "Wine is a constant proof that God loves us and loves to see us happy."

JOHANN STRAUSS, famous musical composer quote, "A waltz and a glass of wine invite an encore."

LOUIS PASTEUR, inventor of pasteurizing quote, "The flavor of wine is like delicate poetry."

WILLIAM SHAKESPEARE, from his book Julius Ceasar quote, "Give me a bowl of wine. In this I bury all unkindness."

MICHELANGELO, sculptor quote, "I feast on wine and bread, and feasts they are."

BEETHOVEN, musical composer quote, "A glass of wine is a great refreshment after a hard day's work."

LUCULLUS, Greek philosopher quote, "Good drinks drive out bad thoughts."

SAINT PAUL, THE APOSTLE, I Timothy, V, 23; Drink no longer water but use a little wine for thy stomach's sake and thine other infirmities.

THE BIBLE, Genesis IX, 20, ascribes wine making to Noah.

HOW TO USE WINE IN COOKING

I have never seen a cook book that stated how to correctly use wine in cooking. The best professional cooks all know how to correctly use wine in cooking but definitely will not tell you. Cook book and magazine food editor recipes that call for wine invariably tell you to add the wine to the recipe and then to cook or heat the item you are cooking. All this causes nothing but a waste of good wine and adds nothing to the item cooked but possibly a very mild low grade grape flavor. The alcohol in the wine quickly completely evaporates with the cooking as well as much of the grape juice that makes up the rest of the wine. Wine tastes like wine only because of the alcohol blended into it. Without the alcohol, wine in nearly all cases is only a low quality grape juice. In many cases it is not even drinkable.

Wine added to gravy, meats, soups, fish, seafood, cakes, cookies, and puddings, is wonderful but add it after the items are prepared and ready to serve. Do not heat any food after the wine is added. If you use wine correctly you will come up with food very different and very fine tasting.

NOTICE TO HOME WINEMAKERS

It is unlawful to produce wine for family use unless you file Form 1541 with the assistant District Commissioner, Alcohol and Tax Division in your district.

Any person may produce up to 200 gallons of wine for his and his family's use tax free providing he has filed Form 1541 which is free of charge and costs nothing to file.

Write for duplicate copies of Form 1541. "Registration For Production of Wine For Family Use". Address your request to:

Assistant District Commissioner
Alcohol and Tobacco Tax Division
Bureau of Internal Revenue

At whichever of the following addresses would fall in your district:
Custom House Building, 555 Battery Street, San Fransico 11, California
Post Office Box 177, Denver 1, Colorado
Peachtree — Seventh Building, Atlanta 5, Georgia
Post Office Box 1144, Chicago 90, Illinois
55 Tremont Street, Boston 8, Massachusetts
708 Minnesota Building, St. Paul 1, Minnesota
2800 Federal Building, Kansas City 6, Missouri
143 Liberty Street, New York 6, New York
Faller Building, 8th and Walnut Street, Cincinnati 2, Ohio
128 Broad Street, Philadelphia 2, Pennsylvania
U. S. Postoffice and Courthouse Building, Dallas, Texas

BRIEF HISTORY OF WINE MAKING

Early wines were of, almost universally, very poor quality. In many cases, so distasteful to drink that they had to be mixed with water and flavoring so that they could be drank at all. Early wines were made by fermenting in open crocks and the wine sealed in jugs and crocks by pouring oil, fats or wax over them. In many cases just an oily wrap was put on top of the wine jugs. Air-borne bacteria continually entered them. The alcohol content was very low running not more than 5 to 6% alcohol. Wild yeasts easily got into the wines and very frequently turned them to vinegar.

The Monk, Dom Pierre Perignon of Hautivilliers, France, at the end of the 17th century, for the first time developed the use of corks and bottles to store wine in instead of jugs, casts, and crocks. He also invented champagne. In 1775 a notable wine discovery was made at Rheingau in Germany. There it was discovered that grapes left to rot on the vines produced a sweetness and bouquet not possible to produce from grapes in their prime.

Wine is made by converting the sugars, glucose and fructose, into alcohol and carbon dioxide. This can be represented by the chemical equation C6H1206 equals 2C2H50H plus 2C02. The reaction, also on occasion, creates small amounts of glycerol, acetic and succinic acids and traces of higher alcohols.

True wine yeast is saccharomyces ellipsoideus. Wild yeast that converts alcohol to acetic acid is mycoderma vini.

In the 18th century chemists discovered that sodium metabisulphite used 4 grains to a gallon killed wild yeasts and bacteria in wine making liquids. Then true wine yeasts were put into the wine making liquid and, of course, the wine produced was perfect every time and with an alcohol content of up to 18%. Before the use of sodium metabisulphite in wines the quality was exceedingly poor and the alcohol content very low. Sodium metabisulphite releases sulphur dioxide as it is mixed with the wine liquid which is called the "must."

This process is called "sulphiting" wine.

AREAS IN THE UNITED STATES THAT DRINK THE MOST ALCOHOLIC BEVERAGES

The month of December is the month that the most alcoholic beverages are drunk with November the second and August the third month. No one knows why people drink more in these months than in any other months. It is not because of holidays as in August there are few and in November and December few. January has as many holidays, including New Years, yet drinking in January is low.

The area of the United States where the individual consumption of liquor is the highest is the district of Columbia or Washington D. C. In fact, it is by far the highest in the whole world. People of the state of Nevada are second, Alaska third, Connecticut fourth and Delaware fifth.

FRENCH METHODS OF MAKING WINE

The methods that I describe are the ones not only used in France but by reliable American commercial wine makers.

There are very few people in the world that know how to make good wine perfectly everytime with a high alcohol content. Using the old recipes, you either end up with a very poor quality of wine at best with 5% to 6% alcohol content or nothing but vinegar or tannin.

In order to make good wine with an alcohol content of 12% to 18%, you must have the following simple inexpensive equipment and supplies. If you use them, it is absolutely impossible to have a wine failure of any kind.

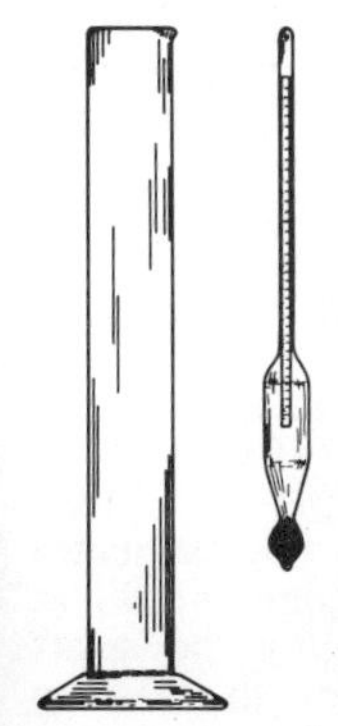

SACCHAROMETER

This is a long hollow glass tube that, when placed in fruit or root juice, tells you the amount of sugar in it and the amount of alcohol this sugar will create. You must also have a saccharometer glass jar or a so-called hydrometer jar. This is simply a tall glass to put the liquid in that you desire to test for sugar content. You then just put the saccharometer into the liquid and take a reading. The saccharometer costs $2.47 plus postage and the saccharometer glass jar, $2.47 plus postage. You can order them as well as all other wine making supplies from Herter's Inc. Waseca, Minnesota. U. S. A.

SODIUM METABISULPHITE

Buy sodium metabisulphite in 4 grain tablets or by the ounce. If you buy by the ounce, also buy a Herter's Model B powder scale which is accurate to 1/10 of a grain and measure out the grain quantities you have to use. Price of the Model B scale is $6.25.

Fruit pulp needs 4 grains of sodium metabisulphite per gallon of fruit pulp applied as follows. Crush the fruit in a crock or polyethylene pail. Add a quart of boiled water for every gallon of crushed fruit and stir in well. Dissolve four grains of sodium metabisulphite for every gallon of the mixture of fruit pulp and boiled water in a cupful of warm water and mix this with the fruit pulp. Leave the mixture stand for two hours. The sodium metabisulphite will kill off all wild yeasts and bacteria in the fruit pulp.

To sterilize bottles before putting wine into them do as follows. Take a gallon jug. Fill it with boiled, cooled water. Put eight grains of sodium metabisulphite into the jug and shake it up well until dissolved. Pour some of this solution into a bottle and shake the bottle until all of the inside of the bottle is wet then pour the solution into the next bottle and repeat until all of the bottles are sterilized. Then pour the sterilizing solution back into the gallon sterilizing solution storage bottle to be used over. The sterilizing solution may leave a slightly pungent odor in the bottles. Actually, this will not affect the taste or aroma of the wine you fill the bottles with. If you desire, you can rinse out the bottles with boiled, slightly cooled, water but this really is not necessary.

If you use corks to cork your wine bottles, place them in a large pot. Put a suitable weight on the corks that will hold them down and cover them with the sterilizing solution. As you use each cork, take it from the pot, dip the cork in boiled water and wipe it dry with a clean cloth dipped in the sterilizing solution. Corks must be dry when put into bottles. Thus, they keep the weight of the wine from pushing out the corks if the wine bottles are laid on their sides. Wine bottles, of course, are often stored on their sides.

FERMENTATION LOCKS

After your wine has fermented in a covered crock for not more than five days, the wine minus the fruit pulp must be removed and final fermentation done in large five gallon or larger plastic polyethylene bottles or glass bottles. Collapsible easily stored plastic polyethylene bottles can be bought from Herter's for $3.06 each plus postage. Five gallon or larger glass bottles can be bought very reasonably at pop bottling plants. They get syrups in them and usually have a surplus of empty ones on hand.

Actually, it is best, if possible, to ferment your wine entirely in large five gallon or larger plastic or glass bottles then use crocks. When you use a fruit pulp to make wine, it is very difficult to get the fruit pulp out of the bottles and, hence, much easier to ferment the fruit pulp in covered crocks for five days, then throw away the fruit pulp and ferment the liquid only in plastic or glass bottles. If, of course, you prefer a light bodied wine, you can just squeeze out the juice of the fruit and put the juice alone in your plastic or glass bottles and ferment it as instructed.

When your wine liquid, or "must" as it is called, is siphoned into the large plastic or glass bottles, you must put a cork or rubber seal or stopper on the mouth of the bottle. Make a hole in the cork or stopper and insert a fermentation lock into the hole. Put a little boiled water into the fermentation lock as the instructions state. As the yeast, which, of course, is still in the liquid or "must", continues to ferment, it keeps on changing the sugar to alcohol and carbon dioxide. The carbon dioxide will force its way up through the water of the fermentation lock and out into the air. The water prevents any wild yeasts or bacteria from getting into the wine and spoiling it and also prevents any flies getting into the wine. The fermentation lock performs another vitally important function when the bubbles stop going up

5 gallon polyethylene plastic jugs. The one on the left has a fermentation lock The one on the right has an airtight plastic cap.

The 5 gallon polyethylene jug on the right has been collapsed to show how easily they can be stored.

through the fermentation lock. The wine has finished fermenting and is ready to put into another bottle to clear or to final bottle. There is no danger at all of the wine being left too long after it has completely finished fermenting.

WINE YEASTS

In the case of grapes and most fruits, their skins contain yeasts, molds and bacteria. Most of the time their skins contain some good wine making yeast. Using the natural yeast found on grape and other fruit skins, if no bad yeast is also found on them, you can get wine from 10% to 11% alcohol content. However, no where in the world today are commercial wines made by this method. Although, in ancient times this was the only method used. Using bakers yeast you can get wine from 10% to 12% alcohol content. Using wine yeast you can get wine from 15% to 18% alcohol content.

It is best to use sodium metabisulphite to kill all yeasts and bacteria in fruit pulp and then add wine yeast or bakers yeast so that you do not take a chance on any bad yeasts spoiling your wine.

YEAST NUTRIENTS

Yeast nutrient is simply chemical foods for wine yeast. They make sure that the wine yeast changes all possible sugar into alcohol and as quickly as possible. In using grapes and most fruits, you do not need yeast nutrient although it does not hurt to use it. In making wines from extracts, flowers, grains, etc., you need yeast nutrient.

INVERT SUGAR

In adding sugar to "must" or the wine liquid so that the alcohol content will be as high as you desire, you will get best results by using invert sugar instead of household white sugar. You can, of course, make excellent wine by using just white household sugar but all of todays best wines are made with invert sugar. Invert sugar gives your wine a smoothness, better taste and converts to alcohol quicker than household sugar. You can buy invert sugar from Herter's, Waseca, Minnesota and it costs no more than household sugar or you can make sugar that is partly inverted as follows.

Put 8 pounds of white household sugar in a large pot. Add 2 pints of water and ½ ounce of citric acid, which you can get from any drugstore, or the juice of four lemons. Over a medium heat, bring to a slow boil. Stir all the time so all of the sugar dissolves. After all sugar is dissolved, boil slowly and very gently without any stirring, if possible, or with only very slight occasional stirring. Allow to cool to just warm, then add just enough boiled water to make one gallon. Store in tightly sealed jars. This is not pure invert sugar but about three fourths of the sugar is inverted. The inversion is done by the acid and heat. One pint equals about 1 pound of household cane or beet sugar.

WINE DISEASES

In the years before the nineteenth century, wine making, at best, was a very uncertain process with the majority of the wine made spoiled or of very poor quality and very low alcohol content.

With the advent of sodium metabisulphite to kill off wild yeasts and molds and bacteria in the "must" and to sterilize utensils and the invention of fermentation locks, wines became very easy to make in top quality. Actually, wine diseases are of no longer any importance or concern if you use the methods for wine making described in this book.

I will describe wine diseases here more as a matter of historical importance than of importance to the modern wine maker.

The two worst wine diseases are acetic fermentation and flowers of wine. Both of these diseases are completely eliminated by the sulphiting process, fermentation locks and by keeping the jugs full when racking after fermentation has been completed. Both of these diseases have to have air in order to ruin the wine. After your wine is fully fermented and polished and has an alcohol strength of 12% or more and has a little sodium metabisulphite in it, they cannot get started in your wine. You then can bottle your wine and not completely fill up the neck of the bottles, filling them up to only about a third of the neck from the top.

Acetic fermentation turns wine to vinegar, and is caused by a wild yeast getting into the wine. It cannot happen if you follow the methods outlined.

Flowers of wine. This is a film that forms on the surface of wine and, if left untouched, eats up the alcohol in the wine. It can occur when you leave the wine in the fermenting crock past the time when it should go into the jugs and by not keeping the glass or plastic jugs full as previously instructed. Using large plastic or glass jugs for your fermenting, it is impossible to get flowers of wine or acetic fermentation into your wine.

FRUITS, ROOTS, FLOWERS, GRAIN AND EXTRACTS ALL MAKE THE FINEST OF WINES

Most all of us have to count our pennies these days. We would all like to drink a little good wine now and then and serve some to our friends but the cost of buying good wine puts it out of the question. If you make your own wine you can afford to have it for yourself and friends.

If you live in an area where native wild grapes, wild elderberries, wild cherries, crow berries, salmon berries, blueberries, black berries or raspberries are found, your wine will cost about 25c a gallon to make or less. Wheat, old potatoes and old carrots, also make fine wine. Domestic fruits such as peaches, pears, plums and apples are wonderful for wine making.

Extracts in fruit or liquor flavors used with yeast nutrient makes excellent wine. If you want, you can use the extracts in combination with grapes or fruits and leave out the yeast nutrient, although it is always good to use yeast nutrient.

If you live in New England, the Middle West, West and Pacific Northwest, plant several Beta grape vines and you will have grapes enough for all of the red wine that you want. Beta grape vines need no winter protection and will stand fifty below zero winters. In the warmer parts of North America, plant Concord grapes for red wine, Niagara grapes for white wine and Catawba grapes for a good medium red wine. In the Eastern states and California, you can grow the French hybrid grapes. No matter what state you now live in from Arizona to Alaska, you can grow grapes.

Grapes for wine making can be grown from Alaska to South America. Here is a vineyard near the Salton Sea in California. The soil is so full of salt that it has to be repeatedly washed out with fresh irrigation water yet grapes even grow well under such conditions.

HOW TO MAKE WILD GRAPE WINE

I will first discuss the making of wine from wild grapes. Wild grapes are usually small and contain little juice. Gather as many as you possibly can. Remove about half of the stems on wild grapes as they contain large quantities of tannin. You need some tannin in good wine but in reasonable quantities. Using tame grapes you need not remove any of the stems. Weigh the grapes. Place the grapes, a small quantity at a time, into the bottom of as large a crock or polyethylene plastic pail as you can procure. Say, for example, a twenty gallon crock. Squash them with a clean piece of 2 x 4 or 4 x 4 wood. Add a quart of boiled water that has been cooled down slightly. Take 4 grains of sodium metabisulphite for about every gallon of grape pulp and dissolve in a cup of warm water then stir in well into the pulp. Leave stand for two hours or more. This will kill off all bacteria and wild yeasts and molds in the pulp and liquid, thus, letting you add pure wine making yeast. Now add boiled lukewarm water at the rate of one gallon for about every three pounds of grapes. Be sure that the crock is not over three fourths full or it will overflow when fermenting. Stir the "must" and boiled water well with a clean wooden stick that has been dipped in the bottling sterilizing solution made up of eight grains of sodium metabisulphite in a gallon of water. Now take some of the "must" of liquid and strain it through a coarse cloth into the saccharometer glass. Carefully place the saccharometer into the liquid in the glass and note the reading on it.

Compare to the chart on the next page.

WHAT THE SACCHAROMETER INDICATES		TO MAKE WINE OF 6% ALCOHOL BY VOLUME ADD. SUGAR		TO MAKE WINE OF 8% ALCOHOL BY VOLUME ADD. SUGAR		TO MAKE WINE OF 10% ALCOHOL BY VOLUME ADD. SUGAR		TO MAKE WINE OF 12% ALCOHOL BY VOLUME ADD. SUGAR		TO MAKE WINE OF 14% ALCOHOL BY VOLUME ADD. SUGAR		TO MAKE WINE OF 16% ALCOHOL BY VOLUME ADD. SUGAR		TO MAKE WINE OF 18% ALCOHOL BY VOLUME ADD. SUGAR	
BACK	FRONT														
Unit Density	Alcohol Strength	in pounds per 10 gals.	in ounces per gal.	in pounds per 10 gals.	in ounces per gal.	in pounds per 10 gals.	in ounces per gal.	in pounds per 10 gals.	in ounces per gal.	in pounds per 10 gals.	in ounces per gal.	in pounds per 10 gals.	in ounces per gal.	in pounds per 10 gals.	in ounces per gal.
1034	3.5	3.60	5.74	6.40	10.24	9.20	14.69	12.00	19.22	14.85	23.76	17.70	28.32	20.55	32.88
1037	4.0	2.90	4.64	5.75	9.21	8.50	13.67	11.35	18.16	14.20	22.70	17.05	27.28	19.90	31.84
1040	4.5	2.05	3.28	4.90	7.88	7.75	12.42	10.60	16.95	13.45	21.49	16.30	26.08	19.15	30.64
1043	5.0	1.40	2.27	4.25	6.81	7.10	11.35	9.90	15.89	12.75	20.43	15.60	24.96	18.45	29.52
1046	5.5	.80	1.28	3.65	5.84	6.50	10.41	9.35	14.95	12.15	19.49	15.00	24.00	17.85	28.56
1050	6.0			2.80	4.54	5.65	9.08	8.50	13.62	11.35	18.16	14.20	22.72	17.05	27.28
1053	6.5			2.05	3.28	4.90	7.88	7.75	12.42	10.60	16.95	13.45	21.52	16.30	26.08
1056	7.0			1.40	2.27	4.25	6.81	7.10	11.35	9.90	15.89	12.75	20.40	15.60	24.96
1059	7.5			.65	1.07	3.50	5.61	6.35	10.15	9.15	14.69	12.00	19.20	14.85	23.76
1062	8.0					2.80	4.54	5.65	9.08	8.50	13.62	11.35	18.16	14.20	22.72
1065	8.4					2.35	3.60	5.10	8.14	7.90	12.68	10.75	17.20	13.60	21.76
1069	9.0					1.40	2.27	4.25	6.81	7.10	11.35	9.95	15.92	12.80	20.48
1072	9.5					.65	1.07	3.50	5.61	6.35	10.15	9.20	14.72	12.05	19.28
1075	10.0							2.85	4.54	5.65	9.08	8.50	13.62	11.35	18.16
1078	10.5							2.10	3.34	4.90	7.88	7.75	12.40	10.60	16.95
1081	11.0							1.40	2.27	4.25	6.81	7.10	11.35	9.95	15.92
1085	11.5							.75	1.20	3.60	5.74	6.45	10.32	9.30	14.88
1088	12.0									2.85	4.59	5.70	9.12	8.55	13.68
1091	12.5									2.15	3.47	5.00	8.00	7.85	12.56
1094	13.0									1.40	2.27	4.25	6.81	7.10	11.35
1097	13.4									.85	1.34	3.70	5.92	6.55	10.48
1101	14.0											2.95	4.72	5.70	9.12
1104	14.5											2.25	3.60	5.10	8.14
1107	15.0											1.50	2.40	4.35	6.96
1110	15.5											.75	1.20	3.60	5.74
1120	17.1													2.90	4.64
1125	17.9													2.05	3.28
1130	18.7													1.40	2.27

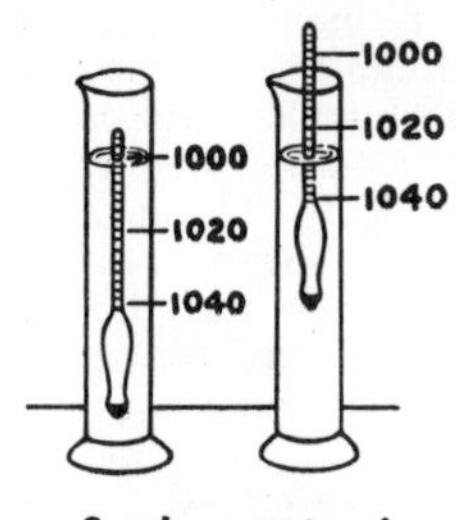

Saccharometer in water on left, in wine at right.

If you have the Herter combination saccharometer and thermometer, it has the alcohol percentage scale in it and you do not need to consult the chart at all.

The sugar must be added to the "must" in the form of a syrup. If you use household white sugar, dissolve it in water then bring the water to a boil and boil for about two minutes, then leave the syrup cool to warm and stir into the "must." If you use invert sugar, this is already a syrup and can be added directly to the "must" and stirred in well.

Now remember this, add only one half of the sugar or invert sugar needed for the initial fermentation. Yeast works better if the "must" does not have too much sugar to start with.

Use wine making yeast if possible. If you use bakers yeast, a cake is more than enough for five gallons and four cakes for up to twenty gallons. Just crumble up the bakers yeast and stir it into the "must." If you use wine yeast, make a "starter" of it as follows. It is best to sterilize a gallon jug with the sterilizing solution. Then rinse it out with boiled water cooled down to warm. Put a half gallon to three fourths of a gallon of boiled, cooled down water into the gallon jug and add a level teaspoon of sugar for every pint of the water.

Put a half gallon to three fourths of a gallon of water into a pot. Add two level teaspoons of sugar for every pint of water. Dissolve the sugar into the water and bring to a boil for about a minute. Leave cool to lukewarm then pour the sugar water mixture into the sterilized jug. Put in the wine yeast and put a fermentation lock onto the jug. Put in a warm place and leave ferment for about three days, then add to the "must." A half gallon, or three fourths of a gallon, of yeast "starter" like this is enough for up to 25 gallons of wine. The "must" will quickly go into a vigorous ferment. If you have no cover for the crock, do as follows. Put a sheet of polyethylene film over the mouth of the crock and put about a four inch ball of absorbent cotton on the inside edge of the crock. With a cotton cord tie the polyethylene sheet to the crock and bind down the ball of cotton. The carbon dioxide given off by the fermenting wine can escape through the cotton batting but wild yeasts cannot enter the crock and neither can fruit flies or wine flies. Wine will ferment in most any warm temperature but it does the best between 65 degrees to 75 degrees. Place the crock where it is warm. The grape skins will come to the top and form a hat or chapeau on the wine. Leave the wine ferment for about four days.

Sterilize 5 gallon or larger plasic polyethylene jugs or glass jugs. Take a piece of small plastic or rubber tubing. Dip it into the sterilizing solution. Then siphon the wine from under the pulp and grape skin hat into the jugs. Add to each jug the amount of the household sugar syrup or invert sugar syrup to make the alcohol content you set. Then put a fermentation lock onto the bottle and leave in a warm place to ferment. The first fermentation in the crock is done simply to get the juice and flavor from the skins and pulp but not have to contend with getting them out of a bottle. This second fermentation is not only an alcohol fermentation but a fermentation of the acidity of the wine. The wine now contains tartaric acid and malic acid. The yeast will attack the malic acid turning it into carbon dioxide gas and a feebler lactic acid. Leave the wine ferment until all fermentatation has stopped. With a fermentation lock, you can tell exactly when the fementation has stopped by when the carbon dioxide bubbles stop coming out of the fermentation lock. Toward the last of the fermentation it may take many minutes for a bubble to go out of the fermentation lock. To make sure that all fermentation has ceased you can give the jug a slight shake. This may start the wine fermenting a little more. Actually, it does not hurt the wine at all if you do bottle it before it has finished the last wee bit of fermenting.

The wine now has its full alcohol content and if this content is 12% or over, this alcohol in the wine will preserve it very well. The wine now should be clear or fairly clear Place one jug on a table. Now take a siphon that you have sterilized in the sterilizing solution and, being very careful not to disturb the sediment in the bottom of the jug, siphon out the wine into a clean sterilized jug on the floor. Leave the wine run against the side of the bottle aerating it. Changing the wine from one jug to the next is called "racking" the wine.

Siphoning the fermented wine from one jug to the next and aerating it.

Fill the jugs up, full, right to the top, full jugs prevent any harmful bacteria from forming in the wine as most of such bacteria have to have air to live on. If the jugs are full, there is no air in them. Put fermentation locks on the jugs. Leave the wine stand for another month but in the coolest part of the basement or out in your unheated garage this time. In fact, if the weather is cold, it is best to put it outside in your garage where it will get a good chilling. Freezing will not hurt the wine but help it. Chilling causes the cream of tartar to settle out of the wine. The sediment in the bottom of crocks or jugs is called "lees." This time the sediment will be mostly cream of tartar. You must get all of the sediment out of wine to have good tasting wine.

Your wine now should have enough alcohol in it to keep it. The wine will be "dry" and not sweet. If you desire the wine made sweet, there are two ways to do it.

1. Add artificial sweetener to the wine.

2. Add sugar in the form of syrup to the wine. If you add sugar do as follows. Mix 2 grams of sodium metabisulphite. This is a pinch in an ounce of warm boiled water for every five gallons of finished wine that you have. Add to every 5 gallons of the wine. The sodium metabisulphite will stop the finished wine from ever fermenting the sugar you add if it picks up a bit of yeast from the air. Actually, adding 2 grams of sodium metabisulphite to every 5 gallons of every finished wine is a good precaution. It prevents the wine from ever being affected by any molds or bacteria.

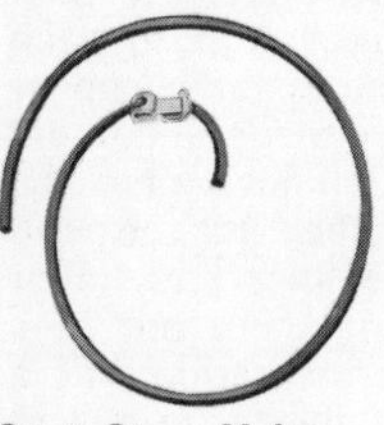

Start-Stop Valve On Your Siphon.

If the following things are true, and they should be at this stage, the wine is now ready to bottle permanently. If these things are not true, "rack" the wine again before bottling.

1. The wine must be brilliantly clear, or "polished." A clear wine is called a "polished" wine. If it is cloudy, it will tend to remain cloudy or form more sediment in the bottle than a good wine should.

2. The wine should have been left where it was as

cool as possible for three to four weeks before bottling as instructed to make sure that all cream of tartar was precipitated.

3. The wine must now have a good aroma free from all hydrogen sulphide or rotten egg odor. If it has such an odor an aerating and racking will eliminate it.

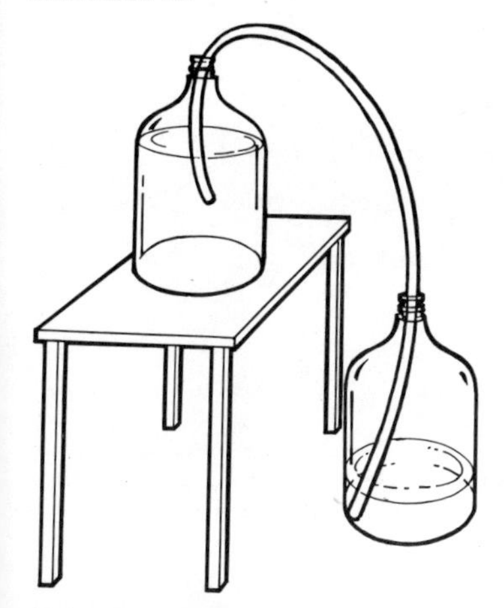

Siphoning wine from one jug to another without aeration.

4. The secondary fermentation must be fully completed.

Large size Ginger Ale and pop bottles make excellent wine bottles. Jugs are also very good. The metal and cork caps can be used to cork bottles and screw on metal and cork caps used to seal jugs. Be sure that all caps are sterilized. The little machines to put on bottle caps can be purchased from Herter's. The use of regular wine bottles and wine corks gives your wine a fancier appearance but does not improve the wine any and is far more expensive.

Use your siphon to get the wine from the large jugs into your bottles or other jugs. Get a start-stop valve for your siphon from Herter's.

Fill the bottles so that the wine comes up to within one-third of an inch of the top. This is important. If you drink the wine after 24 hours or so, it will be quite flat and not good tasting. The wine will not be ready to drink for a month and will be best after one year.

Now siphon, "rack," the wine into sterilized bottles and seal the bottles with the proper seals. Siphon the wine from the large jugs directly into the sterilized bottles or jugs without any aeration. Place the siphon well down into the wine and the other end put into the clean jug or bottle right on the bottom. The jug that you siphon from must be on a table and the jug or bottle that you siphon into must be on the floor.

HOW TO MAKE WINE FROM CULTIVATED GRAPES

If you have to buy cultivated grapes to make wine, the cost of the finished wine will run between 25 cents to 75 cents per gallon depending on where you live and what you have to pay for the grapes. This is high so you must be very careful to make the wine properly so there is no danger at all of spoiling it. Never buy grapes if you can help it unless they are overripe and you can get them for a few cents a pound. The fruit dealers cannot sell overripe grapes for eating but they make the very best wine.

A lug holds a little over a half bushel of grapes. If you are making 50 gallons of wine buy about 6 lugs. For 25 gallons about 3 lugs. For 12 gallons about 1½ lugs. For 6 gallons ¾ of a lug or 1 lug. Do not wash the grapes or stem them.

The taste for different wines varies greatly from one continent to the other. In Europe the French, German, Italian, and Spanish wines are the accepted standards. If wine differs from what these countries can produce, it is not liked in Europe. Europeans do not like any wines made from grapes originating in North America such as Concord grapes, Delaware grapes, Catawba grapes, Beta grapes and many others. They say that they have too much of a musk or "foxy" taste. Americans, however, prefer wines with a musk or "foxy" flavor by a large majority. Wine made from Concord grapes is by far the most popular wine in America and it has a distinct "foxy" flavor and aroma. In other words, whether wine made from one grape or another is excellent depends on the person's taste who is drinking it.

If you are going to make grape wine regularly, buy a wine press or a good kitchen liquifier. Commercial wine today is rarely run through a

The making of wine in California is a streamlined highly commercial process. Here grapes are being hauled to a plant that reduces them into a liquid.

Bringing in tankloads of liquidized grapes to a California winery. California wine making is very automatous and little resembles European wine making processes.

crusher-type wine press but instead is run through a liquifier which reduces the stems, seeds, and skins and pulp all to a liquid. A home meat grinder does a very good job of crushing grapes too.

European commercial wine makers all loudly claim that they use nothing but the juice of the grapes to make their wines. The same is true with American commercial wine makers. Actually, they get as much water as possible into the wine as a watered wine is by far the best wine. This can be done by adding large quantities of water with sugar to adjust the wine to the desired alcohol content or by the winery owner simply ordering water added to the grape juice. I have drank a lot of wine made in every continent in the world and I much prefer a wine that is fermented from a mixture made up of crushed grapes and grape juice and an equal amount of good water. Anyone who honestly knows anything about wine, I find. has the same preference.

Huge wooden wine casks in a California winery. In some cases these casks are strictly for show and are not used at all to store wine.

HOW TO MAKE RED WINE FROM CULTIVATED GRAPES

Buy a polyethylene or ceramic crock with a cover. Mount your wine press, liquifier or meat grinder over the fermenting crock and put in the grapes and run them through. If you do not have a crusher, put the grapes in the bottom of the crock in small batches and crush them with a 2″ x 4″ or 4″ x 4″ piece of clean wood. Do not put in any unripened grapes. It is best that the grapes are overripe. Now for every gallon of crushed grapes and grape juice, take four grain tablets of sodium metabisulphite and dissolve them in a quart or two of lukewarm water and stir the water well into the crushed grapes and grape juice. Leave stand for 24 hours. This will kill all yeast and bacteria in the crushed grapes and grape juice. Grapes all have wine yeast on them but, in some cases, they also have some bad yeasts on them and it is best just to make sure to kill off all yeast and use a wine yeast "starter." Now add about the same amount of boiled and cooled down water that you have of crushed grapes and grape juice and stir in well. Test the liquid with your saccharometer and add half enough sugar for the alcohol content that you desire. Boil the sugar in water for about two minutes before adding and leave cool down then add. Now put in a "starter" from wine yeast and leave ferment at about 65 to 70 degrees for five days. Every evening take off the cover and with a clean spoon break up the hat or "chapeau" of the "must" that forms from grapes, skins, etc. Now put the pulp in a strong coarse cloth and wring it out as dry as possible into large plastic fermenting bottles then put aside the wrung out pulp to make "Pomace" wine later on. If you have a wine press, run the "pomace" through the wine press to get all liquid out of it. Pour the "must" or rest of the liquid from the fermenting crock into the large plastic jugs filling them about three fourths full. Add the other half of the sugar in syrup form dividing it equally between the jugs and put on fermentation locks on all jugs. Leave until all fermentation stops. Now siphon or "rack" the wine into sterilized plastic jugs filling them full right to the top and put fermentation locks on the jugs.

Italian Swiss Colony salesroom and sampling room near a winery in Napa Valley. In my opinion their best product is their unfermented table grape juice.

Leave stand where the temperature is about 60 to 70 degrees. Try to leave the wine for about 105 days. Then take a sterilized plastic jug and place it on the floor and a jug of the wine on a table. With your siphon, siphon the wine into the clean jug leaving it flow down against the side of the jug aerating the wine. Wash out the jug with the sediment in it and repeat. Be sure that the jugs are all full right to the top. Put fermentation locks on them. Now place the jugs where it is cool, not warm. The cooler the better. Freezing will not even hurt the wine. This chilling precipitates more cream of tartar out of the wine.

In about 45 days, "rack" the wine again. This time, however, do not aerate the wine as it is "racked." Before putting the wine into clean sterilized jugs, this time, however, do as follows. Take a pinch or two grams of metabisulphite for every 5 gallons of wine and dissolve it into an ounce of warm sterilized water. Divide into equal parts for each jug before putting in the wine. This will prevent the wine from oxidizing or spoiling.

You should do this to all wines. For the very best red wine, "rack" the wine again about four months later. It is ready for drinking a month after the last "racking" but it is best one year after the last "racking." Bottle and cap after the final "racking."

Wine sampling room in a California winery. Do not stop in at any of these places with the idea that you are going to get a lot of free wine. A small half glass of two kinds is usually the house limit.

Remember that we told you to save the "pomace" or mash, so to speak, when you first took the wine from the fermenting crock. Now place the fresh pressed "pomace" back into the fermenting crock and break it up well. Add a water and sugar solution to the "pomace" equal to the wine taken off. Make the sugar solution so it will yield 12% alcohol when fermented. Add 6 grams of tartaric acid per gallon of "pomace" and sugar and water mixture or three grape leaves cut up. Dissolve this tartaric acid in a glass of warm water. Stir up well. Then treat this second batch of wine exactly as you did the first. You will end up with a wine light bodied and of excellent quality.

MAKING WHITE GRAPE WINE FROM CULTIVATED GRAPES

White grape wine is made in two different manners.

1. Make it exactly as we have described for making red wine from

cultivated grapes. Such a wine will be a trifle more yellow in color than wine made with Method Number 2 but the wine will be of much better taste, aroma and quality.

2. Run the grapes through a wine press twice and use only the juice of the white grapes. Save the skins and make "pomace" wine from them by adding sugar and water to them exactly as we have described for "pomace" wine making in the red wine making instructions.

For Method Number 2, put the juice into a plastic or ceramic fermenting crock.

Dissolve 4 grams of sodium metabisulphite per gallon of juice into the water and stir into the juice. Leave stand for 24 hours. Now add an equal quantity of boiled and cooled water. Take your saccharometer and test the liquid to ascertain the amount of sugar that you need for the alcohol content you desire. Boil half of the sugar into water for about two minutes. Leave cool and add. Add a wine yeast "starter," then immediately put the "must" into 5 gallon plastic jugs filling them about ¾ full. There is one exception here. If you use dead ripe California white grapes, they lack acid so it is best to add the juice of one lemon to every two gallons of the "must" made from such juice. A cup of chopped rhubarb will also work just as well. Put on fermentation locks on the jugs and leave ferment at around 65 degrees or as close as you can get to this, until all fermentation has stopped. Now "rack" the wine into sterilized plastic jugs leaving the sediment behind. Fill the jugs full right up to the top so that there is no air in them. Use old wine or sterilized water to fill them if you run short of wine. Put on fermentation locks. Leave the jugs in a spot as close to 65 to 70 degrees as possible. Leave the wine in the bottles until it is well cleared or "polished". Add 2 grams of sodium metabisulphite or a pinch per five gallons of wine and siphon into bottles and cap. Leave the wine age in the bottles for three months before drinking. A year is even better if you can wait.

HOW TO MAKE ROSE OR PINK WINE FROM CULTIVATED GRAPES

Rose wines or pink wines are simple white wines made with a few black or blue grapes in them to color the wine pink or wine made from black or blue grape "pomace" and sugar and water. There are no grapes in the world that have a natural pink juice.

HOW TO MAKE WINE FROM FLOWERS

Some of the world's finest wines are those with the very finest tastes and finest aroma are made from flowers. It is best to gather flowers on sunny days when the flowers are open. On rainy days some flowers close and there are apt to be insects in them.

DANDELION WINE

Produces about five gallons of a light dry wine. If you desire this wine sweet, sweeten the wine with an artificial sweetener before bottling.

4 gallons of flower heads. 12 pounds of sugar. 1 oz of bakers yeast or wine yeast "starter." 4 gallons of water. 4 lemons. Yeast nutrient speeds fermentation.

The best quality of dandelion wine is made by just using the petals of the flowers. If you do use the whole flower heads, be very sure to have the flower heads without the tinest bit of stalk on them. The stalk of dandelions is very bitter, in fact, is used to make some types of European bitters.

Put the 4 gallons of petals, or heads, of the flowers in a large plastic pail, tub or a pottery crock and pour on 4 gallons of boiling water. Cover with a sheet of polyethylene. Leave soak for seven days. Stir the flowers or petals daily or shake them around well. On the seventh day, pour the liquid into a sterilized 5 gallon or larger plastic jug or glass bottle. Put the heads of the flowers or petals into a clean cloth or a sieve and squeeze out all liquid in them into the fermenting bottle. Boil half of the sugar, six pounds in a quart of water, for about two minutes. Cool to lukewarm and add to the "must." Add the juice of two lemons and grate the peel of the two lemons and add. Crumble and put in a cake of bakers yeast or wine yeast "starter." Put on a fermentation lock. Leave ferment for about seven days. Now siphon into another plastic or glass jug leaving as much sediment behind as possible. Boil the rest of the sugar for about two minutes in a quart of water. Leave cool and add to the "must." Put on a fermentation lock and leave ferment until all fermentation has stopped. Leave clear or "polish" and then siphon into jugs or bottles and cap.

By doubling the amount of water and increasing the amount of sugar accordingly, you can make a very light dry dandelion wine of fine quality.

ROSE PETAL WINE

Makes about 5 gallons of finished wine.

2 quarts of rose petals. 4 gallons of water. 12 pounds of sugar. 1 oz of bakers yeast or wine yeast "starter." 4 lemons.

Rose petal wine is one of the very finest of all wines. Petals from wild or tame roses work equally well. You can mix rose petals of different colors or just use those of one color.

Place the rose petals in a 5 gallon, or larger, plastic or glass jug, in a crock or large pail. Pour 3½ gallons of boiling water over the rose petals. Put on a fermentation lock. Leave for two days shaking the bottle each day a little. Put 6 pounds of sugar in a quart of water and boil for about two minutes. Leave cool to lukewarm and add to the jug. Add 1 oz of bakers yeast or wine yeast "starter." Leave ferment for three days. Then siphon the "must" minus the petals and sediment from the fermenting jug into another sterilized jug. Put on a fermentation lock and leave ferment for 10 days. Boil the other six pounds of sugar in water for about two minutes and cool down to lukewarm and add. Add the juice of the 4 lemons and the grated lemon peel. Put on the fermentation lock and ferment until fermentation has ceased. Then rack into another sterilized jug. Leave until clear. Then siphon into bottles or jugs and cap.

ELDERBERRY FLOWER WINE

Makes about three gallons of wine.

2 gallons of flowers. 2 gallons of water. 6 pounds of sugar. 1 oz of bakers yeast or wine yeast "starter." 2 lemons.

Put the flowers in a sterilized plastic or glass jug. Boil 3 pounds of the sugar for about 2 minutes with a gallon of water and pour over the flowers while still boiling hot. Put in the juice of the two lemons and grate the peels and add them. When the "must" is lukewarm, add the bakers yeast or wine yeast "starter." Fit on a fermentation lock. Leave ferment for seven days. Then siphon the liquid into another sterilized plastic or glass jug, leaving the flowers and as much sediment as possible behind. Remove the flower pulp and wring out the liquid in a cloth and put it in the new plastic or glass jug. Boil three pounds of the sugar about two minutes in a gallon of water. Leave cool to lukewarm and add to the "must." Put on a fermentation lock and leave ferment until all fermentation stops. Then siphon or "rack" into another sterilized clean jug filling it to the top so no air is in the jug. Use old wine to fill up the air space if necessary. Leave "polish" or clear. When clear siphon into bottles and cap.

CLOVER FLOWER WINE

Make the same as dandelion wine.

HOW TO MAKE WINE FROM FRESH FRUITS AND BERRIES — BOTH WILD AND DOMESTIC

In making fruit and berry wines the fruit or berries must not be boiled as they all contain pectin to a greater or lesser degree. Boiling fruit or berries releases the pectin. The pectin stays in your wine and holds particles of solids with it giving your wine a permanent undesirable cloudiness that is impossible to filter out.

You use the sodium metabisulphiting process which we described for making wild grape wine to kill off all bad yeast and bacteria in the fruit.

METHOD NUMBER 1.

This makes wines of a heavy type about the viscosity of the very heaviest commercial wines. In Method Number 1 we ferment the entire fruit pulp. This makes the wine heavily bodied. It in no way affects the alcohol content of the wine. It is entirely a matter of personal preference. Some people prefer a heavily bodied wine, others a lightly bodied wine.

Crush the fruit in a polyethylene pail, tub or in a pottery crock. Add enough boiled water, that has cooled, to make the mix quite liquid. About a quart of boiled water per gallon of fruit pulp is about right. Mix the boiled water in well with the fruit pulp. Take 4 grains of sodium metabisulphite per gallon of the "must" or wine making liquid. Mix it into a half cup of warm water and mix it in well with the "must." Put on a cover and leave the "must" stand for about two hours. The fruit pulp will "bleach" or lighten in color a little. Test the "must" with a saccharometer and decide on what alcohol content you desire the finished wine and, thus, how much sugar you will add to the "must." In the recipes, approximate amounts of sugar are given but this you can and should vary according to the amount of alcohol you desire in the finished wine.

Take about one third of the sugar and boil it for about two minutes in about a gallon of water if you are making about four gallons of wine. The amount of water is not at all critical. Leave the syrup cool and then pour it into the "must" and stir well. Add bakers yeast or a wine yeast "starter" and leave ferment for about five days. Keep the pail, or crock, covered or cover with a polyethylene sheet with a ball of cotton tied down under the edge to let the carbon dioxide escape and to prevent wild yeasts and flies from entering. Then strain the pulp through a piece of clean muslin and wring it out as dry as you can. Put the liquid into a large plastic polyethylene or glass jug. Boil one third of the sugar in about a pint of water for every gallon of "must" that you had and cool and add. Fit a fermentation lock onto the jug and leave ferment for about ten days. The amount of water that you add to the fruit pulp is not critical, simply the more water that you add, the lighter bodied your wine becomes. Be sure, however, to add enough sugar to put the amount of alcohol you desire in the finished amount of wine. Siphon the wine into a clean sterilized jug. Now boil the remaining one third of the sugar for about two minutes in about a pint of water per gallon of your "must." Leave cool and add. Fit a fermentation lock onto the jug and leave ferment until all fermentation stops. Leave stand until clear or "polished" and siphon into jugs or bottles and cap. If the wine is not clear, siphon it into another large sterilized jug filling the jug right up to the very top so that no air is in the jug. Fit on a fermentation lock and leave stand until clear. Then siphon into bottles and jugs and cap.

METHOD NUMBER 2

Crush the fruit in a plastic polyethylene pail or tube or pottery crock. Add one quart of boiled water that has cooled for about every gallon of crushed fruit. This is not critical. The more water you add, the lighter in body the wine will be but it will have the desired alcohol content if you increase the sugar you add accordingly. Actually, half crushed fruit and half water makes wonderful wine.

Dissolve four grains of sodium metabisulphite into a half cup of warm water for every gallon of "must" that you have and mix it in well with the "must." Leave stand for about twenty-four hours. Then strain the "must" through a piece of clean muslin and squeeze out but not too hard. Throw away the squeezed out fruit pulp. Put the liquid in a large polyethylene jug or glass bottle. Take your saccharometer and test the wine liquid and decide on how much sugar you want to add to achieve the alcohol content you desire. Be sure to allow sugar for water you are going to add over the amounts specified in the recipes. You can do this easily by simply judging what the per cent of water you are adding is to the wine liquid or "must."

Boil one third of the sugar for about two minutes in a half gallon of water for every gallon of "must." Leave cool to lukewarm and add the bakers yeast or wine yeast "starter" and leave ferment for about ten days. Now siphon the fermenting wine into another sterilized jug leaving as much of the sediment or "lees" behind as possible. Boil one third of the sugar about two minutes with a half gallon of water for every gallon of the original "must." Leave cool and add. Fit on a fermentation lock and leave ferment for about fourteen days.

Boil the last third of the sugar about two minutes with a half pint of water per gallon of the original "must." Leave cool and add to the "must." Put the fermentation lock back on and leave ferment until all fermentation has stopped. If clear, siphon into bottles or jugs and cap. If not clear, "rack" into another sterilized jug being sure that the jug is full to the top and leave "polish" or clear. Then siphon into bottles or jugs and cap. Fill bottles up to about two thirds of the bottle neck length.

In using either of these methods it is a good idea to mix 2 grams of metabisulphite. This is a pinch in an ounce of warm water for every five gallons of wine you are to bottle. Add this to the wine just before bottling. The small amount of sodium metabisulphite kills off any bad yeast or bacteria that might have gotten into the wine and makes sure that it will not spoil. It does not destroy any of the natural taste or aroma of the wine.

A hot dry year produces fruit with more sugar than usual and less acid than usual. A wet summer produces fruit with less sugar and more acid than normal. It is always best to use a saccharometer to adjust the sugar content of the "must" to the volume of alcohol you desire in the finished wine. Do not try to get by without a saccharometer. One batch of spoiled wine will cost you far more than buying a saccharometer.

By adding your sugar at three different times during the fermentation, the alcohol content of your wine will be higher in your finished wine than if you add all of the sugar at one time.

If wine yeast has too much sugar to start with, it tends to stop fermentation before it has produced the maximum amount of alcohol that it is capable of producing. You can, of course, make good wine by adding all of the sugar at the beginning of fermentation but such wine will rarely test out over 11% alcohol content and most of the time less than this.

In using fruit or berries to make wine, be sure that they are all ripe. Half ripe fruit gives an acid taste to wine and only a few half ripe fruits can give an entire batch of wine an acid taste. After you feel that your fruit or berries are ripe enough, leave them for another three days before picking them. It is best to have your fruit overripe than unripe.

Overripe grapes, or even grapes that have begun to rot on the vines, produce wine of a wonderfully body and taste.

RHUBARB WINE

Rhubarb leaves are deadly poison and so are the roots. They have been used as poison throughout Europe and Asia for centuries. Be sure to use only the stalks for wine making or eating. Rhubarb, no matter how it is made, makes an acid wine and requires sweetening to tone down the acid taste. Best way to do this is to make your rhubarb wine, then after it is finished, add artificial sweeteners to sweeten it somewhat.

For about 4 gallons of finished wine, use the following quantities. 20 pounds of rhubarb stalks. 12 pounds of sugar. 3½ gallons of water. Bakers yeast or wine yeast "starter." Yeast nutrient helps to speed the fermenting.

Lay the rhubarb stalks on a working table and start in the middle of each stalk and crush it. Put the crushed rhubarb in a large polyethylene pail, tub or pottery crock. Add 1½ gallons of boiled water that has been cooled down. Dissolve four grains of sodium metabisulphite for every gallon of "must" in a cup of warm water and stir it in well with the "must." Put on a cover or cover with a sheet of polyethylene with a ball of cotton on one edge and tie it down with a cotton cord. Leave for five days. Then remove the pulp and place it in a clean cloth and wring it out. Put the liquid in a large polyethylene jug or glass bottle. Test the wine liquid or "must" with your saccharometer to ascertain the amount of sugar you need for the alcohol content that you want. Include the water to be added with the sugar. Dissolve half of the sugar in a gallon of water and boil about two minutes. Cool to lukewarm and add. Put on a fermentation lock and leave ferment for about ten days. Dissolve the other half of the sugar in a gallon of water and boil for about two minutes. Cool to lukewarm and add to the "must." Leave ferment until fermentation stops. Siphon or "rack" into another large sterilized jug leaving as much sediment behind as possible. Be sure that the jug is filled right up to the very top with no air in the jug. Fit a fermentation lock and leave until "polished" or clear. Then siphon into bottles or jugs and cap.

RED CURRANT WINE

To produce about one gallon of finished wine. 4 pounds of red currants. 7 pints of water. 3½ pounds of sugar. Bakers yeast or port wine yeast. Yeast nutrient speeds fermentation.

Use Method Number 1. Ferment the pulp.

CHOKECHERRY OR WHISKEY CHERRY WINE

Produces about one gallon of finished wine. 8 pounds of chokecherries. 7 pints of water. 3½ pounds of sugar. Bakers yeast or wine yeast "starter." Yeast nutrient will speed up the ferment.

Use Method Number 2. Ferment the strained diluted juice. You can double the amount of water and increase the sugar accordingly and still have a fine chokecherry wine.

DOMESTIC CHERRY WINE

Make exactly the same as chokecherry wine.

DOMESTIC OR WILD PLUM WINE

Produces about a gallon of heavily bodied port-like wine.

8 pounds of plums—stones and all. 7 pints of water. 4 pounds of sugar. Port wine yeast or bakers yeast. Yeast nutrient speeds the ferment.

Use Method Number 1. Ferment the pulp. You can double the amount of water and increase the sugar accordingly and still have a fine heavily bodied wine.

DOMESTIC OR WILD PLUM WINE

Makes about a gallon of light to medium bodied wine.

5 pounds of plums—stones and all. 7 pints of water. 3 pounds of sugar. Wine yeast or bakers yeast. Yeast nutrient will speed the fermenting.

Use Method Number 1. Ferment the pulp. You can double the amount of water and increase the amount of sugar accordingly and have a fine light wine.

RASPBERRY — WILD OR DOMESTIC WINE

Makes about one gallon of light dry wine. If you desire this wine sweet, sweeten with artificial sweetener after the wine is finished.

4 pounds of raspberries. 2½ pounds of sugar. 7 pints of water. Sherry wine yeast or all-purpose wine yeast or bakers yeast. Yeast nutrient will speed the fermentation.

Use Method No. 2. Ferment the strained diluted juice. You can double the water amount and increase the amount of sugar accordingly and still have a fine raspberry wine.

SALMON BERRY WINE

Quantities same as raspberry wine but use Method Number 1 fermenting the pulp.

CROW BERRY WINE

Quantities the same as raspberry wine but use Method Number 1 fermenting the pulp.

ELDERBERRY WINE — PORT STYLE

Makes about a gallon of heavily bodied port-like wine. 4 pounds of elderberries. Remove the main stems but leave on small branch stems leading to the berries. 7 pints of water. 4 pounds of sugar. Port wine yeast or bakers yeast. Yeast nutrient speeds fermentation. Use Method Number 1. Ferment the crushed pulp. You can triple the amount of water and sugar and still have an excellent medium bodied wine.

ELDERBERRY WINE — MEDIUM DRY

Makes about a gallon of medium bodied dry wine. 3½ pounds of elderberries with no stems of any kind on them. 3 pounds of sugar. 7 pints of water. Sherry wine yeast or all-purpose wine yeast, or bakers yeast. Yeast nutrient helps speed up fermentation.

Use Method Number 2. Ferment the strained diluted juice. You can double the amount of water and increase the amount of sugar accordingly and still have a fine medium dry wine.

ELDERBERRY WINE — LIGHT AND DRY

Makes about a gallon of light dry wine. 3 pounds of elderberries without any stems at all. 2½ pounds of sugar. 7 pints of water. Sherry wine yeast or all-purpose wine yeast or bakers yeast. Yeast nutrient speeds up fermentation.

Use Method Number 2. Ferment the strained diluted juice. You can double the amount of water and increase the amount of sugar accordingly and still have a really fine dry light wine.

PLANTER'S MISTRESS WINE

Produces about a gallon of medium bodied wine.

2 pounds of ripe bananas. ½ pint of orange pekoe tea. 1 level teaspoon of citric or juice of one lemon. 3½ pounds of sugar or 4¼ pounds of honey. Bakers yeast or all-purpose wine yeast. Yeast nutrient will speed the fermentation.

Use Method Number 1. Mash the banana pulp and ferment the pulp, not the skins. You can double the amount of water and increase the amount of sugar or honey accordingly and still have a fine wine. Bananas produce one of the very best tasting fruit wines.

LOGANBERRY WINE

Produces about 1 gallon of wine. 3 pounds of loganberries. 3 pounds of sugar. All-purpose wine yeast or bakers yeast. 7 pints of water.

Use Method Number 1. Ferment the crushed pulp. You can double the amount of water and increase the amount of sugar accordingly and still have a very fine wine.

GOOSEBERRY WINE

Produces about 1 gallon of a heavily bodied wine. 6 pounds of gooseberries, 3½ pounds of sugar. 7 pints of water. All-purpose wine yeast or bakers yeast. Yeast nutrient will speed up the ferment.

Use Method Number 1. Ferment the pulp about three days. You can double the amount of water and increase the amount of sugar accordingly and still have a very fine wine.

GOOSEBERRY WINE — SHERRY STYLE

Produces about one gallon of wine. 5 pounds of dead-ripe gooseberries. 7 pints of water. About 2½ pounds of sugar for a dry wine, 3 pounds for a medium dry wine and 3½ pounds for a medium sweet wine.

Use Method Number 1. Ferment the pulp for five days only. When the wine is bottled, store it in a hot attic for a summer so it gets a slightly burnt sherry taste. If you do not have a hot attic, store the bottled wine near a furnace or radiator during the winter for about six months. Sherry wine and all sherry-type wines get their burnt flavor by storing near heat. You can double the amount of water and increase the amount of sugar accordingly and still have a very fine wine.

PEACH WINE

Produces about one gallon of wine. 5 pounds of peaches—stones and all. 7 pints of water. 3 pounds of sugar. All-purpose wine yeast or bakers yeast. Yeast nutrient speeds up fermentation.

Use Method Number 1. Weigh with the stones. Ferment the pulp. You can double the amount of water and increase the amount of sugar accordingly and still have a very fine wine.

APRICOT WINE

Make exactly the same as peach wine.

PEAR WINE

Make exactly the same as peach wine.

APPLE WINE OR APPLE CIDER

Apples, of course, are one of our oldest domesticated fruits. They played an important part with Adam and Eve in the Garden of Eden. The stone age lake dwellers of central Europe used apples for food a great deal. Remains of apples found in their caves showed that they not only ate tremendous quantities of apples but knew how to rub animal fat on them to keep them for long periods of time. These ancient people also knew how to cut up apples in thin slices and dry them in the sun for storing.

Apples originated in southwestern Asia in the area from the Caspian to the Black Sea. There were no applies of any kind on the North American continent. The first early immigrants who came to America from Europe brought apple seeds with them. The English to Virginia, the Dutch to New York and the French to Canada. The Vikings brought no apple seeds with them. Apple trees moved West faster than the immigrants did. Indians gathered the seeds and had apple orchards around many Indian villages in the West long before any settlers ever reached the villages.

John Chapman, a missionary better known as Johnny Appleseed, traveled all over Ohio and Indiana early in the 19th century, preaching the gospel and planting apple seeds. Apple seeds were planted at Vancouver, Washington as early as 1817.

The apple tree is a strange miracle tree. The trees grown from the seed of a single apple tree, will all differ from each other and the parent apple tree. Every apple seed, in other words, produces a different kind of apple tree. In order to produce apple trees that are alike, you must graft a shoot off from the parent tree onto an apple root. Most all of our really good apples came from the chance finding of apple trees that grew up from someone simply throwing away an apple core. The first Baldwin apple tree was found in Willmington, Massachusetts. The McIntosh by John McIntosh in Dundas County, Ontario, Canada. The Winesap—in a woods in Rhode Island. The Delicious—in a pasture in Winterset, Iowa. The Yellow Newton was found in a woods clearing in Vermont in colonial times. The Whitney Crab was found in a thicket in northern Massachusetts.

In the United States today a bushel of apples is grown every year for every man, woman and child.

APPLE WINE — PORT STYLE

Produces about a gallon of wine. 8 pounds of apples. Crush them well or run them through a meat grinder. 7 pints of water. 4 pounds of sugar. All-purpose wine yeast or bakers yeast. Yeast nutrient will speed the ferment.

Use Method Number 1. Ferment crushed apples for five days only before straining.

When the apple wine has finished fermenting, "rack" it into a sterilized jug. Add about ½ ounce of Clairjus No. 3 per 10 gallons. Stir it in well with the wine. Then fill the jugs right up to the top so that no air is in the jugs and fit on a fermentation lock. The Clairjus will clear the wine. When clear, "rack" into another sterilized bottle leaving all sediment behind then siphon the wine into bottles or jugs and cap. Apple juice contains a great deal of pectin and tends to be very cloudy. You always have to use a pectin settling agent, such as Clairjus No. 3, in order to settle the pectin. Cloudy apple wine, of course, tastes just as good as the clear apple wine but the clear apple wine, of course, looks much much better.

The exact ounces of Clairjus No. 3 to use per 100 gallons of apple juice under various conditions of time and temperature will vary slightly. Use this chart instead of the general amount specified if you desire to save a little Clairjus by balancing the amount exactly to your temperature. You can double the amount of water and increase the amount of sugar accordingly and still have a very fine apple wine.

Temperature In Degrees F.	5 Hours	15 Hours	30 Hours
40		6.0 ozs.	2.0 ozs.
60	9.6 ozs.	3.2 ozs.	1.3 ozs.
100	3.6 ozs.	1.2 ozs.	
120	2.4 ozs.	.8 oz.	

Remember, never boil apples to get the juice for wine making. Boiling apples as well as any other fruit releases more pectin and makes it next to impossible to ever clear the juice.

APPLE WINE FROM APPLE JUICE

You can get apple juice by running apples through an apple press or by buying apple juice or cider at a grocery store.

Produces about a gallon of apple wine or cider. Two quarts of apple juice. 7 pints of water. 2¼ pounds of sugar. All-purpose wine yeast or bakers yeast. Yeast nutrient will speed fermentation.

Use Method Number 2. Ferment the juice diluted and put it directly into a large jug with fermentation lock.

You can double the amount of water and increase the amount of sugar accordingly and still have a very fine wine.

HOW TO MAKE ROOT WINES

Roots such as potatoes, parsnips and carrots make excellent wines. It is best to use old potatoes and carrots such as those six months or a year old as they contain less starch than new roots. Starch boiled into the "must" will remain in the wine unless you use care. In making root wines, you must add a little acid to the "must" in the form of a lemon or orange or two or a stalk of rhubarb or some oats or a piece of old bread to insure a good ferment. A little acid is essential for a satisfactory ferment. You can use citric acid instead of fruit grain or bread if you want. The juice of two lemons equals about a quarter ounce of citric acid. Actually, the juice of one lemon is plenty of acid for a gallon of wine.

Always add the sugar in stages in making root wines or they will not be good. Yeast simply can only handle so much sugar at one time. Yeast will convert sugar to alcohol and carbon dioxide but can only do this if not smothered with too much sugar. Yeast cannot convert starch to sugar or ferment starch into alcohol. Wines made from fruit, as we have carefully explained, must never under any circumstances have the fruit boiled. In making root wines, however, the roots must be boiled in order to make good tasting wine. Wine made from unboiled roots has a very bad aftertaste. When you add raisins or wheat to a root wine, they must be sterilized and cleaned before adding.

Most dried raisins have been heavily sulphited to prevent fermentation. Break up the raisins and drop them into boiling water. As soon as the water comes back again to boiling, turn off the heat, pour off the water and the raisins are ready to use. To clean grain such as wheat, drop it into boiling water, boil for a minute and remove.

When straining boiled roots into a plastic pail, it is a good idea to first cover the pail with a piece of clean muslin and tie a cord around the mouth of the pail and the muslin to hold it tight to the pail. Then put a second clean piece of muslin over the first one and pour your root liquid onto it and leave the liquid drain down into the pail. The first cloth will keep the cooked roots in the second cloth from sagging down into the drained liquid.

Root wines clear more slowly than fruit wines. Root wines clear in definite stages. At first the top inch will clear, then another inch or so until the wine is finally completely cleared. Usually takes a week to two weeks for them to clear completely. If you are in a hurry, you can buy an ounce of isinglass from a druggist. Crumble it into a little wine in a small sauce pan using about ⅛ ounce for each gallon of wine to be cleared. Warm over a low heat stirring until dissolved. Then pour the mixture into the wine. The wine will clear quickly, never slower than two days.

In making root wines, you lose about a quart of water per gallon in boiling and other operations so we allow more water in the recipes.

When boiling roots, always skim off all scum that rises on the water. If you leave in the scum, it will cloud the wine sometimes permanently.

POTATO WINE

Potato wine is one of the easiest of wines to get up to 18% alcohol. Makes a fine white wine.

This recipe produces about one gallon of wine. 2 pounds of old potatoes. 1 pound of raisins. 4 oranges. 4 pounds of sugar. Bakers yeast or wine yeast. 5 quarts of water.

Do not peel the potatoes. Scrub and grate them into a half gallon of water. Over a medium heat bring slowly to a boil and simmer for about one minute. Strain through a clean piece of muslin cloth into a large plastic or glass jug. Boil half the sugar for about two minutes in a quart of water. Cool to lukewarm and add. Add the raisins. Cut up the oranges and orange peel as small as possible and add. Allow to cool to lukewarm and add the yeast. Fit a fermentation lock and leave ferment for about ten days. "Rack" or siphon into another sterilized jug. Boil the rest of the sugar in a quart of water for about two minutes. Leave cool to lukewarm and add. Put on a fermentation lock and leave ferment until all fermentation has stopped. "Rack" or siphon into another sterilized jug filling the jug full right up to the top so no air is in the jug. Leave clear or "polish." When clear, siphon into bottles or jugs and cap. You can substitute rhubarb for the oranges and cranberries or other berries for the raisins if desired.

SNEAKY PETE WINE

This is one of the best wines ever made.

Recipe produces about a gallon of wine. 2 pounds of potatoes. 1 pound of crushed rhubarb stalks. 4 pounds of sugar. Bakers yeast or wine yeast. 5 quarts of water. Yeast nutrient speeds fermentation.

Make exactly the same as the potato wine recipe.

PARSNIP WINE

Use parsnips only after one or two frosts in the fall so that their starch has mostly been changed to sugar. This recipe produces about a gallon of wine. 2 pounds of parsnips. ½ pound of raisins. 2 oranges. 2 lemons. 4 pounds of sugar. 5 quarts of water. Bakers yeast or wine yeast. Yeast nutrient speeds fermentation. Wash the parsnips but do not peel them. Grate the parsnips into a pot with three quarts of water and boil slowly for about five minutes. Skim off all scum as they boil. Strain through a clean muslin cloth into a pot and pour the liquid directly into a large plastic jug or glass bottle. Boil half of the sugar in a quart of water for about 2 minutes. Leave cool to lukewarm and add. Break up the raisins and add. Cut up the oranges and lemons, peel and all, in small pieces and add. Put in the yeast and put on a fermentation lock and ferment for about ten days. Siphon or "rack" the wine into another sterilized plastic jug or bottle. Boil the rest of the sugar in a quart of water for about two minutes. Leave cool to lukewarm and add. If you add it hot, you will kill the yeast. Put on a fermentation lock and leave ferment until fermentation stops. Siphon or "rack" into another sterilized plastic jug or glass bottle filling the bottle full so there is no air in the bottle or jug. Use old wine or sterilized water, if necessary, to fill up to the top. Fit on a fermentation lock and leave until clear or "polished." Then siphon into bottles or jugs and cap.

PARSNIP WHISKEY WINE

This recipe produces about a gallon of wine. 4 pounds of parsnips. 4 oranges. 3½ pounds of sugar. 5 quarts of water. Bakers yeast or wine yeast. Yeast nutrient speeds fermentation.

Make exactly the same as regular parsnip wine but grate the orange peels and age for about twelve months. It then will have a very good flavor.

MANGOLD WINE

Mangels or mangolds can be obtained from farmers from about September to April. Produces about one gallon of wine. 5 pounds of mangolds. This is about one medium-sized mangold. 2 lemons. 2 oranges or 4 stalks of rhubarb or two cups of berries. 4 pounds of sugar. 5 quarts of water. Bakers yeast or wine yeast. Yeast nutrient speeds fermentation. Wash the mangold but do not peel it. Cut the mangold into thin slices and dice the slices in about quarter inch squares. Put them into a pot with a half gallon of water. Slowly boil for about 15 minutes. Skim off all scum as they boil. Put two pounds of sugar into a large plastic jug or bottle. Strain the mangold juice through a clean piece of muslin into a pot and pour the liquid in the jug over the sugar. Shake until the sugar is dissolved. Grate the orange and lemon peels into the jug and cut up the pulp and add. Allow the "must" to cool to lukewarm, then add the yeast. Put on a fermentation lock and ferment for about ten days. Then "rack" or siphon the liquid into another sterilized jug leaving as much sediment behind as possible. Boil the rest of the sugar for about two minutes in 3 quarts of water. Leave cool to lukewarm and add. Put on a fermentation lock and ferment until all fermentation stops. Siphon or "rack" into another sterilized jug. Leave "polish" or clear, then siphon into bottles or jugs and cap.

BEET WINE

This recipe makes about a gallon of wine. 5 pounds of beets. 1 pound of rhubarb. 4 pounds of sugar. 5 quarts of water. Bakers yeast or wine yeast. Yeast nutrient speeds fermentation.

Make exactly the same as the mangold wine. The rhubarb furnishes the acid instead of the oranges and lemons.

CARROT WINE

This recipe produces about one and a half gallons of wine. 6 pounds of carrots. 1 pound of wheat or wheat cereal such as puffed wheat. 2 oranges. 2 lemons. 2 level tablespoons of raisins. 4 pounds of sugar.

Wash the carrots but do not peel them. Grate them into a gallon of water and over medium heat, boil until tender. Strain off the liquid through a clean cloth or sieve into a large plastic jug or glass bottle. Boil half of the sugar in a quart of water for about two minutes. Leave cool and add. Grate the orange and lemon peel into the jug and slice up the flesh of the oranges and lemons and put them into the jug. Add the raisins and wheat. Add the yeast. Fit on a fermentation lock and leave ferment for seven days. Siphon or "rack" the liquid into another sterilized jug. Boil the balance of the sugar in a quart of water for two minutes. Cool to lukewarm and add. Fit on a fermentation lock and leave ferment until fermentation stops. Siphon or "rack" into another sterilized jug filling to the top so that there is no air in the jug. Use sterilized water or old wine, if necessary, to fill up the jug to the top. Fit on a fermentation lock and leave until clear or "polished," then siphon in bottles or jugs and cap.

CALAMITY JANE WINE

Produces about a gallon of wine. 2 pounds of old potatoes. 2½ pounds of carrots. 1 pound of rhubarb. 3½ pounds of sugar. Bakers yeast or wine yeast "starter." 5 quarts of water. Make the same as parsnip wine. 2 oranges and 2 lemons can be substituted for the rhubarb if desired.

HOW TO MAKE WINE FROM THE PEELS OF CITRUS FRUIT

The peels of oranges, grapefruit, lemons and tangerines contain oils that actually contain more good flavor than the flesh of these fruits. All commercial citrus wines and liquors are all flavored, without exception, with the oil from the skins of citrus fruits, never, in any case, from the juice or flesh of the fruits. In making wine from citrus peels, always grate the peels so that the oil gets a chance to get out of the peel and to flavor the wine as strongly as possible.

ORANGE WINE OR CURACAO WINE

The peels of a dozen oranges or more grated. Enough orange vegetable coloring to color the "must" orange. Bakers yeast or wine yeast "starter." 4 pounds of sugar. 1 gallon of water. Yeast nutrient speeds fermentation.

Put the grated orange peels into a plastic pail. Add the cut up flesh of one orange just to give a little acid to the wine and yeast food or one rhubarb stalk. Add a quart of boiling water. Then dissolve one 4 grain tablet of sodium metabisulphite in a half a cup of water and add for every gallon of liquid. Stir well and leave soak for two days. Now pour the "must" into a large polyethylene jug or glass bottle. Boil half of the sugar in a half gallon of water for two minutes. Leave cool to lukewarm and add. Put in the yeast. Put on a fermentation lock and leave ferment for five days. Siphon the "must" into another sterilized jug. Boil the rest of the sugar for two minutes in a half gallon of water. Leave cool to lukewarm and add. Put on the fermentation lock and leave ferment until all fermentation has stopped. Siphon or "rack" into another sterilized jug filling to the very top so that no air is in the jug. Use sterilized water or old wine, if necessary, to fill the jug right to the top. Add artificial orange coloring. Fit on a fermentation lock and leave until clear or "polished," then siphon into bottles or jugs and cap.

TANGERINE WINE

Recipe produces about a gallon of wine.

Tangerine peels make a fabulous wine with a wonderful taste and aroma. Make just as described for making orange wine. Grate the peels of a dozen or more tangerines. Add the flesh of one tangerine to get a little acid into the wine and yeast food or put in a rhubarb stalk.

GRAPEFRUIT WINE

Recipe produces about a gallon of wine. Grapefruit peels make a very good wine. Make just the same as described for making orange wine but use the peels from only about eight grapefruits. Put in the flesh of one grapefruit or a stalk of rhubarb to get a little acid and yeast food into the wine. Color the wine with a little red food coloring so it is pink.

HOW TO MAKE WINE FROM GRAINS

Grains such as wheat, oats, corn, buckwheat, rice and barley all make very fine wines. In making wines from grain, you need a little acid to insure a good ferment and good tasting wine. Oats, corn, rice and barley all are acid and produce enough acid of their own but wheat and buckwheat are not acid. Adding a little rhubarb, an orange or lemon will give your wine plenty of acid to make it taste just right. An old piece of bread per gallon will also do it.

Fruit wines contain a little natural tannin and this helps bring out the flavor of wine. In using grains, they contain no tannin so you can add a tablespoon of freshly made tea per gallon of wine or chop up a grape or maple leaf and add per gallon which will give you all the tannin that you need.

Before putting grain into your "must," it is a good idea to put it into boiling water for a few seconds or about a minute then take it out. This sterilizes the grain killing all wild yeast germs and bacteria that may be on it.

SAKE

The Japanese people drink mostly a clear rice wine and it is very good. The alcohol content of sake should run 18%. In order to get this high an alcohol content, you must use an all-purpose wine yeast and you must add the sugar in stages of one third at a time. Sake is always served warm, never cold.

This recipe produces about one gallon of wine.

1 pound of natural brown rice. ¼ level teaspoon of green tea leaves. 4 pounds of sugar. 1 gallon of water. All-purpose wine yeast. Soak the rice in water overnight then boil until cooked in a gallon of water. Carefully keep all scum skimmed off from the water. Do not strain but put the cooked rice and liquid into a large plastic jug or glass bottle. Add ¼ level teaspoon of green tea leaves, not orange pekoe tea leaves. Boil one third of the sugar in a pint of water for two minutes. Leave cool and add. Put in wine yeast and put on a fermentation lock. Leave ferment for five days. Boil one third of the sugar in a pint of water for about two minutes. Leave cool to luke-

warm and add. Put fermentation lock back on and leave ferment for about another five days. Siphon or "rack" the liquid into another sterilized jug leaving behind as much sediment as you can. Boil the balance of the sugar in another pint of water. Leave cool and add. Put the fermentation lock back on and leave ferment until all fermentation stops. Siphon or "rack" into another sterilized jug filling it full right to the top so that there is no air in the jug. Put on a fermentation lock. Leave stand and clear or "polish." This takes quite a while with sake wine. After the wine is "polished," siphon into jugs and bottles and cap.

IRISH MIST WINE

This recipe produces about a gallon of wine.

2 pounds of wheat or wheat cereal. 1 pound of old potatoes. 3 pounds of sugar. 9 pints of water. 4 stalks of rhubarb or 2 lemons and two oranges. Bakers yeast or wine yeast. Yeast nutrient speeds the fermentation.

Scrub and grate the potatoes and boil them in five pints of water for about 10 minutes. Skim off all scum as they boil. Put the wheat and the cut-up rhubarb or lemons and oranges into a large plastic jug or glass bottle. Strain the boiling liquid from the potatoes into the jug. Boil half of the sugar in two pints of water for about two minutes and add. Leave cool then add the yeast. Put on a fermentation lock. Leave ferment for ten days. Then siphon the liquid in another sterilized jug, put on a fermentation lock and leave ferment until all fermentation stops. Siphon or "rack" into another sterilized jug filling right to the top so that there is no air in the jug. Use old wine or sterilized water, if necessary, to fill up the jug. Put on a fermentation lock and leave "polish" or clear then siphon into bottles or jugs and cap.

FRENCH CANADIAN WINE

Produces about a gallon of wine.

2 pounds of wheat. 2 cups of dried old bread. Bread is acid and gives the "must" enough acid for a perfect ferment. 3 pounds of sugar. Bakers yeast or wine yeast. A cup of black coffee. 5 quarts of water.

Make the same as Irish Mist Wine. This French Canadian Wine is a fabulous wine.

HIGHLAND FLING WINE

This recipe produces about a gallon of wine. 1½ pounds of wheat. 1 pound of oats or oatmeal. Oats are acid and give the "must" acid for a good ferment. 3½ pounds of sugar. Three level tablespoons of chocolate. Bakers yeast or wine yeast. 9 pints of water. Make the same as Irish Mist Wine.

HOW TO MAKE WINE FROM COMMERCIAL EXTRACTS

The finest possible wines can be made from special wine making extracts and from fruit extracts which are used to give fruit flavor to any food.

In making wine from extracts observe the following rules.

1. When you use invert sugar instead of household sugar, you need no acid in the wine in order to assure a good ferment as invert sugar contains enough acid to insure a good ferment.

2. If you use household sugar, you must add a little acid to assure a good ferment. The juice of one lemon per gallon of "must" will do this or a stalk of rhubarb or just a piece of old dried bread.

3. To do the best job of turning the sugar into alcohol, use yeast nutrient which is just a chemical yeast food or, if you do not use yeast nutrient, a little crushed fruit pulp as a food or a crushed piece of rhubarb per gallon will do, a piece of dried old bread, a potato per gallon boiled, mashed and added with the liquid that it was boiled in. A handful of wheat,

oats, oatmeal, wheat or corn cereal. Both corn and oats are acid and will also take care of the acid necessary to ferment your wine properly. You can, of course, make a clear potato wine and flavor it after it is "polished" with any of these extracts.

The following extracts are available from Herter's, Waseca, Minnesota. Here are their descriptions and the amounts to use to flavor a gallon of "must" and the cost.

1. ORANGE EXTRACT. This is a pure oil of orange. Use 1/16 oz. or 2cc per gallon of "must." Cost $.05

2. PEPPERMINT EXTRACT. This is pure peppermint leaf oil. Use 1 oz. per gallon of "must." Cost $.35

3. MOUNTAIN SIDE TANGERINE. This pure tangerine oil makes a fabulous wine. Use ⅛ oz. or 4cc per gallon of "must." Cost $.07

4. ISLAND LIME. This is a pure lime oil. Makes a fabulous wine and also gimlet drinks. Use ⅛ oz. or 4cc per gallon of "must." Cost $.08

5. ANISE. Pure oil of anise. This is the flavoring used for absinthe and Pernod. Absinthe, itself, has no flavor and is acid. Makes a good wine. Use ½ oz. per gallon of "must." Cost $.16

6. JAMAICAN RUM EXTRACT. This is pure molasses sugar cane extract that all rums are made from. Makes a fabulous wine. Use 1/14 oz. or 2cc per gallon of "must." Cost $.07

7. PURE VANILLA EXTRACT. Made from the natural vanilla bean from the lemon yellow orchids of Central America. Makes one of the world's finest wines. Creamy, delicious tasting. Use ⅛ oz. or 3½cc per gallon of "must." Cost $.08

8. COCONUT EXTRACT. A pure coconut oil. Makes a very good wine. Use 3/5 oz. or 18cc per gallon of "must." Cost $.19

9. MAPLE EXTRACT. A pure maple extract makes a fine wine in itself and a very good wine to blend with most any other wine. Use 3/5 oz. or 18cc per gallon of "must." Cost $.19

10. ROOT BEER EXTRACT. A pure root extract with no creosote as in commercial root beers. Makes a very good wine. Use 3/5 oz. or 18cc per gallon of "must." Cost $.36

11. FRENCH COGNAC EXTRACT. Cognac is stilled from dry French wine. This is the real extract. Makes a fabulous wine. Use 1/5 oz. or 6cc per gallon of "must." Cost $.19

12. KENTUCKY BOURBON EXTRACT. This is a true extract from bourbon "must" or mash. Makes a good dry wine. Use 1/28 oz. or 1cc per gallon of "must." Cost $.04

13. SPANISH SHERRY EXTRACT. Spanish sherry is made by storing white grape wine around a stove so it developes a burnt flavor. This is the real extract and makes a fabulous wine. Use 3/5 oz. or 18cc per gallon of "must." Cost $.38

14. FRENCH WILD FIELD VIOLET EXTRACT. Extracted right from the wild flowers. Makes a fabulous very different wine. Good by itself and very good for blending. Use 2 oz. per gallon of "must." Cost $1.08

15. FRENCH MORNING ROSE EXTRACT. Made from the natural flowers. Makes a fabulous very different wine. Use 2 oz. per gallon of "must." Cost $1.18

16. ABSINTHE EXTRACT. Made from natural oil of anise which is the only flavoring ever used in absinthe. Absinthe, itself, is an acid and has no flavor. Makes a good wine. Use 1/14 oz. or 2cc per gallon of "must." Cost $.07

17. GRAND MARINER EXTRACT. Grand Mariner is a French liquor with a burnt orange taste. This extract produces it exactly. Use 2½ oz. per gallon of "must." Cost $1.15

18. CHAMPAGNE EXTRACT. A true white champagne grape extract. Makes excellent wine or champagne. Use ½ oz. per gallon of "must." Cost $.32

19. FRENCH PERNOD EXTRACT. Pernod is a green anise flavored French liquor. This extract produces it perfectly. Makes a good wine. Use ½ oz. or 8cc per gallon of "must." Cost $.27.

20. FRENCH AMER-PICON EXTRACT. Amer-Picon is a delicious liquor made from mountain herbs with a fruity herb flavor. This extract produces it perfectly. Use 2 oz. per gallon of "must." Cost $.62

21. SWEDISH AKAVIT EXTRACT. Akavit is a liquor made from caraway seed and flower extracts. This extract produces it perfectly. Makes a good wine. Use ½ oz. per gallon of "must." Cost $.32

22. FRENCH VERMOUTH EXTRACT. French Vermouth is a spiced French white wine. This extract produces it exactly. Makes a very good wine. Use 1 oz. per gallon of "must." Cost $.36

23. ITALIAN VERMOUTH EXTRACT. Italian Vermouth is a spiced Italian white wine. This extract produces it exactly. Makes a very good wine. Use 2 oz. per gallon of "must." Cost $.72

24. BENEDICTINE EXTRACT. Benedictine is a French liquor made with an herb base. This extract produces it exactly. Use 1/14 oz. or 2cc per gallon of "must." Cost $.15

25. SLOE GIN EXTRACT. Sloe gin is a pink gin flavored with the Sloe berry. This extract produces it exactly. Makes a good wine. Use 1/16 oz. or 2cc per gallon of "must." Cost $.04

26. GERMAN KUEMMEL EXTRACT. German Kuemmel is a liquor made from caraway seed, herbs, and flowers. This extract produces it exactly. Use 1/32 oz. or 1cc per gallon of "must." Cost $.04

27. CHARTREUSE GREEN OR GREEN MONASTERY EXTRACT. This is a green liquor produced from mountain herbs and flowers. This extract produces it exactly. Makes a fine wine. Use 1/7 oz. or 4cc per gallon of "must." Cost $.20

28. CHARTREUSE WHITE OR WHITE MONASTERY EXTRACT. This is a white liquor produced from mountain herbs and flowers. This extract produces it exactly. Makes a fine wine. Use 1/7 oz. or 4cc per gallon of "must." Cost $.20

29. CURACAO WHITE EXTRACT. Curacao is an orange flavored liquor made from small green oranges. This extract produces it exactly. Makes a fabulous wine. Use ¼ oz. per gallon of "must." Cost $.14

30. BURGUNDY RED WINE EXTRACT. Burgundy is a dry red wine. This extract produces it well. Use ½ oz. per gallon of "must." Cost $.32

31. SAUTERNE WHITE WINE EXTRACT. Sauterne is a dry white wine. This extract produces it well. Use ½ oz. per gallon of "must." Cost $.32

32. HOLLAND CHERRY WINE EXTRACT. Made from unfermented cherries. This extract produces this wine exactly. Use 2 oz. per gallon of "must." Cost $.62

33. MIRABELLE WINE EXTRACT. Mirabelle wine is made from French Lorraine white plums. This extract produces it exactly. Makes a fabulous wine. Use 1 oz. per gallon of "must." Cost $.65

34. PRUNELLE WINE EXTRACT. Prunelle is a liquor made from Mount Royal plums which have a dark blue skin and a yellow flesh. This extract produces it exactly. Makes a fabulous wine. Use 2 oz. per gallon of "must." Cost $.62

35. CREAM OF APRICOT EXTRACT. Made of pure apricot extracts. Makes a fabulous wine. Use 2 oz. per gallon of "must." Cost $.60

36. CREAM OF PEACH EXTRACT. Made of pure peach extract. Makes a fabulous wine. Use 2 oz. per gallon of "must." Cost $.60

37. CREAM OF BANANA EXTRACT. Made of pure banana extract. Makes a fabulous wine. Use 2 oz. per gallon of "must." Cost $.60

38. PEAR OF BELGIUM EXTRACT. This is a liquor made of a special pear grown in the central part of Belgium. This extract duplicates it exactly. Makes a fabulous wine. Use 2 oz. per gallon of "must." Cost $.62

USE THE SAME METHOD FOR MAKING ALL WINES FROM EXTRACTS

Use this same method for making all wines from extracts. Vary the amount of sugar, of course, by using your saccharometer so you get the alcohol content that you want. 3 pounds of household sugar or 3¾ pounds of invert sugar makes a nice wine, with the exception of Vermouth, where I usually use 3¼ pounds of household sugar or 4 pounds of invert sugar. Use the extract amount as mentioned in the text. 3 pounds of household sugar or 3¾ pounds of invert sugar. 1 gallon of water. Bakers yeast or wine yeast. Yeast nutrient or some other yeast food.

Boil one third of the sugar about two minutes in a half gallon of water. Allow to cool to lukewarm then pour into a large plastic jug or glass bottle. Then add the full amount of the extract, the yeast and yeast nutrient or other yeast food. Fit on a fermentation lock and leave ferment for ten days. Boil another one third of the sugar for about two minutes in a quart of water. Leave cool and put into the "must" and put the fermentation lock back on. Leave ferment for about two weeks. Boil the remaining one third of the sugar for about two minutes in a quart of water. Leave cool and put into the "must" and put the fermentation lock back on. Leave ferment until all fermentation stops. Siphon into a large sterilized plastic or glass jug filling the jug right to the top so that there is no air in the jug. Put on a fermentation lock. Leave "polish" or clear then siphon into bottles or jugs and cap.

You can, of course, change the color of wines made from extracts by adding approved food colors when you start the "must."

HOW TO MAKE WINE FROM SYRUPS AND MOLASSES

Rum wine, or wine made from molasses, is not only a wonderful wine to drink but one of the very best wines for using as a sauce on cakes, ice creams and sherbets. Wines made from other syrups, such as dark corn syrup, maple syrup and honey, are also very, very good.

RUM WINE

Produces about a gallon and a half of wine. One half cup of molasses. 4 pounds of sugar. 1½ gallons of water. All-purpose wine yeast or other wine yeast. Yeast nutrient speeds fermentation.

Put the molasses in a 5 gallon plastic jug. Boil half of the sugar in a quart of water for about 2 minutes. Cool and add. Put in a gallon of boiled and cooled water. Add the yeast and yeast nutrient. Put on a fermentation lock and leave ferment for four days. Boil the remaining half of the sugar in another quart of water. Cool and add. Put the fermentation lock back on and leave ferment until all fermentation stops. Leave clear or "polish" in the fermentation bottle or in another sterilized jug if you have one. If you put the wine into another jug, be sure that the jug is filled right up to the top and that you have a fermentation lock on it. When "polished" or clear, siphon into bottles or jugs and cap.

INDIAN SUMMER WINE

Produces about a gallon and a half of wine. This at one time was probably the most widely drank wine in the Midwest and West.

One cup of brown corn syrup. 4 pounds of sugar. 1½ gallons of water. All-purpose wine yeast or other wine yeast. Yeast nutrient speeds fermentation.

Make just the same as rum wine.

VIKING VIRGIN WINE

This is the ancient Scandanavian wine and one of the finest wines ever made. The recipe produces about a gallon and a half of wine.

1 cup of honey. 1 cup of crushed lingonberries. These are just a small wild cranberry. Cranberries of any kind work perfectly. 4 pounds of sugar. 1½ gallons of water. All-purpose wine yeast. Yeast nutrient speeds fermentation. Make just the same as rum wine.

FERMENTATION. GENERAL INFORMATION

Make a yeast starter form your wine yeast as described in the copy on making wild grape wine.

Fermentation should begin within 24 hours. If it does not the air may be too cold. In which case move "must" to a warmer place. If it still does not start add another batch of wine yeast starter or yeast nutrient.

IF MUST IS TOO SWEET

If the "must" is too sweet simply add water until the sugar content is down so it will produce wine of about 12% alcohol content or higher.

SWEETENING WINES

I have previously mentioned that you can sweeten wines by adding artificial sweeteners to the finished wine just before bottling it. The artificial sweeteners, of course, will not start the wine fermenting in the bottles as they furnish no food for yeasts. Artificial sweeteners, however, are rather expensive.

You can, of course, also sweeten finished wines with household sugar or invert sugar just before bottling them. In such cases, stir the sugar in well and add 4 grains of sodium metabisulphite to each gallon of wine so that it will kill off any yeast that tries to ferment the sugar.

MAKING WINES WITH OVER 18% ALCOHOL CONTENT

Wines with over 18% alcohol content are known as fortified wines. Examples of such wines are sherry, port, muscatel, etc. Fortified wines contain 20% alcohol. Such fortified wines have grain alcohol or brandy added to them to bring up their fermented in alcohol content. The grain alcohol is usually distilled from finished potato wine of 18% alcohol. The wine is put into a closed kettle with a coil running out of the top and down through a box of ice or refrigeration. The wine is heated in the kettle so that it steams off the alcohol at 170 degrees F. The first 20% of liquid that steams off and is recondensed in the coil and runs out of the coil is nearly 190 proof alcohol. Brandy is made by distilling a grape wine at 170 degrees to get out the alcohol and 212 degrees to get out the water and flavoring thus, taking about the first half that is steamed off. Federal law prohibits the distilling of alcohols or brandies or whiskeys so you must buy such spirits.

HOW TO MAKE VERMOUTH FROM FINISHED WINES

Vermouth is nothing but a poor quality white grape wine flavored with spices. Cinnamon is the spice usually used. Use one level teaspoon of cinnamon per gallon of wine. Slowly boil the cinnamon in one ounce of water per level teaspoon for 25 minutes. Cool until lukewarm. Add to white wine after the first fermentation. Vermouth should run about 17% alcohol by volume. Store the spiced wine in a hot attic or around a stove which will give it a slightly burnt flavor and darken the color a little. Storing the wine in sunlight will have much the same effect.

Wine companies usually make Vermouth by adding alcohol to a poor white grape wine until it is 50% alcohol by volume. They then add cinnamon flavoring. Then store the wine near a furnace or in the sunlight to give it a burnt flavor. The wine is then mixed with white wine until the white wine is about 17% alcohol. Italian Vermouths are usually sweeter and darker than French Vermouths as they are made with a white wine made from green grapes—skins and all. French Vermouth is usually made from just the juice of green grapes which makes the wine lighter.

Actually, red wine makes a better Vermouth than white wine. To make a red Vermouth or spiced wine, add the same amount of cinnamon to a finished red wine the first time you "rack" it.

HOW TO MAKE CHAMPAGNE OR SPARKLING WINES

Selzer Bottle and Champagne Bottle

1. A selzer bottle, or sparkling water siphon as they are sometimes called, is the easiest and surest way to make champagne or sparkling wine and the cost is low. Fill the selzer bottle with a finished wine to the fill level marked on the bottle and put a carbon dioxide cartridge into the selzer bottle. Then put the selzer bottle into your deep freeze and cool it to 22 degrees. Remove and serve. Be sure that the glasses are chilled. A better method is to fill the selzer bottle with a finished wine to the fill level. Place a carbon dioxide cartridge into the selzer bottle. Then put the selzer bottle into your deep freeze and cool it to 22 degrees. Take out and invert or stand the selzer bottle on its head and release the carbon dioxide or pressure entirely by pushing the lever or button. Turn back, right side up, and remove the head and central tube and pour the champagne into chilled glasses from the mouth of the bottle itself. There is no champagne better than this.

2. Buy a 5 gallon champagne or beer steel fermenting tank from Herter's, Waseca, Minnesota. Pour four gallons of finished wine into the pressure tank. Add 1/5 of a pound of sugar per gallon and dissolve it in well. Add an active wine yeast "starter." Be sure that the wine yeast "starter" is really working. You can make a wine yeast "starter" by putting 1/16 of a pound of sugar in a pint bottle with one part of water and 2 parts of wine. Boil for about two minutes. Leave cool to lukewarm then put in a sterilized bottle. Add wine yeast and put on a fermentation lock. When actively fermenting, add to the pressure tank. Leave ferment for two weeks to make sure that all fermentation has stopped. Then put the pressure tank in your deep freeze and freeze to 22 degrees. At 22 degrees, the carbon dioxide will not bubble. Remove the tank carefully so as not to disturb the sediment and bottle and cork using plastic or cork champagne corks and wire them in place. Champagne can exert about 100 pounds pressure per square inch on a bottle or tank usually, however, about 25 to 45 pounds per square inch. Be sure to wear a protective face mask and protective glasses, protective clothing and gloves when handling champagne bottles. A defective bottle can really blow up and become a grenade.

3. Put finished wine in a large polyethylene jug or glass bottle. Add 1/5 of a pound of sugar per gallon. Add wine yeast "starter" and put on a fermentation lock. When the "must" is actively fermenting, usually within 24 to 48 hours, siphon the "must" into champagne bottles and cork and wire down the corks. Remember, the pressure is 100 pounds per square inch.

Put the bottles on their sides with the necks pointing down in a room at about 70 degrees and leave them completely ferment. After the fermentation has completely stopped, tilt the bottles as much up on their mouth ends as possible and leave for at least 10 days. This is called "riffling" and lets the sediment all go down and collect on the cork. Now put the bottles in a deep freeze and cool them to 22 degrees. At 22 degrees, the carbon dioxide will not bubble out or come out of the wine. Carefully remove the cork which has the sediment on it and put in a new cork and wire it down. This is called "disgorging." Then store. Be sure to wear protective face masks and goggles and clothing while handling champagne bottles. Use only bottles in perfect condition without any chips or cracks in them.

Making Champagne at a Christian Brothers' Winery in Napa Valley, California. A still wine is put in the stainless steel tanks, yeast and sugar added and refermented. The fermenting develops 100 pounds of pressure per square inch in the tanks. The tanks are then cooled to 22 degrees which stops the carbon dioxide formed by the fermenting from bubbling out and the champagne is drawn from the tanks and bottled. This, of course, is not at all like champagne made in Europe when the second fermentation is done in each bottle. The bottle is kept on the side and regularly turned so that the sediment all collects in the cork. The champagne bottle is cooled to 22 degrees and the cork with all sediment on it is removed and a new cork inserted.

CHAMPAGNE OF LOUIE BALSAC

Champagne is simply a white or pink dry wine to which enough sugar is added after it is made to cause it to ferment enough in the bottle to put a fair amount of carbon dioxide into the wine causing it to bubble when opened or a wine that has had carbon dioxide added to it in other manners. A little brandy is usually used to add to the wine, that champagne is made from, to make it around 12% alcohol content or slightly higher.

We all know that champagne is terrifically expensive and far beyond the reach of everyone but the immensely wealthy. As you can well imagine, a method of making good champagne inexpensively right in your home with

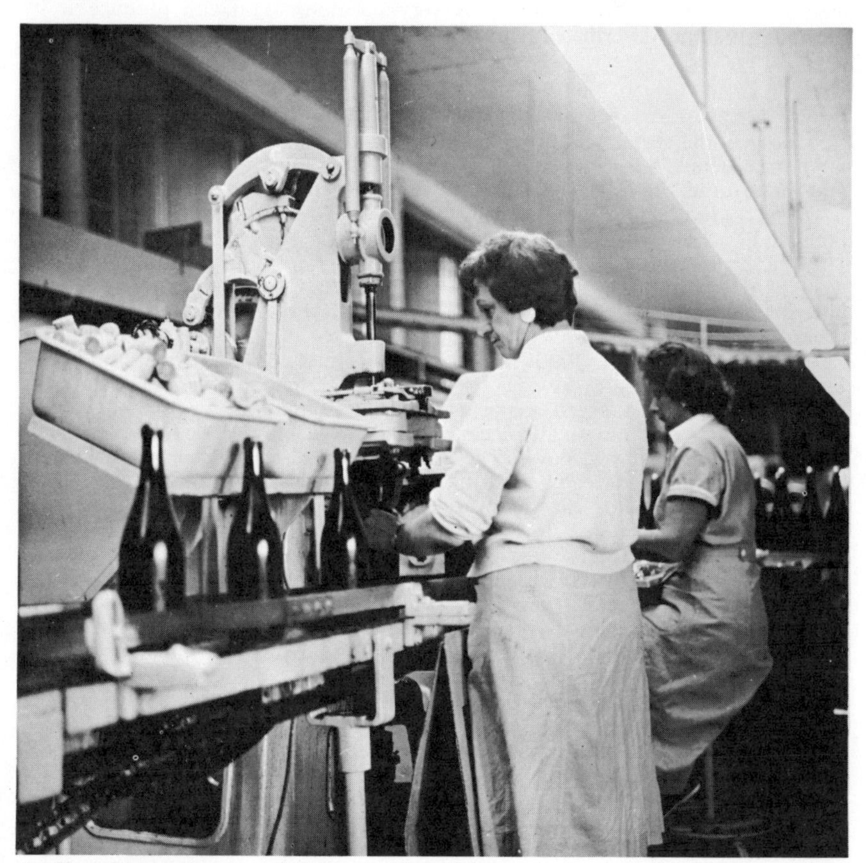

Bottling champagne at a Christian Brothers' Winery in Napa Valley. Three Brothers are the business heads of the wineries and fields but none work in them.

little trouble would be discovered. A man named Louie Balsac in Lyons, France developed this simple method of producing a good champagne at a reasonable cost.

Put your glasses in a refrigerator overnight so that they are really cold. Remove them quickly and put the following in them. The wine and brandy must be kept in your deep freeze overnight. The sparkling water must be kept in your refrigerator overnight and be close to freezing without freezing as possible. The reason that this is all necessary is that your glasses and ingredients must be as close to 22 degrees F as possible to absorb and hold the carbon dioxide that forms the bubbles and lets the bubbles escape slowly like true champagnes do, never rapidly. Take two ounces of sauterne wine which is a very dry white wine. The sauterne made in California is fine. Add two ounces of ice cold plain sparkling water. Add one ounce of ice cold brandy. Do not stir and serve at once. This method produces a crisp, clean tasting champagne that is good.

HOW TO MAKE APPLE CHAMPAGNE

Although it is not generally known France and Belgium produce large quantities of apple champagne. It is very delicious. You can produce it by the same method described in this book for making champagne or sparkling wine.

A BRIEF HISTORY OF BEER MAKING

Beer is the fermentation of malted cereal usually barley malt and some kind of bitters. Acorns, dandelion stems, gentian leaves and flowers, hops and many other items have been used to give beer a bitter taste.

The oldest clay document or tablet in existence, one from Babylonia 6000 B. C., shows the making of beer. In Babylonia, by the year 4000 B. C., 16 different types of beer were made from barley and honey. Bittering agents were used to give beer a bitter taste in 3000 B. C. The use of hops as a bittering agent of beer is, however, fairly recent being first used in the 6th century.

In imperial Egypt 3000 B. C., there were 4 different types of beer. Mothers brought beer every day to their sons in school. Egyptian beer was made of underbaked bread made of crushed germinated or malted barley. The bread was cut into small pieces, soaked in water in a large jug and left to ferment for about two days. The mass or "wort" was then forced through a sieve and was then ready to drink. Modern day beer in Russia is made almost exactly the same except several slices of apples are put into the brew before it is fermented.

All of the early beers were of very poor quality and very low in alcohol content. Air-borne yeasts were allowed to ferment them and most of the time the resulting liquid was more vinegar than beer. Herbs and dates were often mixed in with the beer to make it easier to drink and hold down.

China, in 2300 B. C., had a beer called Kiv. The Inca Indians of South America, far before the time of Christ, made beer from corn called Chicha and Sora. Aztec Indians of Mexico made beer from cactus and called it pulque.

Beer making spread from Egypt to Greece, then to Rome and then to Spain and Germany. The old Germanic tribes quickly learned to make beer from germinated barley and called it Peor or Bior.

They also made a beer called Alo from wheat and honey.

The Bohemians aromatized their beer with myrrh and bittered it with dandelion stems.

In continental Europe, until the 13th century, oats became the most widely used grain for beer making. Until the 14th century, hops was not widely used for beer making. The first record of hop cultivation in Europe was in the 9th century at the Abbey of St. Germain des Pres near Paris. By 840, hops were grown in the Hallertan region of Germany.

Columbus, while exploring Central America in 1502, was given corn beer by the Indians. They should have given him poison. In 1548, the first colonization attempt in Virginia by the British put up a small brewery and made beer from corn. In 1612 two Holland Dutch settlers put up a brewery at the southern end of Manhattan Island. In 1622 Governor Peter Minuit established a brewery at New Amsterdam.

The Pilgrim's landed at Plymouth Rock because they ran out of beer. Here is the exact statement taken from their ship's log.

"For we could not now take time for further search or consideration; our victuals being much spent, especially beer."

In Pennsylvania in 1683, the first brewery was built at Pennsbury Manor near Philadelphia by William Penn.

Thomas Jefferson, Samuel Adams, George Washington, Patrick Henry, Israel Putman and Benjamin Rush were all brewers.

TYPES OF BEER

LAGER BEER

Lager beer is the beer made nearly exclusively in North America. Lager beer is fermented with a yeast that, after fermentation, settles to the bottom. This lager yeast ferments best at 47 to 55 degrees. It is stored, aged and settled at 32 to 35 degrees. The word "lager" simple means storage in German.

ALE BEER

Ale beer is a beer made with yeast that remains in the liquid and does not settle to the bottom. Ale ferments best at 68 to 75 degrees and is stored at 40 to 45 degrees to each.

PILSENER

Pilsener is a very light lager beer with a medium hop flavor. Most all of the beer made in North America is Pilsener.

DORTMUNDER

Dortmunder beer is a very light lager beer with about 10% rice and with a medium hop flavor.

VIENNA

Vienna beer is a medium dark lager beer with a very mild hop taste.

MUNICH

Munich beer is a lager beer very dark brown in color with a very slight hop taste. A small amount of grapes are used in the brew and give it a very slight sweet taste.

BOCK

Bock beer is a lager beer that is a dark brown with a strong hop taste. Originated in the German city of Einbeck whose name was confused with "ein Bock", the German name for goat, and the beer became unfortunately known as bock or goat beer.

STEAM BEER

Steam Beer is a lager beer very pale in color with a mild hop flavor and heavily artificially impregnated with carbon dioxide so that it is very effervescent. It is found in the San Francisco area. You can, of course, impregnate beer by running it through pop machines until it is as much as one third carbon dioxide.

ALE

Ale is a beer fermented with a yeast that ferments throughout the beer including the top and does not settle out when fermentation ceases. Ale is a very pale color and has a strong hop flavor. Usually runs 4 to 5% alcohol by weight. Originated in England in the 15th century and at that time it was made without any hops at all but bittered slightly with acorns. The English people still drink nearly all ales and no lager beers.

CREAM ALE

A beer fermented with a top fermenting yeast. Has a very pale color, a mild hop flavor and flavored with vanilla.

INDIA ALE

A beer fermented with a top fermenting yeast. Has a very pronounced medium yellow color made by adding carrotine which is carrot color concentrate to the beer and a mild hop flavor. Popular in Canada and India.

GUINESS

Guiness stout or ale, both words actually mean the same, is a top fermented beer very dark in color with a mild hop flavor and fermented with a small amount of grapes that give it a slightly sweet fruity flavor.

SPARKLING ALE

Sparkling ale is a top fermented beer with a pale color and medium hop flavor and heavily artificially charged with carbon dioxide to make it very effervescent.

PORTER

Porter is a top fermenting beer with a dark brown slightly reddish color and a mild hop flavor. Runs about 5% alcohol by weight. Has a few dark blue grapes fermented in it to give it a slightly sweet taste and a tinge of red in the color.

STOUT

Stout beer is a top fermented beer with a medium dark brown color and a medium hop flavor. Runs about 5% alcohol content by weight.

HALF AND HALF

This is usually just a mixture of half light pale ale and Porter or Stout.

WEISSBIER

Weissbier is a top fermented beer of a very pale color made from mostly wheat and limited barley malt. Has a strong hop flavor from hops and dandelion stems.

LAMBIC

Lambic is a top fermenting beer made in Belgium. It is medium dark in color, has a mild hop flavor and is made acid by adding a little rhubarb to the ferment.

ACTUAL CONTENTS OF AVERAGE BEER

Beer in general of 4% alcohol content is made up of the following.
9/10 water
4.4 grams carbohydrates or about 170 calories per 12 ounce bottle.
6 grams of protein.
4 mg of calcium.
26 mg of phosphorus
.03 mg of riboflavin.
.2 mg of niacin.
a trace of thiamine.
.2 g of ash.

BEST TEMPERATURES TO SERVE BEER

For Americans 42 to 45 degrees F.
For English 45 to 50 degrees F.
For Germans 45 to 50 degrees F.
For Belgians 50 to 55 degrees F.
For Scandanavians 50 to 55 degrees F.

COMMERCIAL MADE BEERS DO NOT GIVE THE TRUE ALCOHOL CONTENT

On all North American made beers and beer ales, the alcohol content is purposely figured by weight instead of by volume. Alcohol by weight equals only 80% of alcohol by volume.

The United States Brewers Foundation says that the average of alcohol in American-made beers is only 3½% by weight. Very few United States-made beers or ales or malt liquors have more than 5% or 6¼% of alcohol by volume. The only thing strong about American-made beer, ales or malt liquors is the strong taste of the cheap chicken feed most of it is made from.

In Canada the average alcohol content of beers is 7% by volume.

The reason that the United States alcohol content of beers and ales and malt liquors is held so low is that they are by far the most popular drinks in the United States. American brewers have not forgotten prohibition and believe that it is best to keep the alcohol content of beer, ale and malt liquors as low as possible to keep drunkeness down. They still fear a large increase in drunkeness might bring about another prohibition era.

All early beer was ale-type beer, as top fermenting ale beer yeasts were used. In the 15th century, lager beer, or bottom fermenting beer, was invented in Bavaria. Today there are only 200 breweries left in the United States. Of these, only two make naturally carbonated beer. These are Budweiser by Amheuser Busch in St. Louis and Hielman Export of LaCrosse, Wisconsin. If any other breweries begin again to make naturally fermented top quality beer, if they will write me, I will add their names to this list. The tax on beer in the United States now averages 25% of the price that you have to pay for beer.

MALT

Malt is germinated barley or in other words sprouted barley killed by taking away moisture and heat dried and ground or crushed. During the limited germination period of barley, grain enzymes are developed and the grain "modified" so that the ground malt dissolves when mixed into a mash. Thus, starch, the main constituents of all grain or seeds, when mashed, changes to maltodextrins or sugars. There are a number of different types of malt. Such as Crystal for regular light beers. Imperial malt for medium colored beers. Brown or Blown malt for brown and bock beers. Black or Roasted Malt for dark beers and ales.

Malting barley developes enzymes in it that partially change the starches to dextrins and maltose. This is called "modification" of the barley. Depending on how much or long the malt is dried depends on the type of malt produced. American malts are so-called extra pale malts, like Pilsener, or high or hot dried malts like the Munich malts for bock beer. Without the enzymes in malt, other grain starches could not be changed to sugar. Yeast cannot change starches to alcohol and carbon dioxide. Yeast can only change sugars to alcohol and carbon dioxide. In the United States most brewers use the following amounts of materials to produce their beer. Barley Malt 64.63%. Corn meal 22.49%. Rice meal 9.23%. Sugar and invert sugar 2.68%. Barley .84%. Wheat .12%. Grain sorghum .01%.

ADJUNCTS

Adjuncts are materials that are used in beer making to add body or alcohol to the beer other than malted barley. They are lower in cost than malted barley or sugar and, hence, greatly lower the cost of beer production. Their starches must be converted to sugar by malt enzymes so the sugar can be converted to alcohol by yeast.

In early America, beers were made by using such "adjuncts" as corn meal, potatoes starch, squash, and pumpkins. Adjuncts can be used in beer making from 20% to 40% of the total weight of the materials. They add starch, dextrins and sugar to the beer at low cost. They possess no enzymatic power like malted barley does and their starches are converted to sugar by the amylolytic power of the malted barley. Cornmeal, as well as all adjuncts, must be cooked to gelatinize its starches before it can be used as an adjunct. Brewer's rice is a by-product of milling brown rice into white rice and is the best adjunct for making very pale light beer. Budweiser beer has a good deal of rice in it and has its carbon dioxide naturally fermented into it making it the best quality pale beer made in North America. I do not own any stock in the company. This is just the truth. Anyone who tries to make the best possible product should be given a pat on the back. Other adjuncts used with malted barley are unmalted barley meal, wheat meal, oat meal, tapioca starch and milo corn.

SUGARS

Beer brewing sugars are corn sugar, corn syrup or invert sugar. Cane or beet sugars cannot be used to make beer, and if they are used, completely spoil the beer giving it a bad home-brew taste.

MALT EXTRACTS

Malt extracts are made as follows. Malted barley is cooked and the liquid dehydrated. The liquid is often then mixed with corn syrup or even molasses. Few breweries use such malt extracts to make beer as it is absolutely impossible to make good beer from any malt extract. Over cooking malted barley to make malt extracts changes the chemical content of the malted barley entirely ruining it for beer making. Any so-called beer made from it has the characteristic very undesirable "home-brew" taste and odor and is not a true beer at all. In fact, such home brews contain acids and chemicals that can be extremely dangerous. No brewery that makes beer of anything but trash quality would ever think of using any malt extracts to make beer.

HOPS

Hops are a perennial vine that belongs to the mulberry group. Only female hop plants should be grown. The female plant bears cones that look

A hop field in Idaho just after the hops have been picked. Note that poles have been put up over the entire field and wires strung between the poles for the hops to grow on.

like small leafy flowers. These cones have glands that secrete a golden resin called lupulin. This lupulin which contains lupulin acid and humulon acid that gives beer a hop flavor. If male hop plants fertilize these, cone seeds are formed. These hop seeds give beer a very bad bitter acid taste and lupulin and humulon acids are lost entirely. Hops, besides giving beer taste and aroma, help the beer in many other ways. Hops give tannin to the beer which helps protein precipitation when boiling the wort. Hops give off low molecular proteins which act as yeast food. Hops help the biological stability of beer and aids fermentation, foam formation and the ability of beer to hold foam well.

Lager beer should contain about .3 to .6 pounds of hops per 31 gallons of wort. Ale beers which are top fermented takes as much as 1.5 pounds of hops per 31 gallons of wort. You can see as a whole that ale beers contain nearly three times as much hops as lager beers.

WATER

We have pointed out that beer on an average contains at least 91% of water. The water you use to make beer then is highly important. Water, in different areas, varies greatly in their mineral content and in the types of minerals that they contain. Waters may be hard or soft and their hardness can be temporary or permanent. Temporary hardness in water is caused by bicarbonates of calcium, iron or magnesium being in the water. If heated or boiled, the soluble bicarbonates of calcium precipitate out and can be filtered out, thus, softening the water. Permanent hardness in water is caused when the water contains calcium, iron salts, or magnesium other than the bicarbonates, such as calcium and magnesium sulfate and chloride. Boiling will not soften permanently hard water.

Salts, which occur in water, react with the minerals in the malted barley but have marked effects upon many of the fundamental parts of brewing beer. Water for beer making must have no odor and must be free from bacteria. For typical American pale light versions of Pilsener beer, water should be medium permanent hard, never soft. For Dortmund type pale beer and ales, the water should be high permanent hard. For Munich beer or bock, water should be of medium temporary hardness or soft. It pays to travel a few miles, if necessary, to get the best water possible to make your beers. City chlorinated water cannot be used for beer making.

ENZYMES

Enzymes, in general, are organic catalysts of a protein nature and found only in living cells. Barley malt contains enzymes that make good beer making possible.

THE BEER BREWING PROCESS

GRINDING THE MALT

The malted barley must be ground or crushed, separating the husk from the grain and then turn the grain into a coarse meal.

MASHING

100 pounds of malt and adjuncts are used per barrel of water or 31 gallons to make good quality beer. Cheaper beers, of course, do not use anywhere near this amount. Malt must make up 60% to 80% of the mash with adjuncts making up from 20% to 40% of the mash.

The main problem of making beer is actually to make an inexpensive carbonated wine with a malt flavor and body so it has a foam head. In order to do this, you just use inexpensive adjuncts such as cornmeal, oatmeal, etc., that cost only a few cents a pound and a minimum of malt and convert the starches in both the malt and adjuncts into sugars that can be changed into alcohol by yeasts. Using just malt and invert sugar, or corn syrup, beer can be easily made but the cost is prohibitive for commercial production where beer has to sell at a low figure. 25% of this low figure is tax to the government. Making good beer at home where you can afford to use invert sugar, corn sugar or corn syrup making the best beer is not difficult.

Mashing is the process of bringing into solution the substances in the malt and adjuncts so they form a beer making liquid or "wort." First the adjuncts with enough water are boiled so that they form a gelatinous mass. The malt is then mixed in or doughed into the adjuncts. 100 pounds of malt and adjuncts used per 31 gallons of water. The mass is then heated to about 109 degrees and very slowly, the slower the better, brought to 172 degrees. The liquid from the malt and adjuncts is then strained out from the spent malt and adjuncts and is called "wort".

BOILING AND HOPPING OF WORT

The wort is usually boiled in a kettle for 1½ to 2 hours. This boiling is done to inactivate any malt enzymes to completely sterilize the wort, to precipitate higher molecular proteins that cause beer to be unstable. To flavor the wort with hops, the hops are added at the rate of .03 to .5 pounds per 31 gallons for lager beer. .5 to .7 pounds of hops for American Ale beers. 1.5 for British or German ale and stout beers. Hops are then strained out of the wort or sometimes put in the wort in a bag and the bag simply removed. Most every brew master has a different way of putting in the hops and actually all of the results are about the same. The wort is then strained and cooled.

YEAST

Each yeast cell represents an independent organism performing all the necessary functions of life. Yeasts change sugar to carbon dioxide and alcohol with chemical enzymes that it manufactures. The enzymes are lifeless chemicals but have never been produced synthetically. The facts are simply no fermentation without enzymes and no enzymes without life. You can, of course, extract the juice from yeast cells which contain enzymes and use the juice alone to cause fermentation or the change of sugar to carbon dioxide and alcohol.

In 1860 Louis Pasteur showed that the chemical act of fermentation is essentially a life function of the yeast cell.

Brewery yeasts all belong to the species sacchromyces cerevisiae and are in two groups. Ale beer or top fermenting yeasts. Lager beer or bottom fermenting yeasts. Yeast at breweries is added to the wort at the rate of ½ to 1 pound per 31 gallons. No beer that tastes at all like real beer can be made with bakers yeast. Bakers yeast gives beer a bad "home-brew" taste and odor. Lager beer yeast or bottom fermenting yeast at breweries is added to the wort at the rate of ½ to 1 pound per 31 gallons. It costs the breweries nothing as they collect it out of the fermenting tanks. The bottom layer of yeast deposited at the bottom is worthless as it is made up of dead yeast cells, the next layer is made up of live yeast cells and is saved, the top layer is made up of some dead and some live yeast cells and is rarely saved.

The wort is then fermented for 12 to 18 hours in open tanks, then put into closed tanks to ferment. This leaves behind the dead and weak yeast and coarse protein tannin susbtances that settle out. This sediment, if not gotten out of the wort, gives the beer a bad "home-brew" taste. The carbon dioxide gas, given off by fermentation, is collected in a tank, compressed and saved to artificially carbonate the beer. Fermentation stops after 7 to 9 days. The beer is then cooled to 33 degrees and pumped into a storage tank to age. The beer is cooled to as close to 22 degrees as possible and the carbon dioxide is artificially put back in the cold beer the same as it is in carbonating pop and soft drinks.

The beer should not be carbonated like pop but should be made like this. After the beer has fermented for 12 to 18 hours, it should be put into another fermenting tank either open or closed. Thus, leaving behind the dead yeast and other impurities that give beer a bad "home-brew" taste and smell. It then should be fermented until about 1% of the fermentable extract is left. You can quickly ascertain this with a saccharometer for beer testing. The beer should then be put into a closed tank and at a cool temperature of 39 to 43 degrees fermented until all fermentation stops. The carbon dioxide formed during this last fermentation naturally impregnating the beer and carbonating it. Such natural carbonation gives the beer an entirely different taste and aroma and stays in the beer three and four times as long as artificial carbonation.

ALE BEER OF TOP FERMENTATION BEER

Ale beer yeast ferments throughout the beer and rises to the top of the beer. 1/3 to ½ pound of top fermenting yeasts per 31 gallons of wort are used which is much less than lager yeast. Brewers collect this yeast from the top of the wort and save it for the next batch. The wort temperature, when the yeast is added, is 54 to 60 degrees and the fermenting temperature allowed to rise to 70 degrees. Fermentation lasts from six to seven days. The wort is fermented in open tanks. The surface of the wort is first covered by a white foam. Then "rocky heads" or a dense foam with dark masses covers the wort. These dark masses must be carefully skimmed off. Then follows a loose deep foam. The foam then falls and the yeast rises to the top of the wort. Some of the yeast is then skimmed off from the top and saved for future ale making or used to make food. About an inch of yeast is left on the top of the wort to prevent air-borne bacteria from getting into the ale. The ale is pumped through filters into closed tanks and artificially carbonated with carbon dioxide until it contains .45 to .55 of gas by weight.

Ale beer, however, should not be artificially carbonated but should be made like this. The beer placed in closed tanks and sugar in syrup form added at the rate of about 1/5 of a pound per gallon and additional yeast added. Dry hops at the rate of 1/5 to 2/3 of a pound per 31 gallons should also be added. The ale then is allowed to slowly ferment again and the resulting carbon dioxide impregnates the beer naturally carbonating it. Thus, real ale beer actually should be made practically the same as champagne. The ale is then cooled down to as close to 22 degrees as possible and bottled. The cold ale does not give off carbon dioxide gas.

BEER AND ALE HIGHLY PERISHABLE

Commercial beers and ales, with the exception of some malt liquors, have a relatively very low alcohol content, not nearly enough to keep them stable and from spoiling. All good draft beer or ale and all good bottled beer or ale in quart and half gallon bottles should not be pasteurized and must be kept at low temperatures to prevent the beer or ale from spoiling. Pint bottles of beer and ale and canned beer and ale are all pasteurized because they are mostly sold unrefrigerated. Pasteurized beer has a much inferior taste and aroma because of chemical changes caused by pasteurizing. Pasteurized beer and ales produce more hang-over effects than unpasteurized ones.

The spent malt and adjuncts used to make beer are sold as cattle and chicken feed. The extra yeast is sold for human as well as animal food and also for fertilizers, rosins, glues, polishes, plastics, etc.

The great French scientist, Louis Pasteur, in 1860 made possible the making of good beer. He not only was the first to explain the yeast fermentation process, but his pasteurization process made it possible for the first time to keep bottled beer from spoiling. Before Pasteur, beer was nothing but the usual bad home brew. He made good beer a reality.

HOW TO MAKE GERMAN LAGER BEERS

Remember, Beer Making In Homes Is Prohibited By Federal Law

The first thing to remember is that you cannot make real lager beer, or any other kind of beer, with any of the so-called malt extracts or malt syrups. With malt extracts and syrups, you can make nothing but very bad tasting and very bad smelling home-brew full of sediment and with chemicals and acids that can be extremely dangerous. Even the worst and cheapest commercial beers are not made with such products as malt extracts and malt syrups. You cannot have sediment in your bottled beer. Sediment is made up of dead yeast and impurities that give the beer a permanent bad home-brew taste and give you a hang-over.

Here is how to make real lager beer of true lager bottom fermenting beer in your home and it is very simple to make. These are the things that you must have to make lager beer.

1. A fermenting crock. This can be ceramic or plastic. Polyethylene plastic in no way affects the contents or taste of beer. Preferably the crock should have a cover, or a clean cloth or polyethylene sheet cover to keep out flies and bad bacteria. 6 pounds of honest malt concentrate for every 6 gallons of beer. Malt concentrate is not a syrupy so-called malt extract or so-called malt syrup. You can get the malt concentrate from Herter's or breweries at a very low price.

A saccharometer with a built-in thermometer and beer carbonating time indicator.

Two or more 5 gallon or larger plastic polyethylene bottles or jugs with fermentation locks and also with air tight caps. Lager beer yeast. Siphon hose. Bottle caps and capper. Corn sugar, invert sugar or corn syrup.

Hops, if you desire, to give the beer more hop flavor than comes with the malt concentrates.

Take the malt concentrate and put it into a large pot with at least a gallon of water or at least enough water to cover it three inches or more. The more water the better. Put in as much as the pot will hold. Slowly bring to a low boil, the slower the better. Stir well so there is no burning. Simmer the mash for an hour. Remove the mash and squeeze out the liquids into another large pot. Mix water with the mash and keep squeezing it into the pot until the pot is about full. This is called "sparging". You must wash out as much of the concentrate from the malt as possible. If you desire more hops in the beer, put the extra hops in a cloth and then into the wort. Be careful with hops, however, as you can get too much hops in beer and, when you do, you cannot reduce the hop flavor. Boil the wort for about 30 minutes adding water to keep up the water level. Remove the hop sack if you have used one. Now strain the liquid into the fermenting crock and add enough boiled and cooled water to make up 6 gallons. Never fill your fermenting crock more than ¾ full or it will overflow when fermenting.

Leave the wort cool. Test the liquid or wort with your saccharometer and decide on the amount of alcohol you desire in the beer. You can make the beer anywhere from 3 to 12% alcohol. Add half of the amount of sugar in the form of corn sugar, invert sugar or corn syrup. Mix it in well. It will take about 20% more invert sugar or corn syrup than corn sugar for the alcohol content that you desire. Have your lager yeast started in a bottle with a mixture of sugar and sterilized water and a little wort. Be sure that it is working well. Put your lager yeast in the wort. This is called "pitching" the wort. If you have a cover, put it onto the ceramic or plastic crock. If not, cover the crock with a polyethylene sheet. Keep the crock in a place around 50 degrees if you can. Leave ferment from 18 to 24 hours, then siphon into five gallon bottles filling them about three fourths full. Take the balance of the sugar and divide it and add to the bottles mixing in well. Fit fermentation locks onto the plastic bottles. Leave ferment for two to three days. The fermentation will be vigorous. Test with your beer tester the second day and every day after this and if on the red line B., remove the fermentation locks. If you have an extra sterilized 5 gallon plastic bottle, siphon the beer into it and wash out the one that the wort was in and siphon wort into it from the other jug or bottle. Then put on the air tight plastic caps onto the plastic bottles. If they leak at all, seal them with paraffin. The caps must be air tight. Put the plastic bottles in a place as close to 50 degrees or down to 39 degrees as possible and leave until all fermentation has ceased, which will be about a total of 7 to 9 days since you first put in the yeast. The carbon dioxide, formed during this closed fermentation, will impregnate the beer naturally carbonating it. Now put the bottles or jugs in your deep freeze or outside, if the weather is cold enough, and leave them cool down to 22 degrees or colder. Then carefully remove the bottles one at a time, open them up and siphon out the beer and bottle and cap it quickly as possible. At 22 degrees, the carbon dioxide will not leave the beer. Store the bottled beer away from the light. You now will have some real lager beer free from all taste killing sediment and free from the characteristically bad home-brew taste, odor and hang-over qualities.

Here again you must remember that you cannot make real ales or stouts or any other kinds of beer with any so-called malt extracts or malt syrups.

These are the things that you must have.

A fermenting crock with a cover. This can be ceramic or plastic. Polyethylene plastic in no way affects the content or taste of the ale or stout. Preferably the crock should have a cover, or you must cover it with a clean cloth or sheet of polyethylene to keep out flies and bacteria.

6 pounds of ale or stout concentrate for every 6 gallons of ale or stout. This you can secure from breweries or from Herter's at a very low cost.

A saccharometer with a built-in thermometer and beer carbonating indicator.

Two or more 5 gallon or larger plastic polyethylene bottles or jugs with fermentation locks and also air tight caps.

Ale or top fermenting yeast. Siphon hose. Corn sugar, invert sugar or corn syrup. Bottle caps and a capper. Hops, if desired, to give the ale or stout more hop flavor.

Take the ale or stout concentrate and put it into a large pot with at least a gallon of water or at least enough water to cover it three inches or more. The more water the better. Put in as much as the pot will hold up to three gallons. Slowly bring to a low boil, the slower the better. Stir well so there is no burning. Simmer the mash for an hour. Remove the mash and squeeze out the liquids into another large pot. Add water to the mash or "sparge" it or wash out all concentrate that can be washed out and also squeeze this water through the mash and into the pot. You, thus, actually wash out all the good from the mash. If you desire more hops in the ale or stout than comes with the concentrate, put the extra hops into a cloth sack and put them in the wort or liquid. Boil for about 30 minutes adding water to keep up the water level. Remove the hop sack if you have used one. Now strain into the fermenting crock and add enough boiled and cooled water to make up 6 gallons of wort. Never fill your fermenting crock more than ¾ full as it will overflow when fermenting. Leave cool and then test the liquid or wort with your saccharometer and decide on the amount of alcohol that you desire in the ale or stout. Should be made from 6 to 12%. Add half of the amount of sugar in the form of corn sugar, invert sugar or corn syrup. It will take about 20% more invert sugar or corn syrup than corn sugar for the alcohol content that you desire. Have your ale or top fermenting yeast "starter" working well in a bottle with a mixture of sugar and sterilized water and a little wort. You can start this a day or two ahead of time. If you have a cover, put it onto the ceramic or plastic crock. Keep the crock in a place around 60 degrees if you can. Ale and stout are fermented warmer than lager beer. Leave the ale ferment for three days, the surface of the wort first becomes covered by a white foam. Then a heavier foam with dark masses. Skim off these dark masses if they appear. Then a loose deep foam. The foam then collapses and the yeast rises to the top. Skim off all yeast but a one inch layer on the top. Now siphon the ale into the plastic polyethylene bottles or jugs filling them about ¾ full. Leave a day and test with your saccharometer. The wort should be ready for the following, to naturally carbonate it.

Remove the fermentation locks. If you have another large polyethylene jug, siphon the ale into it filling about three fourths full and put on an air tight cap. Wash out the jug the ale was in and siphon the ale from another jug into it, and put on an air tight cap. If you do not have an extra jug, put on air tight cap on the jug the ale is in. Place in as cool a place as you can find and leave ferment until all fermentation ceases, usually in one to three days. The ale, or stout, will be impregnated from the carbon dioxide from this fermentation. Now carefully place the plastic jugs in your deep freeze or outside, if it is cold, and leave cool to 22 degrees or colder. Then one at a time, remove the air tight caps and siphon into bottles and cap. At 22 degrees or colder, the carbon dioxide will not leave the ale or stout. Store away from light. You will have a clear fine ale or stout free from bad home-brew taste, aroma and sediment.

CHAMPAGNE BEER OF ALSACE

Remember Beer Making In Homes Is Prohibited By Federal Law

This is an entirely different beer that actually tastes identical to champagne. A very similar beer is made in the United States called Champale.

Get two 5 gallon polyethylene jugs or bottles with fermentation locks and also with air tight caps. Take a cup and a fifth of pearled barley. This is available at all grocery stores. Put it into a bowl and pour a gallon of hot water on it and leave stand overnight. The next morning take the pearled barley and its water and place it in a cooking pan and keep hot just below boiling, but not boiling, for a half hour. Take one and a fifth cups of wheat, add one gallon of water and put into a cooking pot and boil for one hour. Leave the wheat cool down a little then add the pearled barley and its water to it. Takes a two gallon pot. Now filter the mixture through a strainer removing the spent grains. The remaining liquid, as you now know, is called "wort" and is pronounced "wurt". Now take two ounces of dried hops and put them into a clean cloth bag and put the bag into the wort. You can buy the hops from Herter's, Waseca, Minnesota. Now gently boil the hops with the wort for one hour. Then remove the bag of hops. Put half of the wort in one 5 gallon polyethylene jug and half in another 5 gallon polyethylene jug. Add enough good water to fill each jug about three fourths full. Test the wort with a saccharometer and ascertain the amount of alcohol you desire in the finished beer. You should make this beer about 11½ per cent alcohol. Seems to be just perfect for it. Now take half the sugar and boil it for about 2 minutes in enough water to make it into a syrup. Leave cool and put half in each jug. Yeast or "pitch" this beer, as putting in yeast is called, as follows. Take a bunch of at least a pound of unwashed white, blue or red grapes. They can be any color, but white is usually used. Crush them in a small bowl and place them in a quart bottle—stem and all. Add about twice their volume of water, test the liquid with your saccharometer and add enough sugar to come out 11½ per cent alcohol. Put the bottle in a warm place about 60 to 70 degrees and leave ferment for 24 hours or until you have a good lively fermentation going. If you have no grapes, use a pint of grape juice and wine yeast and make your "starter." Now "pitch" or dump the fermenting yeast "starter," grapes and all, about half in one jug and half in the other. Put fermentation locks on both jugs. Leave ferment for five days. If possible, buy another 5 gallon plastic bottle. Siphon the liquid from one plastic jug into it. Add half of the remaining sugar boiled in water and cooled and put on a fermentation lock. Then wash out the plastic jug that the wort was in and siphon the wort from the remaining plastic jug leaving all sediment behind. Add the remaining sugar to it in cooled syrup form. Then put on a fermentation lock. Leave ferment for about three days checking with your saccharometer beer tester everyday. When it reads B, remove the fermentation locks and screw on the air tight caps for the plastic jugs. Leave ferment until all fermentation stops. This impregnates the wort with carbon dioxide naturally carbonating the beer. Now carefully put the plastic jugs in your deep freeze or outside, if it is cold enough. Leave them cool down to 22 degrees or colder. Then remove and siphon into bottles and cap. The beer at 22 degrees will not give up its carbon dioxide. You will have a clear sediment-free beer practically identical to champagne or Champale. It is wonderful drinking.

INGREDIENTS OF WHISKEY AND WHISKY AND HOW IT IS MADE AND WHAT ONES TO BUY

The word whisky comes from the Celtic word "Uisquebeatha" gradually shortened to "Usquebaugh," meaning "water of life." The Celts were an early central European tribe that inhabited France, Britain and Ireland. The word ferment comes from the latin word "fervere" meaning "to boil". Early people believed that fermentation was a cold boiling process because of the bubbling of fermenting liquids. It was not until the 17th century that brewers discovered that the boiling of fermenting liquids was caused by carbon dioxide gas. Alcohol obtained by distilling was the first organic compound discovered by man. Distilling was invented in India and was brought back to Europe by the crusaders. All chemistry has come from man's discovery of how to distill alcohol from fermented liquids. Acetic acid made by souring wine was the first acid made by man. Early whiskies were flavored with saffron, nutmeg, and cinnamon.

Malted barley used alone to form a mash or by using it with others, grains the "enzymes" in the malted barley and turns the starches to maltose sugar which yeast can turn into alcohol. A German, W. Kuhne, gave the name "enzymes" to the chemicals produced by yeast that turn sugar into alcohol and carbon dioxide.

The word "Whisky" means whisky made in England, Scotland, Ireland and Canada. The word "Whiskey" means whiskey made in the United States.

Whiskeys are in general made as follows.

1. Ground malted barley and ground other grains are mixed with water and boiled. The enzymes in the malted barley change the starches of the grains to maltose sugar which can be fermented by yeast. This process is called "mashing." All mashes are more or less sweet or they could not be used at all to produce alcohol. The word "sour mash" loosely used by some distillers is strictly advertising "hokum."

2. The liquid from the mash is strained from the mash and the mash, itself, washed or "sparged" with water and the spent meal put aside. The liquid or "wort" from the mash is then adjusted so it will make a 16% liquid when fermented.

3. The fermented wort is distilled to get out the alcohol and some of the flavoring from the wort.

There are two kinds of very different stills used to distill the whiskey wort. They are as follows.

POT STILL

A pot still is just a large cooking vessel with a tube leading off the top of it and down through refrigeration of some kind that cools the tube, thus, condensing the hot vapors into a liquid that go out of the tube from the cooking vessel. At the beginning of the tube, distillers sometimes put some baffle plates in the tube so that some of the hot vapors are condensed on the baffle plates and drop back into the cooking vessel to be distilled again. Pot stills, for example, are used to make the best quality of Scotch and Irish whisky and to make North American illegal moonshine whiskey. Using a pot still, the true natural flavors of the fermented wort are distilled into the whiskey. You have to use good materials to make pot whiskey.

PATENT STILL

The patent still was invented in 1831 by Aeneas Coffey an Englishman. It consists of essentially two columns called rectifier and analyzer columns. Each column is subdivided horizontally into a series of chambers by perforated copper plates. The columns are filled with steam and put into the bottom of the analyzer column. The fermented wort at nearly boiling temperature is put in at the top of the analyzer column. The steam forces the alcohol out of the wort and into the rectifier column and the alcohol is condensed from the rectifier column. A patent still whiskey is mostly just pure alcohol and, hence, the whiskey can be made from most anything as the materials used actually flavor the whiskey very little or not at all. Patent stills are fine for making paint solvents but poor for making whiskey. Patent still whisky is made in Scotland, Ireland, Canada and the United States. Scotland, Ireland, and Canada, however, make their good whisky with pot stills. The United States makes no pot still whiskey.

Scotch and Irish pot still whiskies are made of the following ingredients. Malted barley smoked over peat fires, oat meal, wheat meal, rye meal and unmalted barley meal.

Scotch and Irish Patent Still whiskies are made of cornmeal, barley meal, rye meal, malted rye, and oatmeal.

The two most widely sold American-made whiskeys are bourbon and rye whiskeys. Bourbon, of course, is a "corn whiskey." American whiskeys are not made from malted barley smoked over peat fires like Scotch and Irish Pot Still whiskies. American whiskeys are white and clear when made and get their color and most of their flavor from being stored in charred white oak barrels that give the whiskey a reddish brown color and some flavor. If American whiskey, with the exception of "corn whiskey," is stored in a charred oak barrel for two years, it is known as straight whiskey. Blended American whiskies are made of several straight whiskeys and neutral grain ethyl alcohol and flavored and colored as much as 2½ per cent of their volume.

Corn whiskey can be sold as soon as it is distilled for a straight whiskey.

United States Federal Regulations on whiskey material and whiskey making are only very general ones and are as follows.

Whiskey is an alcoholic distillate from a fermented mash of grain distilled at less than 190 proof in such manner that the distillate possesses the taste, aroma, and characteristics generally attributed to whiskey, and withdrawn from the cistern room of the distillery at not more than 110 and not less than 80 proof.

"Rye whiskey," "bourbon whiskey," "wheat whiskey," "malt whiskey," or "rye malt whiskey" is whiskey which has been distilled at not exceeding 160 proof from a fermented mash of not less than 51% rye grain, corn grain, wheat grain, malted barley grain or malted rye grain, respectively.

"Corn whiskey" is whiskey which has been distilled at not exceeding 160 proof from a fermented mash of not less than 80% corn grain stored in uncharred oak containers or reused charred oak containers and not subjected, in the process of distillation or otherwise, to treatment with charred wood.

Bourbon whiskey obviously can be very carelessly made and is usually the worst of American-made whiskeys.

HOW TO MAKE CANADIAN TYPE WHISKEY

As previously mentioned, Scotch and Irish whiskies are usually flavored with sherry wine. The best Canadian whiskies are flavored with port wine. Wine flavoring destroys the harsh, biting alcohol taste and fumes of whiskies and, strange as it may seem, makes them less prone to produce bad hangovers. Nothing mixes and covers over the raw, harsh alcohol molecules like grape molecules.

In Southern Ireland, the Irish import Henessey cognac from France made 120 proof especially for them. It is drank straight in the Pubs. This is the strongest drinking liquor made in the world, yet it is not anywhere near as harsh and biting as American whiskey of 90 proof. Henessey cognac is made from distilled wine and contains, of course, grape juice molecules that cover the alcohol in it.

Canadian whiskies with grape molecules are certainly much better quality than American made whiskeys. They are so high priced, however, that no one can afford them in this country anymore.

Fortunately, for those who care to drink good Canadian whiskies, they can be duplicated here very easily. Purchase a fifth of the cheapest American made Whiskey. Add 1½ ounces of port wine to the fifth and shake it up well. Leave it stand for three hours or more. You then will have as smooth a drinking and tasting whiskey as any made in the world, regardless of price. In fact, it will taste much like the famed Canadian-made Canadian Club Whiskey that is so smooth and free of irritants that it can be drank without any diluting at all. Your American whiskey with the port wine added, you will find, can also be drunk with no diluting at all and will have no bad alcohol taste or fumes.

JOHNSON CLUB WHISKEY

It Is Illegal To Make Whiskey In Your Own Home Even For Your Own Use Without A Government Permit And They Are Hard To Get

It is many years ago that this Norwegian recipe was used and I put it down here just for a matter of record. It would be a blessing if modern distillers would adopt this old pure formula.

Take one bushel of cornmeal and a fourth bushel of malted barley meal. Place them in a large kettle and cover with enough good well water to cover the meal at least four or five inches. Slowly bring to a low boil and simmer for at least one hour, preferably two hours, and keep adding water to keep up the water level as the meal absorbs the water. Stir to keep from burning. This cooking or mashing gives the malted barley enzymes a chance to change the starch in the corn to maltose which is an easily fermented sugar. Yeast cannot change corn starch or any other starch to sugar. Remove the pot from the heat. Leave cool and strain the liquid from the cooked meal into a fifty gallon oak barrel. Add well water to the cooked meal mass. This is called "sparging" it and stir and again squeeze out the liquid. Repeat until all of the liquids possible are washed out of the cooked meal. Add about 100 pounds of corn sugar or invert sugar or cane sugar, if you do not have the others, and stir in well. Fill the barrel about three fourths full by adding good well water. Take a saccharometer and test the solution. By adding sugar or water, adjust the solution so that it will produce 16% alcohol. Add a gallon of top fermenting yeast "starter" or about five pounds of yeast skimmed off from a previous mash or bakers yeast if you have no top fermenting yeast. Put a cover on the barrel as yeast produces alcohol much faster if it does not have too much of a supply of air. Never set a mash where it is windy or drafty as then the yeast will turn the sugar into carbon dioxide and water, not carbon dioxide and alcohol. Leave ferment at not colder than 75 degrees. Test the wort or liquid everyday with a saccharometer. Let the saccharometer go between 996 and 998. Then siphon and run the wort through a pot still, not a patent still, in not less than 3 hours time producing not more than 10 to 12 gallons of whiskey running about 90 proof. Strain the whiskey through a three foot thick layer of hard maple charcoal. Add one quart of dry sherry wine and the juice from a level tablespoon of nutmeg boiled in a half cup of water to the whiskey. Store in oak barrels or in glass jugs with a few oak chips in the bottom. The oak barrels or the oak chips will give the whiskey color. No modern maker has ever equalled this whiskey and will admit it if asked. It is so smooth that you can drink it down like water, needs no mixing with anything. Any Scandanavian worthy of the name was highly insulted if you ever tried to dilute this drink of the Gods.

HOW TO MAKE BRANDY OR COGNAC

This old brandy and cognac recipe is preserved here from the early French immigrant records from Minnesota. At one time they made all of their own brandy and cognac. Today it is illegal to make brandy or cognac even for your own use, unless you have a government permit to do so.

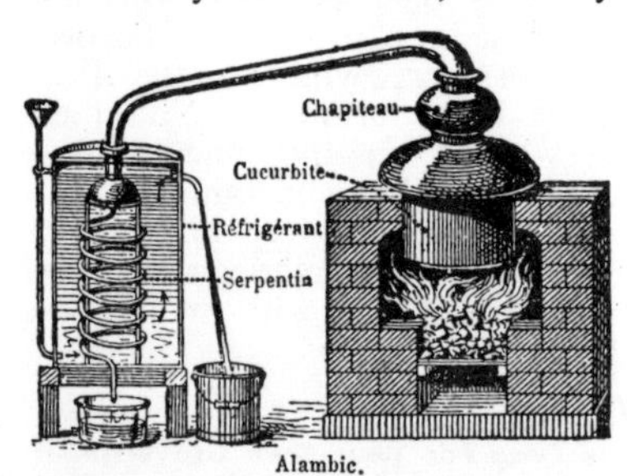

Still called "Alambic" in France and early Minnesota and used to make brandy and cognac.

Stills were made by simply buying a large soup kettle with a cover. Drilling a hole in the cover and soldering on copper tubing. The tubing was coiled and run down through a metal tank and out a hole in the bottom of the tank. The tubing was soldered well around the hole in the tank so that it would not leak. Cold water or ice was used to cool the coil.

A fire not hotter than absolutely necessary was used. The distilled fluid was kept away from fire at all times as it was highly inflammable and explosive.

All brandy and cognac was made by distilling wine. Wine of 16% alcohol content was used and put into the kettle. Just after it was fermented and not bottled the wine was heated until about one-third of the wine turned to steam and went out the tubing and turned back to a liquid in the cooled coils. Alcohol boils off at 170°, water and flavoring at 212° Fahrenheit. This gave brandy that made excellent drinking just plain the way it should be drunk. The brandy or cognac was about half alcohol and half wine derivatives. It was bottled immediately.

HISTORY OF GIN AND HOW TO MAKE AND BUY IT

It is illegal to make gin even for your own use in the United States of America unless you are licensed by the Federal Government to do so. This Belgian recipe is listed merely as a matter of record and is the authentic one brought over to Minnesota by early Belgian immigrants and made here for years by them. Gin originated in Belgium and its real name is genievre, not gin.

It is made as follows.

One measure of ground malted barley mixed with two measures of ground rye. In other words, a 1 to 2 ratio. Each 100 pounds of the ground malt and rye are mixed with 24 gallons of water brought to a very slow boil and boiled slowly for one hour and sometimes two hours. Stir well and add water so there is no burning or loss of water on the surface of the mash. Leave cool and strain out the liquids from the mash. Pour good water on the spent mash meal and wash out all liquids from it into the fermenting vessel. This is called "sparging." Use the spent meal for cattle or chicken feed. Add enough water so the specific gravity is 1.035. Checking with your saccharometer, adjust the sugar content so that the liquid will produce 16% alcohol. You actually will have around 31 to 33 gallons of liquid. Add a top fermenting yeast or wine yeast and a pound of crushed small blue grapes per 10 gallons of wort but remove the skins before adding so the skins do not color the wort red. The Beta grape, native to America, is almost identical to the grape that is grown in Belgium and used. Put the wort in closed containers with fermentation locks. Today, this means large plastic jugs and ferment until all fermentation stops. Then distill off the alcohol at 170 degrees F and flavoring and water at 212 degrees F so you have about 32 per cent distilled liquid or 80 proof liquor. Now put in 12 juniper berries per gallon in a cloth sack and leave them soak in the liquor for a week. Use no coriander or cardamom seed in real genievre. Then remove the bag of juniper berries. Most Europeans prefer the liquor just as it now is but some redistill it although I frown upon this. You cannot flavor genievre with juniper oil as it will not mix with alcohol and water mixtures.

The making of genievre spread to Holland and its discovery falsely credited by some writers to a Professor Franciscus Sylvius.

This is pure "hokum." In Holland genievre was called geneva, simply a Holland spelling of genievre. They also made a similar liquor but without the grapes added to the wort at Schiedam and called it Schiedam. English tourists brought genievre back to England in Queen Anne's time and English distillers began making genievre. They shortened the name to gin and produced a cheaper poor quality product that they called London Dry Gin.

London Dry Gin is made as follows.

The mash is made of 75% cornmeal, 15% malted barley meal, and 10% rye or potatoes, whichever is cheaper. The grapes are left out and this makes the resulting alcohol harsh, and hang-over forming. The wort is fermented off at 190 proof alcohol then flavored with juniper berries and coriander seed and cut with distilled water down to 80 or 90 proof. Some of it is colored a pale yellow with vegetable coloring. Cardamom seeds and even cassia bark and angelica root are used with the juniper berries and sometimes no juniper berries at all but artificial juniper flavoring as it mixes faster. This is exactly the same cheap method used by bootleggers to make gin in the prohibition days. English gin today, no matter how fancy the advertising, label or bottle, is still nothing but bootleg bathtub quality gin. Instead of just dumping the flavoring into the alcohol and water mix, some English gin makers simply put the flavoring in a pocket in the coil of the still and let the alcohol absorb some of the flavoring as it passes through the coil. This is called a "gin head". By using this method, the flavoring goes further and the gin is still worse. Many English gin makers label the gin that they ship into this country "Distilled London Dry Gin" or "Distilled Gin." Nothing could be a worse lie. All English gin is synthetic and none of it distilled from true gin ingredients but fabricated from raw alcohol water and flavoring.

Gin made in the United States is made of a mash consisting of 85% cornmeal, 12% barley malt and 3% rye. It is made exactly like English gin.

You can greatly improve the taste and aroma of both English and American gins by adding one ounce of dry sauterne white wine to a fifth, shaking it up and leaving it set for 24 hours.

HISTORY OF RUM AND HOW TO MAKE IT OR BUY IT

All rum is made from sugar cane derivatives or waste. Sugar cane is related to bamboo and originated in India. Seeds from sugar cane were brought to Arabia and to Europe during the third century. Shortly after the voyage of Columbus to America, sugar cane seeds were brought to St. Dominique in the West Indies.

Rum was first called rumbullion, a Devonshire dialect word meaning rumpus or wild party. The West Indies natives called it Kill Devil as it made them forget that they were slaves. The rum makers called rum, Barbados Waters, to give it a fancy name that they hoped would help sell it better than the word rum which was considered very vulgar. The French thought rum was a good cure for colds and called it "rhum" after the French word rhyrm, meaning a cold.

In 1740 Admiral Vernon of the British Navy issued a pint of rum per day per man and a half pint a day per boy in an effort to cure scurvy. It did not help the scurvy at all but it made it a lot easier to bear it. Admiral Vernon had most of his clothes made from a cloth called, at the time, Grogram and in later days sometimes grograin. Today it is used for the bands on men's hats. His men called him "old grog" because of his fondness for grogram cloth. Soon the daily ration of rum he issued became known as "grog" and rum gained still another name.

Rum is a liquor distilled from the fermentation of sugar cane juice, or juice scums, exhausted molasses, or blackstrap molasses. It is made mostly in the West Indies where it originated.

Here are the different kinds of rum.

JAMAICAN RUM

This rum is made from the scum and washings from the boiling of cane juice to make sugar, molasses and "dunder". Dunder is the residue left in the still from a previous distillation of rum.

Jamaican rum is not made stronger than about 80 proof. It is nearly white in color and colored with burnt carmel. Jamaican rum is made in two grades. One, a rum for drinking, the other, a rum for blending and making rums by mixing with alcohol and water.

DEMERARA RUM

This rum is made from molasses and 1 pint of sulphuric acid and one pound of ammonium sulphate per 100 gallons. Water is added until specific gravity is 1.065. The acid checks undesirable organisms in the fermenting liquid. The fermentation is very rapid being completed in 48 hours. Top fermenting yeast is used. The rum wine runs about 16% alcohol and is distilled out around 80 to 90 proof. It is a very pale light beige color almost white. It is colored all shades of brown from light browns to dark browns and even black. It is also frequently given added rum flavoring. The black rum is usually high in proof being run off at about 125 proof.

UNITED STATES RUM

Blackstrap molasses is exclusively used to make rums in the United States. Blackstrap molasses is simply mixed with water until the saccharometer shows it will produce 16% alcohol. It then is fermented in closed containers with fermentation locks. When fermentation has stopped, it is distilled at 190 American proof which has only a very slight rum flavor and is pure white. It then is cut with water to 80 to 90 proof and colored all different shades of brown with oak chips. Heavy body United States rums are distilled at 160 American proof and stored in oak barrels to darken them and are then cut to the desired proof with water.

CUBAN RUM

Made the same as United States rum and distilled at 190 proof then run through charcoal. It actually is just a pure alcohol very slightly rum flavored. It then is rum flavored and cut to the desired proof with water. For West Indies consumption, it is banana, orange, and pineapple flavored.

PUERTO RICO RUM

Made and flavored the same as Cuban rum.

NATAL SOUTH AFRICAN RUM

Made and flavored the same as Cuban rum.

AUSTRALIAN RUM

Made the same and flavored the same as Cuban rum.

GERMAN RUM

Made by flavoring a mixture of alcohol and water with high ester Jamaican rum.

BLACK RUM

Run off at around 125 proof. Made from sugar cane refuse. Artificially colored. Black Demara rums are made this way.

BARBADOS RUM

Made the same as Cuban rum.

MAKING CORDIALS

The distilling of alcohol from wines and mash was brought back to France from Palestine by the early crusaders. Until the crusaders brought back the knowledge of how to distill there was no distilling done in any part of Europe. The only liquors available were wines and beers with an alcohol content of not more than 16 percent usually much less than this averaging around 6 to 9 percent.

The making of cordials was invented a great many years later during the reign of Louis the XIV of France. He was born in 1638. His father was Louis XIII and Anne of Austria. He ruled from 1643 to 1715. When he was about fifty years old the head of his kitchen added sweetening, flavors, and perfume to alcohol and water making the first cordials. They were called "liqueur cordiale" and "potion cordiale". This was the beginning of cordial liquors. At that time many of the cordials were much better than they are today as they used a good deal of good perfume in making them. Perfumes today are considered too expensive to use in cordials.

It is illegal to make cordials even for your own use in the United States of America unless you are licensed by the government to do so and it is not easy to get a license. These cordial recipes are listed merely as a matter of record and are the ones brought in by the early French immigrants to Minnesota and made here by them for years.

Cordials such as Creme de Menthe, Curacao, Creme de Coca, Creme de Mocha were all very easily made. The only difficult thing about cordials was to pronounce their names. No cordial made in the world is naturally fermented or distilled. They are all just mixtures of pure alcohol sugar or syrup, flavoring and water. If they are a day old or a hundred years old the taste and flavor are the same. Here are the old recipes for the record of the more widely used ones. The alcohol was gotten from a grain, potatoe or wine mash as described for making gin. Sugar used to be used exclusively for lending the sweetness to cordials. Sugar however, has a bad habit of crystallizing out of the mixture and sticking the stoppers or corks in the bottles. Since the discovery of clear corn syrup in America this or invert sugar was used as the sweetening base for all good cordials. Recipes are for four-fifths of a quart. Vodka can be substituted for alcohol as it is nothing but alcohol and water.

CREME DE MENTHE

8 ounces of alcohol or 18 ounces of 80 to 90 proof vodka.
1 tablespoon oil of peppermint.
1 tablespoon green vegetable coloring.
1 cup of clear white corn syrup or invert sugar.

Balance good water.

If you desire white Creme de Menthe, simply leave out the green vegetable coloring.

CURACAO

8 ounces of alcohol or 20 ounces of 80 to 90 proof vodka.
1 tablespoon orange oil.
1 teaspoon orange vegetable coloring.
1 cup of clear white corn syrup or invert sugar.

Balance good water.

CREME DE MOCHA

14 ounces of alcohol or 20 ounces of 80 to 90 proof vodka.
3 heaping teaspoons of instant powdered coffee.
1 cup of clear white corn syrup or invert sugar.

Balance good water.

CREME DE COCA

8 ounces of alcohol or 20 ounces of 80 to 90 proof vodka.
3 heaping teaspoons of powdered chocolate. Mix it in well with the alcohol.
1 cup of clear white corn syrup or invert sugar.

Balance good water.

For white creme de coca use one level tablespoon of clear uncolored chocolate flavoring.

HOW TO MAKE NONALCOHOLIC FRUIT JUICES

At various seasons of the year you are apt to have a surplus of some fruit. Turning it into pure fruit juice for drinking gives you the best possible fruit juice at hardly any cost at all. You can use plums, cherries, currants, raspberries, blueberries, grapes, elderberries, crow berries, cranberries, salmon berries or any similar fruits.

Place the fruit in a large cooking pot and mash it up as much as possible. Put enough water into the pot to well cover the fruit. Simmer the fruit until it is soft enough to mash up well. Keep the fruit well covered with water all of the time. Stir the fruit frequently. The cooking time will vary, depending upon the fruit you are cooking, from 15 minutes to as much as an hour or more. When cooked, empty the pulp and juice into a food mill and run it through. Now strain the pulp through one layer of an old worn dish towel or piece of muslin. Force the juice through the cloth by picking up the ends of the cloth and twisting them to force the juice out of the pulp. Now for every 10 gallons of juice, add one fourth cup of Clairjus No. 3. Stir it in well. Leave the juice stand for 12 hours at as close to 60 degrees as you can. This product cleans and makes the juice clear or quite clear. Some boiled fruit juices just will not ever clear up perfectly. Now siphon off the juice into a large pan leaving as much sediment behind as possible. Heat the juice to 170 degrees. Add 4 grains of sodium metabisulphite per gallon and quickly bottle in jars or jugs that you have just sterilized in boiling water. Fill the jars right up to the top so no air can get into them. Put on sterilized covers. Leave cool and store in a dark place. To serve, add brown sugar to taste. Brown sugar does not change the flavor of the juice as white sugar does. This juice will give you a far better juice than you can buy at grocery stores. It will keep indefinitely and will not spoil or ferment in the jars.

HOW TO MAKE CIDER WITHOUT ALCOHOL

First you must extract the juice from the apples. Quickest method, of course, is with a hand-operated fruit press but most people do not have one. You can, however, extract the apple juice by simply running the apples through a meat grinder and put the pulp and juice into a large pot. Cover with plenty of water. Boil slowly for several hours or until the pulp is mush. Keep the water level up as apples burn very easily. Stir them frequently while they are cooking. Put the apple mush in an old dish cloth and tighten up the ends and squeeze out the liquid into another large pot or crock. For every 10 gallons of apple juice, add ½ ounce of Clairjus No. 3. Stir it in well. Leave the juice stand for 12 hours at as close to 65 degrees as you can. This produces, cleans and makes the juice clear or quite clear. Some apple juices that have been boiled are very hard to clear completely. This is called "polishing" the apple juice. Now siphon off the clear apple juice into a large pan. Be very careful not to get any of the sediment into the pan. Heat the juice to 170 degrees, then add 4 grains of sodium metabisulphite per gallon and bottle in jars or jugs that you have just sterilized in boiling water. Fill the jars or jugs full right up to the top. Juice, so prepared, will keep indefinitely and will not ferment or spoil in the jars or jugs.

WHAT THE PROOF OF ALCOHOLIC DRINKS REALLY MEANS

The early distillers wet gunpowder with the liquor that they made. When the liquor was at least 50% alcohol, the gunpowder would burn. If the liquor was less than 50% alcohol the gunpowder would not burn. The test was 100% proof that the liquor was half or more alcohol so 100 proof liquor came to mean that the liquor was 50% alcohol. 200 proof liquor is pure alcohol.

American liquors are fairly accurate as to the proof marked on their labels. Imported liquors of all kinds vary considerably from the proof marked on their labels. Usually running least in proof than the label reads.

HOW TO TELL IF YOU ARE GETTING LIQUOR NAMED ON THE LABEL OR BOOTLEG LIQUOR

People are prone to refer to the old prohibition days as the days of bootleg liquor. This is not altogether true. Today, there is nearly as much bootleg liquor sold as there was at any time during prohibition.

The tax on liquor has foolishly been made so high that it has recreated bootlegging on a huge scale. It still costs much less than a dollar a gallon to produce whiskey made from alcohol, water and flavoring. In Mexico, you can buy 190 proof alcohol for 85c a quart tourist price and 25c a quart wholesale. Even the cheapest whiskey today sells for over $4.00 a quart, not a fifth but a quart, bringing a minimum of $16.00 per gallon. In a bar even poor whiskey brings $45.00 a gallon by the drink.

If the tax on whiskey was lowered, obviously the amount of tax collected would be much higher as bootlegging would be stopped and, too, people could afford to drink more.

Bootlegging today is done in a number of different ways. Here is just one of the many ways. The federal tax stamp is steamed off from a bottle of good whiskey. The neck of the bottle is soaked in warm water until the plastic sleeve swells. The plastic sleeve seal is then removed. Three-fourths of the good whiskey is poured out and the bottle filled with bootleg whiskey made from alcohol, water and flavoring. The plastic sleeve seal is placed on the neck of the bottle and allowed to shrink and dry back in place. The federal tax stamp is stuck over the plastic sleeve label and stopper making the bottle appear exactly the same as before the bootleg whiskey was added to it. The good whiskey is cut three-to-one with bootleg whiskey and sold to illegal liquor outlets for use in mixed drinks, etc.

There is one easy way however, to tell if whiskey has been cut. Just shake the bottle. If the whiskey in the neck of the bottle runs quickly down into the bottle, the bottle has not been tampered with. If the liquor runs back down in the bottle slowly and tends to hang to the inside glass of the neck of the bottle, chances are it has been tampered with.

HOW TO AVOID ALCOHOLISM AND STILL DRINK

Some people are continually bothered by the fear that they will become alcoholics. To avoid any chance of becoming an alcoholic and still drink do as follows:

1. Never drink any alcoholic beverage with over 12% alcoholic content. This means drinking unfortified wine or beer or whiskey, gin and brandy, etc., diluted down to 12% or less.
2. Always drink after you have eaten food, never on an empty stomach.
3. Drink very slowly. The more slowly the better.

Some would-be authorities on drinking say that if you drink such things as olive oil, mineral oil, milk, cream, etc., before drinking that the alcohol in the liquor you drink will have little effect on you because of the oils and fats. Nothing could be further from the truth. Ordinary foods such as bread, meat and potatoes slow down the absorption of alcohol in your systems but not fats and oils. Drinking alcoholic beverages with a lot of oil or fat in your stomach however can be extremely dangerous. It can give you a permanently bad stomach.

SHANDY

A Shandy is the universal cooling drink served in Africa. It is a great favorite of white hunters as well as townspeople. It does not sound like much of a drink but has a clean, crisp, refreshing taste and is an honest thirst quencher that you can drink anytime of the day. You have to try this drink to appreciate it.

Here is the original recipe.

Use a tall lemonade type glass. Fill it half full of lemonade or Seven Up. Fill the other half with beer not less than 6% alcohol content and preferably 12% alcohol content such as the so-called "malt liquors", Stite, etc. which are simply strong beers. Do not stir and serve at once.

The Shandy was invented by W. D. M. Bell, a Scotchman born near Edinburgh, Scotland in 1880. He went down to Africa to hunt elephants for ivory when he was seventeen years old. He heard of the Alaskan gold rush while down in Africa and immediately went to the Yukon. When the Boer war started he joined some Canadian volunteers and fought in South Africa. Bell stayed in Africa until the beginning of World War I. He returned to England, became a pilot and was sent back to Africa to fly under General Smuts. After the war he remained in Africa until 1932.

Bell like most everyone in his right mind found English beers and Ales which were widely exported to Africa to be much too heavy and actually increase your thirst instead of to quench it. After a particularly bad day after drinking Bass Ale he tried mixing it half and half with lemonade and the Shandy was born. He named the drink Shandy after a camp cook he had at the time. When available he used carbonated lemon squashes instead of lemonade in the drink.

Bell was quite a hunter and killed around a thousand elephants as a professional ivory hunter. For the most part he used only a small 6mm cartridge with a steel jacketed bullet and used brain shots. This is just about the same as shooting them with a .243 Winchester. As might be well imagined he was nearly killed on numerous occasions and it got to the point no one would hunt with him.

ORIGINAL HIGHBALL

The highball originated in early St. Louis, Missouri at a saloon owned by a man named John P. Slaughtery. He catered to the railroad trade a great deal. The railroad engineers liked to stop in for a couple of drinks before going to work. They did not want to drink straight drinks as the railroad companies frowned on engineers who showed any marked signs of drunkenness on duty. If you could chin yourself on a man's breath this did not matter just so long as he did not look drunk. The engineers had an ounce of bourbon put into a tall glass and the glass filled with "ditch" or water. In those days a glass was called a ball by bartenders so the drink was called a highball. Engineers took to the name and made it a part of their railroad language. It still is a mighty fine practical drink, gets the alcohol content down around 12% where it is not too effective.

DOC'S PRESCRIPTION

Doc Holiday will be long remembered for what he said to a man he caught beating up a girl just before he killed him in a gunfight. "The worst thing that I can call you is that you are a human. Horses, dogs, even pigs treat each other better than humans treat each other."

This saying may seem strange and stupid but it has a very deep meaning. When you see how, at times, even the human leaders of nations treat other nations and people, this statement has a lot of truth in it. Doc was right. It is hard at times to call someone something worse than a human.

This is a drink invented by Doc Holiday, a dentist, who became a great admirer of Wyatt Earp. Doc had tuberculosis and strongly believed that the right alcoholic drink would cure him. He finally found that the following drink seemed to help him a little and drank about a fifth of it a day.

1 ounce of applejack.

1 ounce of bourbon.

Mix together well.

There was no orange peel or ice ever used in the drink. He finally succumbed to tuberculosis.

WARD 8

Invented in 1903 in Boston by Patrick Fogarty, a professional bartender. He named it after Ward 8 where politics were particularly corrupt and survival of the fittist was the only law. Mayor Curley was a great drinker of Ward 8.

The original drink was made as follows.
Fill a shaker with cracked ice.
Add 2 ounces of burbon.
½ ounce of orange juice.
½ ounce of lemon juice.
½ level teaspoon of grenadine syrup.
Shake well and strain into a whiskey sour glass.

HOW TO MAKE AN AUTHENTIC MINT JULEP

The inventor of the mint julep was Albert Sidney Johnston, a Confederate general. He was not much of a drinker himself, but served this now famous drink in order to show friends that "mountain dew" or local whiskey could be made quite palatable. He took the name Julep from the ancient Persian word julep which means a medicine to be taken by the mouth made of water and plant gum or crushed leaves.

Here is the original recipe and it has never been equaled. Originally it could only be made in the winter when ice was occasionally available.

Select a good sized catnip leaf, hold it on the inside of a water glass and bruise it severely with a spoon. Fill the glass with cracked ice, now pour whiskey into the glass until it is within half an inch of the top. Take a glass of good water and add two level teaspoons of sugar to it. Dissolve well. Now fill the glass with ice and whiskey to the top with the sugar water. Take three good sprigs of catnip with two or three leaves on each and poke well down into the ice. Do not stir. Sip slowly, do not drink with a straw.

Catnip is a perennial herb weed native to Europe and Asia. It was widely planted here originally for curing stomach disorders. It went wild and is found all over the South, Middle West and East.

The glasses were not frosted as there was a lack of refrigeration and no spring was cold enough to frost a glass. This is indeed a wonderful drink.

A genuine mint julep does not require lime water for the ice, or water, use catnip leaves instead of mint, does not require Bourbon Whiskey and does not require the glass being frosted or made of metal. You can make a much better julep than is served with mint leaves by simply using a half ounce of Creme de Menthe instead of mint leaves.

Whether you serve beer or a tall drink, it is very nice to serve them in a frosted glass. In order to frost glasses, place them in the freezer compartment of your refrigerator for an hour before using them. When you remove them, they will quickly frost themselves as they enter the room temperature air.

SAZERAC

Peychaud made a drink called the Sazerac. The brandy used was blended in France by Mssrs. Sazerac de Forge et fils located in Limoges, France. This brandy or cognac was imported by a John B. Schiller. In 1859 he opened the Sazerac Coffee House at 13 Exchange Alley. He served Mr. A. A. Peychaud's cognac Sazerac cocktail among other drinks. His accountant, Mr. Thomas H. Hardy took over the business in 1870 and changed the name to "Sazerac House". To save money, Mr. Hardy substituted cheap American whiskey for cognac in the Sazerac drinks and the bars in New Orleans are still doing the same thing today. Unless you demand it, you will be getting nothing but American whiskey in your Sazerac in any bar in New Orleans.

Peychaud's Sazerac is made is follows:

Put 1½ ounces of brandy in a glass. Add three drops of anise flavoring. Add ¼ teaspoon of granulated sugar mixed in a level tablespoon of water. Add eight drops of bitters as made by Peychaud.

No absinthe, no Pernod, no ice, no lemon were ever used in this drink. Pernod is just an anise flavored liquor and absinthe a liquor made from the bitter absinthe plant and anise flavored to take away the very disagreeable bad acid taste. Anise flavoring is far superior to either absinthe or Pernod for anise flavoring anything and this Peychaud, as a pharmacist, knew very well.

There were at one time two bars in New Orleans called Sazerac. One was on the right-hand side of Royal Street. The bar is now a barber shop. The word Sazerac is still inlaid in white tile on the sidwalk. Another Sazerac bar was located in the 400 block on Carondelet.

Today, I know of no bar in New Orleans or any place else that serves a true Sazerac.

ORIGINAL COCKTAIL

Mr. Antoine Amedee Peychaud was born in France. He migrated to Santa Domingo and set up a drug store. He was very familiar with the bitters made in the area but disliked them very much. He created a bitters of his own made from alcohol, water, cherry and anise flavoring that he called Peychaud's Bitters. When the Africans rose and drove out the Europeans, he went to Louisiana which at the time was ruled by Spain. He started a drug store called Pharmacie Peychaud on 437 Royal Street. The store is now an antique shop.

Peychaud was a Mason, W. M. of Concorde Blue Lodge, Grand Orator of the Grand Lodge, High Priest of the Royal Arch. His Masonic friends as well as waterfront people liked to use his drug store as a rendezvous point. He served them a drink made from Sazerac cognac. He used a double-ended egg holding cup as the jigger, called in French a coquetier, pronounced Ko-K-Tay. English speaking friends pronounced this "cocktail" and the cocktail was first created. The Sazerac cognac drink became known as a Sazerac.

While in Santo Domingo, Peychaud quickly learned to make the bitters used in some of the drinks served in Santo Domingo. Bitters are not at all difficult to make. Bitters are just something bitter used to add to drinks. Tannic acid is a common bitters base. They can easily be made from thousands of ordinary leaves, roots, stems and barks. Actually, anything bitter that is safe for human consumption, will do. In many cases, adding bitters to a drink greatly hurts the drink. Their use is very limited and they must be used with great care.

The bitters used in Santo Domingo originated at the Orinoco River town of Angostura, Venezuela. The town was renamed Ciudad Bolivar in 1864. It was made as a Voo-doo potion by the natives and used to help stomach disorders and cure scurvy. Similarly coca-cola was first made to cure headaches. An ex-Russian army surgeon named J. G. B. Siegert found it took some of the sweetness out of over sweet alcoholic drinks and its use for such purpose became widely spread. In this area, the bitter flavor of the root of a gentian plant is used to give the bitter flavor. Gentian plants are common in North and Central America. They are known more for their pretty flowers, usually blue in color, rather than their roots. The root of the yellow gentian found in Central America and nearby islands is used to make the bitters from these areas as it is easily come by. At one time the bark from the South American tree, Cusparia Angostura, of the rue family was used to make bitters. It works very well, as good as any material for bitters, but is scarce and today little used. The stems of dandelions, tea leaves, willow and oak bark and acorns all make wonderful bitters. I myself, prefer bitters made from dandelion stems to all others.

To make Central American bitters, proceed as follows:

Put a fourth of a pound of yellow gentian root in a pot and cover it with a pint of water. Boil it for two hours. Keep up the level of the water. Add one half level teaspoon of ground cloves, a half level teaspoon of ground cinnamon, a half level teaspoon of ground nutmeg. Strain the liquid and add to the liquid one level teaspoon of orange flavoring, one half level teaspoon of orange vegetable coloring, 1/16 level teaspoon of cayenne pepper or 6 drops of tobasco sauce. Add a pint of 90 or 100 proof vodka or a pint of half water and half alcohol. Stir well and your bitters are ready to use.

The English and the Germans make bitters by using hops instead of yellow gentian root. Makes a fabulous bitters.

Peychaud did not like Central American bitters at all and I certainly agree with him. He could not understand why anyone used them. He made his own bitters as follows:

4 level teaspoons of cherry flavoring.

4 level teaspoons of anise flavoring.

½ cup of vodka or ½ cup of alcohol and water, mixed half water and half alcohol.

Peychaud was a man who liked to be different so he served his drinks in egg cups called coquetier. I have three of the original cups that he used.

The first cocktail and the best ever made by Peychaud was as follows:

1½ ounces of brandy.

¼ teaspoon of sugar dissolved in one ounce of water.

4 drops of bitters flavoring made by Peychaud.

BLOODY MARY

Invented in 1929 by George Jessel multimillionaire show business figure in Hollywood, California.

After an all night party, at daybreak George Jessel thought it was time to start drinking something that would help settle a squeezy stomach. He concocted a drink made as follows:

Use a standard water glass.

1½ ounces of gin, not vodka.

2 level teaspoons of lemon juice not the juice of half a lemon.

1 level teaspoon of Lea and Perrine's Worchestershire Sauce.

1/8 level teaspoon of salt.

1/16 teaspoon of black ground pepper.

1 ice cube, no more.

Fill the glass to the top with tomato juice.

A girl named Mary Geraghty was at the party and had the first of the new drinks so the drink was called Bloody Mary.

RAMOS GIN FIZZ

The Ramos brothers ran a well-known bar in New Orleans before prohibition. They had eight African Americans in their bar who did nothing but shake drinks. On some drinks that required a lot of shaking, each African would shake the drinks until his arms were tired then hand it to the next one until all eight of the men had given the drink a real shaking.

The Ramos brothers invented the Ramos Gin Fizz.

Have all of the ingredients cold.

1 ounce of gin.

2 level teaspoons of powdered sugar.

White of one fresh egg.

2 ounces of coffee cream or whole milk.

4 drops of orange flavoring.

½ ounce of lemon juice.

½ ounce of lime juice.

Use a cold shaker filled with large ice cubes and shake well for about a minute. Strain and serve in a suitable glass.

Where the Ramos Gin Fizz was invented in downtown New Orleans. The Ramos Gin Fizz was not invented in the Roosevelt Hotel as is sometimes falsely stated.

There is no orange flower water used in this drink or no vanilla. If you put shaved or cracked ice in the shaker you simply dilute the drink too much, something the Ramos Gin Fizz will not stand. Orange flower water is simply water, orange flavored. You never know how much flavoring is in orange flower water. You must use the orange flavoring undiluted or this drink tastes like nothing at all.

THE AUTHENTIC MARTINI DRINK

The martini drink has become America's most popular hard liquor drink for two simple reasons.

1. It gives you more raw alcohol for your money than any other drink and hence more of an alcohol jolt.

2. Americans want an escape from reality and use Martinis as an anesthetic not actually as a drink.

The way Martini drinks are made in America they are about the poorest excuse for an alcoholic drink that you could possibly find, actually no better than drinking Sterno canned heat strained through bread, the national drink of the bum jungles.

Everytime you pick up a magazine some author makes up the name of an American man and says he invented the martini drink. They carefully fail to include any details so you cannot trace the facts at all. Actually they not only do not know the name of the man who invented the martini drink but do not know how to make an authentic martini.

One writer took the name Martiney and said that a man with this name invented the martini and that the first martinis were called Martineys. This is strictly a lie.

The martini drink is strictly German and was invented by J. P. Schwarzendorf, a German music composer born in 1741 and who died in 1816. He composed the operas Lover of Fifteen Years and Pleasures of Love. His nickname was "Martini." He invented two drinks which his friends promptly named after his nickname. The first was called "Martini" and here is the correct and original recipe. It is far superior to the slop called and served as Martinis in American bars and homes today.

Take two ounces of Genievre. Genievre is the original gin first invented in Belgium. It is flavored with the berries from a small bush called the Geneurier or sandy juniper and wild grapes. English and American made gins are very poor copies of the original Genievre but must be used as the original Genievre is not imported into North America although still widely drunk in Europe. Add one ounce of dry white wine such as Rhine wine or Chablis. One sixteenth level teaspoon of ground cinnamon. Stir well and serve as cold as possible. You will note that there is no Vermouth, no olives in the genuine Martini. Vermouth is nothing but a cheap spice flavored white wine and was originally made in order to get rid of wine too poor to sell on its own. The idea of using Vermouth in Martinis was the sole idea of unscrupulous importers of Vermouth who simply wanted to promote its sale and are the kind of people who will do anything to make money. The idea of putting an olive in a Martini was the idea of Robert Agneau, French New York bartender who put in the olive to try to conceal the raw alcohol taste of Martinis served in the United States with the salt in an olive. It helps very little. An American martini is still just a drink for alcoholics who want a quick alcohol jolt regardless of taste.

Schwarzendorf invented another drink which he named the Martini Verboten. This is one of the world's great alcohol drinks but never gained any popularity. It was made for the habitual drinker and alcoholic, Schwarzendorf had many friends in this class. This drink tends to calm down a heavy drinker, to get away from the over dry after drinking mouth of a heavy drinker and it prevents liver damage to the alcoholic as well as nerve damage such as delirium tremens. Here is the original formula. Two ounces of Genievre, or gin. One ounce of apple cider vinegar. Stir well and serve as cold as possible.

The martini found its way to America by isolated music lovers and became popular in the United States over a period of years.

You can verify these facts in the Nouveau Petit Larousse, French Dictionary.

DAIQUIRI

This drink was invented by Adolf L. Zimmerman. He was in Santiago de Cuba in 1898 working on the construction of a sugar refinery. Here is the original recipe.

1½ ounces of light rum.

1 level teaspoon of sugar.

1 ounce of lime juice.

Mix together well and serve. There was no ice in the Daiquiri as none was available in this area at this early date.

HURRICANE

Pat O'Brien from Alabama and Charles Cantrell from the Carolinas own Pat O'Brien's bar in New Orleans. Pat O'Brien's consists of a room with a

Entrance to Pat O'Brien's bar in the French Quarter of New Orleans where the Hurricane drink was invented.

large standard drinking bar for regular drinking, one room with two pianos with two girls playing the pianos and tables and chairs for group singing and drinking. There is a patio in the rear for quiet drinking.

Patio of Pat O'Brien's bar in New Orleans. Note fountain in the rear.

Famous Door Bar on Bourbon Street in the French Quarter of New Orleans. A well known bar that features Dixie Land music.

In the group singing and drinking room, it is the only drinking room in the world where one minute everyone may be singing some ribald song so ribald that it would not even be tolerated in the whore houses of Hong Kong and the next minute Silent Night.

Charles Cantrell invented the Hurricane drink and it is popular at Pat O'Brien's. It is served in a large hurricane lamp glass, a good 12 inches tall.

The drink is made as follows:

4 ounces of light rum.

2 ounces of lemon juice.

2 ounces of Red Passion Cocktail mix.

Fill up the rest of the glass with crushed ice and that is it.

The Red Passion Cocktail mix is a non-alcoholic mix consisting of the following. Sugar, dextrose, water, fruit juices, pulp, true and artifical flavor, phosphoric acid and tartaris acid, vegetable gums, artificial color 1/10 of 1% of Benzoate of Soda. It has nothing to do with Passion fruit or for that matter very little of any fruit at all.

The glass used to serve the Hurricane drink.

Hawaiian Punch is available at grocery stores and contains real fruit juices and used instead of the Red Passion Cocktail mix, in my opinion, makes a far, far better Hurricane but, of course, costs a little more.

Some of the alcoholics who visit Pat O'Brien's can down seven to eight hurricanes in any evening if they are in the middle of their alcoholic career. If they are at the tail end of alcoholism, two will put them in an alcoholic foggy stupor.

It is quite a sight to see some sophisticated gal who does not know that a hurricane contains 4 ounces of rum come into the bar hanging pretentiously on her boy friend's arm and smartly toss down a hurricane like a cocktail. The next minute she has a hard time even seeing her boy friend's arm say nothing about being able to hold on to it and looks about as sophisticated as an Australian bush woman.

The Hurricane drink costs $2.35 including the glass in the regular drinking bar and $2.50 including the glass in the group singing and drinking bar.

MARGARITA

Invented by Red Hinton, a bartender in an early Virginia City bar. He named the drink after Margarita Mendes, his Mexican girl friend. She hit a man over the head with a whiskey bottle. His friend, Robert Arthur, got excited and shot off his revolver to scare her away. He accidently hit her in the top of the head and killed her. He was freed as it was decided that if he had wanted to kill her, he would have shot her through her easiest to hit widest area, which happened to be her chest.

Here is the recipe for the original drink.

Wet the rim of a glass with the juice of a lemon. Place the rim of the glass in a bowl containing salt so that the salt covers the rim of the glass heavily. Put one ounce of tequila in a shaker or bowl.

½ ounce of lime juice.

½ ounce of orange juice.

Mix well and pour into the glass with the salt on its lip.

There is no Triple Sec or ice used to make this drink. There was no Triple Sec or ice in Virginia City when this drink was invented. Triple Sec is simply an oil of orange rind flavored white liquor.

Helpful Hints

HOW TO MAKE FRENCH SOAP

We always have the money to buy good soap in this country and women folk look down on such menial tasks as making soap these days. An H bomb strike in this country would change the whole picture. If you had soap after a few bombs dropped you would have to make it yourself or go without.

The early French fur traders and trappers were the best soap makers because they brought with them the art of extracting perfume to scent soap.

Soap can be made from any grease such as deer fat, beef suet, lard, bear fat, etc.

For this example we will describe soap making using lard as the grease.

Take 10 pounds of lard. If you desire to perfume the lard with flowers spread the lard about one inch thick on wooden boards. Place the boards in a building or sheltered outside spot. Take the blossoms of any strong smelling flowers and stick them into the lard as close together as possible. Do not cover them with the lard just stick them well into the lard. Leave the flower blossoms in the lard for 24 hours, then remove the blossoms. The lard will have extracted most of the perfume from the blossoms. Repeat if you desire a stronger perfume odor. This is the same method used to make perfume in France. In perfume making the lard is distilled to extract the perfume.

If you desire a pine odor to your soap, boil pine needles slightly in soft water and use the water in place of regular soft water as described further on.

Now take the 10 pounds of lard and place it in a kettle with two quarts of soft water or two quarts of pine water. Bring to a boil. Then remove the kettle and set it aside to cool for 10 to 12 hours or over night.

Any dirt or meat particles will settle out and sink to the bottom of the kettle. Now take 4 tablespoons of sugar, 2 tablespoons of salt, 6 tablespoons of powdered borax, ½ cup of ammonia, and mix well into 1 cup of soft water or pine water.

Go outdoors and mix 2 quarts of cold soft water or pine water into 2 cans of Lewis Lye in a granite dish. Stir well. Be very sure you use cold water to mix into the lye. If you use hot water the lye will fume up and explode causing bad burns or blindness. The lye will cause the water to become hot. Leave the lye and water mixture cool down to lukewarm.

Now take the sugar, salt, borax and ammonia mixture and pour it into the cool lye and water mixture. Then add the cool lard. Stir well with a wooden paddle and use a granite pan or kettle. Stir until honey colored. Cut the soap into squares before it becomes completely hard. If you desire the soap in other shapes place a piece of the soap in two piece wooden or metal molds and squeeze to the desired shapes.

This soap is very good for a face, hand, and body soap as well as for washing dishes and clothes.

HOW TO KEEP HEALTHY IN THE WILDERNESS

It is a very serious matter to be taken sick in the wilderness or on a camping, hunting or fishing trip as medical aid is usually not available.

Acidosis or an acid body condition is the big danger. Acidosis is the primary cause of most of mankind's poor health. Indigestion, constipation, high blood pressure are just a few of the serious conditions acidosis can produce rapidly.

The cause of acidosis is nearly entirely an unbalanced diet. To avoid acidosis for example, eat a reasonable amount of fruits, or vegetables, during the same day you eat meat, fish and bread. The tastes of food does not tell its reaction on your body. Fruit juices and fruit which are sour are not acid at all but alkalin. Bread which has a neutral taste is one of the worst and most common causes of acidosis. Try to come as close as you can to a balanced diet every day and you will be in no danger of most serious illnesses.

Here is a brief list of acid and alkalin food:

ACID FOODS

Bread, Corn, Crackers, Cranberries, Eggs, Fish, Beef, Rice, Chicken, Pheasant, Partridge, Quail, Pork, Plums, Veal, Duck, Venison, Elk, Moose, Bear, Rabbit, Squirrel, Clams, Oysters, Oatmeal, Peanuts, Prunes.

ALKALINE FOODS

Almonds, Grapes, Acorns, Apples, Asparagus, Black Walnuts, Yellow water lily root, Bananas, Beans, dried; Beans, Lima; Cabbage, Pine seeds, Carrots, Cantaloupe, Cauliflower, Wild Celery, Celery, Currants, Lemons, Blueberries, Strawberries, Radishes, Raisins, Apricots, Turnips, Lettuce, Algae from a pond, lake, river or slough; Cow Milk, Oranges, Peaches, Peas, Potatoes.

NEVER DRINK COFFEE RIGHT AFTER EATING PEPPERED FRIED EGGS OR SOFT BOILED EGGS

If you drink coffee after eating fried or soft boiled eggs with pepper on them the coffee will taste terrible. To avoid this drink a little water after you have eaten peppered eggs, then drink your coffee and you will enjoy your coffee.

Never drink water just after eating pickled or fried fish. If you do your mouth will taste like a live fish is swimming around in it. Eat some other food after eating fish, then drink water if you are thirsty.

RED PEPPER GOOD FOR RADIATION AND UPSET STOMACHS

Red pepper which is made up of ground up hot red peppers was discovered by the Indians. Red peppers originated in the Americas. Mexican and southern Indian food has always been highly seasoned with red pepper. Most people who were not raised in the southwest do not like food highly seasoned with red pepper. Many believe that eating foods with red pepper is bad in general for your health. This is not true. Our modern day scientists now have proven that people who eat food seasoned with hot pepper resist atomic radiation much better than people who do not eat it. In fact people who use considerable hot red pepper in their foods are almost immune to atomic radiation except in a severe form.

The eating of hot red pepper on foods has also been found to help people with nervous upset stomachs.

APPLES AS A TRANQUILIZER

The apple is indeed a miracle fruit. Every seed in every apple if planted will produce an entirely different apple unlike any apple that has ever before been produced. The apple holds the secret to mutations and contains ingredients that our finest scientists cannot find, duplicate, or even make a good guess as to what they are. The only way that you can reproduce apples of the same kind is by grafting.

The saying that an apple a day keeps the doctor away is no joke, it is absolutely true.

Michigan State University in 1962 released the following information that has been known for over 2,000 years.

Thirteen hundred and eighty one students for a period of three years ate an apple a day for two quarters of each year. Complete records of the visits of these thirteen hundred and eighty students to the University health service doctors were kept and their visits carefully compared to those of the over 17,000 other students attending Michigan State University. The results showed beyond any doubt that the students who ate apples daily had far less of the two illnesses that students most frequently have which are colds and upper respiratory diseases and nervous disorders — such as nervous tension conditions. For all other diseases the students who ate apples regularly had far better health records.

Tests in Belgian and German Universities have shown the same results.

In Ancient times these same things are found to be true of apples. In Scandinavia apples were used to cure all nervous disorders. In the Mediterranean countries apples were used for curing nervous disorders as well as for improving a person's general health. Apple cider was also used for the same purposes and with good results. Apple vinegar was used in England and Europe as a tranquilizer for nervous disorders and for alcoholics.

For a month's time eat an apple a day and you can throw away those sleeping pills. Eat them skin and all — do not peel them. Apple cider and apple vinegar is also very good. A cup of apple cider a day brings good results or three tablespoons of apple vinegar per day.

INDIAN METHOD OF REMOVING HAIR FROM RABBIT, AND SQUIRREL CARCASSES

In skinning rabbits and squirrels it is impossible to keep loose hair from getting onto the meat. This hair is very difficult to remove from the meat and if left on gives the meat a strong gamey flavor. You can leave the meat dry to a glaze then brush off the hair with a stiff vegetable brush. The best method however to remove hair from rabbit and squirrel carcasses is as follows:

Take a candle or an alcohol lamp if you have one. Run the flame over the hair just as you would singe a duck or chicken. The hair will look like it is still there on the meat as the flame will of course only char it. Then wash the carcass in water and the charred hair will quickly wash right off.

HOW TO EASILY TELL IF EGGS ARE REALLY FRESH

Fill a large pot full of water. Put an egg into the water. If it sinks to the bottom and lays on its side it is fresh. If it floats or rests upright on the bottom it is not a fresh egg. It will surprise you to find that many of the premium high priced eggs you buy at grocery stores are not at all fresh.

HOW TO KEEP PANCAKES, MEAT OR EGGS WARM IN CAMP OR AT HOME

Put a small pot full of water onto the fire and get it boiling. Cover the top of the pot with a plate right side up. Put your pancakes, meat, or eggs on the plate. Then place a plate upside down over them. This will keep the meat or eggs, or pancakes well warmed until served.

HOW TO KEEP EGGS FROM STICKING IN A STAINLESS STEEL COPPER BOTTOMED FRYING PAN

When frying eggs in a stainless steel, copper bottomed frying pan the eggs tend to stick to the pan even when the pan is properly greased. This makes the eggs difficult to remove from the pan or to turn over.

To avoid this just before trying to remove the fried eggs from the pan or just before you try to turn over the eggs remove the pan from the burner and leave it set for several minutes on a dead burner or on a stove pad. Then remove the eggs from the pan or turn them over whichever you desire. You will find that when the eggs rest in the pan for several minutes away from heat that they will not stick to the pan.

HOW TO KEEP BACON FROM MOLDING

Bacon is a must item for camp and trail food. It provides some strength giving meat but most important it provides you smoke flavored grease to cook wild game flesh, pancakes and other food items in.

Bacon regardless of the weather molds very easily. With the mold it becomes rancid and loses its good flavor entirely. To prevent bacon from molding take a clean cloth and wash it with vinegar. This will not only prevent it from molding but makes it retain its good fresh taste.

HOW TO KEEP SPAGHETTI AND MACARONI FROM BOILING OVER WHILE COOKING

Just put a tablespoon of beef suet, butter, or margarine into the water. In the case of the beef suet hold the spoon over heat a few minutes until it is melted.

HOW TO PREVENT TOXIC ACTION OF BARBECUED FOODS

When you barbecue foods over a fire of charcoal briquets the charcoal briquets deposit tars on the food. Many people who eat such barbecued foods feel nauseated or sick to their stomachs. In Russia doctors now believe that these tars deposited on the food by barbecuing is a direct cause of cancer.

To avoid charcoal tars getting upon food as you barbecue it take a sheet of aluminum foil and spread it over the burning charcoal. The aluminum foil allows the heat to come through but keeps most of the charcoal tars from getting on the food. Does not spoil the flavor of the barbecued food in fact makes it taste much better.

HOW TO MELT SOLID CHOCOLATE

Grease the pot you use to melt it in with butter. Melt carefully over medium heat.

HOW TO PEEL PEARS AND PEACHES QUICKLY

Use boiling water to scald either pears or peaches. The skins will then slip off easily.

HOW TO KEEP CHEESE FRESH

Whether you store cheese in or out of your refrigerator to keep it fresh, cover it with a cloth moistened with vinegar.

PRESERVING THE VITAMINS IN MILK

Keep milk out of all sunlight. Sunlight quickly destroys and deteriorates milk vitamins.

PREVENTING THE TARNISHING OF SILVERWARE

Place several lumps of alum in the drawers, boxes, or bags that you have the silverware stored in.

HOW TO MAKE POPCORN POP AS LARGE AS POSSIBLE

Keep the popcorn stored in your refrigerator or as cold a place as possible. Keep the popcorn in an open not closed container. The popcorn will absorb some moisture in the refrigerator which of course will turn into steam when you heat the corn causing it to burst as large and fluffy as possible. Popcorn that has become dried out and will not pop can be put in a refrigerator and will pop well after being kept in the refrigerator for several weeks.

GETTING RID OF ANTS WITH LEMON

Take slices of a fresh lemon rind and all and place them where ants are found or where they travel. The ants will leave the area and stay away.

NORWEGIAN METHOD OF GETTING RID OF RATS

If rats get into your home, cabin, or boat they simply must be destroyed quickly. If left unchecked they will actually devour your food faster than you can provide it. The Norwegian, or brown rat that we have in North America is supposed to have originated in Norway. The Norwegian people in Norway are always plagued with both brown Norwegian rats and black rats. They come in on the many ships that land there. Rats are very difficult to get rid of. The Norwegians discovered centuries ago a simple, quick way to get rid of rats that has never been equaled. They brought this unique method to Minnesota with them. It never fails and is very easy to do. Simply take fresh white bread. Sprinkle it medium lightly with lye on one side. The Standard Lewis Lye that you get in grocery stores will do very well. Pour syrup over the lye and spread the syrup evenly on the bread with a wood stick. Place the bread in the runways of the rats, being very careful to cover it so that children or dogs or cats will not be able to get at it. You will have no rats on your premises within three days. If more move in simply repeat.

PICKING UP BROKEN GLASS IN THE KITCHEN

No matter how careful you may be occasionally a glass or cup will get broken. Sweep up the large pieces with a broom and put them into an empty tin can and dispose of them. The small pieces are very difficult to pick up without getting them into the fingers. Take a large gob of absorbent cotton and wet it. This will readily pick up all the small pieces of glass with no danger of the pieces going into your fingers.

HOW TO MAKE COLORFUL FIREPLACE FLAMES

Buy a little copper sulphate at your drug store. Sprinkle it on your fire in the fireplace and you will have beautiful colorful flames. Keep the copper sulphate away from children as taken internally it is poisonous.

EFFECT ON KEEPING CIGARETTES, CIGARS AND PIPE TOBACCO IN A REFRIGERATOR

Keeping cigarettes, cigars, or pipe tobacco in a refrigerator cools the tobacco and keeps it from losing moisture. In some cases it adds moisture to the tobacco. When you smoke such refrigerator cooled tobacco the smoke is entirely different. Because the tobacco is cool and full of moisture it burns more slowly and steam travels with the smoke into your mouth and lungs. The steam, of course, precipitates some of the tars in the smoke. The tars collect on the tobacco.

My friend, famous Dr. Banner from the Mayo Clinic at Rochester, Minnesota, always keeps his cigars well refrigerated.

INDIAN METHOD OF QUITTING SMOKING

Today people have become very conscious of smoking or quitting smoking with all of the talk about cancer being caused by smoking.

Tobacco of course is strictly American. The Indians were the first to cultivate tobacco and the first to smoke tobacco. The European settlers who came to this continent gradually learned to smoke from the Indians. In the early pioneer days most everyone who smoked grew their own tobacco. If you had a good tobacco crop you had enough tobacco for the year. If you did not you went without tobacco. Buying tobacco in many areas was impossible and in other areas beyond the pocket books of the early settlers.

The Indians had much the same problem as they often had a tobacco crop failure and were without tobacco for long periods of time.

Quitting smoking was never considered a problem at all by either the Indians or the early settlers. When your tobacco got low you simply saved a small amount and smoked up the balance. You then would take a piece of leaf tobacco about the size of a dime and place it on an inside cheek of your mouth. Never spit out any tobacco flavor, just leave it there. When the tobacco flavor has completely left the piece take it out and put in a new one. Remove the piece before meals and put in a new piece after meals. After a week to ten days of this, all desire to smoke will leave you. Putting the small bits of tobacco leaves in your mouth is non-habit forming, in fact produces just the opposite effect. These pieces of leaves in your mouth build up a distinct distaste for tobacco after a week to ten days time. Small pieces of pipe tobacco or cigarette tobacco work very well for this. I have quit smoking myself using this method for as much as ten years at a time.

Although this is an ancient method to stop smoking there is none as good as that I have ever heard of including the most scientific ones. My old friend the late Doctor Bernard Gallagher who in his younger days was a doctor at the world famous Mayo Clinic at Rochester, Minnesota used this same method to stop smoking himself. Instead of putting part of a leaf of tobacco in his cheek he simply kept an unlighted cigarette in his mouth and let the raw tobacco taste permeate his mouth.

When you start using this method tell yourself that you are just using it to quit smoking for 24 hours at a time. Do not say to yourself right from the start that you are going to quit smoking for life because this is bad psychology. Before you know it the 24 hours will have stretched out into weeks, and months and years, if you so desire.

SIOUX METHOD OF CRACKING BLACK WALNUTS, BUTTERNUTS HICKORY NUTS AND HAZELNUTS

Black walnuts, butternuts and hickory nuts originated in North America. Even today there are none of these nuts to be found in Europe or Asia.

The flavor of black walnuts is by far the most different nut flavor in the world. Butternuts also have a rich, clean flavor found in no other nuts. Hickory nuts have a flavor much like English type walnuts. Hickory wood used extensively by the Indians to smoke meat gives meat a rich, heavy, spicy flavor. Today many people like pork ribs smoked with hickory wood.

The European cooks have been very slow to learn of these wonderful American flavors. As I write this in 1959 you still cannot buy black walnuts or butternuts or black walnut or butternut flavoring in all of Europe. You can travel to every town in Europe and you cannot buy pork ribs hickory smoked or even maple, apple or pear wood smoked.

The Indians used nuts for flavoring a great deal in their cooking. They also stored them uncracked for winter food. With all of our so called advancement we have never learned how to crack nuts. Might come in handy to know in case of a hydrogen bombing and you had to rely on wild nuts for a part of your diet.

Sioux Indians, whose name means cut throat, rarely scalped their enemies. They simply cut their throats and left it go at that. This custom of theirs soon earned them the name Sioux.

They cracked nuts by this method. After the nuts are picked, spread them out and leave them stay until the shucks are soft and easy to remove. Then remove the shucks and leave the nuts dry.

The method is as follows: Put the nuts into your oven at about 350 degrees and heat them for about 15 minutes or until they open up at the seams. Then crack them by laying the nuts on the open crack and hit them on the edge of the crack with a hammer.

IN CASE OF A HYDROGEN BOMB ATTACK YOU MUST KNOW THE WAYS OF THE WILDERNESS TO SURVIVE

If we have a bomb attack it will be a heavy one with every major city and most of the country wiped out in less than a half hour.

In reading some of the official rot put out about survival in case of a bombing attack it shows that the people putting it out have no first hand knowledge of what they are talking about. I am just going to take the time to say a few words about it here as if an attack comes I do not want my friends dying needlessly. I have been through bombings and have talked to people all over Europe who have been bombed out and what I say here are the true facts of the matter not political dribble.

1. The would-be authorities tell you to go into your basement and put up a wood lean-to against one wall and get under it. This is the surest way to get killed in a bombing attack and is the thing you must not do. If your home is hit all the debris will come down on you and you will not be able to get out. If you have city water the water pipes will burst and flood the basement drowning you like rats in a trap. If you have city gas the gas pipes will break and can let out enough gas to kill you especially in such a confined area. The sewer pipes may break in the area if you have city sewage and the sewage gas will back up in the basement and kill you quicker than the furnace gas. Get in any kind of a cave, ditch or valley as far away from buildings as you can and lie on the ground face down. If at all possible get in a cave.

2. The first bombs will knock out all gas lines, transportation, and electrical lines and the factories controlling them. Food in your deep freeze will spoil. If the weather is cold all canned goods will freeze and spoil.

3. Make the following preparations in general as applied to your particular situation.

a. If the weather is cold, have a wood stove that can be set up in an abandoned house or shelter. Wood is usually available. Coal would not be available.

b. If the weather is cold have a reserve of lots of blankets.

c. Have a reserve of food consisting of dried beans, dried peas, dried potatoes, dried milk, bacon, canned shortening, sugar, peanut butter, powdered coffee, and tea, chocolate, salt, pepper, macaroni, flour and baking powder. Have at least 1,000 matches in a waterproof container. In World War II matches in some countries were $25.00 a box on the black market when available.
Keep such things as flour, sugar, salt, dried milk, dried potatoes in 5 gallon milk cans that have press fit covers.

d. Have a small .22 caliber rifle and at least 1,000 rounds of ammunition. It will kill small game and birds and can be used to protect your home. Bombings bring looting and the looting is done in most all cases by so-called friends who live near you. This is what happened in both World War I and II.

e. Have six number 1½ traps and two twenty foot coils of woven picture frame wire for snares. Have 100 fish hooks in assorted sizes and 200 yards of nylon fishing line in a variety of weights. The above items can supply your family meat, fowl, and fish if properly used.

f. Have a half pint of iodine, a year's supply of laxative and 100 bufferin tablets. If you live in an area where biting flies and mosquitos abound have a year's supply of bug dope and ten yards of bug net.

g. Have 5 one pound cans of tobacco. This is your fortune. If there is any food or material available that you need, the tobacco will get it for you when money will not.

4. When you get away from buildings stay in a cave for 3 days to avoid radiation fall out.

European countries now require that you keep such reserves as they know that if it comes this time all the help you will get will be that which comes from yourself.

To have a reserve of the above is the cheapest kind of insurance. If you never need it give thanks to Christ. If you do need it, it is worth more than anything you have no matter how worldly wealthy you are at the moment.

TABLE OF CONTENTS

Add Your Own Favorite Recipes Here

Other Books Written by George Leonard Herter

PROFESSIONAL LOADING OF RIFLE, PISTOL, & SHOTGUN CARTRIDGES AND RELOADING DATA FOR PROFESSIONAL & AMATEUR TARGET SHOOTERS, GAME HUNTERS & GUIDES

THE TRUTH ABOUT HUNTING IN TODAY'S AFRICA AND HOW TO GO ON A SAFARI FOR $690.00

PROFESSIONAL FLY TYING, SPINNING AND TACKLE MAKING MANUAL AND MANUFACTURER'S GUIDE.

SECRET FRESH AND SALT WATER FISHING TRICKS OF THE WORLD'S FIFTY BEST PROFESSIONAL FISHERMEN.

PROFESSIONAL GUIDE MANUAL VOLUME I.

PROFESSIONAL AND AMATEUR ARCHERY TOURNAMENT AND HUNTING INSTRUCTIONS AND ENCYCLOPEDIA

GUNS, BALLISTICS AND HERETOFORE UNPUBLISHED FACTS ON RIFLES, REVOLVERS, PISTOLS, SHOTGUNS, TELESCOPIC SIGHTS, METAL SIGHTS AND CHRONOGRAPHS.

GEORGE THE HOUSEWIFE AND HOW TO DIET AND NEVER BE HUNGRY

HISTORY AND SECRETS OF PROFESSIONAL CANDY MAKING AND IMPROVING PASTRIES, CAKES AND PIES.

HOW TO GET OUT OF THE RAT RACE AND LIVE ON $10. A MONTH.

If you have enjoyed this book order a copy of George the Housewife and How to Diet and Never be Hungry. It contains recipes from the best 35 New York Restaurants plus many other recipes.

For details on any of the above, write Herter's, Inc., Waseca, Minnesota.